THE ILLICIT TRADE IN ART AND ANTIQUITIES

This new text provides practical guidance on the modern law relating to cultural objects which have been stolen, looted or illegally exported. It explains how English criminal law principles, including money laundering measures, apply to those who deal in cultural objects in a domestic or international setting. It discusses the recovery of works of art and antiquities in the English courts where there are competing claims between private individuals, or between individuals and the UK Government or a foreign State. Significantly, this text also provides an exposition of the law where a British law enforcement agency, or a foreign law enforcement agency, is involved in the course of criminal or civil proceedings in an English court. The growth of relevant international instruments, which include not only those devoted to the protection of mankind's cultural heritage but also those concerned with money laundering and serious organised crime, provide a backdrop to this discussion. The UK's ratification of the UNESCO Convention on Means of Prohibiting and Preventing the Illicit Import, Export and Transfer of Ownership of Cultural Property 1970 in 2002 is considered. The problems posed in attempting to curb trafficking in art and antiquities are explored and the effectiveness of the current law is analysed.

The Illicit Trade in Art and Antiquities

International Recovery and Criminal and Civil Liability

Janet Ulph

Solicitor, Professor in Commercial Law at the University of Leicester

Ian Smith

Barrister, 11 Stone Buildings, Lincoln's Inn, London

Consultant editor

Sir Michael Tugendhat

Judge of the High Court (Queen's Bench Division)

•HART•
PUBLISHING

OXFORD AND PORTLAND, OREGON

2012

Published in the United Kingdom by Hart Publishing Ltd
16C Worcester Place, Oxford, OX1 2JW
Telephone: +44 (0)1865 517530
Fax: +44 (0)1865 510710
E-mail: mail@hartpub.co.uk
Website: http://www.hartpub.co.uk

Published in North America (US and Canada) by
Hart Publishing
c/o International Specialized Book Services
920 NE 58th Avenue, Suite 300
Portland, OR 97213-3786
USA
Tel: +1 503 287 3093 or toll-free: (1) 800 944 6190
Fax: +1 503 280 8832
E-mail: orders@isbs.com
Website: http://www.isbs.com

British Library Cataloguing in Publication Data
Data Available

ISBN: 978-1-84113-964-7

Typeset by Hope Services, Abingdon
Printed and bound in Great Britain by
TJ International Ltd, Padstow, Cornwall

MIX
Paper from responsible sources
FSC www.fsc.org FSC® C013056

PREFACE

Art and antiquities are stolen every day, not only from the UK but from countries around the world, such as Iraq, Egypt, Libya, China and India. They are smuggled from one country to another. This text focuses upon the extent to which laws can protect vulnerable countries and considers what further steps could be taken in the future. This involves an analysis of not only international laws but also English criminal and civil laws to determine whether enough is being done to deter the illicit trade in art and antiquities and to recover stolen items. In particular, as there is evidence that international criminal syndicates are involved in this trade, there is discussion of recent legislation dealing with money laundering, serious organised crime and corruption.

We would like to thank Michael Tugendhat for reading all of the text and for providing both authors with helpful comments and insights.

Janet Ulph and Ian Smith

THANKS

I have written five of the seven chapters and this work would not have been possible if not for the generous support provided by the Leverhulme Trust in the form of a Research Fellowship. I am very grateful to the Trust.

I would like to thank the following people for their encouragement: Michael Bridge, Lionel Smith, Norman Palmer, Ruth Redmond-Cooper, Rob Merkin, Vernon Rapley and Tatiana Flessas. A substantial amount of background work for my research in money laundering was carried out at the Fredric G Levin College of Law at the University of Florida in Gainesville and I would take the opportunity to thank the staff there and, in particular, Professor Fletcher Baldwin. Thanks are due to Anna Barwell and Andrew Fairman for proof reading and discussing points in these chapters with me. I would also like to thank the Hart publishing team for their support.

I would also pay tribute to the late Professor Kaiyan Kaikobad who was all that an academic should be: scrupulous in his research and kind and supportive of others.

Janet Ulph

CONTENTS

TABLE OF CASES

Australia

Canada

European Court of Human Rights

European Court of Justice

Germany

India

Ireland

New Zealand

United Kingdom ....

VAT and Duties Tribunal

United States of America

TABLE OF LEGISLATION

Australia

Canada

China

Egypt

European Union

Directives

Regulations

France

Iran

Italy

Netherlands

New Zealand

Switzerland

Turkey

United Kingdom

United States of America

TABLE OF CONVENTIONS, TREATIES, ETC

1

The Trade in Art and Antiquities

JANET ULPH

I Introduction

1.01 Introduction

Art and antiquities can be beautiful, fascinating and highly valuable. It is unsurprising that those in possession of such objects may find that others covet them. The focus of this text is upon the law relating to cultural objects which have been stolen, looted, or illegally exported, in recent times. These objects may be secretly exported from the original countries in which they were located in order to escape detection. They may be sold on the black market abroad or, where the object is not easily identifiable, offered openly in foreign markets.

London is one of the prime locations in the world where there is a legitimate and healthy trade in works of art and antiquities. Unfortunately, stolen or looted objects may masquerade as legitimate purchases. This text will therefore discuss the dangers posed by the illicit trade in cultural objects, the risk that profits made will be used to further other criminal activities, and the strategies which could be employed to combat this trade. This will include an explanation of how the English criminal law, including money laundering measures, applies to those who deal in cultural objects in a domestic or international setting. As the illicit trade in art and antiquities is one of the most lucrative in the world, the powers of law enforcement agencies to seize these objects will be explained. Trafficking in cultural objects, because it is a global trade, is difficult to suppress; consequently the efforts made by international bodies and governments to combat it must also be considered.

The victims of this illicit trade will be anxious to recover their art and antiquities. This text will detail how they may do so, using private civil proceedings. These actions for recovery are often complex, because there will usually be competing claims between private individuals, or between individuals and governments, which may involve issues such as the application of foreign laws and the enforcement of foreign judgments. An analysis of the obstacles facing any claimant in attempting to recover cultural objects will therefore be provided.

1.02 The Loss of Legal Rights to Claim

Over the centuries, individuals, museums and states have been wrongly deprived of cultural objects. The surrounding circumstances have often involved the abuse of the poor by the rich, or of the defenceless by the powerful. Where works of art or antiquities have been taken a long time ago, such as the Elgin Marbles, it will be too late to bring a legal claim. The dispossessed individual or state can nevertheless argue that, on moral grounds, the object should be returned. There has been heated debate about objects taken centuries ago.[1] The history behind the loss of each object will vary, and the moral issues will be stronger in some cases than others. For example, paintings and other works which were taken during the Holocaust period and which have ended up as part of a UK national collection, are viewed as a special case.[2]

However, this text will be primarily concerned with the law. The focus is therefore necessarily limited to objects which have been taken in recent years.

1.03 The Illicit Trade in Cultural Property

In 2002, the UK Government became a party to the Convention on the Means of Prohibiting and Preventing the Illicit Import, Export and Transfer of Ownership of Cultural Property 1970 (hereafter the UNESCO Convention 1970). All signatory states are encouraged to protect cultural property within their territories against 'the dangers of theft, clandestine excavation, and illicit export'.

This text reflects the concerns of the Convention, dealing with the three situations which are usually encompassed within the phrase 'illicit trade in cultural property'. First, the phrase may refer to paintings, statues and other cultural objects which have been stolen or misappropriated from a museum, or other public building, or private collection. Recent examples include the thefts of artefacts from the Egyptian Museum on 28 January 2011 during a period of civil unrest. Secondly, it may allude to the trade in objects of antiquity which have been secretly removed from archaeological sites or monuments. This has been a particular problem in Iraq since the 1990s, due to armed conflict. However, it has also affected many other countries, such as Africa, China, Italy, Central and South America, Turkey, Bulgaria, Iraq, Egypt and England.[3] A report by a House of Commons Select Committee noted: 'Such objects have an owner and a victim – usually a State or a landowner – but their entry into and passage through the trade is more difficult to trace and quantify';[4] in other words, these objects are not on any database and their loss may not be detected until years later. Thirdly, the phrase may refer to the export of an object without

[1] See eg JH Merryman, 'Thinking About the Elgin Marbles' (1985) 83 *Michigan Law Review* 1881, reproduced in JH Merryman (ed), *Thinking About the Elgin Marbles: Critical Essays on Cultural Property, Art and Law,* 2nd edn (The Netherlands, Kluwer International BV, 2009) (hereafter Merryman, *Elgin Marbles)*; C Hitchens, *The Parthenon Marbles: the Case for Reunification* (London, Verso Books, 2008); S Waxman, *Loot: The Battle over the Stolen Treasures of the Ancient World* (New York Times Books, 2008); J Greenfield, *The Return of Cultural Treasures,* 3rd edn (Cambridge, CUP, 2007); J Cuno (ed), *Whose Culture? The Promise of Museums and the Debate over Antiquities* (Princeton NJ, Princeton University Press, 2009).

[2] In order to redress historic wrongs which were committed during the Nazi era, the UK Government established a Spoliation Advisory Panel in 2000 to make recommendations in relation to any claim relating to Holocaust items: *Official Report,* 8 May 2000, Vol 349, c 491. The Spoliation Advisory Panel has received only a small number of claims and has generally been successful in resolving them. However, certain museums lacked the statutory powers to de-acquire objects and were consequently unable to comply with any recommendation by the Panel to restore an object to the victim's family: this problem has been successfully dealt with by the Holocaust (Return of Cultural Objects) Act 2009. See generally, NE Palmer, *Museums and the Holocaust* (Leicester, Institute of Art and Law, 2000); C Woodhead, 'Moral claims against museums: the emerging concept of moral title to objects of cultural heritage' (2009) 2 *International Journal of the Inclusive Museum* 1.

[3] UNESCO, Information Kit, *The Fight Against the Illicit Trafficking of Cultural Objects, The 1970 Convention: Past, Present and Future* (2011) CLT/2011/CONF.207/6. See also C Luke and JS Henderson, 'The Plunder of the Ulua Valley, Honduras, and a Market Analysis for Its Illicit Antiquities' in Brodie et al, (eds), *Archaeology, Cultural Heritage and the Antiquities Trade* (Gainesville, University Press of Florida, 2006) 147, 148.

[4] Culture, Media and Sport Committee, House of Commons Session 1999–2000 7th Report *Culture Property: Return and Illicit Trade* (3 vols) (London 2000) (The Select Committee Report) [8].

permission, in contravention of a country's export regulations. This does not necessarily mean that the object was stolen: the owner of the object may decide to secretly smuggle it out of the country or more brazenly to use forged documents to remove it. This is a particular problem in countries with extensive restrictions on exporting cultural objects, such as Italy.

1.04 Big Business

Thieves and looters are usually motivated by greed. However, this is not always so. There is some evidence that thieves of works of art may steal from museums for their private pleasure: to enjoy the power of possession over an object by viewing it and handling it at will.[5] Even so, these thieves may eventually be tempted to sell the work because of its high value. In contrast, the excavation of antiquities which has taken place at archaeological sites in Iraq and other countries appears to be entirely motivated by a desire for money. An insatiable demand amongst collectors for certain types of antiquities has driven up prices and has led to extensive looting.

The removal of antiquities has become highly organised in recent years. They are taken and swiftly transferred to a chain of middle-men dealers, to be rapidly sold and resold. These transactions have been aided by a market culture where traditionally no questions relating to provenance were usually asked. Any lurking suspicions were suppressed. Corrupt customs officials might be prepared to provide false export documents. Restorers and scholars might unwittingly assist the trade: restorers might agree to clean objects of dirt, thereby eliminating information of where they had been buried; scholars might be persuaded to confirm their authenticity. This process of legitimisation ensured that these objects would realise high prices when sold in international markets.

Looted antiquities are often high-value items, and huge profits can often be made by dealers.[6] These lucrative transactions have brought this trade to the attention of terrorists[7] and international organised crime groups. It is increasingly recognised that professional criminals are involved in the illicit trade of art and antiquities. In the early 1990s, it was observed that only the drug trafficking trade was greater, in relation to the value of the assets transferred.[8] This view was echoed in the Report of the Law Reform Commission of Ireland published in 1997, in which it was observed that:

[5] S Mackenzie, 'Criminal and Victim Profiles in Art Theft: Motive, Opportunity and Repeat Victimisation' (2005) X(4) *Art Antiquity and Law* 353, 357. See also, M Durney, 'Understanding the Motivations Behind Art Crime and the Effects of an Institution's Response' (2009) 2(1) *The Journal of Art Crime* 83; J Conklin, *Art Crime* (Westport, CT, Praeger, 1994) 119.

[6] MM Kersel, 'From the Ground to the Buyer: A Market Analysis of the Trade in Illegal Antiquities' in Brodie et al (eds), *Archaeology, Cultural Heritage and the Antiquities Trade* (Gainesville, University Press of Florida, 2006) 188, 189–94.

[7] Bogdanos comments, in relation to objects stolen from the Iraq National Museum which were found in the possession of insurgents in Iraq, that 'the cosy cabal of academics, dealers, and collectors who turn a blind eye to the illicit side of the trade is, in effect, supporting the insurgents who are killing our troops in Iraq': M Bogdanos, 'Thieves of Baghdad' in PG Stone and J Farchakh Bajjaly (eds), *The Destruction of Cultural Heritage in Iraq* (Woodbridge, The Boydell Press, 2008) 109, 124 (hereafter Stone and Farchakh Bajjaly, *Destruction of Cultural Heritage in Iraq*).

[8] NR Lenzner, 'Illicit International Trade in Cultural Property: Does the Unidroit Convention Provide an Effective Remedy for the Shortcomings of the UNESCO Convention?' (1994) 15 *University of Pennsylvania Journal of International Business Law* 469, 472–73. See also, M Olivier, 'The UNIDROIT Convention: Attempting to Regulate the International Trade and Traffic of Cultural Property' (1996) 26 *Golden Gate University Law Review* 627. However, any estimate will lack precision and, for example, Podesta estimates that the illicit trade in cultural objects is the *third* most profitable illegal trade in the world, after drug and arms trafficking: JM Podesta (2008) 16 *Cardozo Journal of International and Comparative Law* 457, 461.

> It is estimated that art smuggling is second only to drug dealing as the most lucrative crime in the world. In South America alone, it is estimated that between 2 and 10 billion dollars worth of art objects are lost each year through theft and smuggling. In Ireland, conservative figures suggest that more than £2 million of antiques are removed from this jurisdiction each year. The objects tend to re-emerge in markets in wealthy developed countries.[9]

The Select Committee on Culture, Media and Sport, in its 7th Report of 2000, added a note of caution to such speculation, remarking that, as the trade was an underground and secretive activity, it was difficult to provide an accurate estimate of the profits being made.[10] Whilst sources such as the Museums Association and the Metropolitan Police estimated that billions of profits were made each year and that profits had increased over the preceding 10 years, the Antiquities Dealers Association suggested that much lower figures would be more accurate.[11] However, the Select Committee went on to conclude on this issue that:

> Although it is hazardous to extrapolate from domestic insurance claims, there have been estimates of the value of collectable items stolen annually within the United Kingdom of £300 million or more.[12] Even assuming that only a small proportion of such collectable items constitutes cultural property likely to enter an international market, that figure indicates the worldwide scale of stolen cultural goods likely to be susceptible to entry into the illicit trade. Readily identifiable cultural goods are often likely to be transferred across international boundaries because of the reduced likelihood of detection and the increased ease of sale.[13]

1.05 The Impact of Laws which Protect Good Faith Purchasers

Illegal excavation of antiquities, or theft of objects from museums, churches and private collections, may occur in many countries around the world. As the trade in these objects is international in scale, international instruments will be considered in Chapter 2. However, this text will be primarily concerned with scrutinising the robustness of English laws. Even so, the impact of the domestic laws of other states should not be overlooked. For example, the laws of some states, such as France and Switzerland, provide generous protection for a good faith purchaser after a relatively short period of time against claims by the owner from whom the art or antiquity was stolen.[14] Any thief or fraudster sending an object abroad may be tempted to divert the goods through one of these countries, arranging a sale to a business partner. Once the purchaser has obtained good title through the generosity of a particular system's laws, the object can be sold with impunity within that country. This is why there are references to the 'illicit' trade in cultural property. The original appropriation

[9] The Law Reform Commission of Ireland, *Report on the Unidroit Convention on Stolen or Illegally Exported Objects* (1997) LRC 55 [1.4].

[10] In order to obtain a better understanding of the size of the problem, the Ministerial Advisory Panel had recommended that art theft should be a reportable offence: Report of the Ministerial Advisory Panel on Illicit Trade, Department for Culture, Media and Sport, December 2000 [74], [91].

[11] The Select Committee Report [9], [11].

[12] The Committee referred to J Butler, 'The Art and Antiques Squad' in KW Tubb (ed), *Antiquities Trade or Betrayed: Legal, Ethical and Conservation Issues* (London, Archetype Publications, 1995) 226.

[13] The Select Committee Report [12].

[14] See *Winkworth v Christie Manson and Woods Ltd* [1980] Ch 496, and other examples, discussed in the Report of the Ministerial Advisory Panel on Illicit Trade, Department for Culture, Media and Sport, December 2000, Annex A [14]–[16]. Switzerland has been a popular staging post for illicit material in the past, but has now begun to tighten up its laws: P Gerstenblith, 'Recent Developments in the Legal Protection of Cultural Heritage Antiquities' in Brodie et al (eds), *Archaeology, Cultural Heritage and the Antiquities Trade* (Gainesville, University Press of Florida, 2006) 68, 77.

of the item may have been illegal; however, its later transfer may result in the original owner, whether a private individual or a state, being divested of the legal title to it.

1.06 Terminology

Cultural Goods, Cultural Property, Cultural Objects and Cultural Heritage

Terminology can be employed quite loosely in this field. Nevertheless, the precise meaning of a particular phrase will need to be ascertained where it is used in an international instrument, European Directive or domestic legislative measure. For example, the phrase 'cultural goods' is used in Regulation 116/2009, set out in an Annex to this text, and this phrase is carefully defined by the Regulation.

The phrase 'cultural property' is used in two leading international conventions. For example, Article 1 of the UNESCO Convention 1970 refers to 'cultural property' and provides a very wide definition of tangible and portable objects of importance for 'archaeology, prehistory, history, literature, art or science'. The definition is set out and discussed in Chapter 2.[15] The drafters of the UNIDROIT Convention on Stolen or Illegally Exported Cultural Objects 1995 (hereafter, the 'UNIDROIT Convention') preferred the phrase 'cultural objects' which more closely reflected the domestic laws of countries such as France. It has been suggested that the phrase 'cultural property' places emphasis upon the property law aspects of cultural objects, thereby encouraging people to view them as commodities to be bought and sold.[16] The phrase 'cultural object' is seen as more neutral and one which clearly acknowledges an item's cultural value. This rather subtle refinement has not been adopted in this text: it is hoped that the phrase 'cultural' will suffice to highlight the special status of these objects to humankind or to groups within a society.[17]

The phrase 'cultural heritage' is wide in scope and can refer to land, tangible objects and intangible knowledge which has a message which can be passed from one generation to another. This text focuses upon tangible portable objects alone. Consequently, any references to cultural heritage will merely be acknowledging the fact that the objects in question have a significance for successive generations.[18]

Looting

This phrase refers to objects which are illicitly unearthed, or which are forcibly removed from a temple, monument or other culturally significant structure, and taken from their country of origin.[19] Since the Second World War, scientific techniques for recovering information about the past have improved dramatically. Unfortunately, at the same time, looting of archaeological sites has increased exponentially.[20] One may add to this that the rapid expansion in easy travel and communications has unfortunately facilitated the stripping of archaeological sites on an industrial scale.

[15] See 2.14. The 1954 Convention for the Protection of Cultural Property in the Event of Armed Conflict (the 'Hague Convention') also uses the phrase 'cultural property:' see 2.04.

[16] See J Blake, 'On defining the cultural heritage' (2000) *International and Comparative Law Quarterly* 61, 64, 66.

[17] For a detailed discussion of these concepts, see B Hoffman (ed), *Art and Cultural Heritage: Law, Policy and Practice* (Cambridge, Cambridge University Press, 2005) 14–18.

[18] It may therefore implicitly suggest a need to preserve and protect: LV Prott and P O'Keefe, 'Cultural Heritage' or 'Cultural Property; (1992) (1) *International Journal of Cultural Property* 307.

[19] S Mackenzie and P Green, *Criminology and Archaeology* (Hart, Oxford, 2009) 1.

[20] P Gerstenblith, 'The Public Interest in the Restitution of Cultural Objects' (2001) 16 *Connecticut Journal of International Law* 197.

Market Nations and Source Nations

Merryman has suggested that the world can be divided into source nations and market nations.[21] In source nations, such as Iraq, China, Egypt, Mexico, Greece and Italy, the supply of desirable cultural objects will often exceed the internal demand. In market nations, such as France, Germany, Japan, Switzerland and the United States, the demand may exceed the supply. The demand for cultural objects in the market nation encourages exports of these things from source nations. This distinction is useful but simplistic, not least because some market nations, such as the UK, could also be viewed as source nations for certain types of cultural objects.

Patrimonial Laws

A patrimonial claim refers to a claim by a foreign government asserting ownership over property.[22] This type of claim should be sharply distinguished from a personal claim by a foreign sovereign to recover unpaid tax, which may be refused by the English courts on public policy grounds as a penal law. In *Government of the Islamic Republic of Iran v The Barakat Galleries Ltd*,[23] the Court of Appeal accepted that the Iranian Government had title to antiquities which had been illegally excavated. This was therefore a patrimonial claim which was being brought to recover them from the defendant art gallery and, on the facts, it succeeded. The phrase can also be found in the UNESCO Convention, where Article 9 is clearly referring to assets owned by the state when it provides that a Contracting State can call upon other states for assistance when its 'cultural patrimony' is in jeopardy from 'pillage of archaeological or ethnological materials.'

Pillage

This phrase can be found in Article 4(3) of the Convention for the Protection of Cultural Property in the Event of Armed Conflict 1954 (the 'Hague Convention'), which provides that Contracting States must undertake to prevent 'any form of theft, pillage or misappropriation of, and any acts of vandalism directed against, cultural property'. It is also referred to in Article 9 of the UNESCO Convention, as discussed above. Arguably 'pillage' is a loose phrase which connotes intentional or reckless conduct with an international dimension which leads to destruction and perhaps also theft.

Provenance and Provenience

Provenance is concerned with information about the history of an object and, in particular, the succession of previous owners. It is important for any and every cultural object. If an object is offered for sale accompanied by documents which reveal its entire history, then it is clear (assuming that the documents are genuine) that it is not stolen or a forgery. In contrast, provenience is only relevant as regards objects of antiquity. Provenience is concerned with the location of the object and its stratified context. Stratigraphic analysis aids our

[21] JH Merryman 'Two Ways of Thinking About Cultural Property' (1986) 80 *American Journal of International Law* 831, reproduced in Merryman, *Elgin Marbles*, 82, 83.

[22] *Government of India v Taylor* [1955] AC 491 (HL) 511 (Lord Keith). See also *USA v Inkley* [1989] QB 255 (CA) 265; *Re State of Norway's Application (No 2)* [1990] 1 AC 723 (HL) 807.

[23] *Government of the Islamic Republic of Iran v The Barakat Galleries Ltd* [2007] EWCA Civ 1374; [2009] QB 22 (CA) [134], [149].

understanding of the evolution of human culture. As Gerstenblith has observed, 'Controlled scientific excavation of archaeological sites relies on an understanding of stratigraphy; remains of past cultures are deposited in layers (or strata), and each stratum represents a particular time period.'[24]

Repatriation, Restitution and Return

'Repatriation' refers to the return of human remains or other property of cultural significance either to its country of origin or to a group of indigenous people. It does not suggest that the state has requested the return of the object. It is often used in situations where an object is returned at the request of a particular group, or where the object is simply purchased and taken back to its country of origin.[25]

The phrase 'restitution' is employed in the international arena in the context of disputes between states. According to UNESCO's *IGC Guidelines for the Use of the Standard Form Concerning Requests for Return or Restitution,* the phrase 'restitution' should be used in cases of 'illicit appropriation'.[26] In other words, the use of the phrase indicates that the objects were taken unlawfully, in contravention of the laws of the source country and the 1970 UNESCO Convention. The phrase 'restitution' might therefore be applied where an object was stolen from a museum: it indicates past wrongdoing.

In contrast, the phrase 'return' is quite neutral. It does not suggest that the object was appropriated in contravention of any law. If a state seeks the 'return' of an object, it may simply be doing so on the basis of cultural co-operation, rather than because the object has been misappropriated in the past. The return of an object may imply an ex gratia act by the donor.

This text is concerned with wrongdoing, but focusing upon English domestic law rather than public international law. In English private law, 'restitution' is frequently used to refer to situations where the defendant has been unjustly enriched at another's expense. In order to avoid any confusion, the neutral phrase 'return' will generally be used.

II Cultural Loss

1.07 Introduction

Fraud in commercial dealings is unfortunately all too common. A court will frequently be invited to determine which of two innocent parties should suffer a loss as a consequence of the wrongdoing of another.[27] However, the consequences of theft and fraud involving commonplace items, such as grain, oil, machine parts and consumer durables, are normally purely financial. The position is different where cultural objects are involved. The Select

[24] P Gerstenblith, 'Controlling the International Market in Antiquities: Reducing the Harm, Preserving the Past' (2007) 8 *Chicago Journal of International Law* 169, 171.

[25] Examples are helpfully provided in the Museum Association's Policy Statement on Repatriation of Cultural Property; this Statement can be found on its web-site. See also MG Simpson, *Making Representations: Museums in the Post-Colonial Era* (Routledge, 1996).

[26] Intergovernmental Committee for Promoting the Return of Cultural Property to its Countries of Origin or its Restitution in Case of Illicit Appropriation, UNESCO 1986 (revised 1996).

[27] See J Ulph, *Commercial Fraud: Civil Liability, Human Rights and Money Laundering* (Oxford, Oxford University Press, 2006) ch 11. In relation to theft, see 5.33–5.51.

Committee suggested that 'the problem of the illicit trade should be measured not only in monetary terms but also in terms of its impact on cultural heritage and on the legitimate trade in cultural property'.[28]

Measuring the trade in monetary terms is important. Huge profits can be made from the illicit trade in cultural property, which can then be used to subsidise further criminal activity. As international organised criminal syndicates become richer, they become more powerful and more able to influence and even destabilise governments. However, apart from these considerations, there are further losses caused by this trade, which are considered below.

1.08 Thefts from Museums: Damage and Destruction

Theft of cultural property has become an increasingly important problem in recent years even in the most politically stable countries, where criminals may take cultural objects from churches, museums and private collections. One example is the theft of five irreplaceable paintings by Picasso, Matisse, Braque, Modigliani and Léger from the Museum of Modern Art in Paris in May 2010.[29] Their value in monetary terms would be impossible to calculate accurately. The public have been deprived of the pleasure of viewing them. However, more importantly, there is always the risk that they will have been damaged in the process of being removed. Paintings may be damaged as they are cut from their frames;[30] objects can be dropped in making a getaway. Until stolen items are recovered, there will be the constant anxiety that they have been damaged, stored in poor conditions, or even destroyed.[31]

1.09 Objects Unearthed or Removed from Monuments

Where objects of antiquity are dug out of the ground or forcibly removed from some ancient monument, their removal not only robs a vulnerable country of information about its history, but may partially strip the cultural object itself of its identity. Information relating to the depth at which an object is buried (stratification) might well have indicated its age, for example.[32] The impairment of the accumulation of knowledge about particular types of antiquity, such as Cycladic figurines which have been subject to large-scale looting, makes it easier for forgeries to be accepted as genuine and to circulate in the market; conversely, a genuine object, which has been looted, will be all the more difficult to identify as authentic.[33] For example, Dacian people in Transylvania, mysterious contemporaries of the Romans, are believed to have created marvelous bracelets of gold. It is believed that looters took about two dozen of them from the Sarmizegetusa Regia archaeological site in Romania

[28] The Select Committee Report, [12].

[29] See the Report of the Ministerial Advisory Panel on Illicit Trade, Department for Culture, Media and Sport, December 2000 Annex A [29]–[30] for a list of some of the museums which have been burgled in recent years.

[30] It has been reported that a theft of a Van Gogh painting from the Khalil Museum in Cairo, Egypt, on 21 August 2010 involved cutting the painting from its frame. Paintings stolen from the Isabella Stewart Gardner Museum in Boston in 1990 had also been forcefully removed from their frames.

[31] There are suggestions that these paintings have been destroyed: H Samuel, '£100m masterpieces stolen from French museum "crushed by rubbish truck"' *Daily Telegraph* (9 October 2011), discussed in Derek Fincham's *Illicit Cultural Property* blog.

[32] C Renfrew, *Loot, Legitimacy and Ownership: The Ethical Crisis in Archaeology* (London, Duckworth, 2000). See also S Mackenzie and P Green, *Criminology and Archaeology* (Oxford, Hart Publishing, 2009) 2.

[33] P Gerstenblith, 'Controlling the International Market in Antiquities: Reducing the Harm, Preserving the Past' (2007) 8 *Chicago Journal of International Law* 169, 172.

between 1999 and 2001. Twelve bracelets, which are at least 2,000 years old, have been recovered and are available to the viewing public at the Romanian National History Museum in Bucharest. However, there is a question mark over whether the bracelets could be forgeries. The problem is that the Dacians lacked a written language. Consequently, very little is known about them; the main source of information is drawn from the description of their Roman conquerors, who would not necessarily have been impartial in their observations. It is uncertain whether the bracelets were used as part of a religious ceremony or not.[34] It is precisely in this sort of situation that archaeological objects can reveal so much about the past and where, if an archaeological site is damaged and stripped of key items, an artful forger has scope to create his own version of the past.

Looters are usually looking for objects which can easily be sold, and have no respect for the historical record. Thus, frescoes may be torn off walls and crudely cut up into sections which are easier to transport, without any regard being paid to the integrity of the original ensemble. The sections are likely to be sold individually rather than reassembled. Furthermore, other artefacts are often damaged or destroyed in the process of excavating particular objects which are seen as attractive and desirable. It has been estimated that looters only take 5 to 10 per cent of what could originally be found on any given site, destroying the rest in their search for sellable objects.[35] As a consequence, both the site and the individual object lose much of their significance. Valuable historical data will have been lost for ever. The removal abroad of a substantial number of items may erode a group's sense of identity.[36] The Law Reform Commission of Ireland has lamented the 'lost familiarity' with history that results from the transfer of cultural objects from their country of origin, leading to situations where communities become isolated from their own culture.[37]

III The Global Market in Art and Antiquities

1.10 A National and International Market

The UK has a prominent international market in cultural property, along with the United States, France, Hong Kong, Switzerland and Thailand. In 1999, the UK enjoyed 26 per cent of the global market and exports accounted for £629 million.[38] There are a number of associated services providers which depend upon the market, such as restorers and export agents. The British Government has therefore been keen to support the licit market in art and antiquities, because it benefits the domestic economy. Moreover, a market which deals in legitimate objects can be said to provide a public benefit in terms of stimulating interest in both domestic and global culture.

[34] T Watson, 'Ancient Transylvanians likely controlled untold riches in gold, suggests a new study of a cache of priceless, snake-shaped bracelets' (2011) January *National Geographic News* 13.

[35] S Melikian, 'A Degree of Destruction Unprecedented in the History of the World – And Yet I Support Collecting' *The Art Newspaper* (London, October 1995, No 52) 27.

[36] G Green, 'Evaluating the Application of the National Stolen Property Act to Art Trafficking Cases' (2007) 44 *Harvard Journal on Legislation* 251, 252.

[37] (1997) LRC 55 [1.12]. See further, P O'Keefe and L Prott, *Law and the Cultural Heritage, Volume 3 – Movement* (London, Butterworths, 1989) 11 [108].

[38] Department for Culture, Media and Sport (DCMS) (2001) 'Creative industries mapping document 2001', citing Market Tracking International (MTI), *2000: The Art and Internet Report.* See also, House of Commons Culture, Media and Sport Committee, *Sixth Report of Session 2004-05: The Market for Art*, 2005, Part 2.

The share of the global market which a particular country enjoys will vary according to a large number of factors, including its system of regulation and taxation and the state of its economy.[39] For example, there was a shift of the art market from New York to London in 2008, which was generally attributed to the weak rate of exchange of the US dollar. Both Sotheby's and Christie's are multinational organisations, well able to take account of changes in the market in a particular country.[40] However, the projected sale price is always significant: a seller or an auction house may choose one country rather than another in which to sell an object, in order to achieve the best price. Consequently, efforts made to regulate one market to prevent the illicit trade in cultural property need to be matched by a similar effort in all other countries. If this does not occur, sellers in possession of objects which they know or suspect have been stolen by looting or other means are likely to choose to sell these objects in a country which makes little effort to curb this trade and where they can be confident of making a lucrative deal.[41]

The UK Government has become concerned that business will be lost elsewhere due to two EU harmonisation measures. First, since 1999, the rate of value added tax has been raised on works of art imported into the UK from outside the EU from 2.5 per cent to the EU minimum rate of 5 per cent. Secondly, the UK has been forced to introduce a right, given to artists and their heirs, to a proportion of the resale price of their works of art (*droit de suite*). This right applies to all transactions involving art market professionals, such as auction houses and dealers.[42] It is difficult to predict the extent to which the UK share of the market may shrink as a consequence of these measures. However, their existence means that every effort will be made to ensure that any measures taken to counter the illicit trade in cultural property are necessary and proportionate, and do not simply have the effect of damaging the UK's share of the market.

IV Iraq and the Pattern of Trade

1.11 Iraq

The risk of cultural objects being misappropriated and smuggled across borders is a worldwide problem. However, circumstances may arise whereby a country becomes particularly vulnerable to theft, looting and misappropriation. Iraq serves as an example. Prior to the twentieth century, those who dug objects up in Iraq could keep them. A law was introduced in 1922 which forced finders to share their spoils with the Iraq National Museum. The country was stable then and, over the years, the Museum in Baghdad amassed an impres-

[39] It was ever thus: for example, the decline of the art market in the 1680s mirrored the state of the country's economy at that time: I Robertson, 'Art, Religion, History, Money' in Robertson (ed), *Understanding International Art Markets and Management* (London and New York, Routledge, 2005) 37, 40.

[40] D Gledhill, 'Sotheby's brings down the hammer on UK jobs' *The Independent* (14 January 2001).

[41] S Mackenzie and P Green note that it was reported that certain dealers moved to the more congenial environment of Brussels after the enactment of the Dealing in Cultural Objects (Offences) Act 2003: 'Criminalising the Market in Illicit Antiquities: an Evaluation of the Dealing in Cultural Objects (Offences) Act 2003 in England and Wales' in S Mackenzie and P Green (eds), *Criminology and Archaeology: Studies in Looted Antiquities* (Oxford, Hart, 2009) 164.

[42] Artist's Resale Right Regulations 2006, SI 2006/ 346. These regulations were made pursuant to the Resale Right Directive, 2001/84/EC.

sive collection of antiquities.[43] Illegal excavations were rare. However, the position changed in the 1990s, in the aftermath of the First Gulf War of 1991.[44] The country became more and more impoverished. The Iran-Iraq war in the 1980s had already placed a strain on the economy. This was followed by economic sanctions in the 1990s, imposed by the United Nations Security Council Resolution 661.[45] After the end of the first Gulf War, Iraq's regional museums were ransacked and artefacts were taken. The circulation of objects from Iraq became increasingly common in the international markets. Whilst some Iraqi families may have sold inherited property to make ends meet, there is no doubt that most of the items would have been stripped from archaeological sites. Artefacts from some of the world's oldest civilisations (such as Sumerian, Assyrian and Babylonian) found their way on to the black market in other countries.

After the invasion of Iraq by coalition forces in April 2003, the looting of archaeological sites escalated, particularly in the south of the country where there was acute poverty.[46] In Baghdad, government buildings, including the Iraq National Museum, were looted by civilians.[47] An estimated 15,000 treasures were stolen or destroyed. Looters beheaded ancient statues. Although a significant amount was returned when an amnesty was declared a few months later, at least 7,000 artefacts are still missing.

Iraq illustrates that, where there is armed conflict, cultural objects become peculiarly vulnerable. Local people, living in deprived conditions, may see the taking or excavating of cultural objects as an opportunity to earn money for survival.[48] Conflicts may erode legal and social controls within a country so that it is difficult to protect museums and sites of importance. There may be difficulty in protecting objects even where they are removed to a place of safety.[49]

1.12 Pattern of Trade

The international nature of the licit and illicit art markets presents particular difficulties in preventing wrongdoing. As regards works of art or antiquities, their passage to the London market may involve being moved from country to country over a period of some years. Most source nations now have legislation in place to assert ownership over excavated material, so some form of smuggling from a source nation is inevitable. The same is true for all stolen objects. They will normally be taken to countries where it is easier for 'good faith' purchasers to obtain a good title to them. In this process, false papers can be created to give an object some form of history. The object can then be exported with the proper paperwork to be subsequently offered on the open market in London or elsewhere.

[43] L Al-Gailani Werr, 'The Story of the Iraq Museum' in Stone and Farchakh Bajjaly, *Destruction of Cultural Heritage in Iraq* 25.

[44] M Gibson, 'The Acquisition of Antiquities in Iraq, 19th Century to 2003, Legal and Illegal' in Stone and Farchakh Bajjaly, *Destruction of Cultural Heritage in Iraq* 31, 34.

[45] B Crossette, 'Iraqis, Hurt by Sanctions, Sell Priceless Antiquities' *The New York Times* (23 June 1996).

[46] PG Stone, 'The Identification and Protection of Cultural Heritage during the Iraq Conflict: A Peculiarly English Tale' in Stone and Farchakh Bajjaly, *Destruction of Cultural Heritage in Iraq* 73, 78; DG Youkhanna, 'The Looting of the Iraq National Museum' in ibid 97, 107.

[47] See eg Stone and Farchakh Bajjaly, *Destruction of Cultural Heritage in Iraq*.

[48] UNESCO Information Dossier on the Promotion of the Return or Restitution of Cultural Property: http://unesdoc.unesco.org/images/0013/001394/139407eb.pdf.

[49] Some items from the Iraq Museum, including furniture from palaces in Nimrud, were damaged due to poor storage from the 1990s onwards: L Al-Gailani Werr, 'The Story of the Iraq Museum' in Stone and Farchakh Bajjaly, *Destruction of Cultural Heritage in Iraq* 25, 27.

The route of smuggled items depends upon the location of the source country, the type of item taken, and market demand for that type of object. For example, there is anecdotal evidence of objects that were smuggled out of Iraq being transferred to Syria, Saudi Arabia, Iran and Turkey. These items were then given false papers relating to their provenance.[50] Any objects taken out of China, such as jade, might go via Hong Kong, Macau or Taipei, because there is a strong demand for these objects in the Asian market.[51]

The size of the object may affect the choice of route and destination. Small items, such as amulets or cylinder seals from Iraq, have become particularly popular with collectors. Cylinder seals are usually inscribed or decorated with semi-precious stones. They were used by their owners to make identifying marks on wet clay tablets by being rolled across them. They are the Mesopotamian equivalent of English seals and date back as far as 2500 BC, or earlier. They are frequently found in tombs and, as they are usually no larger than a person's little finger, they can be easily taken and concealed in someone's luggage or pocket.

Although small packages of drugs are also easy to smuggle, they are easy to identify as prohibited substances, and the penalties applied when someone is found in possession of drugs are usually severe.[52] In contrast, there are few risks involved in smuggling an object which has been unearthed from an archaeological site: it will not have been recorded on any database; if it has been cleaned, it may be impossible to identify its source with sufficient certainty. It may well be impossible to prove that any offence has been committed.

Once these objects are removed from their source country, the routes which they take can be convoluted. For example, poorer quality items may be released on to the market straight away, to be sold at auction to trusted middlemen. There is even evidence of dealers selling objects and then arranging to buy them again.[53] The items may circulate and recirculate through the auction houses, meanwhile stimulating interest in artefacts of that type amongst collectors and so gradually pushing up their price. The higher quality items may then be sold privately, their value having been raised by the sale prices of items sold at auction.

The profits to be made, particularly by intermediaries such as dealers, are so large that elaborate organisation becomes worthwhile. Thus, it is not only small objects that are looted, but much bigger items, such as heavy tombstone-shaped slabs of limestone with hieroglyphics (known as steles). Their removal requires advance planning; they may need to be detached from a wall of a building, and they are likely to be difficult to transport. They may also need to be stored for some time before sale. One method is to ship them and then store them in a warehouse. A number of countries operate a system whereby goods arriving by ship at a port can be stored in a warehouse without incurring customs duties: these warehouses are known as 'freeport warehouses'. These cultural objects can eventually be loaded on board another ship for their final destination. In 1995, a freeport warehouse

[50] See M Gibson, 'The Acquisition of Antiquities in Iraq, 19th Century to 2003, Legal and Illegal' in Stone and Farchakh Bajjaly, *Destruction of Cultural Heritage in Iraq* 35–36.

[51] K Polk, 'Whither the Criminology in the Study of the Traffic in Illicit Antiquities?' in S Mackenzie and P Geen, *Criminology and Archaeology* (Oxford, Hart Publishing, 2009) 13, 15.

[52] See *R v Simms* [2010] EWCA Crim 1449 [10], where the defendants attempted to argue – as a defence –that they thought that they had been involved in smuggling antiquities from Iraq, rather than drugs.

[53] There was clear evidence that one dealer, Medici, sold and then repurchased objects, because he left the Sotheby's labels on the objects: P Watson, 'Convicted Dealers' in Brodie et al (eds), *Archaeology, Cultural Heritage and the Antiquities Trade* (Gainesville, University Press of Florida, 2006) 93, 94. If the object is stolen, and therefore represents the proceeds of crime, this activity could be viewed as money laundering: see 3.34.

in Switzerland was raided by Swiss and Italian law enforcement officials, who found approximately 10,000 unprovenanced antiquities valued at £25 million.[54]

The potential to make thousands or perhaps millions of pounds induces criminals to steal from private and public collections and to encourage the looting of archaeological sites. Every effort appears worthwhile, because these objects are seen in purely financial terms. Yet this is the problem: these objects have special characteristics which contribute to their financial value but which make them irreplaceable and sometimes in reality priceless.

V The Special Characteristics of Cultural Objects

1.13 Intrinsic Values

Cultural objects are not defined solely by their physical characteristics.[55] They can help to inform us as human beings: 'Art tells us who we are and where we came from.'[56] They possess a special status because of their intrinsic values.[57] These values reflect the intellectual effort or ingenuity with which an object was created (including the colour, line and shape and general composition). But these objects are also repositories of information relating to the human condition, society and history.[58] Furthermore, some objects are seen as possessing religious or spiritual qualities.[59] Merryman has commented: 'A cultural object embodies or expresses or evokes some aspect of the culture of its time and place.'[60] It is precisely these attributes which prompt members of the public to go to museums to admire these objects and to learn more about them.

Cultural objects have arguably become increasingly important in this mechanised and electronic age. Humans are largely detached from the production of goods. As our relational distance from food and other basic commodities lengthens, arguably our relationship with cultural property becomes more significant. Heritage property is distinctive in an increasingly homogenised world. It may be helpful in creating a sense of cultural identity, establishing common bonds, and bringing communities together. It is a source of information relating to our past, assisting us in understanding how the world and our nation have evolved. As the market in cultural property can therefore legitimately be regarded as distinct, it should be approached with an expectation that the moral responsibilities of market participants might not necessarily be the same as those who trade in ordinary commodities.

[54] Report of the Ministerial Advisory Panel on Illicit Trade, Department for Culture, Media and Sport, December 2000 Annex A [38]; N Brodie, J Doole and P Watson, *Stealing History: The Illicit Trade in Cultural Material* (Cambridge, the McDonald Institute for Archaeological Research, 2000) 27.

[55] M Govan, 'Art as Information' (2001) 19 *Cardozo Arts and Entertainments Law Journal* 109, 123.

[56] A Elsen, 'Why do we Care about Art?' 27 *Hastings Law Journal* 951, 952. For further discussion of the notion that art is special and is a mirror of culture, see PM Bator, 'An Essay on the International Trade in Art' (1982) 34 *Stanford Law Review* 275, 304–06.

[57] S Guest, 'The Value of Art' (2002) VII(4) *Art Antiquity and Law* 305.

[58] Thus, even if one could make exact copies of the Elgin Marbles, using the same marble, they would not possess the value of the originals because the historic context would differ. If this were not the case, the repatriation debate would not exist. This association of the Elgin Marbles with a great culture has been described as 'special' value: S Guest, 'The Value of Art' (2002) VII(4) *Art Antiquity and Law* 305, 313.

[59] For example, the Willamette Meteorite: S Vincent, 'Indian Givers' in K Fitzgibbon (ed), *Who Owns the Past?* (New Brunswick, New Jersey and London, Rutgers University Press, 2005) 33, 35.

[60] JH Merryman, 'Counterfeit Art' (1992) 1 *International Journal of Cultural Property* 27, reproduced in Merryman, *Elgin Marbles* 468.

Unfortunately, not all those operating in the market see cultural objects in this edifying way. A number of dealers and collectors see the art market as similar to other markets. They take risks and hope to make a sizeable profit.[61] Indeed, markets do not generally operate in a neutral way:[62] they encourage participants to see the goods being bought and sold in financial terms. The price paid for art and antiquities has continued to rise throughout the twentieth century and the early twenty-first century. For example, on 5 May 2004, Picasso's 'Boy with a Pipe' was sold for $US93 million (together with the auction house's $US11 million commission). It is calculated that the increase in capital value earned the seller the equivalent of 64 per cent interest per annum over 54 years.[63] The fact that huge profits can be made encourages middlemen to treat cultural items as they would any ordinary commodity.

But do all buyers see their purchases in financial terms? Gibson has suggested that the collapse of the stock market in the USA and elsewhere in the late 1980s and the soaring prices for legitimate objects of antiquity prompted investors to seek out cylinder seals and other items which had been smuggled out of Iraq.[64] But, for some at least, part of the attraction might have been to possess and control the object, in a manner which one cannot do with shares in a company. Sagot-Duvauroux has observed that individual investors appear to wield more power in the art market than in the stock market: whereas the owner of a cultural object enjoys power over it, an investor in shares is merely one of many owners of rights in a company, each of whom may well be acting independently.[65] The attraction of possessing something which was not only aesthetically pleasing but also unique (rather than owning a portion of homogeneous, substitutable shares) might (for some) prove irresistible.

Cultural objects are therefore complex dualities: treated as any other commodity in financial terms, and yet also providing a human dimension in terms of creativity and information. The relationship is a strange one. A high value for an object of antiquity is not necessarily a good thing. The more that a type of object of antiquity is desired, whether for its aesthetic qualities or its historical associations, the more this type of object will become an attractive investment, and the more likely it will be that such objects will be looted to satisfy market demands. In contrast, in the contemporary art market, consisting of the work of living artists, a high value is seen in an entirely positive light. This market is highly dependent upon saleability, in order to reassure purchasers that the object is worthy of being collected and preserved. If an object does not sell, its claim to be a work of art comes into question. The market is small and difficult for newcomers to break into, which serves the purposes of both sellers and buyers.[66] Yet contemporary works of art also clearly possess intrinsic values. The materials used often have very little value in themselves, and artists often rely upon novelty, unusual materials, and non-traditional forms of communication. They may be highly conceptual in nature, such as 'The Lights Going On and Off', by Martin

[61] In relation to antiquities, see N Brodie, J Doole and P Watson, *Stealing History: The Illicit Trade in Cultural Material* (Cambridge, the McDonald Institute for Archaeological Research, 2000) 9.

[62] See M Sandel, 'Markets and Morals', Reith Lectures 2009: A New Citizenship (BBC Radio).

[63] I Robertson, 'The Economics of Taste' in Robertson, *Understanding International Art Markets and Management* 1.

[64] M Gibson, 'The Acquisition of Antiquities in Iraq, 19th Century to 2003, Legal and Illegal' in Stone and Farchakh Bajjaly, *Destruction of Cultural Heritage in Iraq* 34.

[65] D Sagot-Duvauroux, 'Art Prices' in R Towse (ed), *Handbook of Cultural Economics* (Cheltenham, Edward Elgar, 2003) 58.

[66] Singer has suggested that both buyers and sellers are interested in barriers to entry, in contrast to other types of market, where the barriers to entry exist for the sellers' benefit alone: LP Singer, 'Phenomenology and Economics of Art Markets: an Art Historical Perspective' (1988) 12(1) *Journal of Cultural Economics* 27.

Creed. There has been a move away from placing emphasis upon the formal elements of a creation, and towards concentrating on the emotional and intellectual response to the work, requiring the viewer's mental participation.[67] It is a world away from antiquities, and yet there is a common thread: these are all creations which speak to a particular time in history and a social context.

1.14 Intrinsic values and English law

Since the UK's acceptance of the UNESCO Convention, courts should recognise the intrinsic values of cultural objects. In *Government of the Islamic Republic of Iran v The Barakat Galleries Ltd,* the Court of Appeal emphasised the importance of each nation's cultural heritage and it was noted that the Convention made it necessary for states to be alive to their moral obligations to protect and respect cultural property.[68] The Court endorsed the comments made by Finlay CJ in *Webb v Ireland,* in which he stated that 'one of the most important national assets belonging to the people is their heritage and knowledge of its true origins and the buildings and objects which constituted keys to their ancient history.'[69]

The criminal courts take account of whether criminal acts involve cultural property rather than commonplace items in relation to sentencing. Thus, in *R v Hakimzadeh,*[70] the appellant stole various books, maps and pages from books belonging to the British Library and the Bodleian Library in order to improve his own library of books of historical significance. He pleaded guilty to 14 counts of theft, but appealed against the sentence of two years' imprisonment. The Court of Appeal observed:

> In our judgment, it is apparent that this kind of offending, where cultural property is concerned, is very different from offending where the seriousness can only be gained by the value in the open market of items which can readily be replaced and purchased, whether they may be goods in a supermarket or ordinary books which are still in print and available and it is simply the replacement value of items lost. Cultural property cannot be valued in the same way as cash or readily replicable items, and the gravamen is the damage to rare items of historical, intellectual and cultural importance, and that is why, in our judgment, a significant element of deterrence is always necessary to deter others from such crimes which diminish the intellectual and cultural heritage of the nation.[71]

Although the Sentencing Guidelines Council had published definitive guidance in relation to sentences imposed from 5 January 2009 onwards for theft and burglary, they did not expressly deal with cultural property. However, the Court of Appeal noted that, as a scholar, the appellant had been in a position of trust: he was expected to treat the books as an important cultural and historical resource. The Court therefore used the recommended guidelines for the more serious case of theft in breach of trust to assist them. But certain mitigating factors were taken into account, including the fact that the materials had not been taken for commercial gain and had now been returned, and the applicant's sentence was reduced accordingly.

[67] T Godfrey, *Conceptual Art* (London, Phaidon Press, 1998) 4; D Watkins, 'The Value of Art or the Art we Value?' (2006) XI(3) *Art Antiquity and Law* 251, 258.

[68] *Government of the Islamic Republic of Iran v The Barakat Galleries Ltd* [2007] EWCA Civ 1374, [2009] QB 22 (CA) [2] (Lord Phillips of Worth Matravers).

[69] *Webb v Ireland* [1988] IR 353 (Supreme Court of Ireland) 383.

[70] *R v Hakimzadeh* [2009] EWCA 959, noted by K Warner (2010) XV *Art Antiquity and Law* 95.

[71] [2009] EWCA 959 [13]. This principle was subsequently applied in *R v William Simon Jacques* [2010] EWCA Crim 3233, where there were no mitigating factors.

1.15 The duality of cultural objects and European law

Cultural objects have a dual nature: on the one hand, cultural objects can be seen in financial terms as objects of commerce; on the other hand, they can be seen as vessels of information, prompting both cerebral and emotional responses to our past and our sense of identity. This 'duality' has confronted the European Court of Justice in dealing with cases involving the European market. The Treaty of Rome of 1957 laid down a general principle of free movement of goods. However, it was accepted that certain types of cultural property should be excluded from the market integration process. Consequently, domestic legislation designed to protect 'national treasures possessing artistic, historic or archaeological value' was permitted.[72] But this exception forced the European Court of Justice to consider what measures a state might legitimately take to 'protect' its national treasures. This has meant that the Court has been obliged to assess objects from a cultural and non-economic perspective, whilst simultaneously accepting that the movement and transfer of these objects involve economic consequences. This point is illustrated by the decision in *EC Commission v Italy*.[73] In this case, the Italian Government attempted to justify the severe export restrictions and taxation which it imposed upon any articles having artistic, historical, archaeological or ethnographic interest by arguing that they were art treasures and not commercial goods. It was contended that, as a consequence, these restrictions did not infringe the basic principle of free movements of goods. However, the European Court rejected this argument, suggesting that:

> 'The Products covered by the Italian Law, whatever may be the characteristics which distinguish them from other goods in commerce, nevertheless share with those latter the characteristic of being able to be valued in money and so to be the object of commercial transactions.'[74]

In essence, the Court ruled that this exception did not allow states to impose onerous taxes on the export of cultural objects, as this did not protect such objects but merely imposed a burden on the owner.

The Treaty of Rome of 1957 made little mention of cultural matters otherwise.[75] Cultural objects were seen as promoting national interests, rather than European or international ones. However, in more recent years there has been increasing interest in developing a common cultural policy, for political reasons, in order to promote a sense of European citizenship and to foster European integration. Article 151 of the 1992 Maastricht Treaty consequently provided a legal basis for promoting culture. Its objective had been to celebrate a 'common cultural heritage', whilst recognising the importance of regional diversity. This approach has been adopted by Article 167 of the 2009 Lisbon Treaty, which superseded Article 151 and which provides:

> The Union shall contribute to the flowering of the cultures of the Member States, while respecting their national and regional diversity and at the same time bringing common cultural heritage to the fore;
>
> Action by the Union shall be aimed at encouraging co-operation between Member States and, if necessary, supporting and supplementing their action in the following areas:

[72] EEC Treaty, art 36; replaced by EC, art 30.

[73] *EC Commission v Italy* Case 7/68 [1969] CMLR 1 (ECJ).

[74] [1969] CMLR 1 [5].

[75] Although provision was made for cultural links with third countries: EEC Treaty, art 131, replaced by EC, art 182. See R Craufurd Smith, 'From Heritage Conservation to European Identity: art 151 EC and the Multi-faceted Nature of Community Cultural Policy' (2007) *European Law Review* 48, 50.

improvement of the knowledge and dissemination of the culture and history of the European people,
conservation and safeguarding of cultural heritage of European significance,
non-commercial cultural exchanges,
artistic and literary creation, including in the audio visual sector.

The terminology of Article 167 is vague and aspirational in tone. Article 167(5) expressly provides that any measures adopted to fulfil these objectives do not include harmonisation of the laws or regulations relating to cultural property which form part of the domestic law of the Member States.

1.16 The Duality of Cultural Objects and the Importance of Experts

A feature which makes the market in art and antiquities distinct from other markets is the impact of connoisseurship. In relation to artistic matters, people's preferences are strongly influenced by institutions or persons who collectively possess a monopoly in relation to taste.[76] As regards works of art, their judgments assist in determining what is valuable, and bring order to a market which is concerned with values which are difficult to assess objectively. In relation to antiquities, the contributions of archaeologists can heighten interest in material from a particular country or period of history.

The views of experts are therefore likely to affect any valuation of an object. These experts will include archaeologists, art critics, art historians, dealers, galleries and auction houses. The views of private collectors have also carried great weight over the centuries.[77] Museum officials are also influential: they may act as arbiters of taste in the choices which they make in terms of borrowing works for temporary exhibitions or in purchasing works for their collections. The response of the public may also be significant. The popularity of public exhibitions may enhance the reputation of an artist or ignite interest in the antiquities of a particular country. However, the response of the public cannot be characterised as an untutored one. Although objects of art and antiquities have the potential to induce emotions in those who engage with them, information and objective critical assessment assists in validating those feelings.[78]

From a legal perspective, the opinions of experts may be essential not only in gauging an object's authenticity in a world which is awash with forgeries,[79] but also in identifying objects for the purposes of criminal prosecution or civil action for recovery. For example, neo-Assyrian gold earrings, estimated to be over 3,000 years old, were offered for sale by Christie's in New York in 2008. Christie's claimed that the previous owner had acquired them in 1969. However, the Director of the National Museum in Baghdad, the late Donny George Youkhanna, was able to identify the earrings as unique and as belonging to the

[76] I Robertson, 'The Economics of Taste' in Robertson, *Understanding International Art Markets* 1, 4. See further, R Towse, 'Introduction' in R Towse (ed), *Handbook of Cultural Economics* (Cheltenham, Edward Elgar, 2003), in which she argues that, as consumers cannot have full information, they must rely upon experts, leading to supplier-induced demand: ibid 2–3.

[77] See ME Mayo, 'Collecting Ancient Art' in K Fitzgibbon (ed), *Who Owns the Past?* (New Brunswick, New Jersey and London, Rutgers University Press, 2005) 133. See also I Robertson, 'Art, Religion, History, Money' in Robertson (ed) *Understanding International Art Markets* 41.

[78] S Guest, 'The Value of Art' (2002) VII(4) *Art Antiquity and Law* 305, 306–308.

[79] See J Ulph, 'Markets and Responsibilities: Forgeries and the Sale of Goods Act 1979' [2011] (3) *Journal of Business Law* 261. In the Report of the Ministerial Advisory Panel on Illicit Trade, Department for Culture, Media and Sport, December 2000 Annex A [46], it is noted that a substantial number of Cycladic figurines had been forged to satisfy the intense demand in the market for such figurines.

Government of Iraq as part of the 'Nimrud treasure'. They were subsequently returned to Iraq.[80]

The courts may well depend upon experts when called upon to interpret the wording of any statutory definition of cultural property. The legislature may have tried and failed, or simply have neglected to consider a proper definition which captures the intrinsic values contained within certain types of cultural property. Indeed, cultural objects are so diverse, and their intrinsic values are so difficult to identify at times, that the opinion of experts may be needed in relation to the application of any statutory provisions which specially affect them. For example, experts have been used in helping to determine whether video installations can be classified as 'sculptures', which attract a lower rate of customs duties on importation.[81]

Although the use of experts may make legislative schemes costly and unwieldy to administer, if an attempt is made to avoid this problem by simply ignoring cultural characteristics altogether, not only would it be ethically dubious, but it may bring different problems in its wake. In particular, there is a risk that it would contravene human rights legislation, by unjustly depriving an individual of his property. Thus, in *Kozacioğlu v Turkey*,[82] the Grand Chamber of the European Court of Human Rights accepted that, whatever the difficulties in putting a financial value to these intrinsic values, this did not provide an automatic excuse for avoiding the problem altogether.

In *Kozacioğlu v Turkey*, the applicant had owned a building which had been classified as a 'cultural asset' by a public body on behalf of the state. It was compulsorily acquired, but the compensation paid simply reflected the fact that it was a two-floor building and did not take account of its cultural value. The relevant statute expressly stated that the value of the compensation could *not* reflect 'a property's age, rarity and artistic features'. The Expropriation Act (Law no 2942), which provided for the procedure for valuation, supported this approach, stating that the valuation must be on the basis of objective criteria. The applicant argued that the compensation paid was inadequate and that there had been a violation of Article 1 of the First Protocol of the European Convention on Human Rights. Article 1 consists of three rules:

> Every natural or legal person is entitled to the peaceful enjoyment of his possessions. No one shall be deprived of his possessions except in the public interest and subject to the conditions provided for by law and by the general principles of international law.
>
> The preceding provisions shall not, however, in any way impair the right of a state to enforce such laws as it deems necessary to control the use of property in accordance with the general interest or to secure the payment of taxes or other contributions or penalties.

The Court accepted that the applicant had been lawfully deprived of his possessions within the meaning of the second sentence of Article 1, which permits such deprivation if it is done in the public interest. Here, the legislation was made in pursuit of a legitimate aim, which was to protect Turkey's cultural heritage.[83] But the Court observed that the three rules in Article 1, although distinct, must be balanced against each other; together

[80] '3,000 year old earrings returned to Iraq from US' *Daily Telegraph* (22 August 2010).

[81] See *Haunch of Venison Partners Ltd*, Decision of the VAT and Duties Tribunal (London) of 8 December 2008, discussed in the context of import duties at 3.58. Witnesses included a director at the National Portrait Gallery, a programme leader at the Courtauld Institute of Art, and a writer, lecturer and art critic: ibid [19].

[82] *Kozacioğlu v Turkey*, App no 2334/03 (Grand Chamber); [2011] 53 ECHR 3.

[83] The Court made reference to the Convention for the Protection of the Architectural Heritage of Europe, adopted on 3 October 1985, which encouraged states to take statutory measures to protect the architectural heritage and to prevent damage to protected properties: ibid [54].

they provide a framework against which a particular legal principle may be judged.[84] There must be a reasonable relationship of proportionality between the aim of protecting the nation's heritage and the means employed to achieve that aim.[85] The Court considered that a compulsory purchase scheme which did not provide full compensation was not necessarily unfair.[86] Furthermore, states have some discretion in how they implement particular policies, provided that it was not manifestly without reasonable foundation.[87] Nevertheless, it was decided that the law was disproportionate and unfair in these circumstances because, although the building's historic significance could be ignored to avoid paying more generous compensation, if the property had depreciated in value due to its listed status as a cultural asset, the state could take advantage of this fact in reducing the compensation payable.[88]

The one dissenting judge, Judge Maruste, remained unconvinced that additional compensation should be provided to reflect an asset's cultural and historic values, observing:

> The reason there are no clear rules and common standards is the obvious difficulty – if not impossibility – of assessing and calculating the pecuniary value of unique historical and cultural objects. (What is the rarity value of the Eiffel Tower or the Palace of Westminster? The answer is that no such rarity value exists, because there are no other Eiffel Towers or Palaces of Westminster on the market.) In respect of ordinary property the value is evident and clear – it is the market value average, which can be calculated on the basis of a statistical analysis of the market. In respect of a unique item that forms part of the cultural heritage, this method cannot be used. Its value is a matter of (subjective) assessment and, if not agreed, is subject to litigation.

However, the majority observed that other states took account of a property's historical value in attempting to arrive at a fair price by way of compensation; the UK, for example, did so in deciding upon the property's 'intrinsic qualities'.[89] The majority accepted that, although there are no straightforward objective criteria which can be applied to recognise the intrinsic values in cultural property, this should not prevent a legislative scheme being created which makes a reasonable attempt to take account of such matters, even if it is inevitably going to be an imperfect process. The case therefore demonstrates the uneasy relationship between culture and money: the applicant succeeded in arguing that the cultural qualities of his house should be properly recognised in Turkey's legislative scheme, but that those qualities should be reflected in hard cash.

1.17 The Duality of Cultural Objects and International Conventions

The duality of cultural property poses problems for those drafting international conventions, as well as domestic statutes, which aim to protect cultural material. A suitable definition must be found which distinguishes cultural objects from commonplace ones. Although the sale price of similar objects could be seen as introducing some element of objectivity,

[84] *Kozacioğlu v Turkey* [2009] ECHR 2334/03 (Grand Chamber) [48]; *Pye (Oxford) Ltd v UK* [2008] 1 EGLR 111 (Grand Chamber) [52]; *Sun v Russia* [2009] ECHR 31004/02 [23]; *Islamic Republic of Iran Shipping Lines v Turkey* [2007] ECHR 40998/98 [86]; *Allgemeine Gold- und Silberscheideanstalt AG (AGOSI) v UK* (1986) 9 EHRR 1.

[85] *JA Pye (Oxford) Ltd v UK* [2008] 1 EGLR 111 (Grand Chamber) [55]; *Gabric v Croatia* [2009] ECHR 9702/04 [35]; *Sporrong and Lönnroth v Sweden* (1982) 5 EHRR 35 [69]; *James v UK* (1986) 8 EHRR 123, 145 [50].

[86] *Kozacioğlu v Turkey* [2009] ECHR 2334/03 (Grand Chamber) [65].

[87] ibid [53]. In relation to a state's margin of appreciation, see further, *JA Pye (Oxford) Ltd v UK* [2008] 1 EGLR 111 (Grand Chamber) [55], [71], [75]; *AGOSI v UK* (1986) 9 EHRR 1 [48].

[88] *Kozacioğlu v Turkey* [2009] ECHR 2334/03 (Grand Chamber) [69].

[89] ibid [34], [35], [71].

financial valuations are not necessarily helpful. Some cultural objects are aesthetically more pleasing and will attract much higher prices because of this. The uniqueness of each item contributes to the unpredictability of its price. Unsurprisingly, the categories of items listed in the UNESCO Convention 1970, which is discussed in Chapter 2, are fairly vague.[90] When the UK Government became a party to the UNESCO Convention in 2002, it confined the definition of 'cultural property' to the list of objects to be found in two sources: one source was the Annex to Council Regulation (EEC) No 3911/1992 (now Council Regulation 116/2009) on the export of cultural goods; the second source was the Annex to Council Directive 93/7/EEC on the return of cultural objects unlawfully removed from the territory of a Member State.[91] The categories of objects listed in the Annexes to the Regulation and Directive are basically the same; they are accompanied by thresholds relating to age and/or financial value and represent a much narrower definition of cultural property than the one provided by the UNESCO Convention.

1.18 The Duality of Cultural Objects: Justifying Misconduct

Where dealers and collectors are indifferent to the history of an object and turn a blind eye to suspicious circumstances, unprovenanced cultural objects can be bought and sold with relative ease. The dual nature of such items assists those who wish to excuse any irresponsible behaviour. Some dealers may view cultural objects as commodities, valued according to their yield of potential profit. In the context of looted antiquities, they will assert that some source countries have unduly retentive laws, and will argue that these antiquities should be freely traded to generate wealth and to satisfy educated collectors.

However, those trading in illicit antiquities often prefer to emphasise the intrinsic values which cultural objects possess. Thus, one justification for exporting objects from the country of origin is based on the argument that cultural objects have a 'universal' dimension. It is suggested that the free movement of cultural objects is beneficial because it increases accessibility, boosting exposure to and appreciation of other cultures. This argument obviously has a pearl of truth. There is no doubt that cultural objects have an educative value. It is obviously worthwhile to create opportunities for the public to learn more about other cultures through examining cultural objects. However, it is not necessarily a good reason for criticising the patrimonial laws of source states. If objects are taken abroad for temporary public display in museums and international galleries, this should promote the exchange of knowledge about different cultures. In contrast, those objects which are sold on the markets to private collectors will not be accessible to the public.

A further argument made is that the dealer or collector is saving objects which might otherwise be destroyed.[92] This argument has been employed in relation to artefacts taken from Afghanistan. Following the collapse of the communist regime in 1993, many items were stolen from the National Museum of Afghanistan in Kabul – according to some estimates, as much as 70 per cent of its collection was plundered. Subsequently, Islamic

[90] See 2.14.

[91] Directive 93/7/EEC has been transposed into UK law by the Return of Cultural Objects Regulations 1994: see 5.08 and 6.02 The list of cultural objects to be found in Directive 93/7/EEC, together with financial guidelines in the 1994 Regulations, are set out in an Annex to this text. Regulation 116/2009 is also set out in the Annex.

[92] S Mackenzie, 'Dig a Bit Deeper: Law, Regulation and the Illicit Antiquities Market' (2005) 45 *British Journal of Criminology* 249. See further, N Brodie, 'Consensual Relations? Academic Involvement in the Illegal Trade in Ancient Manuscripts' in S Mackenzie and P Green, *Criminology and Archaeology: Studies in Looted Antiquities* (Oxford, Hart, 2009) 48.

fundamentalists systematically destroyed ancient Buddhist and Gandharan statuary kept in a storeroom in the National Museum which they considered to be idolatrous. In March 2001, the Taliban destroyed pre-Islamic sculptures in Afghanistan, including two giant Buddhas of Bamiyan.[93] This type of wanton destruction has enabled traders to call into question the moral principle, reflected in the 1970 UNESCO Convention, that ancient works should remain in their country of origin. Dealers have argued that they are saving these types of artefacts from destruction and that collectors will take care of them.[94]

At first glance, this argument may appear persuasive. If an antiquity is destroyed, it means the obliteration of information contained within the object. There is a moral duty to preserve these objects at all costs. Even so, it should be noted that, once saved, these objects have usually joined the market in licit and illicit goods, rather than being donated to a museum for safe-keeping. Furthermore, objects which are 'saved' may end up being hoarded secretly afterwards.[95] It is suspected that many objects from Afghanistan found their way onto the international market and have ended up in private hands. The result is that the public will be deprived of them for years to come.

It has been suggested that a number of antiquities finding their way on to the market are chance finds.[96] It is argued that, if dealers were not ready to trade in these antiquities, farmers working in the fields in source countries would throw such objects away: the fact that the farmer can make a profit from the object will protect it from reckless destruction. It has also been argued that some cultural objects are so common that they may be seen by locals – although not by the international community – as only valuable in terms of their components, so that limestone reliefs might simply be seen as a source of lime, until it is appreciated that they have a market value in the West.[97] But is this attempt to justify the illicit trade in cultural property somewhat misleading? Tubb and Brodie argue that 'chance finds' lying on the ground are usually worth very little, because exposure to the weather will have damaged them. They suggest that the truly valuable objects are those found in tombs.[98] Objects hidden in tombs or buried in the ground do not need to be 'saved'. As Gibson observes, 'Artefacts are safest in the ground, awaiting their careful exposure by trained archaeologists, who can extract much greater information from them through knowledge of the context in which they resided.'[99]

[93] See 2.11.

[94] T McGirk, 'A Year of Looting Dangerously' *Sunday Review, Independent on Sunday* (24 March 1996) 4–8.

[95] A notable exception relates to the ransacking of the Iraq National Museum: approximately 4,000 objects were subsequently returned. See DG Youkhanna, 'The Looting of the Iraq National Musem' in Stone and Farchakh Bajjaly, *Destruction of Cultural Heritage in Iraq* 97, 104.

[96] S Mackenzie, *Going, Going, Gone: Regulating the Market in Illicit Antiquities* (Leicester, Institute of Art and Law, 2005) 56–57.

[97] M Gibson, 'The Acquisition of Antiquities in Iraq, 19th Century to 2003, Legal and Illegal' in Stone and Farchakh Bajjaly, *Destruction of Cultural Heritage in Iraq* 31.

[98] KW Tubb and N Brodie, 'From Museum to Mantelpiece: The Antiquities Trade in the United Kingdom' in R Layton, PG Stone and J Thomas (eds), *Destruction and Conservation of Cultural Property* (London, Routledge, 2001) 102, 106.

[99] M Gibson, 'The Acquisition of Antiquities in Iraq, 19th Century to 2003, Legal and Illegal' ch 4 in Stone and Farchakh Bajjaly, *Destruction of Cultural Heritage in Iraq* 31, 37.

VI Changing Attitudes

1.19 The Impact of Philosophical Debate: Internationalists and Nationalists

If a cultural item is viewed purely as an object of commerce, any disputes in relation to it could be decided by reference to legal principles. The key policy issue would be the extent to which the law should protect the rights of the original owner. Any debate would centre on how national laws respond to this issue. However, as discussed, cultural items possess intrinsic values and their dual nature is recognised at international and European levels, as well as by English law. Even so, there are those who take the view that cultural items should be freely traded for scientific, educational and cultural purposes. In recognition of the fact that these items are more than mere commodities, it is argued by 'cultural internationalists' that all countries have an interest in the preservation of cultural objects, because they form part of a common human heritage; they suggest that, where items can be transferred from one country to another with relative ease, there will be immense benefit to the public because these items assist them in learning about other cultures.[100]

Yet there are various arguments which can be made against this school of thought. O'Keefe and Prott observe that there is a desire in Western societies for exploration and change which leads to a vigorous interest in cultural objects from elsewhere. This prompts Western societies to attribute a positive value towards movement of cultural objects, which is not shared by other societies: 'It is important . . . to appreciate that the values related to movement . . . are not universally dominant; that where they seriously threaten other values important to a community, such as tradition and stability, insensitive promotion of them is a form of ethnocentrism which may prevent appropriate appreciation of the differently ranked values of the other culture.'[101]

'Cultural nationalists' argue, on moral rather than legal grounds, that all artefacts should be returned to their source country because they form part of that country's history and cultural heritage and therefore foster a sense of community.[102] The arguments of cultural nationalists have a persuasive strength where a particular source nation has been stripped of its most important treasures by conquest in earlier centuries; but it is submitted that these arguments are at their weakest when wide-ranging claims are made to any and every object which was once on the land that forms part of the current boundaries of a particular country but which were donated to another nation consensually in the distant past.

The focus of this text is upon the law relating to objects which have been recently removed; it is not concerned with the repatriation or return of objects taken centuries ago. Consequently, the debate between nationalists and internationalists has been presented very briefly. Even so, the debate cannot be ignored. Various source materials have been sub-

[100] This issue is discussed by JH Merryman, 'A Licit International Trade in Cultural Objects' (1995) 4 *International Journal of Cultural Property* 13, reproduced in Merryman, *Elgin Marbles* 244, 245. See further, A Sljivic, 'Why Do You Think It's Yours? An Exposition of the Jurisprudence Underlying the Debate Between Cultural Nationalism and Cultural Internationalism' (1998) 31 *George Washington Journal of International Law and Economics* 393, 413–14.

[101] O' Keefe and Prott, *Law and the Cultural Heritage, Volume 3 – Movement* (London, Butterworths, 1989) 10 [105]. The Law Reform Commission of Ireland, Report on the Unidroit Convention on Stolen or Illegally Exported Objects (1997) LRC 55 [1.15].

[102] JH Merryman, 'Thinking about the Elgin Marbles,' (1985) 83 *Michigan Law Review* 1881, 1911–12, reproduced in Merryman, *Elgin Marbles* 24; DN Chang, 'Stealing Beauty: Stopping the Madness of Illicit Art Trafficking' (2006) 28 *Houston Journal of International Law* 829, 844.

ject to scrutiny from this perspective.[103] More importantly, the debate appears to have changed the attitudes of museums in relation to their acquisition policies. Moreover, after 1970, when the UNESCO Convention came into being (and long before the UK became a party to it), UK museums became cautious about acquiring objects which might be seen as the national patrimony of another country Museums are now guided by ethical codes of conduct and are expected to check the provenance of objects before accepting and accessioning them in their collections.[104] Critics have suggested that the emphasis upon provenance has the effect of driving objects onto the black market.[105] Yet the exercise of due diligence in acquiring objects will deter the illicit trade in art and antiquities.

The current caution being shown by museums and the scientific community when presented with a novel item should be warmly welcomed. In this regard, the guiding principles of the Archaeological Institute of America's Code of Ethics are to be applauded.[106] The Code's second principle states that its members should 'Refuse to participate in the trade in undocumented antiquities and refrain from activities that enhance the commercial value of such objects.' Its third principle provides that archaeologists should report any suspicious circumstances to the appropriate authorities. These principles might once have been described as representing a 'nationalist approach',[107] but this would betray a lack of awareness of the activities of serious organised criminals. From a legal perspective, these principles offer sensible advice. As museums, archaeologists and dealers become alive to the risk that they may become unwitting accomplices to money launderers, a healthy scepticism in relation to unusual transactions is advisable.

VII Combatting the Illicit Trade in Art and Antiquities

1.20 Challenges

The United Nations Economic and Security Council requested the United Nations Office on Drugs and Crime (UNODC) to convene an intergovernmental meeting on preventing and combatting trafficking in cultural property.[108] Simon Mackenzie prepared a background paper for this meeting, which was held in November 2009. The paper summarised the challenges which confronted the international community as follows:

> The main characteristics of the transnational crime problem of looted and smuggled cultural property/heritage are:

[103] For example, the 1970 UNESCO Convention is seen as largely based on a nationalist retention perspective: see JH Merryman, 'The Retention of Cultural Property' (1988) 21 *University of California Davis Law Review* 477, reproduced in Merryman, *Elgin Marbles* 170, 197. See further, B Hoffman (ed) *Art and Cultural Heritage: Law, Policy and Practice* (Cambridge, Cambridge University Press, 2005) 14.

[104] In relation to UK museums, see 5.15. As regards US museums, after ratification of the UNESCO Convention, relatively few actively collected antiquities: WG Pearlstein, 'Cultural Property, Congress, the Courts, and Customs – The Decline and Fall of the Antiquities Market?' in K Fitzgibbon (ed), *Who Owns the Past?* (New Brunswick, New Jersey and London, Rutgers University Press, 2005) 9, 13

[105] PM Bator, 'An Essay on the International Trade in Art' (1982) 34 *Stanford Law Review* 275, 317–19.

[106] The Code of Ethics was adopted in 1990 and amended in 1997.

[107] JM Podesta, 'Saving Culture, but Passing the Buck: How the UNESCO Convention Undermines its Goals by Unduly Targeting Market Nations' (2008) 16 *Cardozo Journal of International and Comparative Law* 457, 470.

[108] See Resolutions 2004/34 and 2008/23.

(a) A crime problem in poorer 'source' countries which provides a source of income for local populations;
(b) Difficulty in enforcing the relevant laws in source countries due to lack of resources as well as varying levels of corruption;
(c) A ready market for looted objects in rich market countries providing a demand for the international transportation of looted [cultural property];
(d) Difficulty in telling illicit objects apart from licit ones once they are mixed together in the chain of supply – compounded by a culture of privacy in the antiquities market (buyers are reluctant to ask too many searching questions about provenance);
(e) A conflicted law enforcement and policy response to the issue in some market countries, since market and free trade principles tend to weigh against restrictive controls on the cross-border movement of [cultural property];
(f) An existing trade infrastructure (dealers, collectors, museums) which has a history and developed culture of dealing in [cultural property] without necessarily knowing about its provenance or provenience.[109]

1.21 Market norms: a culture of privacy

No one expects purchasers to make a detailed investigation of the history of everyday items.[110] Traders dealing in wheat, or metals, or other materials, will assume that they will be rapidly resold or put to work in producing other goods. Transactions are often speedily concluded, leaving no time for lengthy investigation of title. But, as discussed, cultural objects are quite distinct. It might have been anticipated that a different market norm would have evolved, because these objects need to be preserved for future generations: sellers might have been expected to thoroughly check the provenance of an object. However, as Mackenzie's paper indicates, this has not been the case.

An obvious strategy which could be employed to combat the illicit trade in art and antiquities might be to tackle the market norms which exist in the art world, where it is not usual to ask questions about an object's provenance. But if changes are to be made, what form should they take? It might be thought that the answer would be to create a situation, through appropriate laws or codes of conduct, which would put pressure upon collectors to avoid purchasing undocumented artefacts.[111] This is a major problem: in 2000, the ITAP Report concluded that the great majority of antiquities on the market were advertised without a stated provenance.[112] In his 2009 background paper Mackenzie echoes this:

> Where it is known that a substantial amount of looting happens around the world, and there have also been many high profile cases of seizure of looted objects in market countries (often in the hands of major auction houses), one would have thought that great effort would be expended by buyers in order to ensure so far as possible that they are not dealing in illicit objects. This has not been the case, however. Research with high level antiquities dealers has shown them to be more

[109] *Protection Against Trafficking in Cultural Property* UNODC/CCPCJ/EG.1/2009/CRP.1 [11].

[110] J Ulph, 'Good Faith and Due Diligence' in N Palmer and E McKendrick (eds), *Interests in Goods,* 2nd edn (London, LLP, 1998) 403.

[111] P Gerstenblith, 'Controlling the International Market in Antiquities: Reducing the Harm, Preserving the Past' (2007) 8 *Chicago Journal of International Law* 169, 174.

[112] Report of the Ministerial Advisory Panel on Illicit Trade, Department for Culture, Media and Sport, December 2000 Annex A [51]. This point has been echoed by Mackenzie, who suggested that 80–90% of the items being sold were unprovenanced articles: S Mackenzie, *Going, Going, Gone: Regulating the Market in Illicit Antiquities* (Leicester, Institute of Art and Law, 2005) 32–50.

concerned with collecting these prized objects, wherever they may have come from, than with playing a part in protecting archaeological sites in foreign countries.[113]

If the goods are accompanied by details of their history, it might be thought that there would be no need for questions: one might assume that they have not been misappropriated or illegally exported. And yet the solution is not so simple. Unfortunately, it is often easy enough for criminals to create false documents in relation to previous purchases and to forge letters from experts.[114]

Should the law do more to alter these market norms? Any changes will only be reluctantly accepted. Dealers have strong financial reasons for not revealing their sources: they may be afraid that, if they do, they will be cut out of the next profitable transaction. How do you persuade business people to ask questions when they have operated in an environment for years where secrecy and confidentiality have been the key concerns? Money laundering measures, supported by the threat of imprisonment, may provide a solution. This area of law, along with other criminal law offences, will be considered in Chapter 3.

1.22 Identification

The fact that it may be extremely difficult to distinguish illicit objects from licit ones 'once they are mixed in the chain of supply' is one of the main stumbling blocks in fighting crime. The large number of fakes and forgeries circulating in the market creates further problems. It is impossible to bring a criminal prosecution if the object in question may or may not be something removed last week from a source country rather than two centuries ago. One cannot send the accused to prison where there are accusations based upon guesswork.

The need for identification of objects is often overlooked in welcoming convictions of dishonest dealers and other accessories. For example, it is doubtful if Tokeley-Parry could have been successfully prosecuted for handling stolen goods, as explained in Chapter 3, if not for the fact that he kept detailed entries of his acquisitions in journals. His prosecution then led to further successful prosecutions.[115] The same is also true in relation to the prosecution of Medici and his associates after the discovery in 1995 of thousands of antiquities stored in a freeport warehouse in Switzerland. There were thousands of photographs providing evidence of the original condition of the looted antiquities, freshly unearthed, and their appearance after being cleaned up.[116] Medici kept sales records and correspondence; like Tokeley-Parry, this proved to be his undoing.

1.23 Law Enforcement and Policy Responses

Tackling the trafficking in art and antiquities requires a co-ordinated response by the global community. However, one difficulty is that, unless the government of a source nation

[113] *Protection Against Trafficking in Cultural Property* UNODC/CCPCJ/EG.1/2009/CRP.1, at [9].

[114] See *Kingdom of Spain v Christie Manson and Woods* [1986] 3 All ER 28. See further, the Sevso Treasure, involving forged Lebanese export documents, and which is discussed in the ITAP Report (Report of the Ministerial Advisory Panel on Illicit Trade, Department for Culture, Media and Sport, December 2000) Annex A [41].

[115] See 3.21.

[116] JH Merryman, AE Elsen and SK Urice, *Law, Ethics and the Visual Arts*, 5th edn (The Netherlands, Kluwer Law International, 2007) 404–405; N Brodie, J Doole and P Watson, *Stealing History: The Illicit Trade in Cultural Material* (Cambridge: the McDonald Institute for Archaeological Research, 2000) 27. See further, P Watson and C Todeschini, *The Medici Conspiracy: The Illicit Journey of Looted Antiquities from Italy's Tomb Raiders to the World's Greatest Museums* (New York, Public Affairs US, 2007).

asserts ownership of the unexcavated antiquities buried in its soil, then these antiquities will be viewed as belonging to no one. If a person takes ownerless property into his possession, it will not be clear to foreign eyes that he has contravened the law in any respect. It is for this reason that governments should enact patrimonial laws clarifying ownership of cultural property. It will then be easier to both secure a criminal conviction and to bring a civil claim to recover the property before the English courts.[117]

1.24 The Way Ahead

In discussing strategies to combat the illicit trade in cultural objects, one must not lose sight of the desired outcomes. One objective is to deter future trade in illicit objects and one of the key issues will be to tackle the traditional market norms which have tolerated irresponsible and furtive dealing. It may be that the criminal law is particularly effective in this regard. But there will be governments and individuals who are more concerned with recovering items which they have *already* lost. Money laundering measures, and forfeiture of cultural objects to the state in which they are currently located, will not assist them directly. Civil suits are often at least as important for victims as criminal sanctions. Unfortunately, claimants seeking the return of objects by bringing civil actions are faced with the twin difficulties of identification and proof of ownership.

It is clear from Mackenzie's paper that there is no simple way of eliminating or even reducing the illicit trade in cultural objects. A number of different strategies will be needed. It is an international problem, and there must be a concerted effort by all governments. It may be that the burden falls on some countries more than others to carry out many of the prosecutions against traffickers, but source nations are expected to protect and preserve their national treasures. A determination to protect cultural property has the potential to divide one country from another; however, increasingly, it now has the potential to bring all nations together to stamp out corruption and trafficking in all types of illicit goods.

[117] See also, *Government of the Islamic Republic of Iran v The Barakat Galleries Ltd* [2007] EWCA Civ 1374, [2009] QB 22 (CA).

2

International Initiatives

JANET ULPH

I Introduction

2.01 Obstacles to International Agreement

Demand for art and antiquities has grown at a phenomenal rate since the Second World War. The art market has flourished. Yet one unfortunate result is that people have pillaged archaeological sites in their search for valuable items. Another modern scourge is the huge increase in the incidence of theft from private homes, museums and places of worship. Although there is general agreement between governments that the illicit trade in cultural property needs to be suppressed, the manner in which this might be achieved remains controversial.

Unfortunately there are major obstacles, both legal and cultural, which stand in the way of achieving international consensus. The domestic laws of states vary enormously, particularly in relation to the concept of ownership of property. Where an object is stolen and a dispossessed owner attempts to recover it from a good faith purchaser, legal systems approach the problem of acquisition of title in different ways. In the common law systems (for example, England, Australia and Hong Kong), there is a doctrine of *nemo dat quod non habet* (no one can obtain a better title than his seller). Although exceptions to this rule exist, a person in possession of a stolen object is generally in a weak position and may be forced to surrender it: this is so, regardless of whether he acted in good faith.[1] In contrast, the vast majority of civil law systems (such as Italy and France) provide a good faith acquirer with greater protection on the basis that, where movables are concerned, possession represents title (*en fait de meubles, la possession vaut titre*[2]). The fact that national laws vary in this manner is exploited by traffickers, who will tend to sell stolen or illegally excavated objects in countries which offer more generous protection to those who obtain objects in good faith.

The response to this trade has varied from one nation to another for political and economic reasons. There is a tension between the concerns of 'source' nations, from which articles are routinely taken, and those of the 'market' states, in which they are usually sold. Some source nations have reacted to the theft or illegal export of heritage items by taking

[1] See 5.33–5.37.

[2] Code Civil 1804, Art 2279.

extreme measures, such as legislating in favour of total export bans[3] or decreeing that there will be no limitation period in making a claim for the return of a cultural object.[4] However, in order to obtain the return of these objects, these source nations depend upon the co-operation of market nations. Market states have been concerned to avoid overly severe restrictions which might hamper the vitality of the legitimate market in cultural objects. Importing states have wished to exercise their own judgement on the matter.[5] As a consequence, long-standing norms in the USA and elsewhere have been to resist any automatic acceptance of foreign export prohibition laws.[6]

Nevertheless, the scale of theft and looting in the second half of the twentieth century has proved impossible to ignore. In *Government of the Islamic Republic of Iran v The Barakat Galleries Ltd*, the Court of Appeal observed that:

> The unlawful excavation and trafficking of antiquities has become very big business. In 1970 the signatories to the UNESCO Convention on the Means of Prohibiting and Preventing the Illicit Import, Export and Transfer of Ownership of Cultural Property (ratified by the United Kingdom in 2002) recognised not only that it was incumbent on every state to protect the cultural property within its borders against the dangers of theft, clandestine excavation and illicit export, but also that it was essential for every state to become alive to the moral obligations to respect the cultural heritage of all nations and that the protection of cultural heritage could only be effective if organised both nationally and internationally among states working in close co-operation (recitals 3, 4 and 7).[7]

This chapter will focus upon the major international conventions and instruments which may objectively have an impact upon the illicit trade in cultural property.

2.02 The Scope and Significance of International Initiatives

The market in cultural property is a global one. If only a small number of countries are parties to a treaty which is intended to curb illicit trafficking in art and antiquities, the thieves will merely sell their ill-gotten gains elsewhere. But, even if such a treaty is widely accepted, its impact will be insignificant if it is only concerned with emphasising the importance of cultural objects and with providing guidelines to assist in their protection. Early initiatives often suffered from this drawback,[8] but were doubtless more palatable as a consequence. Even so, they would have been invaluable in providing a foundation for subsequent endeavours. Although the major conventions which came later were far more

[3] For example, China has banned the export of any object made in China before 1911: see the Law on the Protection of Cultural Relics 2002, as amended in 2007. See further, AM Kaus, 'Safeguarding China's Cultural History: Proposed Amendments to the 2002 Law on the Protection of Cultural Relics' (2009) 18(2) *Pacific Rim Law and Policy Journal* 405.

[4] PM Bator, *The International Trade in Art* (Chicago, The University of Chicago Press, 1982) 38–39.

[5] ibid 52.

[6] PM Bator, 'An Essay on the International Trade in Art' (1982) 34 *Stanford Law Review* 275, 327–30. Lenzner comments that it has been said to be a 'blank cheque' rule if there is a policy whereby any object considered to have been illegally exported from its country of origin must be returned: NR Lenzner, 'Illicit International Trade in Cultural Property: Does the Unidroit Convention Provide an Effective Remedy for the Shortcomings of the UNESCO Convention?' (1994) 15 *University of Pennsylvania Journal of International Business Law* 469, 482.

[7] [2009] QB 22 (CA) [2] (Lord Phillips of Worth Matravers).

[8] See eg the 1966 UNESCO Declaration of the Principles of International Cultural Co-Operation. See also, the 1956 UNESCO Recommendation on International Principles Applicable to Archaeological Excavations, Arts 27 and 28. The 1969 European Convention on the Protection of the Archaeological Heritage, Art 5, required Contracting States to inform a state of origin of any materials which are suspected of being illicit; the revised Convention of 1992, Art 10, is stronger in tone, requiring public authorities to pool information and to inform a state of origin of any suspected illicit materials.

ambitious, their scope was still restricted. Thus, the UNESCO Convention on the Means of Prohibiting and Preventing the Illicit Import, Export and Transfer of Ownership of Cultural Property 1970 and the UNIDROIT Convention on Stolen or Illegally Exported Cultural Objects 1995 rely upon the civil law alone in relation to the return of objects. Although the Convention for the Protection of Cultural Property in the Event of Armed Conflict 1954 provides for the creation of criminal offences, it is limited to conflict situations.

In addition to the major conventions, various multilateral and bilateral agreements have been made. For example, Commonwealth nations agreed to a '*Scheme for the Protection of Cultural Heritage within the Commonwealth.*' It was adopted unanimously by all 53 Commonwealth states in 1993. An obligation is imposed to return any item of cultural heritage of national importance which has been illegally exported from another Commonwealth country.[9] Good faith purchasers will receive reasonable compensation if they are forced to relinquish an object in accordance with this scheme. Once a government is aware of the whereabouts of an object, it has five years within which to make a claim. Contracting States are required to make it an offence to unlawfully import or export an item of cultural heritage covered by this scheme.

The large number of bilateral and multilateral agreements which exist between individual states assist in protecting states from looting and pillaging. The UNESCO Convention 1970 has provided an impetus for making such agreements. For example, on 14 January 2009, the US Government concluded a Memorandum of Understanding with the Government of the People's Republic of China, which forbids Chinese works of art that are more than 250 years old from being imported into the USA. In order to combat the illicit trade in cultural objects, a Model Treaty exists which provides a text that can be used as a basis for establishing bilateral agreements.[10]

In order to combat the illicit trade in cultural property in an effective manner, there needs to be co-ordination and consensus between nations. This has not yet been achieved. A number of states have ratified one or more of the major cultural property conventions, but not all; some states may have signed up to other international agreements relating to cultural heritage as well.[11] This chapter will consider the obligations imposed by the major conventions. However, it is increasingly appreciated that organised criminal groups have become involved in the illicit trade in art and antiquities and that the profits from this trade may be used to finance other types of crime. It is recognised that the networks set up for trafficking in drugs are being used as conduits not only for cultural objects but also for weapons.[12] Consequently, this chapter will move on to consider whether other initiatives, which have been designed to combat serious crime, money laundering, and corruption, may have an important impact upon the trade in cultural property.

[9] This was a response to the decision in *Attorney-General of New Zealand v Ortiz* [1983] 2 WLR 809 (HL), in which their Lordships held that New Zealand had no standing to recover a historic carving. See also (1993) 19(4) *Commonwealth Law Bulletin* (October) 2015.

[10] Model Treaty for the Prevention of Crimes that Infringe on the Cultural Heritage of Peoples in the Form of Movable Property. The treaty was adopted by the Eighth UN Congress on the Prevention of Crime and the Treatment of Offenders, It was welcomed by UN GA Resolution 45/121 of 14 December 1990. See also the UN Economic and Social Council, Commission on Crime Prevention and Criminal Justice, May 2010; E/CN 15/2010/5.

[11] See eg the 1972 UNESCO Convention for the Protection of the World Cultural and National Heritage; the 1978 UNESCO Recommendation for the Protection of Movable Cultural Property; the 1985 European Convention on Offences against Cultural Property.

[12] T McGirk, 'A Year of Looting Dangerously' *Sunday Review, Independent* (24 March 1996) 4.

II The Convention for the Protection of Cultural Property in the Event of Armed Conflict 1954

2.03 Background

In the past, the plunder of art and antiquities during military campaigns was commonplace. The Romans celebrated the fact that they had seized cultural property: it was a symbol of triumph.[13] The fact that such objects usually possess a high monetary value would only have been a subsidiary consideration for victorious armies; they were prized principally because they were seen as representing the country which had been conquered. These objects might eventually find their way into the museums of the conquering state.[14] However, objects may sometimes be destroyed, rather than seized, to demoralise a nation under occupation. For example, Fisk alleges that 'The Serbs had quite deliberately shelled the Sarajevo library in an act of cultural barbarism, an attempt to destroy the history of Bosnia as surely as their snipers were killing its people.'[15] Cultural property, including not only objects but buildings and other structures, may be deliberately destroyed because it has the ability to unite people in spirit and to give them a sense of national identity.

From the eighteenth century onwards, there was increasing recognition that cultural property deserved to be protected for the benefit of mankind.[16] For example, the Lieber Code, signed by Abraham Lincoln in 1863 during the American Civil War, consisted of regulations to provide guidance to soldiers in an armed conflict. They were instructed that they must not intentionally damage cultural property (such as libraries and classical works of art) and that, if objects were seized, their ultimate ownership should be dealt with in a peace treaty.[17]

During the Second World War, there was an unprecedented level of theft and looting of art and antiquities. Despite the existence of conventions which prohibited pillaging,[18] the Nazis and their supporters seized art treasures from museums and from Jewish families. During that period, certain dealers took advantage of the social confusion to misappropriate property as well.[19] The Nazi regime also targeted for destruction any works of art that they considered to be 'degenerate'. In response, the Allied Powers agreed to the Declaration by the United Nations on Forced Dispossession of Property in Enemy Controlled Territory

[13] LD DuBoff and CO King, *Art Law*, 4th edn (St Paull, Minnesota, Thomson West, 2006) 27.

[14] See, for example, Napoleon's acquisitions for the benefit of the Louvre: K Fitzgibbon, 'Chronology of Cultural Property Legislation' in K Fitzgibbon (ed), *Who Owns the Past?* (New Brunswick, New Jersey and London, Rutgers University Press, 2005) 3; JH Merryman, AE Elsen and SK Urice, *Law, Ethics and the Visual Arts* 5th edn (The Netherlands, Kluwer Law International, 2007) 4–6.

[15] R Fisk, 'Foreword' in P Stone and J Farchakh Bajjaly (eds) *The Destruction of Cultural Heritage in Iraq* (Woodbridge, The Boydell Press, 2008) XI.

[16] K Chamberlain, *War and Cultural Heritage* (Powys, Institute of Art and Law, 2004) 7–8.

[17] Similar concerns were expressed in the Declaration of Brussels of 1874. For details of these instruments, see www.icrc.org. See further, D Schindler and J Toman, *The Laws of Armed Conflicts*, 4th edn (Leiden, Martinus Nijhoff, 2004).

[18] Hague Convention of 1899, Convention (II) with Respect to the Laws and Customs of War on Land and its Annex: The Hague, 29 July 1899. This Convention was later amended in 1907: the Hague Convention (IV) respecting the Laws and Customs of War on Land and its Annex, 18 October 1907. See also the Washington Pact of 15 April 1935 (the Roerich Pact). This Treaty on the Protection of Artistic and Scientific Institutions and Historic Monuments established the neutrality of monuments, museums, scientific artistic, educational and cultural institutions.

[19] See *City of Gotha v Sotheby's; Federal Republic of Germany v Same* (2008) 9 September, unrep. See also J Greenfield, *The Return of Cultural Treasures*, 3rd edn (Cambridge, Cambridge University Press, 2007) 238–44 .

1943.[20] This Declaration provided for the return of cultural objects removed from occupied territories, even where they had ended up in the hands of good faith purchasers. The wanton damage and destruction of historic buildings, museums, and works of art during the Second World War was appalling and led to the Convention for the Protection of Cultural Property in the Event of Armed Conflict 1954 (the Hague Convention).[21]

2.04 The Hague Convention 1954: 'Cultural Property'

The Hague Convention 1954, together with its two Protocols, focuses upon the risks posed to cultural property in the event of war or other armed conflict. There had been other initiatives beforehand, but the Hague Convention is significant because it provided a comprehensive set of principles. The Convention has 123 Contracting States; the First Protocol currently has 100 Contracting States; the Second Protocol has 55.

The Hague Convention begins by formally recognising that recent armed conflicts have led to damage and destruction, and it is observed in the Preamble that 'the preservation of the cultural heritage is of great importance for all peoples of the world and that it is important that this heritage should receive international protection.'

Article 1 of the Hague Convention provides:

> For the purposes of the present Convention, the term 'cultural property' shall cover, irrespective of origin or ownership:
>
> (a) movable or immovable property of great importance to the cultural heritage of every people, such as monuments of architecture, art or history, whether religious or secular; archaeological sites; groups of buildings which, as a whole, are of historical or artistic interest; works of art; manuscripts, books and other objects of artistic, historical or archaeological interest; as well as scientific collections and important collections of books or archives or of reproductions of the property defined above;
> (b) buildings whose main and effective purpose is to preserve or exhibit the movable cultural property defined in sub-paragraph (a) such as museums, large libraries and depositories of archives, and refuges intended to shelter, in the event of armed conflict, the movable cultural property defined in sub-paragraph (a);
> (c) centers containing a large amount of cultural property as defined in sub-paragraphs (a) and (b), to be known as 'centers containing monuments'.

It is clear from the beginning of Article 1 that the definition supplied is intended to be indicative rather than exhaustive. Even so, it might be thought that the definition is narrow because it provides that objects should be of 'great importance'. This constraint will exclude many cultural objects. However, this requirement is not as limiting as it may first appear because the Preamble explains that 'damage to cultural property belonging to any people whatsoever means damage to the cultural heritage of all mankind, since each people makes its contribution to the culture of the world'. In other words, it is sufficient if an object, *irrespective of origin or ownership*, is of great importance to a group of people; it does not need to be demonstrated that it is valued by a particular state.[22]

[20] The Declaration of London, 5 January 1943.
[21] Convention for the Protection of Cultural Property in the Event of Armed Conflict, 14 May 1954, 249 UNTS 216, 240.
[22] Chamberlain, *War and Cultural Heritage* 29.

2.05 The Hague Convention: Measures to Safeguard and Protect

The Hague Convention is intended to protect and preserve cultural property. Article 3 of the Hague Convention calls upon Contracting States to take measures 'as appropriate' during a time of peace to safeguard cultural property from the risks associated with war. The phrase 'as appropriate' means that states enjoy considerable discretion in choosing how they will comply with this provision. This flexibility will be seen as an attractive feature by states contemplating whether to ratify the Convention or not. But a Contracting State is expected to formally identify and document heritage assets property, and take account of their location in terms of planning decisions, so that this property is kept at a safe distance from military targets.

A series of obligations are imposed in the event of military conflict. Contracting States must respect cultural property, whether situated in their own territory or in the territory of another Contracting State, by not using it for purposes which expose it unnecessarily to the risk of damage or destruction; nevertheless, according to Article 4(2), this obligation may be displaced if military necessity 'imperatively' requires it.[23] This additional provision may appear to be a cause for consternation. Yet, as irresponsible governments may well be tempted to locate weapons close to heritage sites, in the hope that they will therefore be protected from attack, this provision can be justified on the ground that it may reduce the likelihood of this happening. For example, in the first Gulf War, there were reports that Iraqi MiG fighter planes had been dispersed within heritage sites such as Babylon.[24]

Where there is an international conflict, Article 5 provides that an occupying force should 'as far as possible' support the national authorities in protecting cultural property and should take necessary measures to preserve such property. This might mean, for example, that if archaeological objects are found during military operations, they should be handed over to the national authorities upon the cessation of hostilities.[25] However, the lengths to which an occupying force should go to protect cultural property during a period of conflict remains uncertain. Apart from any principles established in implementing domestic legislation, much must depend upon both political will and resources. For example, from the beginning of the first Gulf War, cuneiform tablets, ancient scrolls and other antiquities were illegally removed from Iraq. In order to have cut off the trade in antiquities, it is estimated that a further $2 million would have been needed for vehicles, weapons and communication equipment.[26] This money was never found, and the looting continued. When Iraq was invaded in 2003 by US led coalition forces, troops did not receive orders to protect the National Museum of Iraq in Baghdad, which was devastated by looting between 10 and 12 April 2003. The US Government only ratified the Hague Convention in March 2009. One advantage of ratification is that the government of a Contracting State can no longer appear aloof and detached from any theft and looting which may be taking place in the occupied country.

[23] Art 4(4) of the Convention adds that no reprisals should be taken against cultural property.

[24] See S Cole, 'War, Cultural Property and the Blue Shield' in Stone and Farchakh Bajjaly, *Destruction of Cultural Heritage in Iraq* 65, 70. Fears were expressed that Colonel Gaddafi had hidden missiles in the Roman ruins at the World Heritage site at Leptis Magna: T Coghlan, 'Wonder of the ancient world at risk as Gaddafi uses ruins to hide deadly rockets' *The Times* (14 June 2011).

[25] See UNESCO's Recommendation on International Principles Applicable to Archaeological Excavations 1956. See further, Chamberlain, *War and Cultural Heritage* 43.

[26] S Breitkopf, 'Lost: the Looting of Iraq's Antiquities' (2007) *Museum News* January/February.

2.06 The Second Protocol of 1999: Protection and Preservation

The preamble to the Second Protocol emphasises that the Protocol is intended to provide enhanced protection for cultural property in the event of armed conflict. It fulfils this aim by providing more detail on a variety of matters in order to supplement the main Convention. Article 6 is particularly important in clarifying the concept of 'imperative military necessity' that exists in Article 4(2) of the Convention, whilst at the same time reducing its scope. Article 7, which is concerned with taking precautions in advance of an attack, goes further than the Convention in attempting to protect cultural property from incidental damage.

Article 5 of the Second Protocol builds upon Article 3 of the main Convention, which was concerned with safeguarding objects. Article 5 directs Contracting States to take measures as appropriate against foreseeable risks and it gives examples, such as the 'preparation of inventories' and the 'designation of competent authorities for the safeguarding of cultural property.' Preparation of inventories is vital: the task of secretly removing a heritage object abroad is made considerably easier if there is no record of its existence. If the description of an object is properly recorded, there is some hope that it can be identified if it is later publicly offered for sale.

The level of detail in the Second Protocol ought to have proved attractive in clarifying an occupying state's obligations and yet it has not been popular. Only 55 states have ratified it. This may suggest that governments prefer the wide discretion provided by the more loosely worded provisions of the Hague Convention itself.

2.07 The Blue Shield: Special Protection for Property of Very Great Importance

In times of war, it is easy for cultural property to be destroyed quite accidentally by shelling. A monument may be used to shield troops or to store weapons without any appreciation of its cultural significance. Article 17 of the Hague Convention consequently provides that cultural property of 'very great importance' should be marked with a distinctive blue and white emblem, described as the Blue Shield. It could be used on immovable property, or cultural objects which were being transported to a new location, to highlight their importance.[27] Chapter 3 of the Second Protocol established an alternative regime of 'enhanced protection', which applies where states are parties to the Second Protocol.[28] It is designed to create more effective protection than that afforded by the Hague Convention itself. The Blue Shield scheme is supported by the work of International Committee of the Blue Shield (ICBS), which provides advice and information to strengthen international efforts to protect cultural property, not only in times of conflict, such as in Libya, but also where there is a natural disaster, such as in the wake of Hurricane Katrina.[29] The great advantage of the Blue Shield scheme is that it protects cultural assets from being accidentally destroyed; unfortunately, it creates a risk that they may be deliberately targeted by renegade groups, in order to demoralise the local populace.[30]

[27] States are encouraged to register a limited number of refuges and other immovable property of 'very great importance' in the International Register of Cultural Property under Special Protection: Hague Convention 1954, Art 8.

[28] Hague Convention, Second Protocol, Art 4.

[29] See S Cole, 'War, Cultural Property and the Blue Shield' in Stone and Farchakh Bajjaly, *Destruction of Cultural Heritage in Iraq* 65, 67.

[30] ibid, 69.

2.08 The Illicit Trade in Art and Antiquities: the Obligation to Return

The Hague Convention itself was not directly concerned with preventing the illicit trade in cultural property. Even so, some of its provisions are relevant. By Article 4(3), Contracting States are required to prohibit, prevent and, if necessary, put a stop to any form of theft, pillage or misappropriation of, and any acts of vandalism directed against, cultural property. This requirement is absolute: it cannot be waived on the grounds of military necessity. It should be noted that there is a reference to 'misappropriation' rather than removal. Consequently, an army may remove cultural property to a place of safety on a temporary basis in order to protect it without contravening this provision.

The First Protocol to the Hague Convention did, however, address the problems posed by the illicit trade in cultural objects. It applies where there is an armed conflict as defined in Articles 18 and 19 of the Hague Convention. Part I provides that a Contracting State must prevent the export of cultural property from a country which it is occupying during armed conflict.[31] An exception is made where cultural objects are intended to be taken to a safe refuge in another country for the purposes of protection.[32]

Where cultural property has been exported from a country under occupation and has then arrived in the territory of a Contracting State, that state is obliged to take the property into its custody.[33] This provision applies even where an object has a valid export certificate. Nevertheless, it is possible to argue that this merely gives rise to a presumption and that, if it can be established that the export was consensual and legal according to the law of the occupied territory, a Contracting State is not obliged to seize the object.[34]

Paragraph 3 of Part I of the First Protocol is particularly important in relation to returning cultural property when the conflict has come to an end:

> Each High Contracting Party undertakes to return, at the close of hostilities, to the competent authorities of the territory previously occupied, cultural property which is in its territory, if such property has been exported in contravention of the principle laid down in the first paragraph. Such property shall never be retained as war reparations.

Paragraph 3 is powerful: it applies even where the country which had been occupied is not a party to the Protocol. The country under occupation is not subject to a time limit in making a claim for the return of its property. Furthermore, the occupying state, which had been under an obligation to prevent the export of cultural property from the country under occupation, is required to compensate any good faith purchasers who are forced to give up property so that it can be returned.[35] There is no guidance on what constitutes 'good faith' or as to how the compensation must be calculated; it may be that a domestic court would refer to the UNIDROIT Convention for guidance.[36] A possessor cannot resist returning the object: he can only hope to receive compensation if he obtained the object in good faith.

Part II of the First Protocol deals with all other situations, such as where objects are removed before a conflict. This applies regardless of whether the conflict is international or local in character. The Protocol provides that the property must be returned to the competent authorities on the cessation of hostilities.

[31] See First Protocol, Pt I, para 1, which supplements the Hague Convention 1954, Art 5.
[32] See Hague Convention 1954, Art 12 and regs 17 and 18.
[33] First Protocol, Pt I, para 2.
[34] Chamberlain, *War and Cultural Heritage* 144–46.
[35] First Protocol, Pt 1, para 4.
[36] See 2.34.

2.09 The Second Protocol of 1999: Creating Criminal Offences as a Deterrent

The Second Protocol goes much further than the main Convention and the First Protocol because it requires an occupying state to take steps to combat the illicit trade in cultural property by creating criminal offences to deter theft and illicit export. Article 9 of the Second Protocol applies to international and domestic armed conflicts,[37] and provides:

> 1. Without prejudice to the provisions of Articles 4 and 5 of the Convention, a Party in occupation of the whole or part of the territory of another Party shall prohibit and prevent in relation to the occupied territory:
>
>   a. any illicit export, other removal or transfer of ownership of cultural property;
>   b. any archaeological excavation, save where this is strictly required to safeguard, record, or preserve cultural property,
>   c. any alteration to, or change of use of, cultural property which is intended to conceal or destroy cultural, historical or scientific evidence.
>
> 2. Any archaeological excavation of, alteration to, or change of use of, cultural property in occupied territory shall, unless circumstances do not permit, be carried out in close co-operation with the competent authorities of the occupied territory.

Paragraph 1(a) of Article 9 requires states to create offences in relation to the export, removal or transfer of ownership of cultural property where this conduct is illicit.[38] This provision is naturally linked to Article 4(3) of the Hague Convention, which prohibited theft, pillage or misappropriation of such property. Paragraph 1(b) is concerned with the protection of archaeological excavations. Under the Hague Convention, sites are implicitly protected by Article 5, which provides that an occupying force should safeguard cultural property. Paragraph 1(b) reinforces this obligation, and an occupying force might be expected to protect an archaeological site by, for example, the erection of fences surrounding it. One advantage of Article 9 is that it forces a Contracting State to create offences in relation to looting and pillaging of archaeological sites. Paragraph 1(c) of Article 9 is particularly wide in scope, and covers preparatory work carried out with the intention of smuggling cultural objects out of the country under occupation.

Contracting States are required by Article 28 to create criminal offences with which to punish serious violations of the Convention and its Protocol.[39] These offences would apply where any person intentionally commits one of a listed series of acts, or assists another in doing so. The UK's domestic law dealing with theft and handling of stolen goods would not be sufficient to deal with the illicit conduct spelt out in Article 9 of the Second Protocol above. Consequently, before the UK Government can ratify the Second Protocol, new offences will need to be created.

Although the UK Government has signed the Convention, it has not yet ratified it.[40] There is concern that Article 28 provides insufficient guidance in relation to the proposed offences. For example, there is no guidance on the mental element required to establish an offence. The type of breach which may be committed varies from the serious (such as deliberate destruction of cultural property which cannot be justified on grounds of military necessity) to the

[37] Hague Convention, Second Protocol, Art 3. As regards domestic conflict, it will not apply to minor outbursts of violence, including riots: ibid, Art 22.

[38] 'Illicit' is defined in Art 1(g) of the Second Protocol as meaning meaning 'under compulsion or otherwise in violation of the applicable rules of the domestic law of the occupied territory or of international law.'

[39] ibid, Art 15.

[40] The Government announced its intention to do so: see DCMS Press Notice 053/04, 14 May 2004.

relatively trivial. As Chamberlain observes, the vagueness of the provision leads to a situation where the enabling laws of Contracting States may greatly differ from each other, and he notes that this will have repercussions where extradition is sought.[41] The Government has drafted a Cultural Property (Armed Conflict) Bill,[42] which is discussed in Chapter 3,[43] which would create new criminal offences. This has not yet been enacted and this delay is unfortunate because the Second Protocol contains a series of important deterrents in fighting the illicit trade in art and antiquities.

III Convention Concerning the Protection of the World Cultural and Natural Heritage 1972

2.10 Introduction

At first sight, this Convention may seem to have little relevance to the illicit trade in cultural property, as it is simply concerned with protection and preservation. However, the destruction of artefacts may well have an impact upon this illicit trade. If a particular type of object becomes a rarity because of the destruction of similar objects, it will have a scarcity value, driving up the price for surviving pieces. The annihilation of cultural property enables thieves to portray themselves as the 'saviours' of cultural heritage.

This Convention grew out of a number of initiatives to preserve the world's natural scenic areas and historic sites. It is commonly referred to as the World Heritage Convention,[44] and it was ratified by the UK in 1984. Contracting States undertake to draw up an inventory of significant natural and cultural properties called a Tentative List. From this list, a Contracting State can nominate a property which may eventually go before the World Heritage Committee for inscription on the World Heritage List.[45] The Convention demonstrates a desire shared by many nations to co-operate to preserve international cultural heritage. However, it is concerned with protecting objects of 'outstanding universal value';[46] its scope therefore appears to be narrower than the Hague Convention.

Each Contracting State has a duty of 'ensuring the identification, protection, conservation, presentation and transmission to future generations of the cultural and natural heritage' within their territory. Even so, it should be noted that this duty has a large discretionary element: a Contracting State must do 'all it can to this end, to the utmost of its own resources and, where appropriate.'[47] The same point can be made in relation to the obligation to 'ensure that effective and active measures are taken for the protection, conservation and presentation of the cultural and natural heritage situated on its territory';[48] the obligation goes no further than what is possible and appropriate for each country.

The World Heritage Convention places pressure upon Contracting States to preserve the universal cultural heritage. It is concerned with *continuous* protection and respect for cul-

[41] Chamberlain, *War and Cultural Heritage* 89.
[42] Cm 7298.
[43] See 3.73.
[44] 16 Nov 1972, 1037 UNTS 151, 11 ILM 1358.
[45] ibid, Art 11.
[46] ibid, Art 1.
[47] ibid, Art 4.
[48] ibid, Art 5.

tural property. In contrast, the main provisions of the Hague Convention 1954 only apply in the event of war or other armed conflict. There will be an armed conflict where there is an international dispute and an intervention of armed forces,[49] or a serious internal situation such as a war of national liberation.[50] But the Hague Convention will not be of direct assistance where cultural heritage is destroyed in a country which is not being occupied and where there is no significant civil unrest.

2.11 The Buddhas of Bamiyan

The World Heritage Convention does not provide Contracting States with powers to bring either a criminal prosecution or a civil suit. As O'Keefe has observed, 'The world's cultural heritage is the proper concern of the international community as a whole but it is not yet, in peacetime, the object of obligations owed to that community.'[51] Instead, where a cultural object which is part of our universal heritage is destroyed, diplomatic pressure is the only realistic option. A resolution and other protests made by individual states will therefore be the proper response. Unfortunately, diplomatic pressure may not suffice to protect cultural property from destruction.

The damage and destruction of pre-Islamic sculptures in Afghanistan by the Taliban illustrates the problems facing the international community in preserving cultural heritage of outstanding value. The destruction of the Buddhas of Bamiyan in March 2001, for example, did not occur during a period of armed conflict.[52] It is possible, however, to argue that this destruction of the Buddhas involved a violation of Article 4 of the World Heritage Convention, as Afghanistan had ratified the Convention in 1979 and had then nominated the monuments of the Bamiyan valley in Afghanistan for inclusion in the World Heritage List.[53]

The two Buddhas of Bamiyan were among Asia's most important archaeological treasures. The statues were believed to have been created in the sixth century, and the larger one was 53 metres tall. The Taliban objected to them because they were non-Islamic idols. The Taliban first threatened to blow up the Buddhas with dynamite on 17 April 1997. The 2001 Resolution entitled 'Acts Constituting "A Crime against the Common Heritage of Humanity"' documents the history of diplomatic intervention from 1997 onwards.[54] Every effort was made after the first threat to expedite the registration of the Buddhas on the World Heritage List. In addition, appeals were made to the Afghan people to protect the Buddhas.[55] After the first attack on the Buddhas in 1998, the General Assembly of the United Nations passed a resolution which expressed great concern regarding cultural property in Afghanistan.[56] It was emphasised that 'all parties share the responsibility to protect

[49] Hague Convention 1954, Art 18. See also ICRC, 'Commentaries to the Geneva Conventions of 1949'. www.icrc.org.

[50] Hague Convention 1954, Art 19.

[51] R O'Keefe, 'World Cultural Heritage: Obligations to the International Community as a Whole?' (2004) 53(1) *International and Comparative Law Quarterly* 189, 207.

[52] ibid, 195.

[53] ibid. The obligation created by Art 4 of the World Heritage Convention includes not only objects on the World Heritage List but also all property of outstanding universal cultural or natural value (see Arts 1 and 2) which has been identified by the state in accordance with Art 3. The Buddhas of Bamiyan had been nominated in 1981: see the chronology of events in Pt I of UNESCO Doc WHC-01/CONF.208/23, 22 November 2001.

[54] See UNESCO Doc WHC-01/CONF.208/23, 22 November 2001, Pt 1.

[55] UNESCO Press Release No 97-61.

[56] GA/RES/53/165, 9 Dec 1998, 'Situation of Human Rights in Afghanistan'. See also the Security Council's concern in relation to the situation in Afghanistan: Security Council Resolution 1214 (1998).

their common heritage', and this statement was repeated in later resolutions.[57] Nevertheless, the Taliban issued an edict of 26 February 2001, which ordered the destruction of non-Islamic objects in Afghanistan.[58] The General Assembly responded by adopting a Resolution which encouraged respect for 'the multicultural, multi-ethnic and historical heritage of Afghanistan' and which pronounced that it was '*Deeply concerned and appalled* by the Taliban edict of 26 February 2001, ordering the destruction of all statues and non-Islamic shrines in Afghanistan, and by the deliberate ongoing destruction of these relics and monuments which belong to the common heritage of humankind.'[59] It was added that the destruction of the statues in Afghanistan, in particular of the unique Buddhist sculptures in Bamiyan, would be an irreparable loss for humanity as a whole. Consequently, the Resolution strongly urged the Taliban to stop the implementation of their edict and to prevent the 'further destruction of the irreplaceable relics, monuments or artefacts of the cultural heritage of Afghanistan'. Unfortunately, news that the sculptures in Bamiyan had been destroyed was confirmed shortly thereafter. Subsequently, the UNESCO Declaration concerning the Intentional Destruction of Cultural Heritage of 17 October 2003 expressed profound regret at the loss of the Buddhas of Bamiyan. In Part III, it encouraged states to 'adopt the appropriate legislative, administrative, educational and technical measures, within the framework of their economic resources, to protect cultural heritage and should revise them periodically.'

The 2001 Resolution entitled 'Acts Constituting "A Crime against the Common Heritage of Humanity"' makes it clear that diplomatic pressure to protect cultural property should be allied with the fight to curb the illicit trade in cultural property.[60] There are a number of other documents which link vandalism and destruction, on the one hand, with looting and clandestine excavations on the other.[61] The UN has rightly encouraged states to ratify *all* of the main international conventions. The scope of each Convention is confined and one strategy – or one set of strategies – will not suffice to protect our cultural heritage and to prevent destructive acts, looting and illicit excavations.

IV Convention on the Means of Prohibiting and Preventing the Illicit Import, Export and Transfer of Ownership of Cultural Property 1970

2.12 Introduction

The UNESCO Convention 1970[62] is the first international instrument to recognise a general obligation upon states to take steps to prevent the illicit movement or transfer of cultural objects which have been stolen or illegally exported or imported. Article 3 provides

[57] GA/RES/53/165, 9 Dec 1998 [16]; GA/RES/54/185, 17 Dec 1999 [16]; GA/RES/54/185, 17 Dec 1999 [16]; GA/RES/55/119 4 Dec 2000 [19].

[58] UNESCO Press Release No 2001-27.

[59] GA/RES/55/243, 1 May 2001, 'The destruction of relics and monuments in Afghanistan'.

[60] See UNESCO Doc WHC-01/CONF.208/23, 22 November 2001, Pt III.

[61] GA/RES/53/203A, 18 Dec 1998 [21]. See also, GA/RES/53/165, 9 Dec 1998 [16]; GA/RES/54/185, 17 Dec 1999 [16]; GA/RES/54/189A, 17 Dec 1999 [30].

[62] 14 Nov 1970 (1971) 823 UNTS 231, 10 ILM 289.

that: 'The import, export or transfer of ownership of cultural property effected contrary to the provisions adopted under this Convention . . . shall be illicit.' The UK Government acceded to the Convention in 2002.[63]

The Convention is highly significant, because it creates universal principles to which all Contracting States should adhere. But it must be noted at the outset that there is a great deal of flexibility in the Convention's provisions. Article 5 encourages states to take steps to make laws 'as appropriate' to combat this trade. Some variation in domestic laws from one Contracting State to another is therefore permitted.[64] The question of whether an object has been traded illicitly will therefore depend upon the domestic law of the country of origin.

2.13 Background and Policy Concerns

Before the Convention came into being, substantial groundwork had been carried out by UNESCO, which was responsible for two relevant Recommendations. The first was the 1956 'Recommendation on International Principles Applicable to Archaeological Excavations'. States were urged to take measures to curb clandestine excavation of sites and damage to monuments and to prevent the illicit export of antiquities obtained by these means. Museums were pressed to check on the provenance of objects in order to ensure that they had not been stolen or illegally excavated; they were also encouraged to co-operate with each other to facilitate the recovery of objects derived from illegal excavations or theft.[65] The second document was the 1964 'Recommendation on the Means of Prohibiting and Preventing the Illicit Export, Import and Transfer of Ownership of Cultural Property', and it is expressly referred to in the Preamble to the UNESCO Convention. This Recommendation required states to draw up inventories of cultural objects and encouraged the establishment of systems to scrutinise the transfers of cultural property. These Recommendations paved the way for the UNESCO Convention, encouraging states to accept that they needed to work together to curb the flow of cultural property from source nations into public and private collections in other countries.

The Preamble sets out general principles to provide context, which include recognising the intrinsic values possessed by cultural property and explaining why these objects deserve special protection. Later provisions should be interpreted in the light of these concerns:

> *Considering* that the interchange of cultural property among nations for scientific, cultural and educational purposes increases the knowledge of the civilisation of Man, enriches the cultural life of all peoples and inspires mutual respect and appreciation among nations,
>
> *Considering* that cultural property constitutes one of the basic elements of civilisation and national culture, and that its true value can be appreciated only in relation to the fullest possible information regarding its origin, history and traditional setting,
>
> *Considering* that it is incumbent upon every State to protect the cultural property existing within its territory against the dangers of theft, clandestine excavation, and illicit export,
>
> *Considering* that, to avert these dangers, it is essential for every State to become increasingly alive to the moral obligations to respect its own cultural heritage and that of all nations,

[63] The Convention was accepted on 1 August 2002; full accession was achieved on 31 October 2002. See Cmnd 5500. For detail on the UK implementation of the Convention, see K Chamberlain, 'UK Accession to the 1970 UNESCO Convention' (2002) VII(3) *Art Antiquity and Law* 231.

[64] After the UK had signed the UNESCO Convention, the Dealing in Cultural Objects (Offences) Act 2003 was enacted, which is discussed in 3.60.

[65] *Recommendation on International Principles Applicable to Archaeological Excavations*, Arts 29–31.

Considering that, as cultural institutions, museums, libraries and archives should ensure that their collections are built up in accordance with universally recognised moral principles,

Considering that the illicit import, export and transfer of ownership of cultural property is an obstacle to that understanding between nations which it is part of UNESCO's mission to promote by recommending to interested States, international conventions to this end,

Considering that the protection of cultural heritage can be effective only if organised both nationally and internationally among States working in close co-operation,

Considering that the UNESCO General Conference adopted a Recommendation to this effect in 1964.

2.14 Defining 'Cultural Property'

Each international instrument must identify, at least in broad terms, which objects it is concerned to protect for the benefit of future generations. Commonplace items need to be excluded because it would be futile to attempt to preserve and protect every object in existence. A simple, universally agreed, definition of what objects can be described as cultural objects does not exist. Domestic law varies, reflecting national cultural priorities. This is unsurprising, if one accepts that the value of the object lies in the information which it contains and in the response which it prompts in the viewer. The drafters of each Convention must struggle with the challenge of defining an object in a way which recognises that its value may depend, at least at times, upon its significance to the locality or state in which it is situated. The international approach to protecting cultural objects is therefore inevitably affected by the concerns of individual states. Governments may in turn be influenced by the operation of their internal markets, which may put a premium upon an object's aesthetic qualities. But objects should be seen in terms of their social realisation rather than aesthetic appreciation.[66] Consequently, in analysing the key conventions, one must consider the extent to which the definition is sufficiently flexible to cover cultural objects in terms not only of their beauty but also of the information which they contain, or their spiritual or other qualities.

Article 1 provides a general definition of cultural property which, although very broad, is constrained by the fact that the objects must be designated by the state and must be of importance. It is supplemented by an enumerative and exhaustive list of different types of object. It is announced that:

For the purposes of this Convention, the term 'cultural property' means property which, on religious or secular grounds, is specifically designated by each State as being of importance for archaeology, prehistory, history, literature, art or science and which belongs to the following categories:

(a) Rare collections and specimens of fauna, flora, minerals and anatomy, and objects of palaeontological interest;
(b) property relating to history, including the history of science and technology and military and social history, to the life of national leaders, thinkers, scientists and artist and to events of national importance;
(c) products of archaeological excavations (including regular and clandestine) or of archaeological discoveries;
(d) elements of artistic or historical monuments or archaeological sites which have been dismembered;

[66] A Strati, *The Protection of The Underwater Cultural Heritage. An Emerging Objective of the Contemporary Law of the Sea* (Alphen aan den Rijn, Kluwer Law International, 1995) 9.

(e) antiquities more than one hundred years old, such as inscriptions, coins and engraved seals;
(f) objects of ethnological interest;
(g) property of artistic interest, such as:
   (i) pictures, paintings and drawings produced entirely by hand on any support and in any material (excluding industrial designs and manufactured articles decorated by hand);
   (ii) original works of statuary art and sculpture in any material;
   (iii) original engravings, prints and lithographs;
   (iv) original artistic assemblages and montages in any material;
(h) rare manuscripts and incunabula, old books, documents and publications of special interest (historical, artistic, scientific, literary, etc.) singly or in collections;
(i) postage, revenue and similar stamps, singly or in collections;
(j) archives, including sound, photographic and cinematographic archives;
(k) articles of furniture more than one hundred years old and old musical instruments.

The enumerated list spans objects which would interest scientists, such as fossils, as well as modern works of art. Its scope is widened by Article 4, which provides that a state's cultural property need not be created by its own indigent people but could, for example, be created by a stateless person. Nevertheless, the objects need to be designated by a Contracting State as being of importance. Although Article 1(e) refers to antiquities which are more than one hundred years old, it is difficult to see how a state could designate unexcavated items. Bator suggests that states could designate objects which are appropriated in the course of clandestine excavations once their identity becomes known; however, he sees this as designation 'after the fact', and acknowledges that a good faith purchaser will be unfairly disadvantaged because of the lack of advance notice.[67] A response would be that a purchaser should be on notice that any item in the listed categories, such as antiquities or rare manuscripts, may be of 'importance'; as a consequence, its provenance will need to be scrutinised with the utmost care.

It is left to the governing bodies of Contracting States to decide what cultural property is worthy of special protection.[68] As a consequence, heritage is determined by national interest. If a state wishes to do so, it can treat all objects falling within the enumerated categories in Article 1 as designated objects. This makes the scope of the Convention very wide. Indeed, it may encourage source states to impose blanket export restrictions on any heritage objects, in an attempt to ensure that all cultural objects remain within their jurisdiction. This type of blanket ban is controversial.[69] Nevertheless, it can be argued that this definition suits the purposes of the 1970 UNESCO Convention itself. As will be seen, the 1970 Convention is primarily concerned with encouraging Contracting States to protect the cultural property within their borders by establishing registers or monitoring the movement of cultural property.

Although Article 1 enables Contracting States to opt for all-encompassing designations, the UK has not taken this approach. The UNESCO Convention allows Contracting States to make reservations on becoming a party, provided that the reservation is not incompatible

[67] Bator, 'An Essay on the International Trade in Art' (1982) 34 *Stanford Law Review* 275, 381.

[68] The US Convention on Cultural Property Implementation Act limits 'objects of archaeological importance', to which it applies, to objects over 250 years old: 19 USC s 302(2)(1).

[69] For discussion of the views of cultural internationalists and nationalists, see 1.19. See also JH Merryman, 'A Licit International Trade in Cultural Objects' (1995) *4 International Journal of Cultural Property* 13, reproduced in Merryman, *Elgin Marbles* 244, 245.

with the object and purpose of the Convention itself.[70] The UK Government stated, when it became party to the UNESCO Convention in 2002, that it would interpret the term 'cultural property' as being confined to those objects listed in two sources: the Annex to Council Regulation (EEC) No 3911/1992 of 9 December 1992 (now Regulation 116/2009 of 18 December 2008) on the export of cultural goods,[71] and the Annex to Council Directive 93/7/EEC of 15 March 1993 on the return of cultural objects unlawfully removed from the territory of a Member State.[72] This reservation was included because it was thought that it would be simpler if a uniform definition of the term 'cultural property' applied regardless of whether the object was being imported or exported from an EU or non-EU country.

The objects listed in Regulation 116/2009 and Directive 93/7/EEC are accompanied by thresholds relating to age and/or financial value and represent a much narrower definition of cultural property than the one provided by the UNESCO Convention. For example, Article 1 of the Directive 93/7/EC provides that the objects must be 'national treasures' which possess 'artistic, historic or archaeological value' under national legislation. The listed categories in the Annex to Directive 93/7/EEC cover all antiquities, regardless of value, like the Convention. But the definition departs from the one contained in the UNESCO Convention in requiring that objects falling into a number of other categories, such as statues or paintings, must be over a certain financial value to be included. The categories listed in Regulation 116/2009 and Directive 93/7/EEC could be criticised as being too restricted. For example, whereas the UNESCO Convention refers to 'property relating to history, including the history of science and technology,' they only mentions means of transport over 75 years old: it would appear that general objects of an industrial or technological nature which have historic significance will not fall within their definition.[73]

2.15 Protection by States of their own Resources by Collection of Information and Education

Article 5 presses Contracting States to take steps to protect their own resources. These measures are wide-ranging in character. For example, by Article 5(b), states undertake to create and update a national inventory listing important public or private cultural property 'whose export would constitute an appreciable impoverishment of the national cultural heritage'.[74] National inventories are important because the description of objects is vital if there is to be any hope of their eventual recovery. In order to harmonise minimum standards of describing art and antiquities, an 'Object ID standard' has been developed.[75] The 30th General Conference of UNESCO in Paris in 1999 has endorsed the 'Object ID standard' and has urged states and international organisations to support it as part of good

[70] This restriction on reservations applies in relation to all treaties: Vienna Convention on the Law of Treaties 1969, Art 17.

[71] See 3.54. Regulation 116/2009 is set out in an Annex to this text.

[72] Directive 93/7/EEC has been transposed into UK law by the Return of Cultural Objects Regulations 1994: see 5.08 and 6.02. The list of cultural objects to be found in Directive 93/7/EEC, together with financial guidelines in the 1994 Regulations, are set out in an Annex to this text.

[73] For further criticism, see Scottish Law Commission, Report on *Prescription and Title to Moveable Property* (Scot Law Com No 228, 2012) at 3.18–3.19.

[74] 'Cultural heritage' is defined in broad terms in Art 4 as cultural property belonging to the state.

[75] The description should be divided into ten categories of information and an image: in the event of theft, it is expected that this information will be transmitted around the globe and will be sufficient to identify the stolen object. See KY Fanizzo, 'Object ID: a Model of Global Collaboration' (2005) 20 *Journal of Museum Management and Curatorship*.

professional practice. Since 2004, it has been administered by the International Council of Museums (ICOM), and many museums use it.

Inventories may be immensely helpful in recovering objects stolen from museums and private collections, but clandestine excavations present different problems. Objects buried in the ground will not have been catalogued. It is in this situation that the obligation to educate local communities will come to the fore. If local people are made aware of the value of antiquities as part of their common heritage, it will encourage them to protect sites. States are therefore encouraged by Article 5(d) to organise a system of supervision of archaeological excavations and more generally to consider methods to protect sites.

States must foster respect for cultural heritage amongst the public.[76] If the local population is aware of why certain objects are part of their national heritage, they will be motivated to protect those objects, rather than seeing them in a detached way as commodities owned by the state.[77] In this way, education and information become strategic tools to fight the illicit movement of cultural objects.[78] Where a cultural object has disappeared, this must be brought to the attention of the public and the relevant authorities as appropriate.[79] This could be done by, for example, contacting Interpol and the Art Loss Register as well as the International Council of Museums (ICOM) and the International Foundation for Art Research (IFAR).

2.16 Pillaging of Antiquities

One of the most significant problems to have confronted the global community has been the stripping of sites of archaeological importance. This is currently a particular problem in countries such as Iraq and Afghanistan. Article 9 deals with archaeological and ethnological materials which are in immediate danger of pillage. It encourages Contracting States to become involved in 'a concerted international effort' to take measures such as the imposition of export and import controls. This appears to be a relatively weak response to a serious but admittedly complex problem. Much will depend upon the implementing legislation of Contracting States. In the UK, the Dealing in Cultural Objects (Offences) Act 2003, discussed in Chapter 3, makes it a criminal offence to deal dishonestly in tainted objects of antiquity.[80]

2.17 Export Controls

Article 6 requires Signatory States to establish a system of export controls, whereby the exporting state provides a certificate to confirm that the export of a cultural object is authorised. In order to support Contracting States in carrying out their obligations, UNESCO and the World Customs Organisation (WCO) jointly developed a UNESCO/WCO Model Export Certificate. The two organisations also agreed a Memorandum of Understanding. It is hoped that states will adopt the Model Export Certificate in whole or in part. It is thought that, if a common export certificate is universally adopted, it would

[76] UNESCO Convention, Art 5(f).

[77] This was a problem in Iraq, where many older Iraqis knew little about Mesopotanian history and assumed that museum objects were Saddam Hussein's personal property: DG Youkhanna, 'The Looting of the Iraq National Museum' in Stone and Farchakh Bajjaly, *Destruction of Cultural Heritage in Iraq* 105–07.

[78] UNESCO Convention, Art 10.

[79] UNESCO Convention, Art 5(g).

[80] See 3.62.

assist customs officials and police in different countries in the fight against the illicit trade in art and antiquities.[81]

Article 6 adds that objects without a certificate should be treated as illicit. The system of export certification has had a particular impact upon museums. Article 7(a) provides that governments should ensure that, 'consistent with national legislation', their public museums should not acquire an object which has been illegally exported from another Contracting State after the Convention entered into force in 1970. These provisions are now reflected in the professional codes of conduct at international and national level. In order to become a member of the International Council of Museums, an applicant must agree to abide by ICOM's Code of Ethics, which includes a requirement that museums must operate in a legal manner, including complying with the UNESCO Convention. Equally, the Museums Association in the UK has a Code of Ethics which deals with acquisitions. The Code refers to the UNESCO Convention in Part 5 and provides that museum employees are expected to behave responsibly and to exercise due diligence in deciding upon an acquisition or inward loan. If any item lacks a secure ownership history, employees should reject it unless there is a certificate to confirm that it was legally exported before 1970.[82] If there is a suspicion that an object has been illicitly traded, it should not be acquired.[83]

However, the limitations of Article 7(a) are clear: it only applies to museums, and not to dealers or private collectors, and it is only concerned with acquisition policies and not with the return of such objects. Even so, it has made 1970 a highly significant year. Unfortunately, sellers of illicit artefacts are likely to try and circumvent it. One ploy is to conjure up documents to support a fictitious claim that a particular object was exported prior to 1970 and then became part of the private collection of a 'gentleman.'

2.18 Import Controls

Article 7(b)(i) provides that Contracting States must prohibit the import of stolen cultural objects where the objects once formed part of an inventory belonging to a 'museum or a religious or secular public monument or similar institution'. As any steps taken must be 'consistent with national legislation', there is scope for variation from one country to another in satisfying this obligation. Although critics once argued that this undertaking might require states to establish elaborate, costly and highly intrusive border controls, with inspection of every item of luggage, it has not caused problems in practice.[84] The obligation is in any event quite limited. As Article 7(b)(i) refers to 'cultural property', the definition in Article 1 applies, which contains a requirement that the object must be one of importance. It also only relates to objects which have been documented in an inventory; unfortunately, even quite wealthy countries may not have found the resources to catalogue every item in the possession of their museums. It has no relevance in relation to antiquities which lie buried in the ground: as they are unknown, they will not have been catalogued. Article 9, discussed above, deals with these materials.

[81] The Model Export Certificate can be found on the UNESCO website.

[82] See the Museum Association's Code of Ethics at 5.10–5.11.

[83] The DCMS has been concerned to assist the UK museums profession in relation to practical guidance on acquisitions: DCMS Cultural Property Unit, *The 1970 UNESCO Convention: Guidance for Dealers and Auctioneers in Cultural Property*, 6.

[84] See the discussion provided by PJ O'Keefe, *Commentary on the UNESCO 1970 Convention*, 2nd edn (Builth Wells, Institute of Art and Law, 2007) 57–58; see also Bator, 'An Essay on the International Trade in Art' (1982) 34 *Stanford Law Review* 275, 329–30.

2.19 Sanctions

Contracting States are required by virtue of Article 8 to impose 'penalties or administrative sanctions' on persons who deal in illegally exported objects in contravention of Article 6 or objects stolen from museums and other sources listed in Article 7. There were already laws in place in the UK which satisfied this requirement before the Convention was ratified. As regards the import of objects without an export licence (forbidden by Article 6(b)), they are vulnerable to seizure by the authorities in accordance with section 49 of the Customs and Excise Management Act 1979. Article 7(b) forbade the import of inventoried objects which had been stolen; this type of conduct would be covered by the laws relating to theft, handling stolen goods and money laundering.[85] However, after ratification of the Convention, the UK Government passed the Dealing in Cultural Objects (Offences) Act 2003 as a further deterrent.[86] This statute has the advantage of clearly covering the importation of objects which have been unlawfully excavated or removed, even where those activities would not amount to theft.

2.20 The Impact Upon Professionals

Article 5(e) calls for the establishment of ethical codes for curators, collectors and dealers to encourage compliance with the principles of the Convention. The growth in professional codes of conduct in both the public and private sectors has been a worldwide phenomenon. In the UK, museums adopt a cautious approach to fresh acquisitions, for various reasons. First, the Museums Association's Code of Ethics requires museums to refuse any object with a dubious provenance. Museums which do not adhere to this code are not eligible to apply for Government support. Secondly, there would be a danger of committing a criminal offence. Customs officers and police officers have statutory powers to seize goods where there is evidence of theft, of handing stolen goods, or of money laundering.[87] Furthermore, an object is liable to forfeiture under section 49 of the Customs and Excise Management Act 1979 if it is improperly imported, such as where it has been concealed in a container holding goods of a different description.[88]

Under the Convention, states are also expected to impose penal or administrative sanctions 'as appropriate' upon 'antique dealers' who fail to keep a record of the origin of each cultural object, the identity of the supplier, a description and the price of the object, or who fail to inform their purchasers of any export prohibition. It is unsatisfactory that the provision does not extend to all dealers in cultural property.[89] In the UK, if a dealer is registered for VAT purposes, this information should be collected in any event. However, until 2003, there was no obligation imposed upon dealers more generally to keep proper records beyond what was needed for the purposes of accounting to the Inland Revenue.[90] Since 2003, all high-value dealers in any type of goods must keep records of the identities of the

[85] See ch 3.

[86] See 3.60. In relation to the USA, see the Convention on Cultural Property Implementation Act 1983, 9 USC ss 2607; see 3.74.

[87] See 4.05–4.06.

[88] See 4.06.

[89] JB Gordon, 'The UNESCO Convention on the Illicit Movement of Art Treasures' (1971) 12 *Harvard International Law Journal* 537, 553; O'Keefe, *Commentary on the UNESCO 1970 Convention* 75.

[90] See DCMS Cultural Property Unit, *The 1970 UNESCO Convention: Guidance for Dealers and Auctioneers in Cultural Property*, 5.

legal or beneficial owner of an object and the nature of the transaction in order to avoid committing a money laundering offence.[91]

2.21 Obligation to Return Stolen Items

Article 7(b)(ii) requires Contracting States to take appropriate steps to seize stolen inventoried objects and to return them at the request of the state from which the objects originated. There is no duty to return an object which is not stolen but merely illicitly exported.[92] Furthermore, the obligation is not concerned with every stolen object but only those objects which are part of an inventory belonging to a museum or similar institution. The state must produce documentary evidence to substantiate its claim and should make its request through diplomatic channels. The requesting state must also pay 'just compensation' to an innocent purchaser or to a person who has valid title to that property.[93] It is further provided that, 'All expenses incident to the return and delivery of the cultural property shall be borne by the requesting Party.' There is no limitation period specified in the Convention upon the expiration of which any request for the return of an object would not be possible; consequently a Contracting State is free to apply the limitation periods contained in its own domestic law.

2.22 International Conflicts and Countries under Occupation

Article 11 provides that 'The export and transfer of ownership of cultural property under compulsion arising directly or indirectly from the occupation of a country by a foreign power shall be regarded as illicit.' This provision covers more than theft and confiscation of assets; it attacks transfers which may have a semblance of legality but which in fact take place under compulsion, such as under duress. It means that a Contracting State must ensure that its own domestic private law would make such transfers void.[94] It is particularly useful where the occupying power has not ratified the Hague Convention and its Protocols. But the provisions of the Convention are arguably weakened by the emphasis placed upon effective administration, which is often partially or wholly absent in times of civil unrest or war. The object must be identified as an object listed in an inventory. In relation to the theft of property from the Iraqi National Museum in Baghdad, one of the problems encountered was that not all objects could be identified, because part of the inventory was missing. Furthermore, although Iraq became a Contracting State to the Convention in 1973, it was by no means clear that the Coalition Provisional Authority and the Iraqi Governing Council, which governed the country after the Iraq invasion, had sufficient status to make a request for the return of any objects which were identified.[95]

[91] See 3.45.

[92] This was not expressly provided for, due to concerns from the USA and other countries in relation to wide-ranging import controls: O'Keefe, *Commentary on the UNESCO 1970 Convention* 57–58.

[93] Compensation is only payable where this is compatible with a signatory nation's domestic laws protecting good faith purchasers: KT Burke, 'International Transfers of Stolen Cultural Property: Should Thieves Continue to Benefit from Domestic Laws Favoring Bona Fide Purchasers?' [1990] 13 *Loyola of Los Angeles International and Comparative Law Journal* 427, 438.

[94] English law is consistent with this principle: see, for example, *Kuwait Airways Corpn v Iraqi Airways (Nos 4 and 5)* [2002] 2 AC 883 (HL).

[95] C Phuong, 'The Protection of Iraqi Cultural Property' (2004) *International and Comparative Law Quarterly* 985, 991.

2.23 Acceptance by the UK

The UK was slow to accept the UNESCO Convention but, following a Report by the Illicit Trade Advisory Panel (ITAP)[96] which recommended its adoption, the UK accepted the Convention on 1 August 2002. This sent out a strong signal that the UK wished to curb the illicit trade in cultural objects. The fact that the Convention is not retroactive in its application was seen as an advantage; it enabled the UK to accede to the Convention without too much disruption to the art market. No substantial changes to existing law were necessary. The ITAP Panel observed that the UK's current export licensing system would satisfy the undertaking in Article 5(b) regarding the maintaining of a national inventory listing important public or private cultural property.[97] Equally, it was suggested that existing laws would suffice in relation to protection of archaeological sites.[98] It was noted that professional codes of conduct already existed.

A positive feature of the UNESCO Convention is that it permits reservations;[99] this flexibility has made it easier for states to accede to the Convention. Following the recommendations of the ITAP Panel, the UK Government took advantage of this freedom and added various provisos to clarify the law relating to the return of cultural objects.[100] A rider was added to ensure that there was a good fit with existing European law to which the UK was already subject. Consequently, where there is a request for the return of an object from a Member State of the EU, and it falls within the scope of EU Directive 93/7 EC, it will be dealt with in accordance with the Return of Cultural Objects Regulations 1994.[101] Where the Regulations do not apply, the existing civil law provides an effective cause of action.[102] However, the UK Government added a reservation that the United Kingdom, in applying Article 7(b)(ii), would 'continue to apply its existing rules on limitation to claims made under this Article for the recovery and return of cultural objects.' Consequently, a good faith purchaser can plead that an action for the return of an object is time-barred because of the expiration of the limitation period.[103]

Although the UK was not obliged, in signing the Convention, to introduce any new criminal offences, ITAP recommended that the UK should create offences relating to dishonestly dealing in stolen or illegally excavated cultural objects. The result was the Dealing in Cultural Objects (Offences) Act 2003, which is discussed at length in Chapter 3.[104]

[96] Report of the Ministerial Advisory Panel on Illicit Trade, Department for Culture, Media and Sport, December 2000 (chaired by N Palmer) (hereafter 'ITAP Report'). See further, Chamberlain, 'UK Accession to the 1970 UNESCO Convention' (2002) VII(3) *Art Antiquity and Law* 231.

[97] ITAP Report [56].

[98] ITAP Report [57].

[99] If a Treaty does not ban reservations, the only restriction will be that a reservation cannot be made which directly conflicts with the purpose of the treaty: Vienna Convention on the Law of Treaties 1969, Art 19.

[100] Letter LA/Depositary/2002/31.

[101] See 5.08. See also 6.02–6.06. EU Directive 116/2009 is set out in an Annex to this text.

[102] For discussion of the tort of conversion, see 5.09–5.13.

[103] See 5.42. This flexibility permits the private law relating to title and limitation periods to be altered even after accession to the Convention: see the Scottish Law Commission's Discussion Paper on *Prescription and Title to Moveable Property* (Scot Law Com No 144, 2010) [4.18].

[104] See 3.60. The UK Government had welcomed the recommendation of the ITAP Panel: House of Commons, Second Special Report, 'Cultural Property: Return and Illicit Trade: Further Government Response to the Seventh Report from the Culture, Media and Sport Committee, Session 199-2000', No 316 [13]. See further, 3.62.

2.24 The US Cultural Property Implementation Act 1983

The UNESCO Convention required Contracting States to establish a system whereby any cultural object which is exported should be accompanied by a certificate confirming that the export was authorised.[105] This prevents dealers importing objects without a valid export certificate. In principle, this would reverse the position adopted by a number of nations, including the UK, the USA and France, whereby objects which have been illegally exported may still be legally imported.[106] This issue was therefore contentious. Although the US Government signed the Convention in 1972, implementing legislation in the form of the Convention on Cultural Property Implementation Act 1983 was delayed due to tension between those who were concerned to stamp out clandestine excavations and theft, and those who favoured free trade in cultural property.[107] A compromise was eventually reached by way of a reservation on ratification. As the Convention does not force a state to accept other countries' export regulations, the US Government reserved the right to exercise its own judgement in relation to whether it would introduce controls to support another country's export regulations.[108]

In order to assist the US Government in arriving at a decision regarding import controls, the US Convention on Cultural Property Implementation Act 1983 established a Cultural Property Advisory Committee. This Committee evaluates requests from Contracting States for a bilateral agreement and will make recommendations in response. It may suggest that an agreement should be negotiated with the requesting state, or it may advocate an emergency import restriction, or it may report to Congress to explain its reasons why the request should be refused.

This process will satisfy Article 9 of the Convention, which requires Contracting States to take necessary measures to assist a Contracting State whose archaeological and ethnological objects are in immediate danger of pillage. Yet the President will usually only make a bilateral agreement in limited circumstances. The requesting state must provide documentation to show that, despite taking measures to protect its cultural assets, they are in jeopardy, and that the application of import restrictions would be of substantial benefit in deterring pillage and would be consistent with the general interest of the international community in the interchange of cultural property among nations for scientific, cultural, and educational purposes, and that less drastic remedies are not available.[109] This process is time-consuming and does not offer a rapid response to a crisis, such as the extensive looting in Iraq. However, in a crisis, section 2603 of the 1983 Act empowers the President to impose emergency import restrictions at the request of a Contracting State without negotiating a bilateral agreement; even so, the state must have made a request for a bilateral agreement beforehand.[110]

[105] UNESCO Convention, Art 6. See 2.17.

[106] See Bator, 'An Essay on the International Trade in Art' (1982) 34 *Stanford Law Review* 275, 377.

[107] Lenzner, 'Illicit International Trade in Cultural Property: Does the Unidroit Convention Provide an Effective Remedy for the Shortcomings of the UNESCO Convention?' (1994) 15 *University of Philadelphia Journal of International Business Law* 469, 486.

[108] WG Pearlstein, 'Cultural Property, Congress, the Courts, and Customs – The Decline and Fall of the Antiquities Market in K Fitzgibbon (ed), *Who Owns the Past?* (New Brunswick, New Jersey and London, Rutgers University Press, 2005) 9, 14–15.

[109] Convention on Cultural Property Implementation Act 1983, 19 USC s 2602: Agreement to Implement Article 9 of the Convention.

[110] 19 USC ss 2602-06.

The United States Government has signed a relatively small number of bilateral agreements with Mesoamerican, South American, European, and Asian countries. Archaeologists and others concerned with combatting the illicit trade in cultural property have pressed the Committee to increase the number of such agreements under the 1983 Act because it provides a legal basis for seizure of imported objects by US Customs and prosecution for theft under US criminal laws.[111] There has been corresponding pressure from the art trade to curtail the number of agreements in order to avoid inhibiting free trade.

2.25 The Style of the Convention

Article 2 provides that:

> 1. The State Parties to this Convention recognise that the illicit import, export and transfer of ownership of cultural property is one of the main causes of the impoverishment of the cultural heritage of the countries of origin of such property and that international co-operation constitutes one of the most efficient means of protecting each country's cultural property against all the dangers resulting there from.
>
> 2. To this end, the State Parties undertake to oppose such practices with the means at their disposal, and particularly by removing their causes, putting a stop to current practices, and by helping to make the necessary reparations.

The 1970 Convention has been criticised as being a weak response to the problems posed by the illicit trade in cultural property. Bator has described Article 2 as 'rhetorical rather than substantive'.[112] There is considerable debate over the effect of the early provisions of the Convention; Bator has suggested that they can be safely ignored.[113] Yet it can be argued that they are important because the Convention takes a holistic approach to combatting the illicit trade in cultural property. The early provisions establish principles (such as the definition of 'illicit' trade in Article 3) which can be linked to later provisions. Arguably Article 13 pulls many of the threads together by providing that Contracting States must prevent by 'all appropriate means' transfers of ownership which may promote the illicit trade in cultural property. It continues by encouraging co-operation between countries in relation to dealing with claims, returning objects, and recognising a state's right to declare certain objects inalienable. However, this final exhortation is phrased with the caveat that this must be done in a manner 'consistent with the laws of each State'.

O'Keefe argues that the early provisions are intended to have an effect. He suggests that Contracting States must treat objects as illicit if they are viewed as illicit exports in the originating country. He adds that, 'One cannot split State obligations. What one decides is an "illicit" export should be an "illicit" import for other State Parties.'[114] The position remains unclear. However, it could be argued that Contracting States are obliged to accept another state's export licensing system, unless a reservation is made to the contrary (as the US Government has done). States may decide to proceed on this basis and to pass legislation which provides that any object exported without a certificate should be regarded as an

[111] See 3.75.

[112] Bator (1982) 34 *Stanford LR* 275, 377. See also, the criticisms by Lenzner (1994) 15 *U Pa J Int'l Bus L* 469, 480.

[113] Bator, (1982) 34 *Stanford LR* 275, 377.

[114] O'Keefe, *Commentary on the UNESCO 1970 Convention* 41–43. For further discussion, see LV Prott, 'The Preliminary Draft UNIDROIT Convention on Stolen or Illegally Exported Cultural Objects' (1992) *International and Comparative Law Quarterly* 160, 164.

illicit import. Australia has adopted this approach. Section 14 of the Australian Protection of Movable Cultural Heritage Act 1986 provides that where a 'protected' object (meaning a movable object which forms part of a country's cultural heritage) is exported from a foreign country, and where its export is prohibited by the law of that country, it will be an unlawful import into Australia and liable to forfeiture. Furthermore, the importer of a protected object may be guilty of an offence in relation to its import.

2.26 Reflections on the UNESCO Convention

The 1970 Convention has been criticised on the basis that it was designed to appeal to source nations. Market nations were slow to ratify it. It is suggested that this hesitation was due to the fact that the Convention espouses a 'nationalistic' approach to cultural property:[115] it permits source nations to create export regulations which are wide-ranging and restrictive, thereby making numerous objects illegal to export. 'Internationalists' argue that there should be a free market in cultural objects because the information which they contain is relevant to the whole world. They suggest that, if too many constraints are imposed upon the legal market in art and antiquities, it will encourage the growth of a black market in these objects. In response, it should be noted that, although many of the original signatories were source nations, there are a number of market nations, such as the USA and UK, which have subsequently ratified the Convention.[116]

There are currently 120 states which are parties to the Convention.[117] One reason why the UNESCO Convention has gained widespread acceptance is because it permits Contracting States a great deal of discretion: states are merely expected to oppose the illicit trade in cultural property 'with the means at their disposal'. As criminals dealing in looted cultural objects will take advantage of any variations in the laws between states if it is to their advantage to do so, this could be seen as a major deficiency. Yet it may also be a strength. The obligations created by international agreements are often not spelt out with the same degree of precision as one would find in domestic law, not least because they have to accommodate structural differences in official languages; this lack of precision does not mean that they can be ignored.[118] They may influence the development of domestic law in each Contracting State without necessarily obliging the State to introduce radical new legislation. This flexibility has proved attractive. A further appeal of the Convention is that its provisions are not retroactive. It therefore avoids the most controversial issues because it offers no assistance to source nations seeking repatriation of objects looted centuries ago. It is consequently of no assistance to Greece in relation to objects taken before 1970, such as the Elgin Marbles.

A particular weakness of the Convention is that it fails to provide dispossessed owners with a direct right of action against the current person in possession of a cultural object. As a consequence, they will have to continue to rely upon the domestic law of the country in which the object is located. On the other hand, Article 13(c) involves an undertaking by

[115] JM Podesta, 'Saving Culture, but Passing the Buck: How the UNESCO Convention Undermines its Goals by Unduly Targeting Market Nations' (2008) 16 *Cardozo Journal of International and Comparative Law* 457, 462.

[116] The United States signed in 1983, Australia in 1989 and France in 1997.

[117] As of March 2011: UNESCO, Information Kit, *The Fight Against the Illicit Trafficking of Cultural Objects, The 1970 Convention: Past, Present and Future* (2011) CLT/2011/CONF.207/6.

[118] *Commonwealth of Australia v State of Tasmania, The Tasmanian Dam Case* (1983) 46 ALR 625 (High Court of Australia) 807–08 (in the context of the UNESCO Convention concerning the Protection of the World Cultural and Natural Heritage 1972).

Contracting States to admit claims for 'recovery of lost or stolen items of cultural property' brought by dispossessed owners so far as those claims are consistent with national law. In the UK, ratification of the Convention has had the effect of encouraging courts to relax public policy objections to international claims for recovery.[119] It may well influence the development of other legal principles as well.[120]

Nevertheless, the Convention has been valuable in bringing to the world's attention the need to prevent the illicit trade in cultural property. It has encouraged professionals involved in selling and purchasing cultural objects to create and comply with codes of conduct. Great care is taken whenever an object is received which was imported into the UK after 1970. In short, although the Convention may lack sufficient teeth, it has exerted a great influence over a large number of states.[121]

V UNIDROIT Convention on Stolen or Illegally Exported Cultural Objects 1995

2.27 Introduction

The UNIDROIT Convention[122] was opened for signature in 1995 and entered into force in July, 1998. It is concerned with civil claims of an international character relating to the recovery of stolen or illegally exported objects.[123] It is wider in scope than earlier conventions: Chapter II supports claims for the return of any stolen cultural object; Chapter III deals with requests for the return of illegally exported objects. In contrast, the focus of the UNESCO Convention was upon the return of stolen objects inventoried in museums and other institutions. The UNIDROIT Convention goes much further than the UNESCO Convention in another respect: it supports claims by private individuals, whereas the UNESCO Convention only assists where a request is made by a Contracting State.

The Preamble to the Convention explains the philosophy and aims of the Convention. It attempts to strike a balance between the competing concerns of source and market nations. Thus, although disquiet is expressed at the fact that the illicit trade in cultural property has resulted in damage to cultural objects and loss of information, it is also stated that the legal trade in cultural objects should be supported. The Preamble recognises the large number of stakeholders whose interests deserve consideration. Protection of cultural property is a matter which calls for the attention of the international community and the Preamble refers to the 'the well-being of humanity'. But the interests of local stakeholders are acknowledged in considering the damage done to the 'objects themselves and to the cultural heritage of national, tribal, indigenous or other communities', in addition to the 'heritage of all peoples'. In referring to the pillage of archaeological sites, the Preamble implicitly accepts

[119] *Islamic Republic of Iran v Barakat Galleries Ltd* [2007] EWCA Civ 1374, [2009] QB 22 (CA). See 5.07.

[120] *Seghal v Union of India* [2005] FSR 39 (High Court of Delhi) (author's moral rights).

[121] Contrast the the European Convention on Offences relating to Cultural Property 1985, which so far has not been ratified by any state.

[122] (1995) 34 ILM 1330. The text was prepared by the International Institute for the Unification of Private Law. For an excellent discussion of the background to each provision see LV Prott, *Commentary on the UNIDROIT Convention* (Leicester, Institute of Art and Law, 1997).

[123] UNIDROIT Convention, Art 1.

that archaeologists and anthropologists and others are affected in their professional capacity by this illicit trade. The existence of so many different stakeholders with potentially conflicting interests would have made the task of achieving a consensus particularly challenging.[124] It is understandable that, in these circumstances, the aim of the Convention was to create 'common, minimal legal rules', whilst enabling Contracting States to avail themselves of their own more protective rules if they wished and also to make minor variations to the Convention rules.[125] Despite this attempt to balance the interests of all parties, the wide scope of the Convention has made it controversial amongst dealers and it has not been ratified by the UK.

2.28 Definition of Cultural Objects

The drafters of the UNIDROIT Convention found that, although there was no uniform definition of cultural property, international treaties had exerted a significant influence on national legislation.[126] Consequently, although Article 2 of the UNIDROIT Convention refers to 'cultural objects' rather than 'cultural property', it contains a general definition which is similar to the definition found in Article 1 of the UNESCO Convention. The definition is comprised of objects which, 'on religious or secular grounds, are of importance for archaeology, prehistory, history, literature, art or science and belong to one of the categories listed in the Annex to this Convention.' The Annex expands on this simple definition with precisely the same reference to various categories to be found in Article 1 of the UNESCO Convention, and which includes rare fauna, flora, minerals, and fossils. This replication of the UNESCO Convention list is to be welcomed because it provides a sense of continuity and facilitates the ratification of the UNIDROIT Convention. However, it should be noted that the objects must be of importance: there is obviously no need to preserve or impose controls on mass-produced handicrafts from any region of the world.

There is nevertheless one significant difference in the general definition of cultural property between the two Conventions. Whereas the UNESCO Convention requires objects to be 'specifically designated' by the government of each state as being of importance for archaeology, prehistory or other enumerated purposes, the UNIDROIT Convention does not contain such a requirement. The approach is appropriate in the context of a Convention which is intended to assist not only states but also private owners in recovering stolen property. Certain states, such as the UK, currently do not have an elaborate system of classification of movables in their domestic law, and a substantial amount of cultural objects are in private ownership. This broad definition is therefore left to judges in the domestic courts of Contracting States to apply to the facts at hand. However, in an age where cultural property is increasingly valued, it is likely that a court will interpret the definition in a generous rather than restrictive fashion.[127]

[124] Arguably the Convention does not favour either 'internationalism' (free trade) or 'retentionism' (national controls): Prott, *Commentary on the UNIDROIT Convention* 19.

[125] See the UNIDROIT Convention, Arts 3(5), 13(5), 16.

[126] G Reichelt, 'The International Protection of Cultural Property – Second Study', *Uniform Law Review*, 1988-I, 52 (UNIDROIT 1988, Study LXX – Doc 4) 17–20.

[127] See, for example, cases involving cultural property of indigenous communities, *FG Charrier v Bell* 496 SO 2d 601 (1986) concerning native American grave goods (US); *Onus v Alcoa* (1981) 36 ALR 425 concerning Aboriginal artefacts (Australia). See also International Institute for the Unification of Private Law, 'Observations of International Organisations to the Committee of Governmental Experts on the International Protection of Cultural Property' (1992), Document 25 [12].

2.29 Chapter II: Return of Stolen Cultural Objects

Article 3(1) asserts that anyone in possession of a stolen cultural object must return it.[128] Despite this forceful opening statement, the Convention does not make possession a criminal offence: it merely imposes a civil obligation upon individuals or institutions to return the object in question. Even so, the Convention is significant in enabling dispossessed owners,[129] whether private individuals, institutions, or governments of Contracting States, to reclaim stolen property by bringing a direct action before the domestic courts in the country where the object in question is located. Although this provision would not be at odds with English law,[130] it runs counter to the domestic law of various countries with civil law systems which traditionally protect the good faith purchaser.

Claimants will face various difficulties in attempting to recover an item in the courts of another Contracting State. It is therefore likely that only the most significant items will be pursued. First, the claimant must show that he has a proprietary claim to the object and, if the object has not been fully catalogued, identification may be problematic.[131] Secondly, it must be shown that the object was stolen. The domestic court will apply its own national law (including private international law) in arriving at an answer.[132] Nevertheless, Article 3(2) provides considerable assistance by adding that stolen property includes property which has been illegally excavated, or excavated and illegally retained, provided that this does not conflict with the law of the state where the excavation took place. This provision is helpful, because not every country asserts rights of ownership over objects buried in its subsoil. If not for Article 3(2), a possessor could argue that an antiquity which had been secretly dug up was ownerless, and therefore any finder could claim it.

Article 10(1) presents a third obstacle by providing that the Convention is not retroactive: its rules will only apply where the cultural object was stolen after the Convention entered into force in the state where the claim is brought *and* the state where the theft occurred.[133] Furthermore, the claim must be of an international character. If the theft and its transfer to another all happen within one state, the dispute between the owner and possessor will be governed by that state's domestic law. It is by no means clear whether there is an 'international' claim where the object is stolen from a location within a Contracting State, shipped abroad, resold and then returned to the Contracting State.[134] Arguably, the application of the Convention should not be defeated in these circumstances because the cultural object will still have been moved across national frontiers.[135] Where the Convention does not apply (such as in the UK, which is not a party to the Convention), any conflicting claims to the object would not be dealt with by the Convention but by domestic law, including private international law.

[128] There is no reference as to whom the object will be returned, although it is envisaged that it would usually be the owner: see the Explanatory Report prepared by the UNIDROIT Secretariat (2001–2003) *Uniform Law Review* 476, 502.

[129] The Convention does not prevent those individuals or institutions with a lesser proprietary interest from bringing a claim, for example a museum which had possession under a loan agreement prior to the theft.

[130] See 5.09.

[131] Identification is a particular problem in relation to material which has been secretly excavated: see, for example, *Bumper Development Corporation Ltd v Commissioner of Police* [1991] 4 All ER 638 (CA).

[132] Prott, *Commentary on the UNIDROIT Convention* 31.

[133] In contrast, paras 3 and 4 of Pt I of the First Protocol to the Hague Convention 1954 provide that Contracting States will take into custody cultural property imported from any occupied country's territory.

[134] See *Winkworth v Christie, Manson and Woods Ltd* [1980] 1 Ch 496.

[135] Explanatory Report to the UNIDROIT Convention on Stolen or Illegally Exported Objects, Study LXX – Doc 51, 10; Explanatory Report prepared by the UNIDROIT Secretariat (2001–2003) *Uniform Law Review* 476, 494.

2.30 Chapter II: Limitation Periods for Stolen Objects

When can a person in possession of a stolen object argue that it is too late for a claim to be made? This was a hotly debated question during the drafting of the Convention.[136] Prott has argued that a lengthy limitation period is desirable because 'objects can be easily concealed in bank vaults and returned to the market when the limitation period has expired'.[137] The Law Reform Commission of Ireland observed that:

> Some negotiating States argued against imposing any limitation period on the ground that it would add legitimacy to a situation which was from the beginning tainted with illegality. Those who insisted upon the inclusion of time limitations argued that the imposition of such periods, especially of short periods, would encourage potential claimants to act with desirable expedition and thus avoid the disruption of long established possessions. These two schools of thought corresponded roughly with the exporting and the importing countries respectively.[138]

The relevant provisions of the UNIDROIT Convention appear to present a solution which is a compromise between these competing points of view. Even so, it could be argued that on balance, the Convention favours those nations who wish to offer some protection to the possessor because it allows for a limitation defence in most circumstances.[139] There are two parts to Article 3(3). The first part provides that, if a claimant wishes to bring an action to obtain the return of an object, it must be done within a period of three years from the time when 'the claimant knew the location of the cultural object and the identity of its possessor.' This defence is not as generous to the defendant as it may first appear, because the provision does not state that knowledge can be imputed to the claimant. In other words, it may not be sufficient for the defendant to show that he had purchased the item at a public auction more than three years before a claim is made because the claimant might not have been aware of that auction. The absence of any express statement that the three-year limitation period could be activated by constructive knowledge was seen as a serious failing by the Ministerial Advisory Panel on Illicit Trade,[140] and led them to recommend that the Convention should not be adopted by the UK Government. The Panel discussed whether the position could be rectified by declaring that knowledge which could be acquired with reasonable diligence should be imputed to the claimant; however, it was decided that this might be viewed as a reservation rather than a declaration; reservations are not permitted by the Convention.[141]

[136] See the first study carried out in the light of the UNESCO Convention: G Reichelt, 'The International Protection of Cultural Property', *Uniform Law Review* (1985) 42 (UNIDROIT 1986, Study LXX – Doc 1) [45]–[55].

[137] LV Prott, 'The Preliminary Draft UNIDROIT Convention on Stolen or Illegally Exported Cultural Objects' (1992) *International and Comparative Law Quarterly* 160, 163; *Menzel v List* 253 NYS 2d 43; 267 NYS 2d 804, aff'd 298 NYS 2d 979 (1969); *Kunstsammlungen zu Weimar v Elicofon* 536 F Supp 829 (1981), 678 F 2d 1150 (1982); *De Weerth v Baldinger* 836 F 2d 103 (1987); *United States v Herce* 334 F Supp Ill (1971). See also, IFAR Reports No 4, July 1990.

[138] The Law Reform Commission of Ireland, *Report on the Unidroit Convention on Stolen or Illegally Exported Objects* (1997) LRC 55 [3.39].

[139] Contrast the First Protocol to the Hague Convention 1954, para 3, which does not impose any time limit in relation to claims for the restitution of cultural property which has been taken from an occupied territory in contravention of the provisions of the Convention.

[140] This issue is discussed In the Explanatory Report prepared by the UNIDROIT Secretariat (2001–2003) *Uniform Law Review* 476, 508, but it had not been anticipated that this would be a problem because owners would normally be expected to be diligent and courts 'will probably apply their own general rules of law to determine whether the claimant has been diligent.'

[141] Ministerial Advisory Panel on Illicit Trade Report, December 2000 [49]–[53].

The second part of Article 3(3) provides possessors of objects with more significant protection by stating that there is an ultimate cut-off period for all claims of 50 years from the time of the theft. Unfortunately, a degree of complexity is introduced by Article 3(4), which restricts the operation of this second part of Article 3(3) in order to give states greater power to obtain the return of objects which are viewed as possessing a special status. It provides that, if the object forms 'an integral part of an identified monument or archaeological site' or belongs to 'a public collection',[142] this 50-year period will not apply. A 'public collection' is somewhat loosely defined by Article 3(7); in essence it is a group of identified or inventoried objects held by local or national government or a charity.[143] Objects in a 'public collection' were seen as deserving special protection because these objects would lie at the heart of a state's cultural heritage.[144]

Article 3(5) has created a further layer of complexity: it provides that a state may make a declaration (at the time of signature, ratification, acceptance or approval of the Convention[145]) which varies the principle enunciated in Article 3(4). Article 3(5) provides:

> Notwithstanding the provisions of the preceding paragraph, any Contracting State may declare that a claim is subject to a time limitation of 75 years or such longer period as is provided in its law. A claim made in another Contracting State for restitution of a cultural object displaced from a monument, archaeological site or public collection in a Contracting State making such a declaration shall also be subject to that time limitation.

What if one state has made a declaration and another has not? This is dealt with in the second sentence of Article 3(5), and it should not cause too much difficulty in practice. If a state makes a declaration that claims by another state for restitution of objects from an identified monument or archaeological site or public collection would be barred after, for example, 75 years from the date of the theft, it would not be able to make such a claim itself after that period.

Problems may arise where there is a dispute between two Contracting States, both of which have made a declaration. For example, suppose State A has declared a limitation period of 75 years and State B has made a declaration of 100 years: which time limit should govern in the event of a conflict? The Law Reform Commission of Ireland has discussed this issue and has suggested that, although the wording of the Convention was of no assistance, the policy concern of reciprocity should supply the answer. Consequently, the Commission has argued that, 'Given that the purpose of the second sentence was to impose the burden of a declaration on a state wishing to benefit by it, it would seem that State A (with a period of 75 years) which makes a claim in State B (with a period of 100 years) will be bound by the 75 year limit (a declaration being burdensome on the state making it). A claim made by B in A will also be bound by A's 75 year limit, as A must benefit as well as be burdened by its declaration.'[146] This seems the best solution from a pragmatic perspective, but it awaits confirmation by domestic courts.

[142] By Art 3(7), a public collection is a 'group of inventoried or otherwise identified cultural objects' in the possession of a public body. By Art 3(8), this also includes objects which are spiritually or communally significant and belong to and are used by a particular tribe or indigenous community for traditional or ritual purposes.

[143] See the discussion in *Report on the Unidroit Convention on Stolen or Illegally Exported Objects* (1997) LRC 55 [3.54]–[3.57].

[144] *Report on the Unidroit Convention on Stolen or Illegally Exported Objects* (1997) LRC 55 [3.45]; Explanatory Report to the UNIDROIT Convention on Stolen or Illegally Exported Objects, Study LXX – Doc 51, 19.

[145] UNIDROIT Convention, Art 3(6).

[146] *Report on the UNIDROIT Convention on Stolen or Illegally Exported Objects* (1997) LRC 55 [3.49].

The 50-year period will also not apply where, according to Art 3(8), there is a claim for the return 'of a sacred or communally important cultural object belonging to and used by a tribal or indigenous community in a Contracting State as part of that community's traditional or ritual use.' It is possible that the application of Article 3(8) may give rise to uncertainty in certain states, although these groups can normally be identified because there will be special legal provisions which apply to them in a state's domestic law.[147]

It can be argued that the provisions on limitation periods contained in the Convention are reasonable. A 50-year cut-off period for the return of a cultural object might be seen as adequate as a general rule, because it would be unusual for objects to be stored for a longer period than that. On the other hand, although the risk that objects would be placed in storage for a much longer period is low, this must be balanced against the importance of the object to the cultural life of a nation. It is unfortunate that, in drafting a special regime to deal with the most important objects, the Convention has created a degree of uncertainty. It may have been better if it had simply provided that there was no limitation period for these types of object.

2.31 Chapter II: Compensating the Diligent Possessor

There are a number of states which offer significant protection to a good faith purchaser. By facilitating claims to obtain restitution of cultural objects, the Convention radically cuts away at this traditional protection. To make the Convention more palatable to such states, Article 4(1) provides that possessors who are unaware that the object is stolen can claim compensation from the claimant:

> The possessor of a stolen cultural object required to return it shall be entitled, at the time of its restitution, to payment of fair and reasonable compensation provided that the possessor neither knew nor ought reasonably to have known that the object was stolen and can prove that it exercised due diligence when acquiring the object.

By Article 4(5), those who obtain an object gratuitously (such as a museum in receipt of a donation) are in the same position as any other possessor and must satisfy the due diligence test in order to obtain compensation.

The burden of proving lack of knowledge is placed upon the possessor. What sort of conduct will satisfy the 'due diligence' test set out in Article 4(1)? No mention is made of the concept of 'good faith' as such, presumably in order to avoid a situation where judges are tempted to draw upon the interpretation given in their countries' domestic legislation.[148] Article 4(4) defines 'due diligence' further. The court must have regard to the general circumstances of the acquisition, including the character of the parties, the price paid, and whether the possessor consulted any agencies or reasonably accessible registers or obtained information or documents or taken other steps that a reasonable person would have done.

The guidelines in Article 4(4) therefore establish an objective test. A court would naturally consider whether there were suspicious circumstances which would prompt a person to enquire further. This would include whether the property was obtained at an unusual time or place. Unusual packaging, such as mud and straw, might arouse suspicion.[149] A

[147] ibid [3.42]. See further, the International Labour Organization's *Convention Concerning Indigenous and Tribal Peoples in Independent Countries, 1989* (No 169).

[148] Prott, *Commentary on the UNIDROIT Convention* 41.

[149] ibid, 41, 47, citing *United States v McClain* 545 F 2d 988 (1977); 551 F 2d 52 (1977); 593 F 2d 658 (1979) (US).

purchaser should also bear in mind the type of goods on offer, as it may be well known in the trade that there is a high incidence of theft of this type of object; in this situation, further enquiries would be necessary.[150] The 'character' of the parties refers in particular to their expertise. As regards the seller, account would be taken of whether he is a reputable dealer who regularly trades in this field. If there was a sale by auction, the character of the auction house would be considered. If it employed specialists, they would be expected to have the expertise to carry out extensive checks on the provenance of a particular item before dealing with it. As regards the price, the transaction would appear dubious if there was an inexplicable undervalue of the art or antiquities in question. The court is given a wide discretion and will look at the particular facts in deciding whether other steps should have been taken, such as consulting computer databases: for instance, the Art Loss Register and the database run by Interpol.[151] For any prized object, the courts may expect the purchaser to have obtained an 'Ownership of Due Diligence Certificate'. This certificate will confirm that not only have all the major databases been searched, but that experts in the field and major auction houses and museums have been contacted.[152] A high standard of care appears to be required: the *negligent* acquirer of art will not be able to satisfy the test.[153] The overall effect of this provision relating to compensation is to incentivise acquirers, whether private individuals or museums, to be careful and diligent in taking possession of new items.

This objective test is not completely unfamiliar to English lawyers: it is similar to the test of 'good faith' purchase when the person in possession is relying upon the limitation periods as a defence.[154] However, it is a departure from a subjective 'good faith' test which prevails in a number of civil legal systems where a negligent possessor who has failed to check an item's provenance is still assumed to have acted in good faith.[155]

The Convention supports the interests of the claimant in various ways. First, as discussed, it is not every possessor who is entitled to be compensated, but only those who can demonstrate that they have exercised 'due diligence'. Secondly, Article 4(2) provides that the possessor is first expected to make reasonable efforts to recover the value from a prior transferor provided that is consistent with the law of the Contracting State.[156] Thirdly, Article 4(3) provides that, if the claimant is forced to compensate the defendant in order to obtain the return of the object, he can sue a prior seller or other transferor. Even so, if a source nation is poor but wishes to make a claim, it will see the requirement to compensate the possessor as a significant hurdle. However, it can be argued that the possessor's right to 'fair and reasonable' compensation does not mean that the claimant is obliged to pay the full commercial value of the object. The position is unclear. No guidance is provided in

[150] *Nicole de Préval v Adrian Alan Ltd* (24 January 1997, unrep), which involved highly unusual candelabra. See R Redmond-Cooper, 'Good Faith Acquisition of Stolen Art' (1997) II(1) *Art Antiquity and Law* 55. See 5.43.

[151] For discussion of electronic databases, see 7.04.

[152] See PJ O'Keefe, 'The Use of Databases to Combat Theft of Cultural Heritage Material' (1997) II(4) *Art Antiquity and Law* 357, 361.

[153] It was envisaged that it would be very difficult to prove due diligence: M van Gaalen and A Verheij, 'The Consequences for the Netherlands of the UNIDROIT Convention' (1998) III(1) *Art Antiquity and Law* 3, 9; Explanatory Report on the draft text dated 20 December, 1994 (Unidroit 1994, Conf 8/3), No 63, 21.

[154] *Nicole de Préval v Adrian Alan Ltd* (24 January 1997, unrep); *Kurtha v Marks* [2008] EWHC 336. See 5.43. For the interpretation of 'good faith' supplied by the common law, in relation to the exceptions to the *nemo dat* principle: see 5.37.

[155] *Report on the Unidroit Convention on Stolen or Illegally Exported Objects* (1997) LRC 55 [3.74]; UNESCO Comments on the Draft Convention, in *Acts and Proceedings of the Diplomatic Conference*, 97.

[156] See P Jenkins, 'The UNIDROIT Convention on Stolen or Illegally Exported Cultural Objects' (1996) I(2) *Art Antiquity and Law* 163, 166.

relation to this phrase by the Convention itself.[157] The drafters of the Convention assumed that the concept of 'fair and reasonable' compensation permits the court to take account of the financial resources of claimants.[158]

However, states are permitted to apply rules which are 'more favourable to the restitution or return' of cultural objects than those provided in the Convention.[159] Consequently, if a Contracting State does not normally provide compensation when a stolen object is recovered, it is not obliged to introduce legislation providing for payment of compensation. It follows that the question of whether a claimant is obliged to compensate a possessor will depend upon the domestic laws of the nation in which the cultural object is currently located.

2.32 Chapter III: Illegally Exported Cultural Objects

Article 5(1) is concerned with international claims by a Contracting State for the return of cultural objects which have been illegally exported from within its territory. The phrase 'illegally exported' is clarified in Article 1(b) of the Convention, which provides that the right to request the return of an object only applies to the removal of cultural objects which are exported 'contrary to its law regulating the export of cultural objects for the purpose of protecting its cultural heritage.' The onus is therefore on governments to protect heritage items by drafting appropriate export regulations (and Contracting States are required, by Article 17, to supply copies of the regulations to UNIDROIT). The scope of the Convention is limited by the fact that it is not enough to show that a domestic law, such as one of a fiscal nature, was violated: it must be shown that there was a contravention of an export law which was intended to protect cultural property. The wording of a Contracting State's export laws may therefore affect the application of this Convention.

The tone of Article 5(1) differs significantly from its counterpart, Article 3(1), which requires the return of stolen objects. Article 5(1) provides that a Contracting State may 'request' an object's return by applying to the court or other competent authority. The distinction made in the Convention between claims relating to stolen objects and those relating to illegally exported objects may seem odd. There is an overlap in the sense that a stolen object may subsequently be illegally exported. Furthermore, both sets of principles are concerned with wrongdoing. The reason why there is a different set of principles governing each situation is because a number of states are reluctant to recognise foreign public laws. A state's export controls protecting heritage interests are viewed as public laws of a foreign state. This used to be a concern in the UK; however, there is now a greater willingness to accept foreign laws protecting cultural objects since the ratification of the UNESCO Convention.[160]

The fact that a Contracting State may make a request rather than a claim is clarified by Article 5(3), which provides that certain conditions must be satisfied before a court or competent authority can order the return of an object. Article 5(3) provides that the state must establish (with accompanying evidence in accordance with Article 5(4)) that:

[157] *Report on the Unidroit Convention on Stolen or Illegally Exported Objects* (1997) LRC 55 [3.78].
[158] Unidroit Explanatory Report, in *Acts and Proceedings of the Diplomatic Conference* 30 [60].
[159] UNIDROIT Convention, Art 9.
[160] *Islamic Republic of Iran v Barakat Galleries Ltd* [2009] QB 22 (CA) [154].

the removal of the object from its territory significantly impairs one or more of the following interests:

(a) the physical preservation of the object or of its context;
(b) the integrity of a complex object;
(c) the preservation of information of, for example, a scientific or historical character;
(d) the traditional or ritual use of the object by a tribal or indigenous community,

or establishes that the object is of significant cultural importance for the requesting State.

At first glance, it would appear that a Contracting State would always wish to argue that the object was stolen, so that there would be no need to satisfy one of the listed interests. However, there may be situations where Articles 3 and 4 cannot be relied upon because it cannot be shown that the object is stolen. This might be the case where the domestic law of a state vests ownership of buried objects in the finder. In this situation, the object cannot be characterised as stolen.[161] If there have been illegal excavations of sites in a state which does not have cultural patrimony laws, the state may be able to establish that the object needs to be returned to its original location in order to ensure 'the physical preservation of the object or its context', referred to in Article 5(3)(a). This phrase is broad and has the advantage of covering situations other than the original appropriation itself. If an object is taken and handled roughly, for example, or painted over to disguise it, this would amount to physical damage. The final part of Article 5(3) can be seen as a 'sweep-up' provision which ensures that rare, or unique or important items which might not fall within paragraphs (a) to (d) can still be included as objects of 'significant cultural importance'.

Article 5 is flexible in not only covering situations where the object was illegally exported but also situations where it was validly exported with a permit for a short period, such as on loan to a museum, but that period has come to an end and it has not been returned. This meshes with the ICOM Code of Ethics for Museums. Article 2(3) of the ICOM Code requires museums to exercise due diligence in verifying the terms of export before exhibiting objects which have been acquired either permanently or on loan for a period. Article 5(7) of the Museums Association's Code of Ethics would also be compatible with the Convention in requiring its members to exercise due diligence before any agreement is made in relation to an acquisition or inward loan.

There are specific situations where there is no obligation under the Convention to return objects which have been illegally exported. Article 7(1)(a) provides quite sensibly that the Convention provisions do not apply if the export of the object is no longer illegal at the time of the request. According to Article 7(1)(b), the provisions have no application where 'the object was exported during the lifetime of the person who created it or within a period of fifty years following the death of that person.' This provision is intended to ensure that the Convention cannot be used by a state to prevent the work of a modern artist being known abroad by preventing the export of any of the artist's works; it is also intended to ensure that artists can provide for their families after their death.[162] However, a state can make a request for the return of an illegally exported object under Article 5, and Article 7(1)(b) will have no application, where 'a cultural object was made by a member or members of a tribal or indigenous community for traditional or ritual use by that community and the object will be returned to that community.'

[161] Although the UNIDROIT Convention, Art 3(2), provides a presumption that an illegally excavated object is stolen, it gives way to any contrary provision contained in domestic laws where the excavation took place.

[162] *Report on the Unidroit Convention on Stolen or Illegally Exported Objects* (1997) LRC 55 [3.102].

2.33 Chapter III: Limitation Periods for Illegally Exported Objects

Like the position where a claim is made for the recovery of a stolen object, a person in possession can resist the claim by arguing that the claim is stale.

Article 5(5) provides that:

> Any request for return shall be brought within a period of three years from the time when the requesting State knew the location of the cultural object and the identity of its possessor, and in any case within a period of fifty years from the date of the export or from the date on which the object should have been returned under a permit.

Article 3(3) creates the same basic period of limitation in relation to the restitution of stolen objects. However, the two regimes are different in one respect in relation to limitation periods: where a cultural object is illegally exported, the principle spelt out in Article 5(5) governs entirely and no distinction is made between different types of cultural object. There is no counterpart to Article 3(4) where certain types of object are viewed as having a special status so that the claimant has a longer period of time within which to bring a claim.

2.34 Chapter III: Compensating the Possessor

Article 6 makes provision for fair and reasonable compensation[163] 'provided that the possessor neither knew nor ought reasonably to have known at the time of acquisition that the object had been illegally exported'. At first glance, the position appears to be the same as that for stolen objects, which is governed by Article 4. There is a similar provision that those who acquire objects by way of inheritance or otherwise gratuitously are in no better position than the person from whom it was acquired. However, unlike Article 4, there is no need for the possessor to establish that he has exercised due diligence. It is difficult to gauge the significance of this omission. It may be that the purchaser is held to a lower standard of care, particularly as the court is only formally required to consider the circumstances and the lack of an export certificate.[164] Article 6(4) makes provision for the requesting state to pay all the costs associated with securing the return of the object,[165] without prejudice to its right to recover the cost from another person (who might be the criminal responsible for illegally exporting it).

Article 6(3) provides that the claimant state may negotiate with the possessor and may agree upon a different solution. It may be the case that the possessor can retain ownership of the object under the applicable law. It may be agreed that the possessor will transfer the object, either gratuitously or subject to receiving some form of compensation, to a reliable person or institution (such as a museum) located in the territory of the requesting state. By injecting a reasonable degree of flexibility into the compensation scheme, this provision makes it more palatable to those countries whose laws provide strong protection for good faith possessors.

[163] The compensation would take account of the resources of the requesting state, and would consequently not necessarily be its market price: Explanatory Report to the Unidroit Convention on Stolen or Illegally Exported Objects, Study LXX – Doc 51, 33.

[164] It should be recalled that Art 6 of the UNESCO Convention 1970 requires its Contracting States to introduce a system of export certificates and to prohibit the export of cultural property without such certificates.

[165] The Intergovernmental Committee for Promoting the Return of Cultural Property to its Countries of Origin or its Restitution in case of Illicit Appropriation, which acts as an advisory body, administers a fund to support the restitution or return of cultural property of fundamental significance.

2.35 Overview

The UNESCO Convention 1970 could be described as providing the foundation for combatting the illicit trade in cultural property. It places great emphasis upon the protection of cultural objects and the value of educating the public in relation to their importance; it is concerned to ensure that there is a system of export controls to prevent the easy transfer of illicit cultural objects. The UNIDROIT Convention is not an alternative to the UNESCO Convention: it is compatible with it, adding a further way of tackling the illicit trade of cultural objects by focusing upon supporting claims for their restitution or return.

The UNIDROIT Convention contains various other provisions which are intended to facilitate recovery. By Article 8(1), all claims under Chapter II and requests under Chapter III must be brought in the courts of the state in which the object is located. This avoids any difficulty in enforcing a judgment ordering the return of an object. Article 8(2) provides that parties can agree to arbitration. This has the advantage of enabling any dispute to be carried out in privacy. This may be an important consideration where it is alleged that an object is stolen. Arbitration also permits more flexibility in, for example, appointing an expert as arbitrator. Article 8(3) makes it clear that, if a claimant sues the possessor in one Contracting State, proceedings can also be brought in another Contracting State where the object is located to prevent, for example, any further dealings with the object. The Convention can be applauded for concentrating on the return of the cultural object by providing that the claimant can recover the property itself without having to prove that financial compensation would be inadequate in the circumstances.

The UNIDROIT Convention is not retrospective in its operation. By Article 10(1), the provisions of Chapter II of the Convention only apply where a cultural object has been stolen after the Convention entered into force in respect of the state where the claim is brought, and provided that: '(a) the object was stolen from the territory of a Contracting State after the entry into force of this Convention for that State; or (b) the object is located in a Contracting State after the entry into force of the Convention for that State.' As regards the illegal export of an object, by Article 10(2), the provisions of Chapter III will only apply after this Convention entered into force for the requesting state as well as the state where the request is brought. There is no doubt that this principle of non-retroactivity, which applies to treaties in general and has the force of international customary law, benefits market states. Thus, if the UK ratified the UNIDROIT Convention tomorrow, it would have no application as regards objects stolen or illegally exported before that time.

2.36 Ratification and the UK Position

The UNIDROIT Convention seems reasonably well balanced in dealing with the interests of the relevant stakeholders in any dispute: possessors of objects, and those seeking their restitution or return. The Convention appears even-handed in providing that those who have acted with due diligence in obtaining possession of an object will be compensated. It is sensitive to domestic concerns in allowing domestic law to define whether an object is stolen or not. Furthermore, Article 9 permits courts in Contracting States to apply their own domestic law if it offers more advantages to prospective claimants seeking restitution or return of cultural objects. Even so, it has not yet proved popular. There are approximately 31 Contracting States,[166] including various source nations (such as Afghanistan,

[166] As of March 2011: UNESCO, Information Kit, *The Fight Against the Illicit Trafficking of Cultural Objects, The 1970 Convention: Past, Present and Future* (2011) CLT/2011/CONF.207/6.

Italy and China) that have signed the Convention. Interestingly, some countries which offer generous protection to good faith purchasers, such as Switzerland, have signed it. However, the main market nations, the UK, the USA and Japan, have failed to do so. Iraq is not a party to the Convention, and therefore neither the state nor its citizens can rely upon its provisions in order to recover property once located in Iraq.

It could be argued that the UNIDROIT Convention represents a compromise between dealers and those who were actively concerned to prevent the illicit trade in cultural property.[167] Yet many dealers in cultural property in the UK would not be in favour of ratification by the UK Government. First, the Convention challenges the traditional way in which traders have dealt in art and antiquities by encouraging purchasers to make detailed enquiries about provenance. Secondly, the Convention establishes a system where an innocent possessor is expected to return a stolen object and to seek compensation, where possible, from his seller. This scheme would have a significant impact upon dealers, exposing them to the risk of civil suits some years after a sale has been completed. The Report of the Illicit Trade Advisory Panel (ITAP) of December 2000 advised the UK Government that the UNIDROIT Convention had a number of disadvantages. It was suggested that the range of stolen cultural objects to which the provisions in Chapter II applied was too broad and, as the Convention prohibited reservations, it was not possible to narrow it.[168] The limitation periods within which claims must be brought were also criticised as being unfair upon the good faith purchaser; in particular, it was thought that they did not encourage the owner to take obvious and reasonable steps to recover his property.[169] The Report recommended that the UNESCO Convention should be ratified by the UK but concluded that the UNIDROIT Convention, despite having many positive features, should not be adopted.

The question of whether the UK Government should ratify the UNIDROIT Convention is now ripe for reconsideration. The ITAP Report was published in 2000. Since then, the Proceeds of Crime Act 2002 and the Money Laundering Regulations 2007 (replacing the 2003 Regulations) have been enacted, which force dealers to obtain information about the identities of their clients and to report suspicious transactions.[170] Despite the fact that the UNIDROIT Convention caused disquiet amongst traders at one time because of a reluctance to make enquiries about the provenance of objects which they wished to acquire, it should no longer do so. Money laundering measures mean that traders should be making these enquiries anyway. Furthermore, the fact that the Convention is not limited to inventoried objects stolen from museums is to be applauded. Every nation should desire a healthy market in licit cultural objects, which will involve their movement from one country to another as they are traded. However, theft is a different matter and courts should be sympathetic towards claims by previous owners for the return of their possessions. As Merryman has observed, there can be 'no licit trade in *stolen* objects'.[171]

Where there are disputes over the return or restitution of cultural property and the Conventions do not apply, UNESCO has an 'Intergovernmental Committee for Promoting

[167] S Mackenzie and P Green, 'Performative regulation: a case study of how powerful people avoid criminal labels' (2008) *British Journal of Criminology* 138, 145. The authors noted that the Panel included representatives drawn from the trade: ibid, 143.

[168] ITAP Report, para 49.

[169] Yet, as discussed at 2.30, in fn 138 above, the Explanatory Report prepared by the Unidroit Secretariat (2001–2003) *Uniform Law Review* 476, 508, reveals that the drafters had expected domestic courts to require owners to be diligent.

[170] See 3.44–3.45.

[171] Merryman, 'A Licit International Trade in Cultural Objects' in *Elgin Marbles,* 253.

the Return of Cultural Property to Its Countries of Origin or its Restitution in case of Illicit Appropriation', which helps to broker agreements. The Committee also provides a framework for discussion and, in 2009, it suggested that a code of ethical dealing amongst collectors could be developed using the UNIDROIT Convention in part as a basis. The Committee's actions point the way forward. The UNIDROIT Convention is useful in the fight against the illicit trade in cultural property. As time goes by it will be increasingly accepted by other countries, and ratification by the UK Government will be seen as less and less controversial. Although the biggest difficulty may be the limitation periods provided, this obstacle is not insuperable. There is no doubt that the UNIDROIT Convention, in straining to appease every point of view, has made the limitation periods complicated. However, it can easily be seen that there are some cultural treasures which should not be subject to limitation periods. For example, if the Crown Jewels were stolen tomorrow from the Tower of London and only emerged onto the market 50 or 100 years later, any defence by their possessor based upon limitation periods would surely be seen as intolerable.

VI Conventions Tackling Property Crimes and Criminal Organisations

2.37 Introduction

The dismantling of exchange controls, global travel and the rapid development of electronic forms of communication, have facilitated not only the illicit trade in cultural property, but also other serious crimes, such as trafficking in drugs, humans, counterfeit goods and vehicles. The profits made are often then used to support further criminal activity. Money laundering involves disguising the fact that assets have been derived directly or indirectly from crime. For example, suppose that an object is clandestinely excavated and illegally exported and sold. All those who are knowingly involved in dealing with the object or with the proceeds of sale are vulnerable to being prosecuted as money launderers. If convicted, they may be stripped of the benefits which they have received by way of a confiscation regime; this has the advantage of removing assets from the hands of convicted criminals which might otherwise be employed in future criminal activity.

In order to tackle the illicit trade in cultural property, it is not enough for states to protect their sites and buildings: a concerted effort is needed by all nations to co-operate with each other to curb this trade. The problem cannot be tackled effectively by one country alone. Without a global effort, traffickers will simply search for an easy market in another country. The same is true of other types of serious crime. The United Nations has played a significant role in creating co-operative relationships through the medium of international instruments in an attempt to tackle the huge increase in international crime in different fields, including not only cultural property but also other economic crimes, such as money laundering and corruption.

Less controversy surrounds the drafting of conventions tackling drug trafficking and serious crime than the illicit trade in cultural property. At first glance, this might seem surprising because there will inevitably be tensions where domestic criminal law, reflecting a particular social, political and economic outlook, differs markedly from one country to another. One explanation might be that the conventions dealing with drug trafficking and crime do not necessarily need to confront nations' differing laws on ownership. Furthermore, there is a general consensus that crime is a public menace and needs to be tackled. In contrast, protection of cultural property has appeared more complex because of the concerns of market nations to support the legitimate market. However, in the twenty-first century, it is increasingly recognised that organised groups may be involved not only in drug trafficking and other serious crime, but also in the illicit trade in cultural property.

2.38 The United Nations Convention against Illicit Traffic in Narcotic Drugs and Psychotropic Substances 1988

The 'war on drugs' was the impetus for laws tackling money laundering activities. Although there have been successive international conventions to prevent traffic in narcotic drugs,[172] the UN Convention against Illicit Traffic in Narcotic Drugs and Psychotropic Substances, which was adopted in Vienna on 19 December 1988 (the Vienna Convention), represented a major step forward. It directed Contracting States to create offences which not only targeted the principals, such as those who grew and supplied drugs, but also any accessories involved either initially or at a later stage. It was recognised that there will usually be a chain of people who will knowingly deal with property derived from crime, such as the profits from the sale of drugs. These people will all be money launderers. The Vienna Convention therefore dealt not only with drug smuggling but also money laundering in a comprehensive manner. Article 3 of the Convention required states to enact domestic legislation to deter drug trafficking, making it a criminal offence to produce, offer for sale and transport drugs. It also required Contracting Sates to make it a criminal offence to acquire, possess, disguise, convert or transfer the proceeds of drug trafficking. 'Illicit traffic' was defined in Article 1 to include all of these activities.

The Vienna Convention was significant because it provided a blueprint which could be used for tackling money laundering of the proceeds of any type of serious crime in subsequent Conventions. The Convention has received widespread approval and support. One hundred and eighty-four states are parties to the Convention, which was ratified by the UK in 1991.[173] It dealt with a global problem by promoting international co-operation amongst Contracting States. It listed sanctions and, in Article 5, set out procedures for identifying and tracing the proceeds of crime, freezing assets and confiscating them.

2.39 The Convention on Laundering, Search, Seizure and Confiscation of the Proceeds of Crime 1990

In Europe, there had been mounting concern over cross-border crime, and an appreciation that money laundering, whether linked to drug trafficking or not, needed to be stamped on. In November 1990, the UK Government signed the Council of Europe's Convention on Laundering, Search, Seizure and Confiscation of the Proceeds from Crime (the Strasbourg Convention).[174] This Convention was similar in many ways to the Vienna Convention,

[172] International Opium Convention, The Hague (1912); Convention Limiting the Manufacture and Regulating the Distribution of Narcotic Drugs (1931); Convention for the Suppression of the Illicit Traffic in Dangerous Drugs (1939); the Single Convention of 1961 on Narcotic Drugs (as amended by the 1972 Protocol), and the Convention on Psychotropic Substances of 1971.

[173] The Criminal Justice (International Co-operation) Act 1990 enabled the Government to implement both this Convention and the European Convention on Mutual Assistance 1957.

[174] Council of Europe Convention on Laundering, Search, Seizure and Confiscation of the Proceeds from Crime (Strasbourg, 8 November 1990; TS (Misc) 10 (1991); Cm 1561) (the Strasbourg Convention) was signed by

requiring states to create various offences in relation to money laundering. It established a set of principles to enable international co-operation to take place between the public authorities of different states. The Convention had a wide scope and covered any serious criminal offence. On ratification of the Convention, individual states could restrict the definition for their purposes. There have subsequently been a series of European Money Laundering Directives which have imposed obligations upon financial institutions and various other private bodies requiring them to establish procedures for identifying customers and systems for reporting suspicious transactions.[175]

These European and international efforts form the backdrop to national criminal legislation, which is discussed in Chapters 3 and 4. The effect has been to spread the net widely. Stolen cultural property and any proceeds of sale will be treated as the 'proceeds of crime' for the purposes of money laundering legislation. Anyone knowing or suspecting that they are dealing with the proceeds of crime may be convicted of a money laundering offence. Accessories, such as banks, lawyers, accountants, dealers and auction houses, are all vulnerable to criminal prosecution.

2.40 International Carriage: the UNESCO and Vienna Conventions Compared

The UNESCO Convention 1970 asked Contracting States to introduce import controls to combat the illicit trade in cultural property.[176] As mentioned, this obligation was criticised on the ground that it would be costly and complex to administer.[177] It was feared that its implementation would require extensive searching of luggage and cargo. As regards carriage of goods by sea, this would present practical problems, as many commodities are now shipped in containers which have been sealed before shipment. O'Keefe has suggested that much more detailed descriptions of the goods being transported should be required to enable cultural objects to be identified more easily.[178] Even so, there is a substantial risk that those who export cultural property illegally will deliberately misrepresent the nature of the objects being transported in order to mislead customs officials.

In contrast, although the Vienna Convention 1988 has demanding requirements to prevent illicit trafficking of goods, these provisions have not been seen as controversial. Commercial carriers are expected to take appropriate measures to ensure that they do not assist in the commission of an offence. These measures take various forms. For example, it is specified in Article 15 that containers must be tamper resistant with individually verifiable seals. It is easy for smugglers of any types of goods, including antiquities, to conceal an object in a container but, if containers are sealed, it makes it more difficult to smuggle items: they can only be introduced before the container is closed. Commercial carriers are also expected to give their employees appropriate training to ensure that reasonable precautions are taken to prevent their transport operations being used for the commission of offences. As this training is directed not only at trafficking of drugs but at money laundering as well, the Convention would have had a positive impact in making it more

the United Kingdom on 8 November 1990. See further, Council Directive 91/308/EEC, OJ [1991] L166/77; H Nilsson, 'The Council of Europe Laundering Convention: A Recent Example of a Developing International Criminal Law' (1991) 2 *Criminal Law Forum* 419, 422–23. See further, WC Gilmore, *Dirty Money: the evolution of money laundering counter-measures* (Strasbourg, Council of Europe Press, 2004).

175 For the current law, see 3.44–3.45.

176 See 2.18.

177 Bator, *The International Trade in Art* 53.

178 O'Keefe, *Commentary on the UNESCO 1970 Convention* 12.

difficult for international criminal gangs to move objects and money from one country to another.

The strategies which are employed for detecting the movement of drugs and stolen goods (such as high-value cars) may be more effective weapons in detecting hidden cultural objects as well. This fight against crime and money laundering has led to customs methods which are intended to be risk-sensitive and proportionate, with searches triggered by unusual activity or an abnormal pattern of events. Even so, it must be appreciated that it is far more difficult for a customs officer to recognise the significance of a cultural object as compared with a high-value car.

2.41 The United Nations Convention against Transnational Organised Crime 2000

The United Nations has expressed concern that those involved in drug trafficking were often involved in other types of serious international crime, including corruption,[179] and that these activities were becoming increasingly transnational in character. In response, the UN General Assembly produced a series of resolutions which were adopted on 14 December 1990. Resolution 45/121 highlighted this growing threat to the political and economic stability of national institutions. Resolution 45/123 encouraged states to take effective anti-money laundering measures, including the monitoring of large scale cash transactions, in order to combat crime.[180] Resolution 45/108 created an intergovernmental working group to draft proposals to combat international crime. Further resolutions followed which were concerned with matters such as the creation of a crime-prevention and criminal justice programme,[181] and the support of the work of the Commission on Crime Prevention and Criminal Justice as the principal policy-making body in the field of crime prevention and criminal justice.[182] The thrust of these resolutions was that, in order to tackle the problems presented by organised criminal groups, states must assist each other.

In 1999, the UN General Assembly authorised the Secretary General to create an ad hoc committee to draft a new convention. The result was the UN Convention against Transnational Organised Crime, which was open for signature in Palermo, Italy in December 2000.[183] One hundred and fifty-eight states are currently parties to the Convention. It was ratified by the UK in 2006. It is often referred to as the 'Palermo Convention' or 'TOC.' In its Preamble, the link between the illicit trade in cultural property and other serious crimes was emphasised:

> *Strongly convinced* that the United Nations Convention against Transnational Organised Crime will constitute an effective tool and the necessary legal framework for international co-operation in combating, inter alia, such criminal activities as money-laundering, corruption, illicit trafficking in endangered species of wild flora and fauna, *offences against cultural heritage* and the growing links between transnational organised crime and terrorist crimes.[184]

This Convention was intended to combat transnational crime which involved organised criminal groups. Like the UN Convention against Illicit Traffic in Narcotic Drugs and

[179] Resolution 44/71 of 8 December 1989, 45/121 of 14 December 1990; 45/123 of 14 December 1990.

[180] See further, Resolution 47/87 of 16 December 1992.

[181] Resolution 46/152 of 18 December 1991.

[182] Resolution 48/103 of 20 December 1993. See further, the Economic and Social Council Resolutions 1992/22 and 1992/23 of 30 July 1992, and 1993/29 and 1993/30 of 27 July 1993.

[183] Resolution A/RES/55/25 of 15 November 2000, 7 United Nations, *Treaty Series*, 2225(39574) 8 E/CN.15/2006/14.

[184] Emphasis added.

Psychotropic Substances 1988, it contains definitions of common terms to make it easier for the government agencies in one country to co-operate with their counterparts in another country. 'Transnational' is given a wide scope in Article 3 to include not only crimes which are organised in one state but carried out in another, but also crimes committed in one state with effects in another state, or where the offence is carried out by an organised criminal group which commits offences in more than one state. 'Serious crime' is stated to mean conduct constituting an offence punishable by imprisonment of at least four years (or a more serious penalty). These definitions are wide enough to affect the illicit trade in cultural property. It is a trade which is transnational in character because it usually involves the movement of an object from one country to another. Moreover, where a cultural object is stolen and sold to a foreign buyer, both the object itself and its sale price can be described as 'the proceeds of crime' because they have been obtained from the commission of an offence. Anyone knowingly dealing with proceeds of crime may be prosecuted for money laundering, which is a serious crime. Anyone purchasing a stolen cultural object is at risk of being prosecuted for handling stolen goods or for an offence established by the Dealing in Cultural Objects (Offences) Act 2003, which are also serious crimes.[185] The domestic legislation enacted in each Contracting State to implement this Convention should be wide enough in scope to create offences which affect those engaged in the illicit trafficking of cultural property.

Articles 5, 6, and 8 require Contracting States to create offences relating to participation in an organised criminal group, money laundering and corruption. Each Article provides detailed guidance. For example, Article 6 obliges Contracting States to create a series of money laundering offences to deal with situations where, for example, a person concealed an object or transferred it to another knowing that the object represented the proceeds of crime. These offences must extend both to conduct committed within the jurisdiction of a Contracting Party, and outside of its jurisdiction but where it would have been a criminal offence according to its domestic law if committed within its jurisdiction. Thus, a dealer or collector who is knowingly in possession of stolen cultural objects is at risk of being prosecuted according to the criminal laws of any Contracting State.

Article 7 provides that Contracting States shall ensure that judicial, law enforcement and financial regulatory authorities are able to co-operate with each other to tackle money laundering. Comprehensive legislative schemes must be introduced to detect and deter money laundering. Consequently, financial institutions and other bodies susceptible to money laundering will be required to engage in client identification, record-keeping, and reporting of suspicious transactions. States are encouraged to establish financial intelligence units to serve as centres for the exchange of information. The aim is to make it much more difficult for criminals engaged in unlawful trafficking in goods or money to escape detection.

There are further provisions in Articles 11 and 12 relating to the imposition of proportionate but effective sanctions, including identification, seizure and confiscation of the proceeds of crime. Contracting States are expected to freeze assets, which may well include art and antiquities; this will usually mean taking them into the possession of the state with a view to eventually confiscating them. Article 13 is particularly significant because it is aimed at facilitating co-operation between Contracting States for the purposes of international confiscation of proceeds of crime. It enables a state which would have jurisdiction over a serious offence to request another state to confiscate the proceeds of crime. A source

[185] These crimes are discussed in ch 3.

nation might therefore ask a market nation to confiscate an antiquity. If the market nation accepts this request, it will take the object into its possession. But can the source nation then ask for the return of the object? According to Article 14, this will all depend upon the domestic law of the nation which has confiscated the object. It is a country's domestic law which will establish the procedures for disposing of it. Nevertheless, Article 14(2) encourages Contracting States to give 'priority consideration' to returning the proceeds of crime to the requesting state so that it can compensate victims and return objects to their 'legitimate owners'. States are encouraged to conclude bilateral agreements with other states to deal with assets confiscated in accordance with these provisions.

Both the Convention against Transnational Organised Crime (TOC) and the 1970 UNESCO Convention on the Means of Prohibiting and Preventing the Illicit Import, Export and Transfer of Ownership of Cultural Property possess the same central tenet: that states are stronger when they work with each other to present a united front. If there are inconsistencies in national laws, there is a risk that criminal networks will exploit these differences. Under TOC, Member States are expected to enter into bilateral or multilateral arrangements as appropriate to ensure co-operation between their law enforcement agencies. It should be noted that the UNESCO Convention has also led to a growth in bilateral and multilateral agreements, particularly between the USA and other countries. Nevertheless, comparisons between the two Conventions are limited. The UNESCO Convention is concerned with educating the public and the return of inventoried objects. TOC is concerned with the criminal law and its processes, including the creation of offences, the exchange of information, assistance and training, extradition, the establishments of financial intelligence units and sanctions such as confiscation of illicit assets. It could be argued that TOC is a modern convention which confronts the realities of international crime. In flagging up issues such as corruption as well as the illicit trafficking in items of cultural heritage, it is responding to evidence that profits from looted property may be siphoned off by corrupt political figures as well as international criminals.[186]

2.42 The United Nations Convention against Corruption 2003

The Convention against Transnational Organised Crime only deals briefly with corruption and the governments of developing countries pressed for more attention to be devoted to this problem. In 2000, the UN General Assembly called for international co-operation in furtherance of national and international 'measures to combat corrupt practices and bribery in international transactions'.[187] It established an ad hoc committee to pursue this matter further;[188] this initiative eventually led to the UN Convention against Corruption of 2003.[189] There are currently 148 parties to this Convention, which entered into force in 2005. The UK ratified it in 2006.

[186] N Brodie, 'An Archaeologist's View of the Trade in Unprovenanced Antiquities' in B Hoffman (ed) *Art and Cultural Heritage: Law, Policy and Practice* (Cambridge, Cambridge University Press, 2006) 57.

[187] Resolution 55/188 of 20 December 2000, 'Preventing and Combating Corrupt Practices and Illegal Transfer of Funds and Repatriation of Such Funds to the Countries of Origin'.

[188] Resolution 55/61 of 4 December 2000.

[189] Convention against Corruption 2003 (A/RES/58/4). See further, the Inter-American Convention against Corruption (1996); the Council of Europe Convention on the Fight against Corruption involving Officials of the European Communities (1997); OECD Convention on Combating Bribery of Foreign Public Officials in International Business Transactions (1997); the Criminal and Civil Law Conventions on Corruption adopted by Committee of Ministers of the Council of Europe (1999); and the African Union Convention on Preventing and Combating Corruption (2003).

The Convention against Corruption was the first multilateral treaty to tackle the challenge of corruption on a global basis. The Preamble declares:

> *Concerned* about the seriousness of problems and threats posed by corruption to the stability and security of societies, undermining the institutions and values of democracy, ethical values and justice and jeopardising sustainable development and the rule of law,
>
> *Concerned also* about the links between corruption and other forms of crime, in particular organised crime and economic crime, including money laundering,
>
> *Concerned further* about cases of corruption that involve vast quantities of assets, which may constitute a substantial proportion of the resources of States, and that threaten the political stability and sustainable development of those States.

The UN's efforts to stamp out corruption are important in the fight to curb the illicit trade in cultural property. There is a risk that local public officials could be bribed, for example, to turn a blind eye to illegal excavations. The often expressed fear that serious organised crime and corruption has the effect of undermining institutions and the administrative structure of a country is relevant to cultural property. Various strategic measures, such as export certificates, are heavily dependent upon proper administration by the competent authorities.

The Convention requires Contracting States to agree to establish an institutional framework to combat corruption. Chapter II provides that each Contracting State is expected to develop effective anti-corruption policies to promote proper management of public property, transparency, integrity and accountability. States undertake to establish bodies which will implement anti-corruption practices. The Convention does not simply focus upon the conduct of public officials. It is wide-ranging and there are further provisions relating not only to the public sector in general, such as the judiciary and prosecution services, but also the private sector. Each state must establish a comprehensive regulatory and supervisory regime requiring banks, other financial institutions, and bodies susceptible to money laundering, to carry out customer and beneficial owner identification, record-keeping, and reporting of suspicious transactions.[190] National law enforcement and other authorities dedicated to combatting money-laundering are encouraged to co-operate and exchange information at international level. The Convention therefore contributes to the erosion of secrecy in relation to the cross-border flow of money. It calls for the establishment of financial intelligence units to serve as national centres for the analysis and dissemination of information regarding potential money-laundering.

There are certain parallels with the 1970 UNESCO Convention. Corruption is viewed as a global problem and states are expected to collaborate with other Contracting States as a consequence.[191] States are given a wide discretion in choosing how to implement anti-corruption measures. It is recognised that what is needed is a variety of strategies drawing on the resources and expertise of a number of agencies. Thus, for example, codes of conduct will be used to guide public officials in behaving in an honourable and proper manner.[192] This is reminiscent of the codes of conduct drawn up for museum employees and dealers. Equally, the value of both publicity and education of the public is recognised as a strategic tool to combat wrongdoing. States are therefore urged to ensure that not only

[190] Convention against Corruption, Art 14.

[191] Chapter IV deals with international co-operation, including extradition.

[192] See further, the International Code of Conduct for Public Officials contained in GA Resolution 51/59 of 12 December 1996.

anti-corruption bodies but also non-governmental organisations and community based organisations should disseminate information about the prevention of corruption amongst the public at large. However, any further comparisons with the UNESCO Convention are limited by the fact that the Convention against Corruption is far broader in scope.

Chapter III of the Convention against Corruption obliges Contracting States to create offences of bribery of national and foreign public officials, and officials of public international organisations. There are further provisions dealing with embezzlement, misappropriation and other diversion of property by a public official, offering an undue advantage in exchange for a public official's promise to exercise his real or supposed influence, the abuse of functions or position, and illicit enrichment. Further offences which must be created relate to bribery or embezzlement of property in the private sector, laundering of proceeds of crime, obstruction of justice and offences as an accessory. It is made clear that the sanctions imposed should be proportionate and could include, for example, a fine. However, provision is made for seizure and confiscation of assets as well.

Chapter V of the Convention against Corruption is concerned with asset recovery. The wealth of developing countries had at times been plundered by those with power in the public or private sphere, and this chapter provided a form of redress. The return of assets to countries of origin is declared to be a fundamental principle.[193] Article 53 affirmed that Contracting Parties should:

(a) Take such measures as may be necessary to permit another State Party to initiate civil action in its courts to establish title to or ownership of property acquired through the commission of an offence established in accordance with this Convention;
(b) Take such measures as may be necessary to permit its courts to order those who have committed offences established in accordance with this Convention to pay compensation or damages to another State Party that has been harmed by such offences; and
(c) Take such measures as may be necessary to permit its courts or competent authorities, when having to decide on confiscation, to recognise another State Party's claim as a legitimate owner of property acquired through the commission of an offence established in accordance with this Convention.

The measures in this Convention are not limited to the recovery of money. Suppose that antiquities are excavated and sold abroad by means of bribing or influencing individuals in the public or private sphere. Contracting States are expected to ensure that their domestic legislation will permit the source state to bring a civil action in which it can 'establish title to or ownership of property' and, if appropriate, obtain its return. If a cultural object has been swept up by a government to satisfy a confiscation order, the source state should be able to assert its rights to recover the object.

Article 55 of the Convention contains further provisions which require Contracting States to identify, trace, seize and confiscate assets at the instigation of another state in cases of corruption. There is considerable flexibility in relation to implementing these provisions, enabling Contracting States to take account of human rights provisions in drafting appropriate laws. Article 55 may therefore be implemented in a manner which allows a Contracting State to recover cultural property located abroad in the hands of criminals or the government of a state. Even so, Article 55 directs governments to avoid prejudicing the rights of 'bona fide third parties'.[194]

[193] Convention against Corruption, Art 51.
[194] Convention against Corruption, Art 55(9).

2.43 OECD Convention on Combating Bribery of Foreign Public Officials in International Business Transactions 1997

The Organisation for Economic Co-operation and Development (OECD) consists of a forum of states, which is concerned with promoting best practice in domestic and international markets. It has played a significant role in tackling corruption and money laundering. It acts by way of peer pressure to improve conduct. For example, it has working parties to review the domestic laws on bribery of Signatory States. This includes examining each country individually for 'on the ground' compliance. OECD also creates non-binding agreements between states which occasionally lead to conventions. The OECD was responsible for the Convention on Combating Bribery of Foreign Public Officials in International Business Transactions, which is often referred to as the OECD Anti-Bribery Convention. Contracting States are obliged to create criminal offences in relation to bribery of officials in their official conduct, with appropriate sanctions to punish and deter offenders. Like other international initiatives, it emphasises the importance of international co-operation and mutual legal assistance. Thirty-eight states have ratified this Convention to date; the UK Government ratified it in 1998 and it was the impetus for the UK's Bribery Act 2010.[195]

2.44 Council of Europe

The Council of Europe consists of 46 states in the European region. The organisation has granted observer status to five other countries. The Council has been responsible for the creation of conventions in the fields of both criminal and civil law, which are intended to foster co-operation between nations. The Criminal Law Convention Against Corruption 1998 and Protocol requires Contracting States to criminalise bribery of all public officials, including judges, regardless of the country in which they are situated.[196] It also requires criminalisation of corruption in the private sector, criminalisation of the laundering of the proceeds of corruption, and the seizure and confiscation of those proceeds. Forty-one states have ratified the Convention, including the UK in 2003.

The Civil Law Convention Against Corruption was also adopted in 1998, in order to harness the civil law in the fight against corruption.[197] Contracting States promised to ensure that effective civil law remedies would be made available to individuals who had suffered damage due to corruption in their domestic law. Potential defendants include not only the giver and recipient of the bribe but also those who failed to take reasonable steps to prevent the corruption. Contracting States also must legislate to render corrupt agreements or contract clauses null and void. Contracting States are encouraged to co-operate with each other in relation to such matters as obtaining evidence and recognition and enforcement of judgments. However, the UK has not ratified the Civil Law Convention on Corruption; so far only 33 states have done so.

2.45 International Convention for the Suppression of the Financing of Terrorism 1999

One might assume that terrorist activities are far removed from the world of cultural property. But this is not necessarily so. Terrorists may be attracted to the illicit trade in cultural property because of the huge profits which can be made. Consequently, although any

[195] See 4.10.
[196] Council of Europe Criminal Law Convention Against Corruption (ETS 173).
[197] Council of Europe Civil Law Convention Against Corruption (ETS 174).

detailed consideration of terrorist financing lies beyond the scope of this text, it should be noted that states have been encouraged by the UN General Assembly to recognise the links between terrorist groups and serious organised crime, including trafficking in cultural objects.[198] Furthermore, the strategies which are put in place to combat terrorism may indirectly help to curb the illicit trade in cultural property. For example, Resolution 1373 of 2001 of the UN Security Council required any and every government to freeze funds which might be used to further terrorism: the resolution supports money laundering measures which focus upon suspicious movements of capital. States have been urged to co-operate in taking measures to combat terrorism. In practical terms, this resolution is likely to bring enforcement authorities in different nations closer together. The exchange of expertise is reinforced by the UN International Convention for the Suppression of the Financing of Terrorism 1999, which is intended to foster co-operative support between nations. One hundred and seventy-four states are parties to this Convention, including the UK, which ratified it in 2001.

VII Strategic Approaches to Tackling the Illicit Trade in Cultural Property

2.46 International Organisations

The Financial Action Task Force (FATF) is an important intergovernmental body, which acts under the auspices of the Organization for Economic Cooperation and Development (OECD). It issued 40 key recommendations in 1990 in order to provide a comprehensive set of counter-measures against money laundering; these recommendations have subsequently been revised to obstruct the financing of terrorism.[199] They are non-binding 'soft' law and they have been influential in the development of national laws relating to money laundering worldwide. FATF has encouraged states to consider money laundering as a complex problem which needs to be combated in a variety of ways. In particular, it has pressed for greater transparency in matters of company ownership and control so that the activities of criminals who use shell companies as a vehicle for laundering money or assets (including cultural objects) can be more easily detected. The impact of FATF on the illicit trade in cultural property is therefore indirect: it established principles such as due diligence in transacting and confiscation of the proceeds of crime.

There are various other important international organisations which play a role in curbing the illicit trade in cultural property. For example, the World Customs Organisation is particularly noted for its work in areas covering the development of global standards and harmonisation of Customs procedures. There are organisations which provide a basis for a global approach to the prevention of serious crime. The International Criminal Police Organisation (Interpol) is concerned with corruption and money laundering prevention worldwide. It provides an information network for law enforcement. In the context of trafficking in cultural property, it is significant in providing an electronic database detailing

[198] See eg Resolution 65/232 of 21 December 2010.

[199] The recommendations can be found at the FATF/OEDC websites: www.oecd.org or www.oecd.org/fatf.

stolen objects; the resulting publicity may make an object unmarketable.[200] The European Police (Europol) is the European Union law enforcement agency. It also provides an information network. It is particularly concerned with forms of serious organised crime such as drug trafficking, money laundering, trafficking in humans and vehicles. As the illicit trade in cultural property may well involve money laundering, Europol may be useful in providing information to enforcement agencies.

2.47 Bangkok Declaration on Synergies and Responses: Strategic Alliances in Crime Prevention and Criminal Justice 2005

The 1970 UNESCO Convention was important in its day in stressing the importance of protecting cultural property and in encouraging Contracting States to establish certain basic structures in furtherance of this goal. However, times have changed, and the strategies employed in that Convention will not suffice alone in suppressing the theft of cultural property by determined criminals. In 2005, at the Eleventh UN Congress on Crime Prevention and Criminal Justice in Bangkok, it was acknowledged that more effective action needed to be taken against transnational organised criminal groups.[201] This was known as the Bangkok Declaration 2005. This Declaration urged states to take action in response to the increased involvement of organised criminal groups in the trafficking in cultural property and wild flora and fauna, along with trafficking in persons, human organs and drugs.[202] The Declaration linked serious crime to terrorism and encouraged states to stamp out corruption.

The Bangkok Declaration appeared to be influenced by international instruments relating to drug trafficking and money laundering. Emphasis was therefore placed upon the need to punish and deter trafficking in cultural property by way of asset recovery and other appropriate sanctions. The Declaration also reflected an awareness of the fact that criminals are becoming increasingly sophisticated. For example, the UNESCO Convention was significant in obliging Contracting States to establish a certification system for exports. But it is easy enough for fraudsters to create false documents, including export certificates. The Bangkok Declaration therefore encouraged states to exchange technical expertise to combat identity theft and document fraud.

2.48 Resolutions 2004/34 and 2008/23: 'protection against trafficking in cultural property'

The UN Economic and Social Council has issued two resolutions which were both entitled 'Protection against trafficking in cultural property'. They welcomed national, regional and international initiatives for the protection of cultural property and duly cited the Hague Convention, the 1970 UNESCO Convention and the UNIDROIT Convention. As one might expect, they contained references to resolutions calling for the return of cultural property to the countries of origin.[203] However, they went further in urging states to assert

[200] See R Attwood, *Stealing History* (New York, St Martin's Press, 2006) 8 (decapitated head of a king from a statue of a winged bull in Khorsabad in Iraq rendered unmarketable after photos were published on the Interpol website).

[201] Eleventh United Nations Congress on Crime Prevention and Criminal Justice, Bangkok, 18–25 April 2005: Report prepared by the Secretariat (UN publication, Sales No E.05.IV.7), chap I, resolution 1; subsequently endorsed by the General Assembly in its Resolution 60/177 of 16 December 2005.

[202] ibid [12].

[203] GA Resolution 58/17 of 3 December 2003 and 61/52 of 4 December 2006. See also, UNODC/CCPCJ/EG.1/2009/CRP/1.

ownership of cultural property and to publicise that fact with a 'view to facilitating the enforcement of property claims in other States.' This is particularly relevant in relation to objects which are buried in the ground. If there is no legislation vesting ownership in the state, a possessor may argue that the objects are ownerless. These resolutions could be seen as adopting a 'nationalist' perspective in sympathy with the views of source nations. On the other hand, these recommendations can be treated as simply acknowledging that private actions are one of a number of strategies for deterring the illicit trade in cultural property. It can be argued that, as only a relatively small number of states have ratified the UNIDROIT Convention, states should be encouraged to enact appropriate domestic legislation which would enable them to sue to recover antiquities in other countries' courts.

Resolution 2004/34 estimated that the international trade in looted stolen or smuggled cultural property was worth several billion United States dollars per year. Both resolutions expressed alarm at the 'growing involvement of organised criminal groups' in this trade. Resolution 2008/23 called for practical steps to combat the illicit traffic, including encouraging international co-operation such as by the exchange of information between law enforcement agencies and mutual legal assistance, establishing procedures for the seizure, restitution or return of objects, and developing the capacity of monitoring institutions such as the police, customs and tourism sector. The recommendation that there should be co-operation between law enforcement agencies based in different countries might well be complex and expensive to implement. However, this recommendation and others are feasible if they are linked to asset recovery and forfeiture because a portion of any money confiscated could be used to provide financial support for the work carried out by enforcement agencies. In the UK, there already exists a central information hub, responsibility for which is currently allocated to the Serious Organised Crime Agency. Each state could be encouraged to establish similar organisations, which could exchange information with each other.

The resolutions were significant in straddling the civil and criminal law. Growing problems, such as the manner in which the internet can facilitate rapid transactions, were acknowledged. It was suggested that the UN Convention against Transnational Organised Crime might lead to 'innovative and broader approaches to dealing with the various manifestations of such crime, including trafficking in cultural property.' There is no doubt that one of the major features of these resolutions and the Convention are confiscation orders and forfeiture of assets. If convicted criminals are stripped of the assets which they have gained over the years, this is not only a deterrent in itself but it may result in a situation where they no longer have the ability to finance further criminal ventures.

2.49 Resolutions Relating to Crime Prevention

The UN Economic and Social Council Resolution 2010/19, entitled 'Crime prevention and criminal justice responses to protect cultural property, especially with regard to its trafficking' of July 2010 builds upon the resolutions discussed in the preceding paragraph. It echoed many of the recommendations made in those documents. It hovered over both the civil law and criminal law, drawing them together. It emphasised the need to protect cultural objects and referred to the UNESCO Convention 1970; it linked these concerns to unlawful trafficking, the Convention on Transnational Organised Crime and the work of the Commission on Crime Prevention and Criminal Justice. It recognised that a variety of different strategies need to be employed to combat the illicit trade in cultural property. It referred to educating the general population with general awareness campaigns involving the media but added that governments must support and develop the capacities and human resources of the police and the customs services in deterring theft and pillaging of cultural property. It urged Contracting States to take appropriate measures in relation to search, seizure and return of illicit cultural objects. Most significantly, it encouraged Contracting States to maximise the transparency of the activities of those who trade in cultural property. However, although the need for technical assistance was identified, there was no explicit call for a worldwide cultural property register.

Resolution 2010/19 of July 2010 represented a milestone on a road with a clear destination. It drew upon previous recommendations to be found in earlier resolutions and those made by the Twelfth Congress on Crime Prevention and Criminal Justice held in April 2010. The desired objective was to persuade countries to work together, to provide each other with legal and technical assistance, to protect their own cultural heritage, to prosecute the criminals involved in the network of illicit trade in art and antiquities, to search and seize cultural objects, and to return those objects to their rightful owners. The UN General Assembly Resolution 65/230 in April 2011 is based upon this previous work and emphasised that numerous different strategies would be needed to tackle this problem effectively.[204] Resolution 65/230 urged states to create offences to combat the illicit trade in cultural property in all of its forms and to strengthen co-operation and assistance in this area, including the return of objects. It also expressed a determination to tackle networks established by transnational criminal groups.[205] The recommendations made in both resolutions have been subsequently endorsed by Resolution 2011/42 of 28 July 2011.[206]

Subsequent efforts have built upon these themes. In the Report of the Commission on Crime Prevention and Criminal Justice in 2011, there was a series of proposed resolutions which included one relating to the illicit trade in cultural property.[207] This draft resolution was formally adopted by the UN General Assembly on 19 December 2011.[208] It spelt out that the illicit trade in cultural property has continued to grow and that urgent curbs are needed. It reiterated the concerns and strategies discussed in previous documents. It urged states to engage in the widest possible co-operation, including mutual legal assistance and the confiscation and return of stolen cultural property to its rightful owner. However, there was one significant addition: paragraph 9(b) requested the UN Office on Drugs and Crime, UNESCO, INTERPOL, and other competent organisations to 'explore possibilities for the collection, analysis and dissemination of relevant data specifically addressing the relevant aspects of trafficking in cultural property.' This appears to be an attempt to focus minds upon a global database, or an effective exchange of information between domestic databases. If so, it should be welcomed because a key problem in prosecuting a wrongdoer, or suing privately to recover an object, is the identification of the object.

[204] Res 65/230 [12].

[205] The Salvador Declaration on Comprehensive Strategies for Global Challenges: Crime Prevention and Criminal Justice Systems and Their Development in a Changing World is annexed to Resolution 65/230, and echoes this point.

[206] Economic and Social Council Resolution 2011/42, 'Strengthening crime prevention and criminal justice responses to protect cultural property, especially with regard to its trafficking.'

[207] Report of the Commission on Crime Prevention and Criminal Justice of the Twentieth Session of December 2010 and April 2011: E/2011/30, E/CN15/2011/21.

[208] Draft resolution IV, A/66/463, 26; A/C 3/66/L55. Meeting of UN GA of 5 December 2011. Adopted by A/RES/66/180; GA 11198, Sixty-sixth General Assembly Plenary of 19 December 2011.

VIII Conclusions

The strategies to combat the illicit trade in cultural property should be diverse. However, commentators often tend to concentrate upon the UNESCO Convention 1970 as the principal international instrument for suppressing this trade. The 1970 Convention is immensely important. It has been accepted by many states and it provides basic mechanisms for both preserving cultural objects and assisting states in relation to their return. Nevertheless, it has been criticised for providing a relatively weak response. But why should it be assumed that the UNESCO Convention must be the sole vehicle for solving all the problems associated with this trade? It can be argued that the UNESCO Convention simply provides one set of strategies which can be supported by other conventions containing other strategies. It would of course be convenient if everything could be found in one convention. But this is an area which is challenging and contentious. It would surely be naïve to assume that one convention could permanently deal with all the issues.

The US spearheaded the fight against drug trafficking and money laundering. But although successive US governments have engaged in a highly publicised campaign relating to the 'war on drugs', there has been nothing similar in relation to the illicit trade in art and antiquities. In the 1970s and 1980s, there were debates in Congress concerning whether to criminalise trafficking in antiquities. However, various obstacles militated against the use of the criminal law as a weapon. First, whereas it was generally accepted that any theft from a museum or private collection was a crime, the purchase of an object which might have been illicitly exported was not viewed in the same light. Indeed, as many people saw export bans as a political matter, the purchase of illegally exported antiquities was often viewed as unobjectionable. Secondly, there has always been a consensus amongst the public in a substantial number of countries that trafficking in drugs is a vile trade which acts as a catalyst for further crimes. The issues surrounding the illicit trade in cultural property are comparatively complex. There is a wide range of cultural property which may be acquired in a variety of circumstances. It may be difficult to discover sufficient information about an object's provenance to determine whether it is part of the licit or illicit trade. This problem is compounded by the traditional secrecy of the art and antiquities market.

This chapter has demonstrated that international initiatives in relation to serious organised crime, money laundering and corruption, may be highly significant in combatting the illicit trade in cultural property. They employ various strategies in order to punish and deter. Key aspects include the creation of offences which are wide in scope, seizure and deprivation of assets, and support for co-operation between enforcement agencies and exchange of technical expertise. The anti-corruption measures add further elements involving raising public awareness and promoting transparency and ethical behaviour.

Global co-operation, which has received considerable emphasis in international conventions and UN resolutions, is arguably easier to achieve when criminal law violations and seizure of the proceeds of crime is under consideration. Many governments, including the UK Government, have been prepared to ratify conventions dealing with transnational crime, money laundering and corruption. However, significant differences exist between these conventions in relation to asset recovery. The Convention against Transnational Organised Crime envisages seizure and confiscation of criminal assets by the enforcement authorities of a Contracting State. There is no guarantee in Article 14 of the Convention that the confiscated objects will be returned to the requesting nation from which the objects may have been looted. In contrast, Chapter V of the Convention against Corruption does contain the principle of seizure and return. The Convention is ground-breaking in dealing with corruption in its widest sense and in establishing a fundamental principle of the return of assets to their countries of origin.

The trade in stolen cultural objects and illegally excavated antiquities has moved from being an issue shrouded in obscurity, with slightly romantic notions of adventurers engaged in daredevil exploits, to being formally recognised in UN resolutions as a trade involving highly organised gangs of criminals. It is an international entrepreneurial activity. The theft of a cultural object not only deprives the public of information and enjoyment but the profits made are often used to fund other activities, such as trafficking in drugs or weapons. The UN leads the way and it is to be hoped that governments worldwide will provide sufficient information to their citizens to help them appreciate that this trade is in the same league as drug trafficking and other crimes.

3

Criminal Offences Affecting the Trade in Art and Antiquities

JANET ULPH

I Background

3.01 The Role of the Criminal Law

Art crime covers various forms of misconduct such as theft, fraud, illicit excavation of archaeological material and tax evasion. In terms of quantity, the trade in illicit antiquities is far greater than that of stolen art.[1] This chapter will consider situations where those involved in the market in cultural property risk prosecution for a crime. It will consider relevant criminal laws which may apply not only to dealers, auction houses and collectors, but also to a wide range of people involved on the periphery of art and commerce, such as conservators, academics and carriers.

It is impossible to eliminate illegal trafficking in cultural property, but the sanctions imposed by the criminal law have the potential to act as a deterrent, particularly in relation to white collar criminals.[2] There are drawbacks in using the civil law alone to combat art crime. A criminal conviction connotes moral wrongdoing, whereas losing a civil case does not. On a practical level, business people can factor into their profit margins the risk of paying compensation to a victim of theft. Although one can insure against financial loss, no insurance will provide protection from imprisonment. Convicted criminals of economic crimes, such as theft and handling stolen goods, also face being stripped of the proceeds of crime by way of confiscation orders,[3] and they may well end up bankrupt as a result.

In practice, prosecutions for offences involving cultural objects are fraught with difficulty. First, it may not be easy to obtain hard evidence in a market which is notoriously secretive. Secondly, any investigation is likely to be expensive, because the prosecution may need to rely heavily upon experts in identifying a stolen or looted cultural object. Thirdly, the facts may be complex. Where antiquities have been excavated, a common aim is to

[1] B Dobovsek, N Charney and S Vucko, 'Art Crime Archives' (2009) 2(1) *The Journal of Art Crime* 25, 26.

[2] See further S Mackenzie, 'Illicit Antiquities, Criminological Theory, and the Deterrent Power of Criminal Sanctions for Targeted Populations' (2002) VII(2) *Art Antiquity and Law* 125, 142.

[3] Art and antiquities may be swept up by the state to satisfy a confiscation order. For example, a 1915 Renoir painting called *Paysage a Cagnes*, was confiscated when R DeSinone was found guilty of money laundering and mail fraud based upon an investment scam, by the federal court in Rhode Island: *The New York Observer* (22 July 2011). See generally, J Ulph, 'Confiscation Orders, Human Rights, and Penal Measures' (2010) 126 *Law Quarterly Review* 251. See 4.14–4.19.

move them from the source nation to a transit country, before eventually taking them to a market nation such as the UK or USA. Transactions are therefore likely to be international in character and may involve a number of people who have dealt with the object or who have made arrangements in relation to it. It may also be difficult to pinpoint the precise series of events which have taken place after an object has been removed from its original location, unless the suspects have kept careful records.

This chapter will focus upon criminal law offences which may be committed not only by those who misappropriate art and antiquities but also the accessories who knowingly participate in handling stolen objects, in suppressing information about them, or in making arrangements which facilitate the illicit trade in cultural property. This will involve an analysis of traditional offences concerned with acquisitive crime, such as theft and handling stolen goods. The significance and impact of money laundering measures will also be discussed. The chapter will conclude by considering statutes which create special criminal offences in relation to certain types of cultural property.

II Theft

3.02 The Offence

The offence of theft is governed by the Theft Act 1968. If a person is convicted of stealing goods, accessories such as dealers, may be prosecuted for handling stolen goods or money laundering offences. The ingredients of the offence are spelt out in section 1(1) of the Theft Act 1968 as follows:

> A person is guilty of theft if he dishonestly appropriates property belonging to another with the intention of permanently depriving the other of it; and 'thief' and 'steal' shall be construed accordingly.

The offence therefore involves a mental element (*mens rea*): a dishonest state of mind and an intention to deprive another of the property. It also involves a factual element (*actus reus*): appropriation of property which belongs to another. These ingredients will be examined in turn.

3.03 Dishonesty and *Ghosh*

The question of whether the accused acted with dishonest intention is left for the jury to decide.[4] The Theft Act 1968 does not define dishonesty as such, but section 2 of the Act offers some guidance: the accused will not be viewed as dishonest if he thought that he had the legal right to take the property, or that the owner would have consented, or if he thinks that the owner cannot be found by reasonable means. However, it is further provided that the fact that the accused is willing to pay for the item is irrelevant. The statute does not provide further guidance and the matter has been left to the courts.

The current law is to be found in the decision of the Court of Appeal in *R v Ghosh*.[5] It was held that the prosecution had the burden of establishing that, first, the defendant's

[4] *R v Feeley* [1973] QB 530 (CA).
[5] *R v Ghosh* [1982] QB 1053 (CA) 1064.

conduct would appear dishonest if judged objectively by the standards of reasonable and honest people and, if so, that the defendant must have realised that, judged by those standards, what he was doing was dishonest. Usually, the jury will simply be told that dishonesty should be given its ordinary meaning; however, if the defendant specifically pleads that he had not considered his conduct to be dishonest, then the direction in *Ghosh* will be explained to the jury.[6] The second strand of the *Ghosh* test is controversial: it makes it more difficult for the prosecution to prove that the accused was dishonest and mixes up the state of mind of the accused with general standards of dishonesty.[7] The fact that the test is difficult to satisfy is significant. Dishonesty is used as a key ingredient in other offences, such as those created by the Fraud Act 2006. In the context of the market in antiquities, it is an important component of offences created by the Dealing in Cultural Objects (Offences) Act 2003. It may be difficult to prosecute any dealer or other intermediary in possession of a cultural object, if he merely shut his eyes to the probability that it has been looted in the immediate past and failed to make further enquiries.

3.04 An Intention to Deprive Another of Property

The prosecution must prove beyond reasonable doubt that the accused intended to deprive another of his property. However, section 1(2) of the 1968 Act provides that there is no need to show that the accused acted with the intention of making a gain or for his benefit. Further guidance is provided by section 6, which states:

> A person appropriating property belonging to another without meaning the other permanently to lose the thing itself is nevertheless to be regarded as having the intention of permanently depriving the other of it if his intention is to treat the thing as his own to dispose of regardless of the other's rights; and a borrowing or lending of it may amount to so treating it if, but only if, the borrowing or lending is for a period and in circumstances making it equivalent to an outright taking or disposal.

The question of whether there has been permanent deprivation will turn upon the facts: for example, if the accused borrowed a thing for a short period of time (such as where a spade is taken to dig up a buried object) and then abandoned it where the owner could easily find it, this might not amount to a permanent deprivation.[8] A contrasting situation is where property is put beyond anyone's reach[9] or is taken and destroyed (including melting metal to form something new[10]). If an object is taken and then used to provide security for a loan (pawned), and its return is subject to a condition such as repayment of the loan with interest, this will be viewed as a permanent deprivation.[11]

What if a painting or other object is secretly taken from a museum or other institution open to the public? The removal would normally amount to theft. However, it is sometimes the case that people take a famous cultural object as some form of political protest. If they plan to return the object, after they have accumulated sufficient publicity for their cause,

[6] *R v Roberts* (1986) 84 Cr App Rep 117 (CA).

[7] K Campbell, 'The Test of Dishonesty in *Ghosh*' [1994] 43 *Cambridge Law Journal* 349, 354. For further criticism, see EJ Griew, 'Dishonesty – the Objections to *Feely* and *Ghosh*' [1985] *Criminal Law Review* 341.

[8] *R v Mitchell* [2008] EWCA Crim 850 (CA) (getaway car); see further, *R v Vinall (George Alfred)* [2011] EWCA Crim 6252.

[9] See *R v Raphael* [2008] EWCA 1014 (CA). Although the provision is normally straightforward in its application to tangible property, there are difficulties in relation to intangibles such as money: see, for example, *Chan Man-sin v AG of Hong Kong* [1988] 1 All ER 1 (PC).

[10] *Richards* (1844) 1 Car & Kir 532.

[11] Theft Act 1968, s 6(2). See *Phetheon* (1840) 9 C & P 552; *Medland* (1851) 5 Cox CC 292. .

they may not be viewed as dishonest. It can also be argued that they have no intention to deprive another of property.[12] Even so, they may commit a different type of offence. Under section 11 of the Theft Act, it is an offence to remove an object, without lawful authority, which has been available for public display as part of a collection.[13] In order to secure a conviction for this offence, there is no need for the prosecution to prove that the defendant was dishonest or that he intended to permanently take the property.

3.05 Property

The Theft Act 1968 seeks to deter people from interfering with another's possession or ownership of property. Section 4(1) provides:

> 'Property' includes money and all other property, real or personal, including things in action and other intangible property.

As the statute extends to things in action (which depend upon legal action for enforcement), it includes the appropriation of cash or shares.[14] In contrast, according to section 4, land, wild animals and wild plants are excluded. However, the offence does cover theft of portable objects in general, such as works of art. It also includes items forming part of the land. Consequently, antiquities are capable of being stolen, even if they lie buried in the ground.

3.06 Appropriation: Assumptions of the Rights of an Owner

According to section 3(1) of the Theft Act 1968,

> Any assumption by a person of the rights of an owner amounts to an appropriation, and this includes, where he has come by the property (innocently or not) without stealing it, any later assumption of a right to it by keeping or dealing with it as owner.

Although the notion of 'appropriation' has a wide scope,[15] section 3(1) makes it clear that there must be an exercise of some form of control over an object.[16] It would not be enough to show that the accused had physical custody of it. The point of appropriation needs to be identified because the prosecution must establish that, at the moment when the accused chose to exercise control, he had a dishonest intent. This may cause difficulties at times, such as in the context of a loan of an object, when it may be difficult to determine when a dishonest intent was formed. But, in the context of stolen art or antiquities, the evidence of appropriation is normally clear. A thief who takes a painting from a museum wall, or a person who digs an antiquity out of the ground, will obviously be taking control of it.

[12] See *R v Bunton*, discussed by H Wine, 'The Missing Goya: Section 11 of the Theft Act 1968' (2001) VI(4) *Art Antiquity and Law* 301.

[13] *R v Durkin* [1973] QB 786 (CA).

[14] Equally, the accused will be guilty of theft if he causes a bank to debit a customer's account as the debt (owed by the bank to the customer whilst the account is in credit) is a thing in action which is capable of being stolen: *R v Kohn* (1979) 69 Cr App R 395 (CA).

[15] Cmnd 2977, at [34]. See *Pitham and Hehl* (1976) 65 Cr App R 45, where the Court of Appeal confirmed that the interpretation of s 3(1) should be a broad one. Good faith purchasers are given express protection by the Theft Act 1968, s 3(2).

[16] *Merry v Green* (1841) 7 M. & W. 623; 151 ER 916; *Cartwright v Green* (1803) 8 Ves. 405; 32 ER 412; *R v Hudson* [1943] KB 458 (CA); *Thomas v Greenslade*, The Times (1954) 6 November.

3.07 Appropriation: Consent to the Transfer is Irrelevant

The prosecution does not need to show that the property was taken without the consent of the owner.[17] If an owner is tricked into transferring the property to another, this can still be viewed as theft. In *R v Gomez,*[18] a seller was induced by false statements by his assistant manager to sell goods to a buyer. Although the seller could have rescinded the contract of sale, he did not do so; the buyer therefore owned the goods. Even so, the House of Lords upheld the manager's conviction for theft on the basis that there had been a dishonest appropriation of property. *Gomez* established that property may be treated as stolen even where the owner agreed to transfer it. It also established that the accused can be prosecuted for theft in cases of deception.[19] Thus, if a landowner is deceived by the accused into agreeing to allow him to dig up objects buried in the soil, this does not preclude a prosecution for theft. Equally, if the accused persuades naïve and trusting owners that their paintings are worth little and then presses them to sell the paintings to him for a minimal amount, he may be guilty of theft.

An individual may be convicted of theft even where he has received the property by way of a gift if it can be shown that he has acted dishonestly. In *R v Hinks,*[20] the accused had taken advantage of the fact that the original owner was highly susceptible to persuasion and she had exploited the vulnerability of her victim in order to obtain his money. Her conviction was upheld by the House of Lords. In contrast, if a recipient is innocent, he will not be exposed to criminal charges because he will not have the necessary intent.[21]

The fact that the offence of theft has such a wide scope has caused concern.[22] One unsatisfactory aspect is that, after the decision in *Gomez,* there has been no sharp divide between theft and deception, despite the fact that this divide is significant for civil law purposes.[23] This rift between the criminal and civil law is unsatisfactory, not least because there is some interplay between them. For example, section 24(3) of the Theft Act provides that goods will not be regarded as stolen goods 'after they have been restored to the person from whom they were stolen or to other lawful possession or custody, or after that person and any other person claiming through him have otherwise ceased as regards those goods to have any right to restitution in respect of the theft.' The suspect is therefore immune from prosecution once the original owner has lost his right to recover the goods according to the civil law.[24] In *Hinks,* it is doubtful whether the victim could have recovered his gifts of money

[17] *R v Gomez* [1993] AC 442, HL. See further, *R v Lawrence* [1972] AC 626, HL.

[18] *R v Gomez* [1993] AC 442, HL.

[19] There may be grounds for prosecution for fraud under the Fraud Act 2006: see 3.52.

[20] *R v Hinks* [2000] UKHL 53, [2001] 2 AC 241 (HL).

[21] Innocent purchasers receive express statutory protection by the Theft Act 1968, s 3(2): *R v Wheeler* (1991) 92 Cr App R 279 (CA).

[22] See ATH Smith, 'Gifts and the Law of Theft' [1999] *Cambridge Law Journal* 10; J Beatson and AP Simester, 'Stealing One's Own Property' (1999) 115 *Law Quarterly Review* 372; JC Smith, 'The Sad Fate of the Theft Act 1968' in W Swadling and G Jones (eds), *The Search for Principle: Essays In Honour of Lord Goff of Chieveley* (Oxford, Oxford University Press, 2000) 97, 100–01. Contrast S Gardner 'Property and Theft' [1998] *Criminal Law Review* 35.

[23] For example, a purchaser cannot acquire a good title to stolen property under any statutory provision apart from the Limitation Act 1980 or the various exceptions to the principle *nemo dat quod non habet:* see 5.33–5.43. See further *Debs v Sibec* [1990] RTR 91; *White v Green* (1851) 10 CB 919, 927 (Talfourd J). The distinction between theft and deception will also present problems if an insurance policy makes a distinction between theft and fraud and only covers loss due to theft. The distinction is also significant in France and Germany: Law Reform Committee, *Transfer of Title to Chattels* (Cmnd 2958, 1966) para. 5.

[24] Title will be lost, for example, upon the expiration of the limitation period: see the Limitation Act 1980, s 4(2) (good faith purchaser); 5.39–5.43.

from the accused in the civil courts. If the criminal law and the civil law do not mesh well, there is a risk that the limits of a criminal law offence may appear arbitrary. It is vital that the law should be certain and predictable, in line with the protection offered by the European Convention for the Protection of Human Rights and Fundamental Freedoms[25] and the rule of law.[26] People must be able to foresee whether their actions will be characterised as criminal or not.[27]

The decision in *Hinks* means that it will be relatively easy to prove that an object has been appropriated and the focus of any prosecution will be upon the question of dishonest intent. *Hinks* could be defended on the basis that it is concerned with penalising those who damage the established system of property rights, thereby threatening the public good.[28] It sends out a clear signal that certain types of conduct, such as where one person exploits another to obtain property, need to be discouraged in the public interest. These policy considerations should be relevant in the sphere of cultural property. They should apply whenever one person exploits the weakness of another, whether advantage is being taken of the frailty of old folk who are pressurised into handing over valuable items, or the vulnerability of a state suffering from internal conflicts.

3.08 Belonging to Another: Possessory Interests

It must be shown that the object belonged to another. This requirement is easily satisfied where an individual dishonestly takes an object which is owned by someone else (such as a collector) or an institution (such as a museum). However, section 5(1) has a wide scope and provides:

> Property shall be regarded as belonging to any person having possession or control of it, or having in it any proprietary right or interest (not being an equitable interest arising only from an agreement to transfer or grant an interest).

It is therefore sufficient if the prosecution can show that someone has a proprietary interest in the object which the accused has appropriated. Conveniently, it is not necessary to prove that someone else owns it. Suppose, for example, a museum had obtained possession of an object of antiquity for three months for the purposes of an exhibition. If this object is stolen, it can be said to 'belong to another' because the museum will have a possessory title due to the consensual loan (known as a bailment).[29]

Even if a person has a right to possess an object, he may be guilty of theft if he dishonestly retains it beyond the time agreed. The position is the same where there has been a delivery of property by mistake. This could occur where money or a small object is accidentally enclosed within a piece of furniture which is sent to be sold at auction, for example. If it is a tangible object which is in issue, the original owner will usually have retained the legal title, wherever it is.[30] If not, such as where money is involved, he may still possess equitable

[25] The Convention is set out in the Human Rights Act 1998; Art 5 provides that every individual is entitled to the right to liberty and cannot be subjected to unlawful detention; Art 7 provides that there must be no punishment without a legal basis.

[26] *Shukhardin v Russia* (App No. 65734/01) [64]; *Golder v UK* (1975) 1 EHRR 524 [35]. In *Montgomery v HM Advocate, Coulter v HM Advocate* [2003] 1 AC 641, 673, Lord Hope of Craighead observed that 'the rule of law lies at the heart of the Convention'. See further, *Roberts v Parole Board* [2005] UKHL 45, [2006] 1 All ER 39 (HL) [41].

[27] *R v Christian* [2006] UKPC 47, [2007] 2 AC 400 [40].

[28] S Shute, 'Appropriation and the Law of Theft' [2002] *Criminal Law Review* 445, 455.

[29] For discussion of possessory titles, see 5.02.

[30] *Merry v Green* (1841) 7 M & W 623, 151 ER 916; *Russell v Smith* [1958] 1 QB 27.

proprietary rights.[31] But the position is put beyond doubt by section 5(4), which provides that where a person obtains property by another's mistake, and is under an obligation to return it, then the property belongs to the person entitled to its return.

3.09 Belonging to Another: Equitable Interests

A person may be guilty of theft even if he has had the legal title to an object all along but where another has an equitable interest. A detailed discussion of the situations where individuals may have an equitable interest in an object under an express, resulting or constructive trust is beyond the scope of this book. However, one example would be where a trustee dishonestly sells a painting and pockets the proceeds: the trustee will have legal title in the painting but, as he holds the painting for the benefit of the beneficiaries, they will have equitable proprietary interests. According to the Theft Act, the trustee may be guilty of theft in these circumstances.[32]

III Objects Which are Excavated or Removed: Theft and Other Offences

3.10 Theft: Abandoned Objects and Finders

One cannot steal an object which has been intentionally abandoned, because it cannot be regarded as 'belonging to any person' within the meaning of section 5(1) of the Theft Act. If a finder is accused of theft, he may well assert that the object which he has found belongs to him rather than anyone else. But it is not easy to show that, prior to its acquisition, an object was ownerless. An object will only be viewed as abandoned where the original owner has relinquished all intent to control his property without conferring an interest on anyone else.[33] Even where the owner has abandoned an object, another person may subsequently have taken control of it so that it may still belong 'to another' for the purposes of a prosecution.[34]

A criminal court will draw upon civil law principles to determine whether an object was ownerless before the accused acquired it. There is a strong possibility that the object was not ownerless, but belonged to a landowner or occupier prior to its removal. The court will consider whether the object is located on private or public land, and who has physical access to the land, and for what purpose. Thus, the occupier of private premises will normally own any items found upon or in the premises. The occupier will be seen as having an intention to exercise control over any such objects, regardless of whether he is aware of the

31 *R v Webster* [2006] All ER (D) 150 (Nov).

32 Theft Act 1968, s 5(2)(3).

33 *Ellerman Wilson Line Ltd v Webster* [1952] 1 Lloyd's Rep 179 (CA), 180; *Palmer on Bailment*, 3rd edn (London, Sweet and Maxwell, 2009) [26-0121]; D Ormerod and D Williams, *Smith's Law of Theft*, 9th edn (Oxford, Oxford University Press, 2007) para 2.186.

34 For example, if an object is dumped in a refuse site or receptacle over which another person exercises control, it will belong to that person regardless of whether he was aware of the nature of the property. See *Williams v Phillips* (1957) 41 Cr App Rep 5 (DC); *R v Reed* (1854) 6 Cox CC 284. For a recent illustration, involving bags of goods left outside an Oxfam shop which were not viewed as abandoned, see *R v Basildon Magistrates' Court* [2010] EWHC 2358, discussed by D Ormerod at [2011] Crim LR 505.

existence of a particular object or not.[35] It may be different where the public have been given a right of access to the premises or land for some purpose,[36] or where no effort has been made to exercise control.[37] Even so, if a finder picks up an object on private land and takes it, he risks being prosecuted for theft.

If a finder takes an object which he found on land to which the public have access, such as a park or road, the occupier will need to show that he has exercised sufficient control over the land to give him possessory rights over the item instead. Although the occupier does not have to prove that he was aware of the existence of the object,[38] he must exercise general control over the site by, for example, placing notices to the effect that all items found on the land should be handed in as lost property. If no effort is made, a finder may have the better right to possession.[39]

However, if the accused assumed that an object had been abandoned when in fact it belonged to another, the prosecution may fail because there is no evidence that the accused intended to deprive another of his property or that he acted dishonestly.[40] Furthermore, a defence is provided by section 2(1) of the Theft Act, which provides that a person is not dishonest if he believes that the owner cannot be found.[41] A finder who discovers an antique piece of jewellery lying in the road, for example, may be able to successfully rely upon this defence.

3.11 Theft: Buried Objects and Objects Attached to the Land

What if someone goes onto land, whether public or private, armed with a metal detector and digs up buried items? If abandoned objects become attached to or buried in the ground as part of the soil, the presumptive rule is that they belong to the owner or occupier of the land.[42] In *Parker v British Airways Board*, Donaldson LJ suggested that the rationale of this rule could be explained on two grounds. First, if an object was buried, it was part of the soil in which it was embedded and should be treated as part of the owner's land against everyone apart from the true owner of the object. Secondly, the finder would be obliged to damage the land in digging up the object; 'if he is not thereby to become a trespasser, [he] will have to justify his actions by reference to some form of licence from the occupier. In all

[35] *R v Woodman* [1974] QB 754. See Hill J's judgment in *Flack v Chairperson, National Crime Authority* (1997) 150 ALR 153, aff'd sub nom *Chairman, National Crime Authority* (1998) 156 ALR 501 (Fed Ct of New South Wales). See further, *Hibbert v McKiernan* [1948] 2 KB 142 (theft of golf balls).

[36] Such as a shop: *Bridges v Hawkesworth* (1851) 21 LJ QB 75.

[37] Such as where an owner has never as such occupied the house in which the object is found: *Hannah v Peel* [1945] KB 509. For a detailed analysis, see N Palmer, 'Bad Apples and Blighted Windfalls: Finding, Bailment and the Fruits of Crime' in F Meisel and PJ Cook (eds) *Property and Protection, Legal Rights and Restrictions (Essays in Honour of Brian W Harvey)* (Oxford, Hart, 2000) 5–9.

[38] *South Staffordshire Water Co v Sharman* [1896] 2 QB 44.

[39] *Parker v British Airways Board* [1982] QB 1004 (CA). See further, *Bridges v Hawkesworth* (1851) 21 LJ QB 75; *Daniel v Rogers* [1918] 2 KB 228 (CA) 234 (Scrutton LJ); *Russell v Wilson* (1923) 33 CLR 538, 547 (Isaacs and Rich JJ); *Costello v Chief Constable of Derbyshire* [2001] EWCA Civ 381, [2001] 1 WLR 1437 (CA); *Asher v Whitlock* (1865) LR 1 QB 1.

[40] *R v Small* [1987] Crim LR 777 (CA). See AH Hudson, 'Abandonment' in N Palmer and E McKendrick (eds), *Interests in Goods*, 2nd edn (London, LLP, 1998) 595.

[41] A finder would not have been guilty of theft at common law if he had made enquiries to no avail: *R v Thurbon* [1843–1860] All ER Rep 928.

[42] *Waverley B v Fletcher* [1995] QB 334 (CA); *Elwes v Brigg Gas Co* (1886) 33 Ch D 562; *South Staffordshire Water Co v Sharman* [1896] 2 QB 44 (DC); *Parker v British Airways Board* [1982] QB 1004 (CA); *Webb v Ireland* [1988] IR 353 (Sup Ct).

likely circumstances that licence will give the occupier a superior right to that of the finder.'[43]

In contrast, where objects are situated on the land, the occupier would not necessarily have a better title than the finder, unless he manifested an intention to control the land and the things which might be on it. In *Waverley BC v Fletcher*,[44] the Court of Appeal confirmed that a distinction should be made between objects buried in the ground, or attached to the land, and objects which were merely lying on it. This distinction is made in other jurisdictions.[45] In *Waverley*, the defendant used a metal director in a council park and dug up a mediaeval gold brooch which was buried about nine inches below the surface. Here, the Court of Appeal had no difficulty in concluding that the brooch was buried 'in' the soil. But it was acknowledged that, as in *South Staffordshire Water Co v Sharman*,[46] there may occasionally be borderline situations. In *Sharman*, two gold rings were found in the mud after a pool was drained and it was held that the rings were 'in' rather than 'on' the land. In most circumstances, there will be no difficulty in applying this distinction because, if any digging is required, this would suggest that the object is 'in' the ground. But what if a landowner ploughs a field and unwittingly turns up an object which is discovered by a finder?[47] Arguably, it should belong to the landowner who owns the land in which it had been buried.

From a policy perspective, it could be said that a rule which favours the landowner simply encourages a finder to keep his discoveries secret. But, on the other hand, the current rule that a trespassing finder digging up the soil (or detaching objects from a building) does not have a better title than the landowner seems right in principle. It means that, if a finder retains any items which he has uncovered, he runs the risk of being prosecuted for theft. For example, in 1985, over 535 artefacts of the Bronze and Iron Ages were discovered by two people using metal detectors. This became known as the 'Salisbury Hoard'.[48] They sold them to a dealer, who sold them to various purchasers both in the UK and elsewhere. The British Museum acquired part of the Hoard and carried out its own investigation. The two people were caught and convicted of theft. In order to avoid any risk of prosecution, individuals with metal detectors are best advised to make an agreement with the owner or occupier in advance.

3.12 Theft and Patrimonial Laws

It is invaluable if the law is clear in relation to objects which lie buried in the soil, vesting ownership either in the landowner or in the state. If an object has been secretly excavated and sold abroad, the owner is in a better position to recover it in a foreign court if he can easily demonstrate his right to possession. Equally, the state may assert its ownership if it has passed a patrimonial law to that effect. Most countries, including vulnerable ones such as Egypt, Iran, Iraq and Afghanistan, exercise some degree of control over or claim ownership of undiscovered archaeological objects. If a state's domestic law contains clear legal principles regarding ownership, it will mean that an unscrupulous finder who conceals a discovery can be prosecuted for stealing the object (because the domestic law will provide that it belonged to either the landowner or the state).

[43] [1982] QB 1004 (CA) 1010.

[44] [1995] QB 334 (CA).

[45] *Tamworth Industries Ltd v Attorney-General of New Zealand* [1991] 3 NZLR 616 (High Ct Wellington); *Webb v Ireland* [1988] IR 353.

[46] [1995] QB 334 (CA) 341.

[47] See further, J Stevens, 'Finder weepers – landowners keepers' (1996) *Conveyancer* 216, 220.

[48] ITAP Report, Annex A [19].

But the threat of prosecution may have little effect. A significant practical difficulty which would confront a landowner (and any prosecutor) would be that of proving that the object had been found on his land. The task is made easier by technical advances, which enable experts to identify the location of an object from the soil in which it will be encrusted. However, once the object is cleaned, so that all trace of its provenience is removed, the landowner will be in an almost hopeless position if there are no witnesses. These problems confront all source nations, including the UK. There is always the risk that found objects will be secretly hidden away or sent abroad, so that there is little risk of detection. Special legislation dealing with treasure, discussed below, tackles this problem by creating incentives for finders to hand over their discoveries and to publicise their finds.

3.13 Treasure: Criminal Offences

If there is a dispute over an object, the courts will decide who has the better right to possess it. There is no possibility of sharing the value of the object. As discussed in the previous section, if a finder unearths an object, it will be treated as belonging to the landowner. However, an exception is made if the object is viewed as treasure.[49] In this situation, ownership vests in the Crown subject to any prior rights, such as those of franchisees.[50] Before the enactment of the Treasure Act 1996, it was not always easy to apply the Theft Act where ancient objects were found in England and Wales:[51] although the object might 'belong' to another, it was not always clear whether it belonged to the landowner, or to the Crown in accordance with the old law relating to treasure trove.[52] Furthermore, the law of theft was not the best way of dealing with the interests of all those involved. For example, a finder might well anticipate that his discovery would eventually generate 'windfall' profits. In order to avoid being shut out of a share in those profits, finders might be tempted to hide their discoveries. But, in the case of antiquities, there are strong policy reasons for encouraging finders to come forward and to declare their finds publicly. If they do not do so, the information which the objects contain may be reduced. The knowledge of provenience could be lost and researchers will be deprived of the opportunity for further investigation and study.

These policy concerns are largely met by the provisions of the Treasure Act 1996.[53] The Act uses a 'carrot and stick' approach to encourage finders to report their finds. By section 8(1), if the finder believes or has reasonable grounds for believing that he has found treasure, he is under an obligation to notify the Coroner for Treasure[54] within 14 days. If he fails to do so, he may be prosecuted and fined or sentenced to prison for a term not exceeding three months. However, by section 8(4), the finder has a defence where he has a reasonable

[49] For the definition of treasure, see 3.16.

[50] A notable example of a franchisee is the Corporation of London: any treasure found in the City or in Southwark will belong to the Corporation of London, rather than the Crown.

[51] In Scots law, treasure will belong to the Crown by default as unowned property in accordance with the *quod nullius rule*: see Scottish Law Commission, *Discussion Paper on Prescription and Title to Moveable Property* (Scot Law Com No 144, 2010) [2.19]. See further, Scottish Law Commission, *Report on Prescription and Title to Moveable Property* (Scot Law Com No 288, 2012).

[52] A prosecutor was best advised to charge the accused with theft from Crown or landowner in the alternative: *R v Hancock* [1990] 2 QB 242 (CA) 251–52.

[53] The statute came into force on 24 September 1997: Treasure Act 1996 (Commencement No 2) Order 1997, SI 1977/1997.

[54] Formerly, local coroners had jurisdiction over treasure trove. However, the Coroners and Justice Act 2009 created a special post of Coroner for Treasure and relieved local coroners of this responsibility. The Coroner for Treasure may be supported by assistant coroners: ibid, ss 25–26, Sch 4.

excuse to explain why he has not made such a report. The 'carrot' offered to the finder is that he will obtain compensation which reflects a proportion of the object's value.

3.14 Treasure: Code of Practice

The statutory framework created by the Treasure Act is supplemented by a Code of Practice as required by section 11 of the Act. This Code is in its second edition and has effect in England and Wales. It provides more detailed guidance on the operation of the Act. The revised Code of Practice encourages finders to provide information relating to the location of the find. If the finder fails to provide information in full to the Coroner for Treasure, his reward may be reduced or denied. It is recommended, in paragraph 34, that the finder should report not only where the find was made, but also how deep the find was and whether the find-spot is on cultivated land or not, and whether there were any other objects of interest. The finder is instructed by paragraph 47 of the Code not to clean the object, because this will remove evidence relating to how it was made and about the environment at the time of deposition. Even where the object discovered is clearly not treasure, metal detectorists are encouraged to provide information about it to the Portable Antiquities Scheme. This voluntary scheme exists to record archaeological objects found by members of the public in England and Wales. It has been a great success: in 2007, for example, 77,606 finds were recorded.[55] The Portable Antiquities scheme can therefore be seen, along with the Act and the Code, as serving two purposes: generating and recording information about objects from the past, and bringing private individuals together with archaeologists and others to assist in preserving the archaeological record.

3.15 Treasure: Recipients and Offences

A new criminal offence is created by section 8A of the Treasure Act, which was inserted by section 30 of the Coroners and Justice Act 2009. Any recipient of potential treasure must notify the Coroner for Treasure where he believes, or has reasonable grounds for believing, that the object is treasure.[56] A recipient must do so within 14 days of either acquisition or later belief that the object is a treasure. If the recipient fails to report the existence of a suspected treasure, he faces a fine or up to 51 weeks of imprisonment. It is a defence to show that he had a reasonable excuse for his failure to notify the Coroner for Treasure. This new offence can be seen as part of a broader effort by the Government to gather information relating to the archaeological record, which has been given a fresh emphasis by recent amendments to the Treasure Act 1996 by the Coroners and Justice Act 2009.[57]

This provision applies to all acquirers, whether they are purchasers or recipients of objects by way of a gift or under a will. This puts additional pressure upon a finder to report any discovered treasure: if he does not, he risks eventual discovery if his purchaser notifies the Coroner for Treasure of the acquisition. If the recipient of a suspected treasure makes a notification, he may be considered for a reward.[58]

[55] R Bland, 'The United Kingdom as a Source Country: Some Problems in Regulating the Market in UK Antiquities and the Challenge of the Internet' in S Mackenzie and P Green (eds), *Criminology and Archaeology: Studies in Looted Antiquities* (Oxford, Hart, 2009) 88.

[56] The revised Code of Practice, para 25, supports this new offence by stating that any person, other than the finder, who comes into possession of an object which is suspected to be treasure, but which he believes has not been reported, should report it promptly.

[57] Thus, for example, s 26 of the Coroners and Justice Act 2009 stipulates that a Coroner for Treasure must investigate who found the object, where it was found and when it was found.

[58] Treasure Act 1996, s 10, as amended by the Coroners and Justice Act 2009, s 30.

3.16 Definition of 'Treasure': the Code of Practice

The Treasure Act 1996 abolished the old law relating to treasure trove and applies to suspected 'treasure'. The definition of treasure can be found in section 1 of the Treasure Act and in the Treasure (Designation) Order 2002. This definition is fleshed out further in the Code of Practice and its Appendices, which should be read in conjunction with the Act itself. The definition of treasure is important, because it is a key ingredient of the new offences created by the Act, relating to failure to report a suspected treasure.

The Treasure Act states that natural objects, such as wood or minerals, will not be viewed as treasure. The Code explains that human remains and fossils, for example, are not treasure. These principles are clear. Unfortunately, the guidance that is otherwise provided by the Act is complex. A distinction is made between objects in general, and coins.

Where the objects are not coins, the definition includes any object over 300 years old which has a metallic content of which at least 10 per cent by weight is a precious metal (gold or silver). The Secretary of State can designate a class of object over 200 years old which he considers to be of outstanding historical, archaeological or cultural importance. However, references to the old law relating to 'treasure trove' have not been done away with entirely; this is because any objects which would have been 'treasure trove' under the old definition remain so. This old definition had been concerned with objects which mainly consisted of gold or silver and which had been deliberately hidden.

As regards coins, they must be over 300 years old and either there must be at least two coins found together with a metallic content of at least 10 per cent of a precious metal, or there must be at least 10 coins in the 'same find.' Furthermore, if a metallic object is discovered amongst other objects in the above categories in the 'same find', that object will be viewed as treasure too. The definition of 'same find' is expanded upon in paragraph 14 of the Code which provides, for example, that 'the discovery of a silver brooch in an Anglo-Saxon grave could make the other non-precious-metal objects in that grave treasure.' The Code is extensive, providing detailed guidance on various matters, such as the position where objects are found on the foreshore or consecrated ground. Furthermore, reference should also be made to the Treasure (Designation) Order 2002 which added to the definition of 'treasure' groups of base-metal objects, other than coins, of prehistoric date, up to, and including, the Iron Age, from the same find. One example would be Bronze Age gold-covered penannular rings whose surface is gold over a base-metal core.[59]

If an object does not fall within the definition of treasure, there is a risk that it may be auctioned off for a price which is beyond the resources of interested museums. This may mean that the public and academics are deprived of the opportunity to study an object of considerable archaeological importance. For example, a 2,000-year-old bronze Roman helmet was recently found by a metal detectorist at Crosby Garrett near Carlisle. The Tullie House Museum in Carlisle and its supporters had raised £1.65 million in order to acquire the helmet, but their hopes were dashed as the bidding rose higher.[60] The sale price of £2 million was split between the owner, the finder and the auction house. The sale of the helmet has prompted calls for reform of the definition of 'treasure' in order to extend its scope, to ensure that highly significant objects can go to a British museum.[61]

[59] See the Code of Practice, para 12.

[60] 'A record £2m for the Roman helmet found in farm mud' *The Times* (8 October 2010).

[61] Lords Renfrew, Howarth and Redesdale, 'Treasure Act must be updated now' *The Times* (9 October 2010).

3.17 Treasure Act: Procedure

The Treasure Act, as amended, requires all finds of suspected treasure to be reported to the Coroner for Treasure. If a finder gives notice that he has found what he believes or has reasonable grounds to believe is a suspected treasure, a treasure inquest should be held.[62] The Coroner for Treasure will tell the finder, or other person in possession, where to deliver the treasure. But if the Secretary of State has disclaimed, on behalf of the Crown, all interest in the object, the inquest should not go ahead.[63] Instead, the Coroner will notify the occupier or landowner that he will return the object to the finder unless they object.[64] If there are conflicting claims, the Coroner for Treasure will keep the object, pending a resolution of the dispute if necessary by the civil courts.

If an inquest is held, it will be decided if an object is treasure or treasure trove and, if it is, 'who found it, where it was found and when it was found'.[65] The Coroner for Treasure will have the duty of notifying the finder, the occupier and the landowner, of the place and date when he intends to hold an inquest. He is also requested to inform interested parties (such as the local museum).[66]

If the object is found not to be a treasure, the procedure will be the same as if it had been disclaimed. If a find is declared to be a treasure, the Coroner for Treasure will inform the relevant museum, the finder, landowner, occupier and franchisee (if any). If the museum wishes to take it, the object will be valued. The award will normally be split equally between the finder and the landowner, unless another form of agreement has been reached between them or the reward is abated because, for example, the finder was a trespasser, or suppressed information, or failed to make any report, or damaged monuments at the findspot.

3.18 Reflections on the Treasure Act

It could be argued that the penalties which may be imposed by the Treasure Act, which consist of fines or short terms of imprisonment, do not act as a sufficient deterrent.[67] But its strength lies in the fact that it includes all the major stakeholders: finders, occupiers, landowners, museums, the Crown and others concerned with treasure.[68] The Act appears to take account of conflicting interests and to establish procedures which will usually lead to an amicable result. It is bolstered by soft law, such as the revised Code of Practice.[69] This Code encourages best practice by, for example, urging all metal detectorists to abide by the Code of Conduct issued by the National Council for Metal Detecting, which encourages people to act responsibly and to avoid trespassing.

[62] See Treasure Act 1996, s 8(1); Coroners and Justice Act 2009, s 26.

[63] Or, if there is a franchisee, the franchisee has disclaimed all interest.

[64] See the Code of Practice, para 50.

[65] Coroners and Justice Act 2009, s 26(5).

[66] Treasure Act 1996, s 9, as amended.

[67] See, for example, *R v Hancock* [1990] 2 QB 242 (CA).

[68] Contrast the position in certain states in the USA, where a landowner has no rights in relation to treasure trove discovered by a finder, even if the finder is a trespasser: L Izuel, 'Property Owners' Constructive Possession of Treasure Trove: Rethinking the Finders Keepers Rule' (1991) 38 *UCLA Law Review* 1659, 1662. Yet a landowner will be seen as in possession of objects other than treasure trove embedded in the land: ibid, 1673.

[69] See 3.15 and 3.17.

3.19 Further Offences: Ancient Monuments and Archaeological Areas Act 1979

The Ancient Monuments and Archaeological Areas Act 1979 (AMAAA 1979) provides a scheme for the preservation of sites of archaeological value and interest. Ancient monuments which are considered worthy of protection are listed in a schedule to the Act. One way in which the 1979 Act protects monuments is by controlling any works which may affect them. In order to legally carry out repair or alterations works to a scheduled monument, the consent of the Secretary of State for Culture Media and Sport must be obtained beforehand. If this consent has not been obtained, section 2 provides that it will be an offence to execute, cause or permit certain works. The prohibited works are listed in section 2(2) and extend beyond damage and destruction to the monument to other matters which might also affect its characteristics such as flooding, tipping operations, planting and ploughing, on land in or under which there is a scheduled monument.

The offence created by section 2 is one of strict liability, although the accused will not be guilty if he can establish that he did not know and had no reason to believe that the monument was within the area affected by the works or that it was a scheduled monument. This defence may often be relevant, because monuments are defined by the Act to include not only great buildings, structures Roman forts and settlements, but also archaeological sites (including adjoining land) where very little may be visible. Furthermore, a large number of scheduled monuments are in rural locations and the boundaries of the monument site may not be evident.[70] For example, if a fort is scheduled, the monument may extend to the remains of a complex system lying around the fort. This will not be obvious to the untutored eye.

The only penalty for carrying out unauthorised works to a scheduled monument is a fine. Imprisonment cannot be imposed. Furthermore, the fine does not reflect the fact that valuable archaeological information may be lost for ever. In *R v JO Sims Ltd,* a company was convicted for an offence under this section and a fine of £75,000 was initially imposed. However, on appeal,[71] the fine was reduced to £15,000, despite the significance of the site, which was next to Winchester Palace. The Court of Appeal took account of the fact that the company had not deliberately flouted the law. It also considered that any fine must be related to the actual or ostensible means of the defendant; here, the company had a relatively low turnover per annum.[72]

A more general offence to deter damage to certain ancient monuments is created by section 28. This section is aimed at those who are determined to loot monuments and archaeological sites. It provides that anyone who, without lawful excuse intentionally or recklessly destroys or damages a 'protected' monument,[73] knowing that it is a protected monument, will be guilty of an offence. This provision is particularly interesting because an offence may be committed even where the landowner consents to these actions and where it would consequently be impossible to prosecute for theft. However, no offence is committed if the

[70] C Shelbourn, 'Time Crime – looting of archaeological resources and the criminal law in England and the United States' (2008) *Criminal Law Review* 204, 205–06.

[71] *R v JO Sims Ltd* (1993) 96 Cr App R 125.

[72] (1993) 96 Cr App R 125, 129; see further *R v Seymour* (1987) 9 Cr App R (S) 395 (CA) (fine of £3,000). It could be argued that the court should consider the anticipated profits which would be made once the work had been completed: R Cranston, 'Vandals, Romans and Bishops' (1992) *New Law Journal* 1372.

[73] 'Protected' monument refers to any scheduled monument and any monument under the ownership or guardianship of the Secretary of State, Commission or local authority: Ancient Monuments and Archaeological Areas Act 1979 (AMAAA 1979), s 28(3), as amended by the National Heritage Act 1983.

works carried out are authorised in advance by the Secretary of State.[74] Upon conviction on indictment, the accused may be sentenced to a fine and/or a maximum of two years' imprisonment.[75]

There are also various offences linked to the use of a metal detector in a protected place, which include removing objects of archaeological or historic interest which had been located by the use of a metal detector.[76] The deterrent value is low: upon conviction, the accused may be sentenced to pay a small fine.[77] Furthermore, the accused may rely upon certain defences provided by the statute. For example, he may argue that he was not using the instrument to detect objects of archaeological or historical interest and was, for example, using the metal detector to look for something which he had lost.[78] The accused may also plead that, despite taking all reasonable steps to find out, he had not realised that the place where he had been using his metal detector was a protected place.[79]

There are drawbacks in bringing charges under the AMAAA 1979. These offences will be difficult and costly to prosecute, unless the accused is caught red-handed. A successful prosecution may otherwise depend upon research involving soil samples, photographs and casts of footprints. The offences are limited geographically to scheduled monuments. The penalties are not severe, and their value as a deterrent is therefore questionable. Unfortunately, under the AMAAA 1979, any financial penalty does not take account of the damage to the archaeological record. Under the equivalent US legislation, the Archaeological Resources Protection Act of 1979, this type of damage can be considered and may result in much heavier fines being imposed under that law.[80] However, an English prosecutor could choose to bring a charge for going equipped to steal, instead.[81] Furthermore, where there is a very serious case involving dishonesty which deserves a lengthy term of imprisonment, a prosecutor may well prefer to bring a charge of theft.[82]

3.20 The Draft Heritage Protection Bill

The draft Heritage Protection Bill (Cm 7349) will introduce a new system which will bring England's heritage together in one single, publicly accessible register. It will include all heritage structures which are of special historic, archaeological, architectural or artistic interest. Its scope will extend beyond scheduled monuments, discussed above, to listed buildings. If it is enacted in the future, it will repeal the Ancient Monuments and Archaeological Areas Act 1979 and other statutes.

The proposed legislation contains criminal offences relating to heritage crimes which do not depend upon proof of dishonesty. For example, as in the existing law,[83] it will be an offence to carry out non-urgent works to a heritage asset without proper consent.[84] Equally, it will be an offence to remove an object from a site that a person believes or could be

[74] AMAAA 1979, s 28(2), as amended by the Planning Act 2008.

[75] ibid, s 28(4).

[76] The offences are set out in ibid, s 42(1) and (3). Protected place is defined in a similar manner to protected monument: see ibid, s 42(2).

[77] ibid, s 42(1), (3).

[78] ibid, s 42(6).

[79] ibid, s 42(7).

[80] C Shelbourn (2008) *Criminal Law Reports* 204, 209.

[81] Theft Act 1968, s 25. See, for example, *R v Kidd* [1995] Crim LR 406 (CA).

[82] In sentencing a criminal for theft, account can be taken of the fact that cultural property was involved: *R v Farhad Hakimzadeh* [2009] EWCA 959 [13]; *R v Jacques* [2010] EWCA Crim 3233 [7].

[83] AMAAA 1979, s 2.

[84] Draft Heritage Protection Bill, ss 86, 89.

expected to believe contributes to the special interest in the site.[85] A defence will be available where the accused did not know that the site was a registered heritage structure and had taken all reasonable steps to ascertain whether it was a registered heritage structure.[86] This defence is important because not every heritage site will have notices informing visitors of the significance of the site. But, if there are such notices and the accused has merely failed to read them properly, the accused may be unable to rely upon this defence. It will mean that hikers should take care in picking up what might appear to be interesting stones or other objects, as they may unintentionally be committing an offence.

Like the AMAAA 1979, a special offence will be created in relation to the use of a metal detector in a registered heritage structure or open space without a licence. A defence would be available where the accused can show that he did not know, and had taken reasonable steps to ascertain whether it was a registered heritage structure or open space.[87]

IV Accessories and the Criminal Law

3.21 Looted Antiquities: a Web of Relationships

The police investigation and court proceedings involving Jonathan Tokeley-Parry are a useful illustration of the complex web of relationships which may exist between those involved in the illicit trade in antiquities and the variety of offences which may be committed. There will normally be local thieves in the source nation, who may be guilty of theft according to the domestic criminal law which governs them. These thieves will usually need 'business partners' located abroad in order to dispose of excavated antiquities. Tokeley-Parry liaised with people in Egypt, who dealt in stolen property (as well as forgeries).[88] He purchased objects from them and exported them.

The offence of handling stolen goods may be committed regardless of whether the goods were stolen in the UK or overseas.[89] However, if someone is charged with handling stolen goods in the UK, it must be shown that the goods belonged to another. The domestic law of the source state is therefore significant. If a source state has passed legislation claiming ownership of any undiscovered objects of antiquity which are buried or attached to land, these objects can be characterised as stolen if they are unlawfully removed. Egypt had passed such a 'patrimonial' law, which vested ownership of all antiquities found after 1983 in the Egyptian Government. Tokeley-Parry could therefore be charged with handling stolen goods.[90] Tokeley-Parry was convicted in 1997 for handling a stolen door taken from the tomb of Hetepka but, if the facts were to be repeated today, he might well be prosecuted for money laundering.[91] Even so, the domestic law of the source state remains important: a successful prosecution for money laundering would depend upon evidence of an initial offence, such as theft.

[85] ibid, s 87.
[86] ibid, ss 87(2), 89.
[87] ibid, ss 161, 162.
[88] See *United States v Schultz* 333 F 3d 393 (2d Cir 2003), 397–98.
[89] Theft Act 1968, s 24(1).
[90] *R v Tokeley-Parry* [1999] Crim LR 578 (CA). See further, 3.25.
[91] See 3.38.

Amongst other objects, Tokeley-Parry acquired a sculptured head which had been looted. The head was believed to be that of the eighteenth dynasty Pharaoh Amenhotep III (circa 1403–1354 BC). Tokeley-Parry was a restorer and, using his skills, he disguised the sculptured head as a tourist souvenir. He coated it in plastic, painted it in black and gold, and placed it on a base inscribed with the name of a Cairo hotel which sold curios.[92] He smuggled it out of Egypt to Switzerland in his luggage.

Other methods of smuggling an object out of a source nation include putting the object in a container with legitimate goods in preparation for a sea voyage. This method may involve bribing an agent or employee of the carrier. If third parties are used in this way, they may be prosecuted for an offence such as handling or money laundering or dealing with cultural objects in contravention of the Dealing in Cultural Objects (Offences) Act 2003.

Tokeley-Parry did not keep the sculptured head. He had a close relationship with Frederick Schultz, an American dealer, who often financed his activities. Schultz purchased the head and sold it for $1.2 million (and was later prosecuted in the US).[93] In order to facilitate its sale, Schultz and Tokeley-Parry had created false documentation and display stickers which appeared to be from the 1920s. The documents related to a fictitious person called Thomas Alcock, who had supposedly collected Egyptian antiquities in the 1920s. Their activities are not unusual. In response to a rising demand for information about an object's provenance, criminals are increasingly turning to the manufacture of false documents. In doing so, they become vulnerable to charges such as money laundering and fraud.

On another occasion, Tokeley-Parry purchased a stela of Pasenenkhons. This object was a four-foot-high slab of limestone incised with hieroglyphics. Ancient Egyptians created stelae in order to make a tribute to a god or a dead relative. Tokeley-Parry used a friend, who held himself out as a lawyer, to seek advice from an academic. The academic confirmed that it was authentic and confirmed that there was no record of it having been stolen.[94] As will be discussed, academics are now much more wary of becoming involved with research into unprovenanced objects, because of the risk that they have been unlawfully excavated. They would now be at risk of being prosecuted for a money laundering offence if the circumstances were suspicious.

The stela was stored for a while in a Zurich warehouse. This is not unusual: freeport warehouses are useful to all types of traders, including smugglers. Such warehouses handle all sorts of cargo, from machines to antiquities.[95] As they are in a duty free zone, there is less need for formal documentation than might otherwise be required. Smugglers can cover their tracks further by using shell companies.

Many of the individuals concerned will be accessories and their offences may vary in nature. However, their offences are not necessarily minor in character. The criminal law flings its net wide to include accessories, for good reason. Those individuals who appropri-

[92] *United States v Schultz* 333 F 3d 393 (2d Cir 2003) 396–97. This practice is not unique: others have smuggled items by disguising them as cheap souvenirs. See, for example, the allegation that antiquities were smuggled out of Thailand with 'Made in Thailand' stickers on them: discussed in KD Vitale, 'The War on Antiquities: United States Law and Foreign Cultural Property' (2009) 89(4) *Notre Dame Law Review* 1835, 1863.

[93] See P Gerstenblich, '*Schultz* and *Barakat*: Universal Recognition of National Ownership of Antiquities' (2009) XIV(1) *Art Antiquity and Law* 21, 28. See 3.75.

[94] B Meier and M Gottlieb, 'LOOT: Along the Antiquities Trail, An Illicit Journey Out of Egypt, Only a Few Questions Asked' *New York Times* (23 February 2004).

[95] Switzerland has accepted but not yet ratified the UNESCO Convention on the Means of Prohibiting and Preventing the Illicit Import, Export and Transfer of Ownership of Cultural Property 1970. See further, R Plutschow, 'Will Switzerland Finally Ratify the UNESCO 1970 Convention?' (2002) VII(2) *Art Antiquity and Law* 163.

ate an object may be acting under the direction of others. Thieves do not usually steal a cultural object for their own personal gratification: they do so in order to sell it on. Consequently, it is important to consider how the law applies to accessories as well as the main actors.

Although a series of prosecutions of all of those involved in trafficking in cultural objects is feasible, there must be sufficient evidence. Tokeley-Parry had kept detailed notes in journals, and other records existed, such as letters to accomplices. These notes were not only used to convict him but also to prosecute accessories in other countries. It was Tokeley-Parry's evidence which led to the successful conviction of Schultz, who was a prominent dealer, for trafficking in stolen property in the USA.[96]

V Handling Stolen Goods

3.22 Introduction

Theft of objects is usually the beginning of a process in which they are sold to professional handlers, or distributed amongst friends and family, or bartered in exchange for drugs. People who receive these objects in the knowledge that they are stolen may be prosecuted for handling. This is seen as a serious offence, and a maximum sentence of 14 years can be imposed, which is clearly more substantial than the maximum term of seven years for theft. Severe deterrents are seen as necessary because, if a criminal knows that a stolen object will be rapidly sold to others, he has an additional incentive to steal: if there is a system in place whereby an object can swiftly change hands from one dealer to another, it may be impossible to track down, and this will reduce the prospect that the prosecution can marshal sufficient evidence for a successful prosecution.[97] Furthermore, professional handlers may encourage criminals to focus upon certain types of goods because there is a ready market for them. This is true in relation not only to thefts from private collections in the UK, but also abroad. For example, there was evidence of targeted looting from the National Museum in Kabul in Afghanistan.[98]

Some form of strategic planning by professional criminals often exists. Handlers may encourage looters to take small items, which can easily be hidden. For example, large numbers of cylinder seals have been taken from Iraq and other countries in recent years. The seals have a picture of a story on their face and are usually carved out of hematite stone or other materials. They are easy to smuggle because they are small (often the size of a pebble); they fetch high prices in market nations because they are often objects of beauty. Alternatively, handlers may demand large stone friezes, with the intention of shipping them abroad to be eventually sold and featured as a statement piece in an office lobby in New York or other large city. In this situation, appropriate stonecutting equipment will be needed so that they can be removed from their sites. Attwood observes that there was evidence of this form of targeted looting after the fall of Saddam Hussein in Iraq.[99]

[96] *US v Schultz* 333 F 3d 393 (2d Cir 2003). See 3.75.

[97] AP Simester, JR Spencer, GR Sullivan and GJ Virgo, *Criminal Law Theory and Doctrine*, 4th edn (Oxford, Hart, 2010) 548.

[98] T McGirk, 'A Year of Looting Dangerously' *Sunday Review, Independent on Sunday* (24 March 1996), 4–8.

[99] R Attwood, *Stealing History* (New York, St Martin's Press, 2004) 7.

3.23 The Broad Scope of the Offence

Section 22(1) of the Theft Act 1968 provides:

> A person handles stolen goods if (otherwise than in the course of the stealing) knowing or believing them to be stolen goods he dishonestly receives the goods or dishonestly undertakes or assists in their retention, removal, disposal or realisation by or for the benefit of another person, or if he arranges to do so.

The original thieves cannot be charged with handling: the phrase 'otherwise than in the course of the stealing' was intended to exclude thieves, so that they are not subjected to the heavier penalties associated with this offence.[100] However, in other respects, the offence is broad in scope. The definition of 'stolen' goods is widened by section 24 of the Theft Act to include property obtained by blackmail or fraud or by obtaining a wrongful credit,[101] whether in the UK or elsewhere. It is further provided that the offence applies in relation to other property, including proceeds of sale, which directly or indirectly represent the 'stolen' property.

Where the accused is charged with handling objects which have been illegally excavated abroad, it is vital that a source nation's laws are clear in relation to ownership of cultural property, so that title in unexcavated objects is vested either in the landowner or the state. If the law of the source state is unclear, the court may conclude that the object had been previously ownerless; in these circumstances, the accused will not have committed the offence of handling stolen goods.

3.24 Property

The definition of goods is wide and is similar to the law of theft. By section 34(2)(b), unless the context suggests otherwise, goods include money[102] and portable property, including objects unearthed from the land, but not land itself. Hence, items such as gold, jewellery and antique furniture are included,[103] as well as stolen art or antiquities. For example, Raymond Scott, an unemployed antiques dealer, was convicted of handling stolen goods in 2010: he had been found attempting to sell Shakespeare's First Folio, originally published in 1623, which had been stolen from the University of Durham.[104]

3.25 The Mental Element (*Mens Rea*)

The offence requires the prosecutor to establish beyond reasonable doubt that the accused handled stolen goods dishonestly, 'knowing or believing' that the goods were stolen.[105] The test for knowledge or belief is subjective: the fact that the circumstances are so suspicious that a reasonable man would be put on enquiry is not sufficient.[106] No offence is committed if the accused merely harbours suspicions.[107] Knowledge means a 'true belief' that the goods

[100] *R v Bloxham* [1983] 1 AC 109 (HL) 115.

[101] Theft Act 1968, s 24(4)(5).

[102] This includes choses in action such as money deposited in a bank account, which will be a debt owed by the bank: *R v Forsyth* [1997] 2 Cr App Rep 299 (CA).

[103] JL Schneider, 'Stolen Goods Markets' (2005) 45 *British Journal of Criminology* 129.

[104] 'Antique dealer jailed for handling stolen Shakespeare First Folio' *The Guardian* (2 August 2010).

[105] In relation to everyday commodities, the name of the owner should be included in the charge: *R v Gregory* [1972] 1 WLR 991 (CA).

[106] *R v Forsyth* [1997] 2 Cr App Rep 299 (CA).

[107] *R v Hall* (1985) 81 1 Cr App R 260 (CA).

were stolen.[108] This would be the case where, for example, the thief informed the accused that this was the case. The meaning of 'belief' has proved more difficult to identify. It is something short of knowledge.[109] One useful guideline is that 'belief' indicates the mental acceptance of a fact as true or existing;[110] it is where a person, although not certain that the goods are stolen, accepts that there could be no other reasonable conclusion.[111]

It should also be noted that, according to section 22(1), the prosecution must show that the conduct of the accused was 'dishonest'. The *Ghosh* test, applied in relation to theft, is also applied here.[112] It would ordinarily be satisfied where the accused knew or believed that an object had been stolen. In contrast, if the accused has taken possession of a cultural item which he believes to be stolen but can provide evidence that he intended to hand it over to the proper authorities, he would not be dishonest, and would therefore not be guilty of handling.

A prosecutor who is faced with a dealer who has failed to make enquiries about the provenance of an object and who has shut his eyes to the possibility of wrongdoing is unlikely to succeed in establishing either that the dealer knew or believed that the goods were stolen or that the dealer was dishonest. In contrast, if a dealer has kept extensive written records, as in the case of *R v Tokeley-Parry*,[113] they may provide sufficient evidence to satisfy these requirements. Furthermore, the prosecution is aided by section 27(3) of the Theft Act, which allows it to bring forward evidence of other incidents where the accused has been found in possession of stolen items in the preceding year for the purpose of proving that he knew or believed that the goods were stolen.[114]

3.26 Handling

The concept of 'handling' is defined widely by section 22 to create two distinct offences.[115] Its first limb relates to receiving goods; its second limb deals with undertaking, assisting or arranging to retain, remove, dispose or realise goods by or for the benefit of another person.[116] Prosecuting authorities need to take care in setting out separate counts in the indictment where different forms of handling are relied upon.[117] It must be established that the accused possessed the appropriate knowledge or belief at the relevant time. In the case of receipt, it must be present at the time of receipt.[118] In the case of other forms of handling which are continuing (such as assisting), it must exist at some point during that time period, although not necessarily at the beginning of the period.

[108] *R v Saik* [2006] UKHL 18, [2007] 1 AC 18 [26]. See further, *R v Montila* [2004] UKHL 50 [27].
[109] *R v Hall* (1985) 81 Cr App R 260 (CA).
[110] *R v Grainge* [1974] 1 WLR 619 (CA); *R v Adinga* [2003] EWCA Crim 3201 (CA).
[111] *R v Hall* (1985) 81 Cr App R 260 (CA).
[112] *R v Roberts* [1986] Crim LR 122 (CA). See also *R v Ghosh* [1982] QB 1053 (CA); 3.04.
[113] [1999] Crim LR 578 (CA).
[114] It is not a precondition for bringing forward such evidence that the accused had been convicted on these occasions: *R v Bradley* (1979) 70 Cr App Rep 200. The prosecution may also bring forward evidence of any conviction of theft or handling within the last five years but must give at least seven days' notice of its intention to do so: Theft Act 1968, s 27(3)(b). The evidence should be admitted only where the defendant's knowledge or belief is in issue: *R v Duffus* (1983) 158 JP 224 (CA).
[115] *R v Bloxham* [1983] 1 AC 109 (HL) 113.
[116] *R v Nicklin* [1977] 1 WLR 403 (CA).
[117] *R v Alt* (1972) 56 Cr App R 457 (CA). See further, *R v Nicklin* [1977] 1 WLR 403 (CA).
[118] *R v Brook* [1993] Crim LR 455 (CA); *R v Williams* [1994] Crim LR 934 (CA).

3.27 Receiving

In relation to receipt, the key ingredient is control; however, evidence of an intention to exercise control over the property needs to be stronger and more convincing in a criminal case than in an equivalent civil case.[119] The accused will be found guilty of 'receiving' goods only if he exercises some form of control over the object,[120] even if this is by indirect means through the use of an agent who is authorised to receive them.[121] Touching an object is not enough.[122] The fact that the stolen goods were discovered on the premises of the accused would not suffice; there must be some evidence that the goods had been delivered by invitation or arrangement.[123] In contrast, in the civil law, the fact that the owner or tenant is not aware of the existence of certain goods stored on his premises does not prevent the court from concluding that the owner or tenant had possession of them on the grounds that he had exclusive control of the premises.[124] The difference between civil law and criminal law must be understood in the light of the different purposes for which the location of possession needs to be determined. It is common for people to share premises, or for other people to have access to them; any number of people might have the opportunity to leave stolen goods on an owner's premises and, as the typical punishment for handling is imprisonment, it is vital that the scope of the offence is clear and carefully confined.

3.28 Arranging, Undertaking or Assisting

Where the accused has not received stolen property but has nevertheless meddled in some way, he may be prosecuted for handling under the second limb of section 22(1) because he has arranged to receive goods which he knows or believes have been stolen[125] or because he has undertaken or assisted in retaining, removing, disposing or realising goods. The scope of this second limb of the offence is defined by section 22(1) in very broad terms. For example, it can include transporting goods because this conduct may assist in their removal; it may also include storage, as this will aid their retention.[126] But merely using goods would not by itself be seen as assisting in their retention in the criminal law.[127] Anyone who assists in the disposal (including negotiating a sale)[128] of stolen goods or in their destruction may be liable for handling.

In *R v Bloxham,*[129] Lord Bridge of Harwich stated that:

> The offence can be committed in relation to any one of these activities in one or other of two ways. First, the offender may himself undertake the activity *for the benefit of* another person. Secondly, the activity may be undertaken by another person and the offender may assist him.

In *Bloxham,* the accused innocently bought a stolen car. When he did not receive the registration documents as promised, he became suspicious and sold the car for a low price to an

[119] It is important to identify the point of receipt because the prosecution must show that the accused had the relevant *mens rea* at that point: *R v Brook* [1993] Crim LR 455 (CA).
[120] *Hobson v Impett* (1957) 41 Cr App Rep 138 (DC) 141. See further, *R v Healey* [1965] 1 All ER 365 (CA).
[121] *R v Cavendish* [1961] 1 WLR 1083 (CA).
[122] *R v Healey* [1965] 1 All ER 365 (CA).
[123] *R v Cavendish* [1961] 1 WLR 1083 (CA). See further, *R v Lloyd* [1992] Crim LR 361 (CA).
[124] *Flack v Chairperson, National Crime Authority* (1998) 156 ALR 501 (Fed Ct of New South Wales).
[125] *R v Park* (1987) 87 Cr App R 164 (CA).
[126] *R v Brown* [1970] 1 QB 105 (CA); *R v Pitchley* (1973) 57 Cr App R 30 (CA).
[127] *R v Kanwar* [1982] 1 WLR 845 (CA).
[128] See *R v Watson* [1916] 2 KB 385 (CA).
[129] *R v Bloxham* [1983] AC 109 (HL) 113.

unknown person who was prepared to take it without its documents. The accused was prosecuted for dishonestly undertaking the 'disposal or realisation' of stolen property 'by or for the benefit of another person'. The House of Lords held that the accused had been wrongly convicted of handling. It was held that a purchaser could not be described as acting 'by or for the benefit of another person' in reselling because his actions were for the benefit of himself, and not anyone else. Consequently, if an innocent purchaser of a cultural object subsequently becomes suspicious of its provenance, he is not guilty of handling if he disposes of it to another.

3.29 Recipients and Innocent Purchasers

The Theft Act 1968 allows the prosecution to follow the stolen property from one hand to another or to trace value from one asset to another in establishing that the objects in the hands of the accused are, or represent, stolen goods. The relevant provisions are set out in section 24(2). If the stolen objects, such as looted cylinder seals, are passed down a chain of dealers who all take in bad faith, the police can follow the seals and all of those who had control of them or became involved in some way may be prosecuted for handing.[130] Equally, if a thief steals a painting and exchanges it for a car, a person who takes the car with the knowledge or belief that it represents stolen property can be convicted of handling stolen goods.

The prosecution must establish all the ingredients of the offence. It is sometimes suggested that possession of a stolen item raises an inference of handling, particularly where the item is discovered in the hands of the accused shortly after the theft has taken place.[131] There is a risk that a person may be prosecuted in these circumstances, if he cannot offer a convincing explanation.[132] Even so, there must be sufficient evidence to convict.[133]

Although a dishonest purchaser can be prosecuted for receiving, innocent purchasers cannot. They do not have the necessary *mens rea*. Furthermore, they receive express protection from section 3(2) of the Theft Act, which provides that where an interest in property is transferred to a good faith purchaser, his assumption of rights in relation to that property will not amount to theft.

3.30 Offences Committed Abroad

If a person in this country handles property derived from an offence committed abroad which was viewed as theft, blackmail or fraud according to the domestic law of that country, he can be prosecuted for handling. The prosecution must prove that a criminal offence was committed abroad.[134] Patrimonial laws are therefore highly significant, because they may provide the necessary evidence to establish that an item imported from abroad is stolen. For example, in *R v Tokeley-Parry*,[135] Tokeley-Parry arranged for an associate, Mark

[130] There is a difficulty where money is paid into an account and then withdrawn to pay someone who takes in bad faith: the bank receives the money paid into the account and it is different money which is paid out to the recipient. In *R v Forsyth* [1997] 2 Cr App Rep 299, the Court of Appeal dismissed this argument and emphasised that s 24(2) was concerned with control of property.

[131] *R v Smythe* (1980) 72 Cr App Rep 8; *R v Nicol* (CA, 11 March 1997).

[132] See, for example, *R v Lincoln Magistrates Court Ex p Field* (19 July 1993).

[133] *Warren v DPP* (5 December 2000).

[134] *R v Okolie* (CA, *The Times* 16 June, 2000). See further, *R Cruickshank Ltd v Chief Constable of Kent CC* [2002] EWCA Civ 1840 (CA).

[135] *R v Tokeley-Parry* [1999] Crim LR 578 (CA).

Perry, to bring certain Egyptian antiquities to England. Tokeley-Parry was convicted of handling two panels of a door of the tomb of Hetepka and a figure of Horus. It was evident that these antiquities were stolen because their removal contravened Egyptian law, which declared that all antiquities belonged to the state and provided that if they were held by an individual without a licence or if they were removed from Egypt, they would be treated as stolen.

It can be seen from *R v Tokeley-Parry* that the importing of a stolen object from abroad could be covered by the second branch of the section 22(1) offence. However, the conduct must fall within the scope of the statutory provision. As Lord Bridge observed in *R v Bloxham*, 'First, the offender may himself undertake the activity *for the benefit of* another person. Secondly, the activity may be undertaken by another person and the offender may assist him.' If the accused excavated an object in Egypt and then took it back to the UK, he may be guilty of theft but not handling. His conduct would not fall within the statutory definition because he would be acting for himself and not for the benefit of another. However, in *R v Tokeley-Parry*, it was Mark Perry who had brought the antiquities to England. As Tokeley-Parry had assisted Perry in their removal from Egypt, he had acted on behalf of another (Perry) in handling the stolen items. Tokeley-Parry could therefore be convicted of handling, and was sentenced to six years' imprisonment.

3.31 The Goods Must be Stolen

According to section 24(3) of the Theft Act,

> But no goods shall be regarded as having continued to be stolen goods after they have been restored to the person from whom they were stolen or to other lawful possession or custody, or after that person and any other person claiming through him have otherwise ceased as regards those goods to have any right to restitution in respect of the theft.

A person will therefore not be guilty of handling if he took possession of an object after it had been returned to the owner. The same is true if the object was in 'lawful' possession or custody, such as under the control of the police,[136] before the accused had possession of it. No offence will have been committed if the owner has ceased to have any 'right to restitution'. Clearly, this would be the case if the owner has abandoned the object. But it is also so where an owner's claim is time-barred.[137] As a consequence, the person in possession of a cultural object can assert that it belongs to him and is no longer 'stolen'. This defence is important because it is not uncommon for thieves to hide objects for some years, before releasing them back onto the market. Limitation periods vary from country to country, but may be quite short.

It is not enough that the accused thought that an object was stolen: it must on the facts be stolen or otherwise derived from criminal conduct (blackmail or fraud).[138] The market

[136] *R v Dolan* (1855) Dears CC 436; *R v Schmidt* (1866) LR 1 CCR 15; *R v Villensky* [1892] 2 QB 597. The question of whether the police have taken possession of the goods will turn upon the facts and whether the police have decided to take control: *Re AG's Reference (No 1 of 1974)* [1974] 2 All ER 899 (CA); *R v King* [1938] 2 All ER 662 (CA). If the goods are no longer stolen goods, it is not open to the police to charge the accused with attempted handling instead: *Haughton v Smith* [1975] AC 476 (HL).

[137] See 5.39–5.43.

[138] Theft Act 1968, s 24(4). See *R v Saik* [2007] 1 AC 18 (HL) [7]; see further, *Anderton v Ryan* [1985] 1 AC 560 (HL).

in art and antiquities is awash with fakes:[139] if it was discovered that the accused merely had a fake in his possession, he could not be convicted of handling unless fraud could be established.[140]

VI Money Laundering Offences

3.32 The Nature of Money Laundering

Money laundering is the process of disguising the origins of property which has been acquired through criminal conduct. The aim is to confer on the property the appearance of having been derived from legitimate business activity. For example, profits made from drugs trafficking by international criminal syndicates may be used to purchase goods (which may include licit art and antiquities) which are subsequently sold. The proceeds of sale will appear to be derived from a legitimate activity of buying and selling goods. However, those profits, which originally stemmed from crime, may be used to support further criminal activity, such as the illicit trade in art and antiquities.[141] Although it is estimated that billions of dollars of profits are generated each year from money laundering activities worldwide, it is impossible to assess the scale of the activity, because so much of it remains hidden.

3.33 Legislative History

Although the money laundering process helped criminals to avoid prosecution for their conduct and provided direct financial support for further criminal activity, for many years it was not a criminal offence. During the twentieth century, governments became increasingly concerned about the impact of money laundering activities upon their economies. Initially, international efforts were directed at preventing the traffic in illegal drugs;[142] but it was soon appreciated that criminal gangs were involved in other serious crimes and efforts were directed towards curbing money laundering more generally.

It was recognised that it was desirable to change national laws in two respects: to criminalise money laundering itself and to strip criminals of the proceeds of crime.[143] In England, a succession of statutes of increasing severity reflected these concerns. Initially, there were two statutory regimes: one dealing with drugs,[144] the other with serious crimes.[145] The Proceeds of Crime Act 2002 took effect in 2003 and replaced earlier laws, removing the distinction between drug-related crime and other crime, thereby making the law simpler and more effective.

[139] For example, the fear has been expressed that 'the accepted Cycladic corpus may be largely corrupted by fakes': C Chippindale and D Gill, 'Art versus archaeology?' in KW Tubb (ed) *Antiquities: Trade or Betrayed: Legal, Ethical and Conservation Issues* (London, Archetype Publications, 1995) 131, 138.

[140] The accused may be guilty of another offence: see eg the Criminal Attempts Act 1981.

[141] See 'Protection against trafficking in cultural property', UNODC/CCPCJ/EG.1/2009/CRP.1; see 2.48. See I Snaith, 'Art, antiques and the fruits of crime: laundering, investigation and confiscation: Part 1' (1998) III(4) *Art Antiquity and Law* 371.

[142] See the United Nations Convention against Illicit Traffic in Narcotic Drugs and Psychotropic Substances, discussed in 2.38.

[143] See Recommendation 1 of the 40 Recommendations by the Financial Action Task Force, revised in 2012.

[144] Drug Trafficking Act (DTA) 1994.

[145] See the Criminal Justice Act 1998.

The Proceeds of Crime Act 2002 introduced a code of law which is largely independent of the ordinary criminal law. This partition extends beyond the principal money laundering offences to cover the ancillary supporting orders which a court can make. The 2002 Act provides vigorous powers of search, seizure, detention, forfeiture and confiscation of property, which are all administered by the Crown Court. If, in contrast, the police are investigating theft, fraud or some other form of acquisitive crime, they will use the Police and Criminal Evidence Act (PACE) 2004 orders and warrants. If, however, terrorist activity is suspected, separate powers are provided in the Terrorism Act 2000, which has created terrorist property offences.[146]

If the police suspect that an individual can be prosecuted for a criminal offence for handling a stolen object or for an offence under the Dealing in Cultural Objects (Offences) Act 2003, they can seize the object to be used in evidence for the prosecution.[147] Once the investigation and prosecution have come to an end, an application to court can be made under section 148 of the Powers of Criminal Courts (Sentencing) Act 2000 or under the Police (Property) Act 1897 for an order for the return of the object to its owner.

3.34 The Principal Offences

Three principal money laundering offences are set out in sections 327–29 of Part 7 of the Proceeds of Crime Act 2002.[148] These offences are wide in scope, and those who assist by, for example, conspiring, inciting, aiding, abetting, counselling or procuring the commission of one of these offences can also be prosecuted for money laundering. However, the offences are not limited to accessories. It should not be overlooked that a person may be prosecuted for money laundering not only where he deals with the proceeds of crimes committed by third parties, but also where he deals with the proceeds of his own crimes. For example, suppose a dealer pays a customs official a bribe of £200,000 to facilitate the import of stolen art and antiquities. The payment of a bribe in these circumstances will be an offence under the Bribery Act 2010.[149] If the official transfers the £200,000 between bank accounts, or uses the money to purchase an item, he may also be charged with a money laundering offence. This is because the £200,000 will be characterised as 'criminal' property. Furthermore, by section 340(4), it does not matter who carried out the conduct, who benefited from it or whether the conduct occurred before or after the enactment of the 2002 Act.

The penalties are severe: defendants may be fined or sentenced to six months' imprisonment as a summary offence or jailed for up to 14 years upon indictment. In addition, upon conviction, a confiscation order will be made, which will be a debt owed to the state which reflects the benefit gained from the crime.[150]

3.35 Criminal Property

All three principal offences require evidence that the accused was involved with 'criminal property'. In order to understand this notion, reference must be made to the interpretation in

[146] The Terrorism Act 2000, as amended by the Anti-Terrorism, Crime and Security Act 2001, came into force on 10 February 2001.

[147] See 4.05–4.07.

[148] They came into force on 24 February 2003: SI 2003/120. Part 7 of the Proceeds of Crime Act (POCA) 2002 has been amended by the Serious Organised Crime and Police Act 2005, ss 97–109, which came into effect on 1 July 2005.

[149] See 3.48.

[150] See 4.14–4.19.

section 340. It is made clear that money laundering is not limited to cash: it can include all types of portable property, as well as land.[151] Property is 'criminal' property where it can be said to be the proceeds of crime. It includes any benefit from criminal conduct and any property which represents such a benefit 'in whole or part and whether directly or indirectly'.[152] The definition therefore encompasses not only the original property obtained from a crime, but any other property which a criminal has received in exchange.[153] Thus, if a thief sells a stolen painting for cash, the cash can be viewed as criminal property. However, a good faith purchaser (of the painting, for example) cannot be accused of a principal money laundering offence because the property in his hands is no longer 'criminal' property.[154]

The burden is upon the prosecution to show that when any type of property is transferred to the accused, it is or it represents the benefit obtained from criminal activity.[155] This burden of proof may be difficult to satisfy, as the sole purpose of money laundering techniques is to disguise the provenance of property which may be mixed and exchanged over a period of time and which may originally derive from crimes committed abroad. It is particularly problematic to gather sufficient evidence where the accused is an accessory who has become involved in a series of transactions at a much later stage in the process.[156]

If the prosecution bring charges of money laundering against a dealer on the basis that he has an object in his possession which is derived from crime, it must be clear that an offence has been committed. In *R v Montila*, the House of Lords observed that the intention of both domestic legislation and the main international conventions was to target particular activities: the concealment and dealing in the proceeds of crime.[157] If the object is from a legitimate source, the prosecution would fail: no conviction for money laundering can be secured on the basis of bad intent alone. However, the courts have been remarkably flexible in relation to the evidence which the prosecution must bring forward. In *R v Anwoir*,[158] the Court of Appeal stated:

> there are two ways in which the Crown can prove the property derives from crime, (a) by showing that it derives from conduct of a particular kind or kinds and that conduct of that kind or those kinds is unlawful; or (b) by evidence of the circumstances in which the property is handled which is such as to give rise to the irresistible inference that it can only be derived from crime.[159]

There is therefore no requirement imposed upon the prosecution to precisely delineate the offence which generated the property to be laundered. This guidance is particularly relevant where a defendant is found in possession of millions of pounds in his luggage and is unable to explain where the money has come from and appears to acknowledge that it may be derived from unlawful activity.[160] But it may be equally relevant where someone is found in possession of a number of artefacts and is unable to explain how he came to be in

[151] POCA 2002, s 340(9).

[152] ibid, s 340(3)(a).

[153] See the example provided in *R v Loizou* [2004] EWCA Crim 1579, [2005] 2 Cr App Rep 37 (CA) [32].

[154] *R v Aminat Adedoyin Afolabi* [2009] EWCA Crim 2879 (CA) [33]–[35].

[155] POCA 2002, s 340(3). This interpretation was confirmed, obiter, in *R v Montila* [2004] UKHL 50, [2004] 1 WLR 3141 (HL) [41].

[156] See the discussion of the policy issues by the Court of Appeal in *R v Montila* [2003] EWCA Crim 3082, [2004] 1 All ER 877 (CA).

[157] *R v Montila* [2004] 1 WLR 3141 (HL) [27]–[38].

[158] *R v Anwoir* [2008] EWCA Crim 1354, [2009] 1 WLR 980.

[159] ibid [21].

[160] *R v F* [2008] EWCA Crim 1868, [2009] Crim LR 45. See further, *R v Ferrel* [2010] UKPC 20; *R v Albert Yip* [2010] EWCA Crim 1381.

possession of them and is attempting to secretly import them into this country. The decision in *Anwoir* has been criticised by writers, and it has been argued that the effect of the decision is to erode the importance of the underlying crime, known as the 'predicate' offence.[161] There is no doubt that the direction in *Anwoir* makes it easier to prosecute a defendant. In order to establish that the property in issue was derived from crime, it is now sufficient to bring forward credible circumstantial evidence relating to the provenance of the object; it can then be left to the jury to decide whether this evidence has given rise to an irresistible inference that the accused was laundering ill-gotten gains.[162]

3.36 International Criminal Activity

The accused may be exposed to a charge of money laundering whenever he is involved with property which represents the proceeds of crime. In order to deal with international crimes, where the criminals have travelled abroad to carry out their operations, criminal conduct is defined as conduct which constitutes an offence in any part of the UK, or would constitute an offence if it occurred in the UK.[163] Consequently, if a cultural object is stolen from a museum overseas, and sold and resold before eventually reaching the market in the UK, all of the dealers in the chain are vulnerable to prosecution for money laundering in accordance with the Proceeds of Crime Act 2002.

However, a person does not commit any of the three principal money laundering offences if the relevant conduct, although a criminal act in the UK, was carried out abroad and was not unlawful under the criminal law then applying in that country or territory.[164] The Proceeds of Crime Act 2002 (Money Laundering: Exceptions to Overseas Conduct Defence) Order 2006, SI 2006/1070 expands on this exception. It makes it clear that the defence can only be relied upon where the conduct is such that, had it occurred in the UK, it would have constituted an offence which would have been punishable with a maximum of 12 months' imprisonment. The defence would appear to be available if the conduct in question, had it occurred in the UK, would involve committing an offence under the Treasure Act 1996. For example, under the Act, the maximum term of imprisonment for failure to report a find of treasure is three months' imprisonment.[165] Consequently, if objects of antiquity are secretly dug up abroad but the source nation does not assert rights of ownership (so that this conduct cannot be characterised as a serious offence such as theft), it would appear that anyone dealing with the object or the proceeds of sale reasonably believing that it was legitimate to do so could plead this section by way of a defence.

3.37 Mental Element: 'Suspect'

What if a dealer is investigated for buying and reselling a stolen object of antiquity? If the prosecutor brought charges for either handling stolen goods or an offence under the Dealing in Cultural Objects (Offences) Act 2003, he would have to establish that the dealer

[161] D McCluskey, 'Money laundering: the disappearing predicate' (2009) *Criminal Law Reports* 719, 720; D Bentley and R Fisher, 'Criminal property under POCA 2002 – time to clean up the law?' (2009) *Archbold News* 7.

[162] See *R v MK, AS* [2009] EWCA Crim 952 [12].

[163] POCA 2002, s 340(2).

[164] ibid, s 327(2A), s 328(3), s 329(2A). These sub-sections were inserted by the Serious Organised Crime and Police Act 2005, s 102.

[165] Treasure Act 1996, s 8(3).

was dishonest according to the *Ghosh* test.[166] This is a difficult test to satisfy. In contrast, if a charge is brought for money laundering, there is no need to establish dishonesty.

As the principal money laundering offences are triggered by normal commercial activities involving transferring, acquiring and possessing goods, money and other property, traders in art and antiquities and their professional advisers are at risk of prosecution. Although the prosecutor need not establish that the accused was dishonest, it must be shown that the accused 'knows or suspects'[167] that the property constitutes or represents a benefit derived from crime.[168] Suspicion is enough. The test for 'suspect' is a subjective one, involving a lower standard than actual knowledge.[169] In particular, suspicion can include situations where the defendant engages in wilful blindness, by deliberately refraining from enquiry.[170] The leading case on the meaning of the term is *R v Da Silva*.[171] The Court of Appeal held that the prosecution did not have to show that there were reasonable grounds for the suspicion.[172] It merely had to prove that the defendant assisted another in retaining criminal proceeds thinking that there was a possibility, which was more than fanciful, that the other person had been engaged in or had benefited from criminal conduct. But Longmore LJ suggested that: 'A vague feeling of unease would not suffice.'[173]

The lower threshold for establishing the mental element (*mens rea*) for a principal money laundering offence means that all those involved in dealing in cultural property should beware. This includes not only dealers and auction houses, but also conservators who remove all evidence of provenience, and academics who authenticate an object and, in doing so, assist in giving it legitimacy. In particular, dealers, academics, conservators and others need to be aware that they cannot plead as a defence that they had a contractual obligation to hand over property to their client. If they know or suspect that an object represents criminal property, they have an obligation to report that fact to the authorities: their contractual duties to their clients are overridden by the obligation to avoid committing the offence of money laundering.[174]

3.38 Concealing the Proceeds of Crime

Section 327(1) of the Proceeds of Crime Act 2002 makes it an offence to (a) conceal, (b) disguise, (c) convert or (d) transfer criminal property, or (e) remove it from the jurisdiction.[175] This offence includes concealing or disguising the nature, source, location, disposition, movement or ownership of criminal property or any rights with respect to it.[176] In principle, this will cover those who attempt to secretly import an object, provided that

[166] See 3.03.

[167] POCA 2002, s 340(3)(b).

[168] ibid, s 340(9); *Prosecution appeal (No 11 of 2007) R v W* [2008] EWCA Crim 2 (CA) [15].

[169] *R v Saik* [2007] 1 AC 18 (HL) [32].

[170] ibid [62]. In contrast, the offence of conspiracy requires proof of intention or knowledge: ibid.

[171] *R v Da Silva* [2006] EWCA Crim 165, [2007] 1 WLR 303 (CA). See *R v Aminat Adedoyin Afolabi* [2009] EWCA Crim 2879 (CA) [18]; *Shah v HSBC Private Bank (UK) Ltd* [2010] EWCA Civ 31; *K Ltd v National Westminster Bank plc* [2006] EWCA Civ 1039, [2007] 1 WLR 311; *R v Haigh* [2007] EWCA Crim 167 (CA); *Shah v HSBC Private Bank Ltd* [2012] EWHC 1283.

[172] [2007] 1 WLR 303 (CA) [16]. See further, *K Ltd v National Westminster Bank plc* [2007] 1 WLR 311; *Squirrell Ltd v National Westminster Bank plc* [2005] EWHC 664 [13]–[15].

[173] *R v Da Silva* [2007] 1 WLR 311 [16]. A fleeting thought would not be sufficient: ibid [17].

[174] *K Ltd v National Westminster Bank plc* [2006] EWCA Civ 1039, [2007] 1 WLR 311 (CA) [9]–[10].

[175] As amended by the Serious Organised Crime and Police Act 2005. The statutory predecessors to this section were s 49(2) of the Drug Trafficking Act 1994 (DTA 1994) and s 93C(2) of the Criminal Justice Act 1988 (CJA 1988).

[176] POCA 2002, s 327(3).

there is an underlying crime (a predicate offence), such as theft or bribery, so that the object can be seen as the proceeds of crime.[177] If a person alters the appearance of a stolen object, such as by painting an object of antiquity to look like a tourist souvenir,[178] he will be guilty of disguising it contrary to section 327(1)(b).[179] If the object is then sold and the proceeds of sale are changed into a different currency, the process of changing the currency would be seen as 'converting' property within section 327(1)(c).[180] Although section 327 is not concerned with merely receiving criminal property, its transfer will fall within the ambit of section 327(1)(d).[181] If an object is smuggled out of the country, this would be caught by section 327(1)(e) which makes it an offence where the defendant 'removes' the property from England, Wales, Scotland or Northern Ireland.[182]

This offence may be committed where the accused exercises control over criminal property. But the offence is wider than this, and includes situations where the accused allows another to use his bank account as a conduit for transferring funds.[183] Consequently, if the accused permits others to transfer assets to him or to use his premises for the storage or movement of any criminal property, he could be charged under this section. For example, Anthony Hershel Blok, a senior partner in a firm of solicitors, was charged with a number of money laundering offences connected with the theft of a painting of 'Girls on the Beach' by Sir William Orpen. One of the offences was transferring criminal property. Blok accepted £75,000 in cash in two bags in suspicious circumstances, which he paid into court as bail security for his client. He provided false evidence when questioned about the money. He was convicted in 2009 at Croydon Crown Court of money laundering activities.[184]

Auctioneers are vulnerable to prosecution where a client deposits a suspicious object for sale. Regardless of whether the object is subsequently sold or returned to the client, their conduct could fall within the scope of section 327(1)(d) of the 2002 Act. However, provided that an auctioneer did not know or suspect that the object represented the proceeds of crime, he would not have committed an offence. What if the auctioneer is suspicious, but is obliged by the civil law to comply with the client's demand? In this situation, the auctioneer should make an authorised disclosure in accordance with section 327(2)(a) and section 338 (as discussed below[185]) in order to protect himself.

The three principal money laundering offences are broad in scope, and overlap. Consequently, even if the accused has not exercised any form of control over an object but has merely transported or stored it in accordance with another's instructions, this may fall within this section as well as under the following sections 328 and 329.[186]

[177] *R v Abida Shaheen Amir, R v Urfan Akhtar* [2011] EWCA Crim 146 (CA).

[178] See 3.21.

[179] *R v Esimu* [2007] EWCA Crim 1380 (CA) (adding false number plates to vehicles); *R v Ashmore* [2006] EWCA Crim 2996 (CA) (stripping parts from cars to add to others).

[180] *R v Saik* [2007] 1 AC 18 (HL).

[181] *R v Abida Shaheen Amir, R v Urfan Akhtar* [2011] EWCA Crim 146 (CA).

[182] See *R v Adrian Dulgheru* [2006] EWCA Crim 1598 (CA).

[183] *R v Fazal* [2009] EWCA Crim 1697, [2010] 1 WLR 694 (CA) [21].

[184] The Law Society News, 19 August 2009; Solicitors Disciplinary Tribunal Case No 10395-2009 (date of hearing 1 December 2010). See also 'Solicitor jailed over bid to sell stolen £500,000 painting' (2009) *Antiques Trade Gazette* 13 July; 'Art Hostage' blog.

[185] At 3.41.

[186] For example, cash couriers can be prosecuted under POCA 2002, s 327(1)(d), or its statutory predecessors, as in *R v Loizou* [2005] 2 Cr App Rep 37, as well as under POCA 2002, s 328.

3.39 Arrangements

According to section 328(1) of the Proceeds of Crime Act 2002:[187]

> A person commits an offence if he enters into or becomes concerned in an arrangement which he knows or suspects facilitates (by whatever means) the acquisition, retention, use or control of criminal property by or on behalf of another person.

The phrase, 'becomes concerned in an arrangement' is clearly directed towards those who become involved at a later stage, after property has been obtained by a criminal act.[188]

This section is aimed at those who facilitate transactions such as agents. These people may never take physical possession of the criminal property concerned. It particularly affects banks,[189] lawyers[190] and accountants, dealers and auctioneers. It could be used against anyone involved in importing an object into the UK on behalf of others which is the product of a criminal act such as theft. Thus, if an export agent is used to inspect a container before it is sealed, and the agent falsely misdescribes its contents to enable stolen antiquities to be imported, he could be prosecuted under this section. An auctioneer could also be prosecuted under this section if he knows or suspects that he is involved in selling stolen property.[191] Auction houses are therefore best advised to withdraw a work once questions are raised regarding its origins and to make an authorised disclosure to the authorities.

3.40 Acquisition, Use and Possession of the Proceeds of Crime

According to section 329, it is an offence to acquire, use or have possession of criminal property.[192] This section appears to be directed at those who receive property for their own benefit, such as those who acquire property from criminals.[193] However, it can also be applied to those who store goods or money for the benefit of another.[194]

A commercial or consumer buyer will not commit an offence under this section provided he has supplied 'adequate consideration' in acquiring, using or taking possession of the property.[195] Guidance on what amounts to 'adequate consideration' is provided by section 329(3):

> (a) a person acquires property for inadequate consideration if the value of the consideration is significantly less than the value of the property;
> (b) a person uses or has possession of property for inadequate consideration if the value of the consideration is significantly less than the value of the use or possession;
> (c) the provision by a person of goods or services which he knows or suspects may help another to carry out criminal conduct is not consideration.

[187] As amended by the Serious Organised Crime and Police Act 2005. As regards the prior law, see the DTA 1994, s 50 in relation to drug trafficking; in relation to other crimes, see CJA 1988, ss 93A, as amended by the CJA 1993, s 29.

[188] It does not apply where property is not criminal property at the time when the arrangement comes into effect: *R v Geary* [2010] EWCA Crim 1925.

[189] A typical example would be where a bank transfers its customer's money from one account to another, where the money represents the proceeds of crime: *K Ltd v National Westminster Bank Plc* [2007] 1 WLR 311; *UMBS Online Ltd v Serious Organised Crime Agency* [2007] EWCA 406 (CA).

[190] *R v Allpress, Symeou, Casal, Morris and Martin* [2009] EWCA Crim 8, [2009] 2 Cr App R (S) 58 (solicitor).

[191] *R v Griffiths* [2006] EWCA Crim 2155 (CA).

[192] As amended by the Serious Organised Crime and Police Act 2005. As regards the prior law, see DTA 1994, s 51; CJA 1988, s 93B.

[193] *R v Taylor* [2005] All ER (D) 267 (Apr) (CA).

[194] *R v Allpress, Symeou, Casal, Morris and Martin* [2009] EWCA Crim 8 (Martin had been prosecuted under this section because he had stored drug money belonging to his brother).

[195] POCA 2002, s 329(2)(c).

This defence would also be available to those who take possession of a work of art or antiquity by way of a lease (such as to display in an office) rather than by purchase, provided an adequate consideration has been supplied.

The notion of 'consideration' was reviewed in *Hogan v DPP*.[196] Irwin J, providing the leading judgment of the Divisional Court, noted that, in relation to the question of the adequacy of the consideration, good faith is irrelevant: consequently, if a purchaser pays the full value for stolen goods, he will not have committed an offence under section 329.[197] It was held that the burden fell upon the prosecution to prove either that no consideration was paid or that, if it was, it was not adequate; this was so regardless of whether the accused knew or suspected that the object represented the proceeds of crime.[198] Irwin J suggested that, if the burden were placed on the defence instead, it would not accord with the language of the Act and it would erode the presumption of innocence to which all defendants are entitled under Article 6(2) of the European Convention.[199]

The decision in *Hogan v DPP* appears reasonable where the transaction involves ordinary commodities (as in the case itself, which was concerned with stolen scaffolding). It means that, in the ordinary conduct of business, buyers are not expected to enquire about the source of the money or the provenance of the goods in order to avoid a conviction under section 329. Nevertheless, it can be argued that the position is highly unsatisfactory where unique or special items, such as cultural artefacts, are involved and where it can be argued that purchasers should be expected to take care in investigating their provenance. Even so, it is always open to the prosecution, upon finding that a person is in possession of a stolen cultural artefact, to challenge whether the consideration is 'adequate'. Cultural objects with a full and satisfactory provenance command exceptionally high prices on the open market: it is likely that any surreptitious purchase of cultural property will be at a price which is 'significantly less than the value of the use or possession' of the object, and will thus fall foul of section 329(3)(b) of the Act. Furthermore, a dealer could be charged with a different money laundering offence in addition, if the facts will support it. If a dealer had disguised the object, for example, he could be charged with an offence under section 327.

In summary, there does not appear to be a requirement that, because the accused is a purchaser, the only possible charge is under section 329. For example, a charge under section 328 would appear appropriate where the accused purchases looted cultural objects and places them in a container and completes the bill of lading or other shipping documents with a false description relating to the contents, in order to import them into the UK. Indeed, if dishonesty can be shown, the accused could also be charged with handling stolen goods. There might also be the possibility of a charge for the offence set out in the Dealing in Cultural Objects (Offences) Act 2003, discussed below.[200]

3.41 Defence: Authorised Disclosure

An important defence is supplied for each principal money laundering offence by sub-section (2)(a) of sections 327, 328 and 329.[201] These sub-sections provide that a person

[196] *Hogan v DPP* [2007] EWHC 978 (DC).

[197] ibid [17].

[198] ibid [27].

[199] Art 6(2) is set out in Sch 1 to the Human Rights Act 1998 and provides: 'Everyone charged with a criminal offence shall be presumed innocent until proved guilty according to law.'

[200] See 3.55.

[201] Law enforcement authorities enjoy a further defence under sub-section of POCA 2002, sub-s (2)(c) of ss 327–29, when carrying out their enforcement functions.

does not commit an offence if he makes an 'authorised disclosure'. According to section 338, an authorised disclosure is one made to the relevant authorities either before an offence is committed or afterwards, if there is a good reason for the delay. Once a person becomes suspicious, he should therefore make a disclosure as soon as possible either to the Money Laundering Reporting Officer within his organisation or to the relevant authority, which is currently the Serious Organised Crime Agency (SOCA).[202] SOCA is due to be replaced by the National Crime Agency (NCA) in 2013.

If an expert in the field is asked to undertake research on the provenance of an article, he should make a report to SOCA as soon as he begins to have any doubts over the apparent owner's title.[203] After making an authorised disclosure, the discloser[204] should not take any further steps for a period of seven days from the next working day after the disclosure is made. This is known as the 'notice period'.[205] SOCA must make a decision within this period. If consent is received from SOCA, the discloser can go ahead with any arrangement or transaction. If the discloser hears nothing within the notice period, the discloser will be treated as having received authorised consent at the end of the period.[206] If, however, SOCA refuses consent, it has a limited time in which to pursue the matter further by seeking a restraint order.[207] There is a moratorium period of 31 days starting with the day on which the person receives the refusal notice;[208] after that time, the transaction may proceed.[209] If these statutory requirements relating to authorised disclosures and appropriate consents are satisfied, there is no risk that an offence will be committed. Individuals will be protected not only in relation to the principal money laundering offences (ss 327-29) but also in relation to the offence of 'tipping-off'[210] and the offence of 'prejudicing an investigation'.[211]

3.42 Care and Conservation: the Position of Restorers

In earlier times, the main objective was to maintain an object so that it was preserved for posterity. Yet, where restoration work has been carried out, it may become difficult to distinguish a genuine object from a fake by determining the date of its creation.[212] Furthermore, restoration work can result in the removal of features which would accurately identify an object's provenance. For example, in 1990, it was estimated that 80 per cent of all antiquities coming onto the market had been illegally excavated.[213] It may be impossible to investigate their past if subtle signs of their illegal excavation, such as surface accretions including deposits from the burial environment, have been obliterated.[214] There

[202] In relation to SOCA's establishment and general functions, see the Serious Organised Crime and Police Act 2005.

[203] See eg *Spencer v S Franses Ltd* [2011] EWHC 1269 [212].

[204] By POCA 2002, s 339(5), the discloser is the person making a disclosure under ibid, ss 330, 331, 332 or 338.

[205] ibid, s 335(5).

[206] ibid, s 335(3).

[207] For discussion of restraint orders, see 4.07.

[208] POCA 2002, s 336(8).

[209] ibid, s 335(4).

[210] An individual must not 'tip off' a person where an authorised disclosure has been made and he knows or suspects that a money laundering investigation is being carried out which might be prejudiced: ibid, s 333.

[211] An individual must not make a disclosure which he knows or suspects will prejudice an investigation into money laundering, confiscation or civil recovery proceedings: ibid, s 342.

[212] *Thomson v Christie Manson & Woods Ltd* [2004] EWHC 1101 [147].

[213] G Norman, 'Great Sale of the Centuries' *The Independent* (24 November 1990).

[214] KW Tubb, 'Ethical Considerations in Conservation' (1997) II(1) *Art Antiquity and Law* 41, 43. See further, DA Scott, 'An Examination of the Patina and Corrosion Morphology of Some Roman Bronzes' (1994) 33 *Journal of the American Institute for Conservation* 1.

is a serious risk that a process of 'conservation' will be used as the last step in the money laundering process.[215]

What if a private owner instructs a conservator to clean and restore an object? At one time, as the conservator would have a contract with the owner, the owner's instructions would have been obeyed automatically. But attitudes have changed. It is now increasingly appreciated that the work of archaeological conservators should involve not only care of an object but also information retrieval. Professional bodies take a leading role in emphasising the importance of contextual information and the need to behave ethically. For example, the Institute for Conservation (ICON) asserts that archaeological conservators are trained to have the knowledge, skills and equipment to preserve the historical record and its website directs readers to the Treasure Act 1996.[216] The International Centre for the Study of the Preservation and Restoration of Cultural Property (ICCROM) is dedicated to the preservation of the cultural heritage of all mankind, and is concerned with research into internationally agreed sets of ethics.[217]

The principal money laundering offences created by the Proceeds of Crime Act 2002 mesh with these ethical concerns. Conservators who remove the specks of soil and other debris from an object of antiquity which might have assisted in identifying its original location, and ignore the possibility that it might have been looted, run the risk of being prosecuted for assisting in disguising the source of the object, contrary to section 327(3) of the Proceeds of Crime Act. These offences, and the special criminal statutes which focus upon those in possession of cultural objects, should have the effect of altering the behaviour of all conservators, not merely those operating in the field of archaeology. In short, the law and ethics have begun to converge in this area. Conservation work should be recorded in writing. This is part of a bigger picture where all participants in the market will expect there to be a paper trail for recent transactions in relation to the care and custody of an object. This information will mean that the object will obtain the best price on the open market; it will also serve to discourage the trade in stolen property.

3.43 Academics and the Principal Money Laundering Offences

In the past, academic archaeologists and others were commonly approached to provide expert information in relation to an antiquity which had no provenance. From an academic perspective, this would be a golden opportunity to carry out research and perhaps to publish a paper discussing the antiquity. Unfortunately, academics have been exploited by unscrupulous dealers in possession of objects which in all probability have been looted. The dealer may not trust his seller, and the academic could be used to provide much needed reassurance, in a market where forgeries abound,[218] that the object was genuine rather than a forgery. An academic may also be able to confirm that the object is not officially recorded as stolen, enabling the dealer to confidently present an object as genuine, so that one more looted item can make its successful debut in the market.

[215] R Elia, 'Conservators and Unprovenanced Objects: Preserving the Cultural Heritage or Servicing the Antiquities Trade' in KW Tubb (ed), *Antiquities: Trade or Betrayed: Legal, Ethical and Conservation Issues* (1995) 244.

[216] See www.icon.org.uk and its conservation website on archaeological materials.

[217] See www.iccrom.org/eng.

[218] In relation to forgeries, see J Ulph, 'Markets and Responsibilities: Forgeries and the Sale of Goods Act 1979' (2011) *Journal of Business Law* 261.

An academic's opinion can assist in establishing an object's historical context, thereby enhancing its commercial value. Academic research of objects, such as Egyptian stelae[219] or manuscripts from Afghanistan,[220] can have the unfortunate effect of stimulating demand in the market for items of that type. In response, there may be widespread looting to satisfy this new demand. Many archaeologists now refuse to publish papers on objects if there is a possibility that they have been looted.[221] Article 2 of the Archaeological Institute of America's Code of Ethics exhorts its members to refuse to participate in any activity which enhances the commercial value of undocumented antiquities. A similar statement can be found in Article 1.6 of the European Association of Archaeologists' Code of Practice. However, other academics defend research carried out on unprovenanced items, on the basis that academic study promotes knowledge and scholarship which benefit the public as a whole; it is suggested that to restrict such research is akin to censorship.[222]

The principal money laundering offences created by the Proceeds of Crime Act 2002 can be said to partly meet these ethical concerns. Those academics who, in carrying out research on behalf of a client, assist in validating an object of antiquity could be charged with an offence under section 328 of the Proceeds of Crime Act: they may be accused of becoming concerned in an arrangement which they know or suspect facilitates the use of criminal property by another person. Consequently, if an academic agrees to carry out research on an object without any provenance, he should make an authorised disclosure to SOCA if he is suspicious.[223] But he must not make the client aware of this disclosure, because the academic might be guilty of 'tipping off' in these circumstances. If the academic has not heard anything by the end of the notice period, the research may proceed – without contravening the law.

The fact that academics should become familiar with making this type of disclosure to SOCA should make them far more conscious of the risks which they run in handling unprovenanced works of art or antiquities. However, avoiding criminal liability may not be their only concern. Suppose an academic suspects that an object lent by a client is looted, and makes an authorised disclosure? There is no certainty that the client will be prosecuted. SOCA may decide not to proceed either with criminal charges or with a civil recovery order[224] for various reasons, such as evidential difficulties. In this situation, the academic must return the object to its apparent owner,[225] regardless of his suspicions. This is not a satisfactory result for any academic who does not wish to become involved in the illicit trade in cultural property, even indirectly by taking temporary possession of an object before returning it.[226] On balance, it would appear advisable for academics to refuse to deal with objects which lack information regarding provenance.

[219] B Meier and M Gottlieb, 'LOOT: Along the Antiquities Trail, An Illicit Journey Out of Egypt, Only a Few Questions Asked' *New York Times* (23 February 2004).

[220] N Brodie, 'Consensual Relations? Academic Involvement in the Illegal Trade in Ancient Manuscripts' in S Mackenzie and P Green (eds), *Criminology and Archaeology: Studies in Looted Antiquities* (Oxford, Hart Publishing, 2009) 45, 49.

[221] ITAP Report Annex A [47].

[222] J Boardman, 'Archaeologists, Collectors and Museums' in J Cuno (ed), *Whose Culture? The Promise of Museums and the Debate over Antiquities* (Priceton NJ, Princeton University Press, 2009) 107.

[223] In relation to authorised disclosure, see 3.40. Note that SOCA is due to be replaced by the National Crime Agency in 2012.

[224] In relation to civil recovery orders, see 4.20–4.22. See further, S Young, *Civil Forfeiture of Criminal Property: Legal Measures for Targeting the Proceeds of Crime* (Cheltenham, Edward Elgar, 2009).

[225] The academic could be sued for conversion if he refuses to transfer it. As regards liability in conversion, see 5.09–5.13.

[226] See the discussion of the Schoyen Aramaic incantation bowls, which University College London was obliged to return to the apparent owner, by N Brodie, 'Consensual Relations? Academic Involvement in the Illegal Trade in Ancient Manuscripts' in Mackenzie and Green, *Criminology and Archaeology* (2009) 54–55.

3.44 Reporting Suspicious Transactions

There are certain typical stages in the money laundering process. The first stage is 'placement'. If money has been stolen, for example, it may be paid into a bank account. The second stage in the process is 'layering', which refers to the series of dealings designed to conceal its origins, as the money is moved between accounts in order to create layers of transactions. 'Integration' is the final stage: the money is legitimised by being invested in shares, for example, or used to purchase an item or service. The same process of movement and concealment will be used for stolen objects. A history will be built up as they pass from one dealer to another by way of purchase or loan.

It is easier to detect money laundering at the earlier stages. Consequently, additional measures exist which are intended to detect money laundering and to support the principal money laundering offences. There are important obligations which are imposed upon a large number of businesses (the 'regulated sector'[227]). These businesses include not only financial institutions, lawyers and accountants, but also dealers in 'high value' goods, such as precious metals, or objects of antiquity or works of art. Dealers in art and antiquities are therefore affected by these money laundering measures if their business involves:

> the trading in goods (including dealing as an auctioneer) whenever a transaction involves the receipt of a payment or payments in cash of at least 15,000 euros in total, whether the transaction is executed in a single operation or in several operations which appear to be linked, by a firm or sole trader who by way of business trades in goods.[228]

By section 330 of the Proceeds of Crime Act 2002,[229] dealers and other professionals working in the regulated sector must report suspicious property and financial transactions as soon as is practicable, where this information has come to them in the course of their business. They must make these reports if they know or have reasonable grounds to suspect that someone is engaged in money laundering and can identify the person or the whereabouts of any of the laundered property, or where they believe (or it is reasonable to expect them to believe) that the information will assist in identifying that other person or the whereabouts of any of the laundered property.[230]

A failure to make a report is an offence. The test is objective: an offence can be committed where the accused is merely negligent (as opposed to reckless). There is a risk that professionals who are honest but do not have efficient systems for detecting money laundering could be convicted. If an employee makes a report to a firm's nominated officer for receiving reports, this officer must take care to avoid committing an offence by failing to disclose information.[231]

Various defences are available. In relation to international criminal activity,[232] it is a defence that the relevant conduct was known or believed to have occurred overseas and was

[227] POCA 2002, Sch 9, as substituted by Proceeds of Crime Act 2002 (Business in the Regulated Sector and Supervisory Authorities) Order 2007, SI 2007/3287, with effect from 15 December 2007.

[228] ibid, Sch 9, Pt 1(1)(q) as amended by SI 2007/3287. Certain high value dealers with a low turnover are excluded: ibid, Pt 1(2).

[229] As amended by the Serious Organised Crime and Police Act 2005.

[230] POCA 2002, s 330(3A), as amended by the Serious Organised Crime and Police Act 2005, s 104. But they will commit an offence if they 'tip off' their client: See further, ibid, s 333.

[231] ibid, ss 331, 332. It should be noted that, according to ibid, s 332, the test is a subjective one of 'knows or suspects' in relation to nominated officers who are not employed in the regulated sector.

[232] See further, 3.41.

legal under local law.[233] In relation to sections 330 or 331, the accused can plead that he had a reasonable excuse for not reporting a transaction or that he has disclosed the matter to the authorities and obtained their consent.[234] However, the Act actively encourages reporting because those who report and obtain consent are protected: they cannot be convicted of a money laundering offence governed by sections 327–29. Moreover, by section 337, their clients cannot sue them for breach of confidence. These new measures are intended to deter professionals who might otherwise be tempted to turn a blind eye to the suspicious conduct of their clients. They support the main money laundering offences, helping to curb criminal activity and organised crime. The effect of these measures is to encourage transparency in commercial dealings.[235] Inevitably, there is a price to be paid both in terms of a loss of confidentiality in relationships[236] and in economic terms, as professionals who are involved in financial transactions are transformed into unpaid detectives.

The fact that the prosecution merely has to show that a dealer or other has been negligent in failing to make a report is significant. There is a danger that someone who receives an object could be accused of a failure to report even where there may not be enough evidence of knowledge or suspicion to convict him of a money laundering offence.

3.45 The Money Laundering Regulations 2007

Money laundering regulations have existed since 1993.[237] These regulations required financial institutions to establish identification procedures ('know your client' procedures) which might involve checking passports and demanding evidence that an address is authentic. Internal monitoring systems also had to be established so that suspicious transactions, which might indicate that a client was involved in money laundering, could be identified. Initially the measures only applied to financial institutions but were extended to a wide range of professionals in the regulated sector. From 2003,[238] these regulations were applied to auctioneers and dealers in 'high value' goods who receive cash of at least 15,000 euros in respect of a transaction.[239] High value dealers in goods may now need to register with the authorities and to follow additional guidelines provided.[240] The requirement that dealers and auctioneers should establish identification and verification procedures is acknowledged in the CoPat Due Diligence Code for Dealers.

The current law can be found in the Money Laundering Regulations 2007, which came into force on 15 December 2007. The 2007 Regulations implemented the European Third

[233] POCA 2002, ss 330(7A), 331(6A) and 332(7).

[234] In relation to defences, see sub-ss (6) and (7) to POCA 2002, ss 330, 331, as amended by the Serious Organised Crime and Police Act 2005.

[235] *Kurtha v Marks* [2008] EWHC 336 [140]; see also *Rachmaninoff v Sotheby's and Eva Teranyi* [2005] EWHC 258 [35]. See further, NE Palmer, 'Keeping the score: the Rachmaninoff claim and the circumspection of auction houses' (2005) X(3) *Art Antiquity and Law* 317.

[236] For further discussion of the tension between transparency and confidentiality, see NE Palmer, 'Adrift on a Sea of Troubles: Cross-Border Art Loans and the Spectre of Ulterior Title' (2005) 38 *Vanderbilt Journal of Transnational Law* 947.

[237] The Money Laundering Regulations 1993, SI 1993/1933.

[238] See the Money Laundering Regulations 2003, SI 2003/3075, which replaced the Money Laundering Regulations 2001, SI 2001/3641.

[239] In the Money Laundering Regulations 2007, SI 2007/2157, 'high value dealers' are defined by reg 3(12) as 'a firm or sole trader who by way of business trades in goods (including an auctioneer dealing in goods), when he receives, in respect of any transaction, a payment or payments in cash of at least 15,000 euros in total, whether the transaction is executed in a single operation or in several operations which appear to be linked.'

[240] In relation to registering with HM Revenue and Customs, see Notice MLRB Registration Guide for High Value Dealers, February 2011, or visit the HMRC website.

Money Laundering Directive of 26 October 2005.[241] The Directive set out fresh measures to combat money laundering, which took account of the revised recommendations made by the Financial Action Task Force (FATF) in 2012. FATF had expressed concern that money launderers created facades, either using shell companies or trusts, to conceal their activities. The Directive tackled this problem by demanding that professionals in the regulated sector should establish procedures to identify the true beneficial owners of property.

The definition of 'beneficial owner' proved particularly difficult for those drafting the UK regulations. It is, of course, vital that terms such as this one are clear, so that people can comply with the law and avoid committing an offence.[242] Regulation 6(1) of the Money Laundering Regulations 2007 provides that, in relation to companies, the beneficial owner is the person who owns or controls more than 25 per cent of the shares or voting rights in the company. In relation to trusts, by regulation 6(3), a beneficial owner is anyone who has control of the trust or anyone who is the beneficiary of 25 per cent or more of the trust capital or, where there are no people with existing equitable interests in capital, 'the class of persons in whose main interest the trust is set up or operates.'

It is quite common to give someone else possession of a tangible object on a temporary basis. The object will be on loan: this is known as a bailment, and the recipient has possession but not ownership. This is analytically quite different from a trust, where legal title is transferred to the trustee and the beneficiary has an equitable interest.[243] However, regulation 6 of the 2007 Regulations does not expressly cover loans. This may have been due to a concern to target inter-bank transfers. Suppose that an object is deposited with an auction house for sale but it is agreed that, if it fails to sell, another person will take possession of it? Although this arrangement might seem odd, it may be the case that high value dealers, including auction houses, do not need to concern themselves with the question of why a customer appears to be acting under the direction of others. On the other hand, the concept of a 'beneficial owner' is drafted sufficiently widely by Regulation 6(6) to include those who 'benefit' from an entity or arrangement. Regulation 6(9) adds: 'In any other case, "beneficial owner" means the individual who ultimately owns or controls the customer or on whose behalf a transaction is being conducted.' It is therefore at least arguable that loans of tangible objects are caught by the regulations. The CoPat Due Diligence Code for Dealers appears to reflect this viewpoint: it is provided that dealers should ask the seller to confirm that the object belongs to him and is his 'unencumbered property'.

Dealers, auctioneers and others should make enquiries whenever they doubt 'the veracity or adequacy of documents, data or information previously obtained';[244] they must also continue to monitor transactions.[245] The CoPat Due Diligence Code for Dealers provides the example of where the asking price for an object does not equate to its market value; the Code suggests that, in this situation, a dealer should be suspicious, and should report the matter to the police.

More broadly, the 2007 Regulations expect dealers and other professionals in the regulated sector to carry out checks which are proportionate to the risks presented. They must therefore carry out identification checks on customers with different levels of scrutiny

[241] Directive 2005/60/EC on the prevention of the use of the financial system for the purpose of money laundering and terrorist financing (European Third Money Laundering Directive).

[242] If a principle of law is not stated with sufficient precision to enable people to regulate their conduct, it will not be Convention compatible: *Commission v Italy* [1988] ECR 3249 [12].

[243] *MCC Proceeds Inc v Lehman Brothers International (Europe)* [1998] 4 All ER 675 (CA).

[244] MLA 2007, reg 7(1)(d).

[245] MLA 2007, reg 8.

according to the business profile of the customer.[246] Certain categories of customer present higher risks than normal, such as those who have held important political positions. Professionals are expected to obtain information regarding their customers which is sufficient in the circumstances, with an understanding of those occasions on which more rigorous ('enhanced') or simplified due diligence processes might be appropriate.[247]

The regulations should create greater transparency in commercial transactions. A blanket of obscurity in relation to control of an object assists those dealing in stolen or looted cultural objects. As Tugendhat J remarked in *Rachmaninoff v Sotheby's and Eva Teranyi*:[248]

> There is a dark side to the confidentiality surrounding the identity of an auctioneer's principal. The public and the law have increasingly come to recognise the potential for abuse by criminals of works of art, and of those who deal in them (consciously or unconsciously), for money laundering, and for disposing of the proceeds of crime. The less the legal risks involved in committing a work for auction, the more attractive the market in works of art and manuscripts becomes for criminals. The policy of the law, both in this jurisdiction and elsewhere, is to look more sceptically than would have been proper in the past upon those who have very valuable property for which they have no provenance.

These Regulations help to reinforce the provisions of the Proceeds of Crime Act, particularly in relation to monitoring and reporting suspicious transactions, but may be costly for high-value dealers to administer. Nevertheless, the European Commission has suggested that their scope could be extended further to include dealers involved in smaller cash transactions.[249]

3.46 Relationship Between Handling and Money Laundering

The law relating to money laundering and handling stolen goods is intended to penalise those who encourage and stimulate criminal activity.[250] These offences are separate from the original offence, such as theft. In relation to handling, section 22(1) of the Theft Act expressly provides that the offence is committed 'otherwise than in the course of stealing'. Much will depend upon the facts: if two or more people combine and carry out a theft, they are all thieves; in contrast, if one steals property and then asks another (X) to take care of the stolen property, X will be a handler rather than a thief. Where there is insufficient evidence to prove that the accused stole the property, the accused may be charged instead with handling.[251] The divide between theft and handling is reinforced in section 22(1) by the statement that the retention, removal, disposal or realisation of the property must be 'by or for the benefit of another person'. The original thief cannot therefore also be characterised as a handler because the thief will be acting for his own benefit in transferring property to another (who might be either a handler or an innocent purchaser).

246 Member States could exempt certain institutions that carry on business on an occasional or limited basis: see the Money Laundering Regulations 2007, SI 2007/2157, reg 2(7) and Sch 2, para 1.

247 In relation to simplified due diligence, see the Money Laundering Regulations 2007, SI 2007/2157, reg 9; in relation to enhanced due diligence, including politically exposed persons, see ibid, regs 11(5) and 14(1)(b), Sch 2.

248 *Rachmaninoff v Sotheby's and Eva Teranyi* [2005] EWHC 258 [35]. See further, *Kurtha v Marks* [2008] EWHC 336 [140]; NE Palmer, 'Keeping the score: the Rachmaninoff claim and the circumspection of auction houses' (2005) X(3) *Art Antiquity and Law* 317.

249 European Commission Report on the Application of Directive 2005/60/EC on the Prevention of the Use of the Financial System for the Purpose of Money Laundering and Terrorist Financing. Brussels. 11.04.12. at p 5.

250 In relation to handling, see *R v Bloxham* [1983] AC 109 (HL).

251 *Ryan and French v DPP* [1994] Crim LR 457 (CA); *AG of Hong Kong v Yip Kai-Foon* [1988] AC 642 (PC); *R v Cash* [1985] QB 801 (CA). See further, *R v Bellman* [1989] AC 836 (HL); *R v Shelton* [1986] 83 Cr App R 379 (CA).

A person cannot be charged with handling unless an offence has already been committed: the goods must be 'stolen' (or obtained by blackmail or fraud). Similarly, a money laundering offence depends upon a 'predicate' offence, such as theft, fraud or other serious crime, which will result in property being categorised as 'criminal property' for the purposes of a money laundering offence. In relation to stolen art and antiquities, the position should be straightforward. If an object has been stolen, it is criminal property; the same is true of the proceeds of sale. Anyone dealing with the object or any property which represents the proceeds of crime is vulnerable to prosecution for a money laundering offence as well as handling stolen goods.

Good faith purchasers cannot be convicted of handling stolen goods or money laundering, because they do not have the *mens rea* needed to be convicted of either offence. They also receive express statutory protection.[252] Furthermore, a good faith purchaser cannot be accused of handling, because he is not seeking to benefit the thief and is therefore not acting 'for the benefit of another person'. In contrast, a bad faith purchaser will be acting for the benefit of the thief by paying for stolen items.[253]

Both offences are concerned with those who conceal or retain property. The offences also cover arrangements to receive or retain. Nevertheless, the scope of the principal money laundering offences appears far wider and more flexible: for example, section 328 may well extend to include conspiracies. Since its enactment, the Crown Prosecution Service has increasingly chosen to bring charges under the Proceeds of Crime Act for a principal money laundering offence, rather than prosecuting criminals for handling stolen goods under section 22 of the Theft Act 1968.[254] The sentence of a maximum of 14 years' imprisonment is the same regardless of whether the conviction is for handling or money laundering. One reason for doing so is that it is easier to secure a conviction under the Proceeds of Crime Act by proving that the accused knew or suspected that the property constituted or represented a benefit from criminal conduct. In contrast, a successful prosecution of the handling offence depends upon proof that the accused handled the goods 'knowing or believing' them to be stolen and mere suspicion is insufficient. However, the most significant difference between the money laundering provisions and other criminal offences is the fact that there is no need to show that the accused had a dishonest intent. It is therefore easier to prosecute someone who has received property or who has been caught up in a property transaction for a money laundering offence.

VII Bribery

3.47 Introduction

The UK is a signatory to a number of international instruments which combat corruption, although the main impetus for the Bribery Act 2010 was the OECD Convention on Combating Bribery of Public Officials 1997 (the OECD Anti-Bribery Convention).[255] The Bribery Act 2010, which came into force on 1 July 2011, is intended to contribute to these international efforts by promoting high ethical standards in business dealings. The Act has

252 See the Theft Act 1968, s 3(2); POCA 2002, s 329(2)(c).
253 *R v Deakin* [1972] 1 WLR 1618 (CA).
254 *R v Christopher Thompson* [2010] EWCA Crim 1216.
255 See 2.43. See also the UN Convention on Corruption of 2003, discussed in 2.42.

swept away England's earlier legislation on bribery.[256] However, as the Act is not retrospective, there may still be prosecutions going forward under the old law. The new Act created two core offences relating to the provision and acceptance of a bribe. There is a new discrete offence of bribing foreign officials. In addition, a commercial organisation may commit an offence if it fails to prevent its employees from engaging in bribery.

3.48 Paying and Receiving a Bribe

The Bribery Act 2010 created two core offences where a person offers a bribe ('active bribery') or receives a bribe ('passive bribery').[257] The prosecution is *not* obliged to show that a person accused of giving a financial advantage or receiving it is dishonest or corrupt. Instead, the mental ingredient required is more neutral and, depending upon the offence, consists of intention, knowledge or belief.

The Act provides six scenarios where the accused will be prosecuted. Either or both the briber and the bribee may face prosecution. The first two cases are concerned with the briber (active bribery) and are dealt with in section 1 of the Act. First, an offence will be committed where the accused offers, promises or gives a financial or other advantage with the intention that it will induce a person (not necessarily the recipient of the advantage) to 'improperly' carry out a 'relevant function or activity', or where the advantage is intended as a reward for his improper performance. The second case is where the accused knows or believes that the acceptance of this advantage would itself constitute an improper performance of a relevant function or activity.[258]

The other four situations, which are listed in section 2, deal with recipients of bribes (passive bribery). Case 3 is concerned with a situation where the accused requests, agrees to receive, or accepts an advantage with the intention that a 'relevant function or activity' should be performed 'improperly' (whether by the recipient or some other individual).[259] Cases 4 to 6 are concerned with situations where the bribee's acceptance of the advantage would in itself constitute an improper performance of a function or activity, or where the bribee requests, agrees to receive or accepts an advantage as a reward or where he improperly performs in anticipation of an advantage. In these last three cases, it does not matter whether the accused was aware that the performance would be improper or not.[260]

The offences deal with situations where the bribe will have an impact on someone's performance of a 'relevant function or activity'. This includes work as an agent or an employee, regardless of whether the activities being carried out are of a public or private nature.[261] An offence may be committed where the person is expected to act otherwise than in good faith, or in an impartial manner, or in accordance with a position of trust.[262]

In essence, the Bribery Act is concerned with relationships between the parties involved in a transaction and its context. It will promote ethical conduct in transacting. Its provisions may make employees, agents, and any other person who is expected to act in good faith or

[256] The previous law, consisting of offences created by the common law and the Prevention of Corruption Acts 1889–1916, was widely seen as complex and inadequate. For the background, see the Law Commission, *Reforming Bribery* (Law Com No 13, 2008).

[257] It has been suggested that these provisions are largely similar in operation to the offences which they replace: G Sullivan, 'The Bribery Act 2010: Part 1: an Overview' (2011) *Criminal Law Reports* 87, 94.

[258] Bribery Act 2010, s 1.

[259] ibid, s 2(2).

[260] ibid, s 2(3).

[261] ibid, s 3(2).

[262] ibid, s 3(3)-(5).

impartially, more conscious of the need to comply with their obligations. It will have a general impact upon the art world. For example, sellers will need to take care to avoid committing an offence in paying 'finder's fees' to those who bring in new business. In ordinary circumstances, it is perfectly acceptable for sellers to pay their agents commission for enabling them to sell a painting or other object to a buyer. However, the Act will force sellers, buyers and dealers to consider the context in which the transaction is taking place. For example, if a seller pays a commission to an employee of the buyer, this may well be viewed as a bribe (unless the buyer is aware that a commission is being paid) because the employee would normally be viewed as in a position of trust.

In the context of the illicit trade in art and antiquities, it is important to note that the 'relevant function or activity' need not have any connection with the UK. Even so, 'improper performance' is judged against the expectation of what a reasonable person in the UK would expect[263] (and not by the local conditions in the country in which the bribe took place[264]). Thus, an offence may be committed where an English dealer bribes a local person in a source country (working for the police, customs or the port authorities, for example), to allow him to remove an antiquity and/or export it. A defence is available where the financial advantage is permitted according to written law of a particular country, but not if it is merely a local custom.[265] Consequently, it is not a defence to suggest that looting of a particular antiquity has become so widespread in a country that it is tolerated.

3.49 Bribery of a Foreign Public Official

This new offence will be committed where the prosecutor can establish that a person (either directly or through a third party) offers, promises or gives a financial or other advantage to a foreign public official (or to another person at the official's request, assent or acquiescence) with the intention of influencing that official and obtaining or retaining an advantage in the conduct of business, where the foreign public official was neither permitted nor required by law to be so influenced.[266] A 'foreign public official' is broadly defined by section 6, to include anyone exercising a public function who is the holder of any legislative, administrative or judicial position. Although a prosecutor may choose to bring a charge under the first of the core offences (paying a bribe) instead, the advantage of creating this separate offence is that its existence demonstrates the UK Government's commitment to its international treaty obligations to deter the bribery of public officials.[267]

If any public official is bribed to turn a blind eye to excavation of antiquities, or to allow an antiquity to be smuggled out of the country, the briber will almost inevitably commit an offence under this section. In 1992, Jonathan Tokeley Parry and an accomplice were investigated by Egyptian police who suspected that they were involved in illicit dealings in Egyptian antiquities. They allegedly paid bribes to certain corrupt members of the Egyptian antiquities police to ensure that their names were removed from police records.[268] If the facts were to be repeated now, there could be a prosecution for bribery of a public official under the Bribery Act 2010.

[263] ibid, s 4.
[264] ibid, s 5(1).
[265] ibid, s 5(2).
[266] Bribery Act 2010, s 6.
[267] OECD Convention on Combating Bribery of Foreign Public Officials in International Business Transactions (1997).
[268] See the main judgment in *United States v Schultz* 333 F 3d 393 (2d Cir 2003) 397.

3.50 Negligent Failure by a Commercial Organisation to Prevent Bribery

In the past, large organisations would usually avoid any responsibility for acts of bribery or corruption on the part of their representatives because of the difficulty in proving that the 'controlling mind' of the organisation possessed the requisite knowledge. The rules on attribution of knowledge would ordinarily mean that an organisation would only be guilty of an offence if senior managers were aware of a particular form of misconduct. However, the Bribery Act 2010 creates an exception in the context of bribery, representing a radical departure from existing law. A commercial organisation, such as a company or partnership or auction house, will be exposed to the risk of prosecution if it can be shown that it has negligently failed to put in place 'adequate procedures' to prevent bribes being paid by anyone performing services on its behalf.[269]

A commercial organisation can only be prosecuted for this offence if it can be shown that one of its representatives has been involved in bribery,[270] and it will only be vulnerable where it cannot bring forward evidence that adequate measures had been put in place to prevent this happening. Even so, this new offence caused consternation amongst traders generally, including those operating in the art markets. On 30 March 2011, the Secretary of State issued guidelines, as required by section 9 of the Act, detailing the measures which organisations could take to protect themselves from breaching the new law before it came into force on 1 July 2011. This gave organisations, such as auction houses, time to introduce new training procedures for employees.

The Ministry of Justice identified a number of general principles which have been carried through into the formal guidance.[271] These principles consist of: proportionality in terms of procedure, risk assessment, due diligence in terms of assessing the other parties to an agreement, monitoring transactions, and top-level commitment to ensuring that there is a culture amongst all employees and associates that business is to be conducted in an ethical manner. These principles appear familiar. The concept of proportionality underpins much of the human rights legislation. Risk assessment, due diligence, monitoring and reviewing transactions are all part of the legislative strategies in place to combat money laundering. However, interestingly, the Government rejected the argument that transparency should also be a guiding principle, accepting that a degree of privacy and confidentiality may be vital in commercial transactions.[272]

This new offence has some relevance in relation to deterring the illicit trade in cultural property because it will affect auction houses, art galleries and other commercial organisations operating in the art market. For example, if one of the representatives of a gallery (whether an employee, an agent or other intermediary) pays a bribe to facilitate the illicit removal and export of an object from another country (whether to a public official[273] or to a shipping agent), the organisation is vulnerable to prosecution.

[269] Bribery Act 2010, s 7.

[270] However, a successful prosecution of the representative is not a prerequisite as long as there is evidence to the criminal law standard: Bribery Act 2010: Joint Prosecution Guidance of the Director of the Serious Fraud Office and the Director of Public Prosecutions 10.

[271] Guidance about commercial organisations preventing bribery (section 9 of the Bribery Act 2010), CPR(R)/11, published on 31 March 2011, 14–15.

[272] ibid 15.

[273] As regards bribery of public officials to facilitate dealings in looted African art, see 'Repatriation of Cultural Property' in JH Merryman, AE Elsen and SK Urice (eds) *Law, Ethics and the Visual Arts*, 5th edn (The Netherlands, Kluwer Law International BV, 2007) 365.

3.51 The Global Reach of the New Legislation

The new legislation can be expected to have an important impact upon traders, not least because of its wide extra-territorial reach. As regards the core offences, or the offence of bribing a public official, there is a jurisdictional base where any element has occurred in the UK or alternatively where the accused has a close connection with the UK.[274] A close connection would include where a person is a British citizen, or is someone ordinarily resident in the UK, or is a company incorporated in the UK, regardless of where the act or omission which forms part of the offence took place. As regards the further offence of negligently failing to establish anti-corruption measures, any organisation incorporated in the UK or which has a business presence in the UK, may commit an offence as a result of its association with someone who is performing services on its behalf and who commits an offence of bribery, wherever that may occur.[275]

The penalties are severe: upon conviction, the maximum term of imprisonment for individuals will be 10 years, whilst both individuals and commercial organisations face unlimited fines. In response, large corporations will establish strict measures to combat corruption, and this emphasis upon ethical conduct in business may have a 'trickle down' effect to small firms and individuals.

VIII Fraud

3.52 The Fraud Act 2006

The Fraud Act 2006 came into force on 15 January 2007. It created a new broad statutory offence of fraud which is triggered by dishonesty.[276] Three offences are created, all of which are essentially concerned with deceit. Although the new set of offences replaces existing deception offences under the Theft Acts 1968 and 1978,[277] the common law offence of conspiracy to defraud was spared abolition through a concern to avoid creating a lacuna in the law.

The three offences created by the Fraud Act are fraud by false representation, fraud by failure to disclose and fraud by abuse of position. Each offence is concerned with the dishonesty of the accused and his intention to make a gain for himself or another, or cause a loss or create a risk of loss for another. There is no need for the prosecution to show the effect of the conduct of the accused upon the intended victim. Moreover, unlike the previous law, there is no need to show that the accused obtained a particular benefit.

If a seller takes an object illegally from its country of origin and attempts to conceal that fact by making false statements about its provenance or by providing false documents which he has created, he may be guilty of fraud by false representation under section 2 of the Act. This is equally true if the seller attempts to conceal his knowledge that others have illegally imported the object into the UK by deliberately misleading the buyer. In each case,

[274] Bribery Act 2010, s 12.

[275] ibid, s 7.

[276] The concept of dishonesty will involve the application of the much criticised *Ghosh* test: see 3.04.

[277] For the background, see Law Commission Consultation Paper, *Legislating the Criminal Code: Fraud and Deception* (Law Com No 155, 1999); Law Commission Report, *Fraud* (Law Com No 276, Cm 5560, 2002).

the seller would be motivated to make these false statements in order to obtain a benefit, namely an increase in the price.

There is a further offence of dishonest failure to disclose, where there is a legal obligation to do so. This offence is set out in section 3 of the Fraud Act and it may affect the way in which dealers in the art market operate. It has been common for dealers to suppress information about an object which would have a negative impact upon the price. Is a seller at risk of being charged with fraud by failing to disclose information in these circumstances? A prosecution may fail if the seller has merely kept silent in relation to the history of the object. It is possible to avoid conviction whilst behaving in a morally disreputable manner. If the seller has not made a false representation, then he cannot be charged with an offence under section 2. Although section 3 of the Act creates a further offence where there is a dishonest failure to disclose information which the accused is under a legal duty to disclose, this may not necessarily apply. Although dealers are guided by a code of due diligence, it does not impose a legal obligation upon sellers to divulge all the information in their possession. Although it has been argued that an obligation is imposed by section 12 of the Sale of Goods Act 1979 upon sellers to disclose an item's history,[278] this is by no means clear: section 12 implies a term that the seller should have a right to sell the goods in question and, if the seller is in breach of this section, he will be liable to return the price or pay damages. But, unlike insurance contracts where a duty of utmost good faith is demanded, this section does not impose an obligation to disclose.

The final offence, contained in section 4, is abuse of fiduciary position. Agents owe fiduciary duties to their principals. Consequently, if a purchasing agent was aware of the fact that an item was stolen but kept this information secret in order to claim his commission, he might be charged under this section.

3.53 Relationship between Fraud and Money Laundering

If someone obtains property by fraud and then passes it to someone else who is aware of the circumstances, that person can be prosecuted under section 329 for money laundering: the recipient will have acquired criminal property. However, prosecutors have attempted to bypass the Fraud Act altogether and to prosecute the principal fraudster for money laundering. It has been argued that, when money is received by the fraudster, it is 'criminal' property and the fraudster can be prosecuted under section 329.[279] However, it appears doubtful that a prosecution would succeed in this situation, which would widen the principal money laundering offences considerably. The mere fact that this is in issue demonstrates the attractions of prosecuting for money laundering rather than an offence which depends upon proof of dishonesty.

IX Exporting Cultural Objects

3.54 Exporting from the UK to Countries outside the EC: a Community Licence

If a person in possession of an object wishes to export it to a territory *outside* the European Community and that object falls within the definition of 'cultural goods' contained in an

[278] Fraud Advisory Panel, *Fraud Bill: Guidance for Industry*, April 2006.

[279] *R v Kausar* [2009] EWCA Crim 922; *R v Nawaz, R v Noreen* [2010] EWCA Crim 819 [13].

Annex to Council Regulation (EEC) No 116/2009,[280] then an application for an export licence (a 'Community Licence'[281]) must be made. The system of licensing is administered by the Export Licensing Unit at the Museums, Libraries and Archives Council on behalf of the Secretary of State for Culture, Olympics, Media and Sport.[282] A Community Licence is needed regardless of whether the export is on a permanent or temporary basis. This licence will be valid throughout the EU.[283] It may be general or specific and may be limited in time and/or subject to conditions.[284]

The current system of Community Licences was originally established in the wake of Council Regulation (EEC) No 3911/92.[285] However, a number of amendments were subsequently made and eventually the Regulation was replaced by Regulation 116/2009, which codified its provisions. The Export of Objects of Cultural Interest (Control) Order 2003 was amended to take account of this change.[286] The preamble to Council Regulation 116/2009 states that it is concerned to standardise export controls which Member States of the EC should apply at their external borders. It is intended to ensure that the seller has no incentive to move cultural goods from one EC country to another in order to take advantage of more liberal export laws.

The question of whether an object is caught by the definition of 'cultural goods' contained within Regulation 116/2009 is a significant one, because a failure to obtain a Community Licence can lead to prosecution. A list of 'cultural goods' which require a Community Licence can be found in the Annex to the Regulation which, given its importance, is set out at the end of this text. The specific requirements for each type of object vary according to criteria linked to age and value. As a general principle, objects must be over 50 years old; archaeological objects are an exception to this rule. If an object does not fall within the definition of 'cultural goods', it may still require an export licence under UK domestic law,[287] as discussed in the following paragraph.

3.55 UK Domestic Law Relating to Exports of Cultural Objects

Regulation 116/2009 will not be engaged if the goods are not 'cultural goods' within the meaning of the Regulation or, even if they are 'cultural goods', it is only proposed to export them to another Member State within the EC. In these situations, UK national law will apply instead. The Export of Objects of Cultural Interest (Control) Order 2003 provides that any object of 'cultural interest' will need an export licence issued on behalf of the Secretary of State for Culture, Media and Sport, for any destination except the Isle of

[280] OJ L39/1, Art 1.

[281] See the Export of Objects of Cultural Interest (Control) Order 2003, SI 2003/2759, art 1(2) and the European (Amendment) Act 2008, s 3(6).

[282] For the change in designation of the Secretary of State, see Secretary of State for Culture, Olympics, Media and Sport Order 2010, SI 2010/1551. Although many of the functions of the Museums, Libraries and Archives Council will be transferred to the Arts Council, guidance on export licensing could still be found on its website in January 2012 at www.mla.gov.uk.

[283] Regulation 116/2009, OJ L39/1, Art 2(3).

[284] Export of Objects of Cultural Interest (Control) Order 2003, SI 2003/2759, art 3(1).

[285] The Regulations was brought into effect by SI 1992/3092, which was subsequently replaced by the Export of Objects of Cultural Interest (Control) Order 2003, SI 2003/2759.

[286] The amendments were made by the Export of Objects of Cultural Interest (Control) (Amendment) Order 2009, SI 2009/2164 with effect from 28 August 2009. The order was made in exercise of the powers conferred on the Secretary of State by the Export Control Act 2002.

[287] Regulation 116/2009, OJ L39/1, Art 2(4).

Man.[288] 'Cultural interest' is defined by article 1(2) and Schedule 1 of the Export of Objects of Cultural Interest (Control) Order 2003 to include objects which are more than 50 years old (with certain limited exceptions, such as postage stamps, personal documents or objects created by the exporter or his family). Like Community Licences, these licences granted by the Secretary of State may be general or specific and may be subject to conditions.

3.56 National Treasures and the Waverley Criteria

There is an uneasy relationship between export controls and ownership. For example, some countries, such as Italy, make wide-ranging ownership claims and ban all exports from their countries. This might seem at odds with the general principle that goods should move freely within the European Community.[289] However, Article 30 EC lists various exceptions to this principle, one of which is 'the protection of national treasures possessing artistic, historic or archaeological value'.[290] This exception means that a Member State is entitled to define what it considers to be its national patrimony. The exception is construed narrowly because it is expressly provided that any prohibitions or restrictions must not 'constitute a means of arbitrary discrimination or a disguised restriction on trade between Member States.'[291] Regulation 116/2009 reinforces the exception contained within Article 30. The Preamble states that, although its definition of 'cultural goods' is intended to identify national treasures, it is not exhaustive, and that states are free to designate other objects in addition as worthy of special protection in relation to trade with third countries. Article 2 adds that an export licence may be refused where a cultural object is dealt with by national legislation which has designated it as a national treasure of artistic, historical or archaeological value.

In the UK, for many years restrictions have been in place to preserve national treasures.[292] As part of this earlier scheme of restrictions, a committee, under the chairmanship of Lord Waverley, was established to make recommendations on the control of the export of cultural property which might be of special national, historical or artistic interest.[293] As regards national treasures, three questions are posed (which became known as the 'Waverley criteria') to decide whether an object was of such importance that its export should not ordinarily be permitted.[294] The three criteria are as follows:

1 Is the object so closely connected with our history and national life that its departure would be a misfortune?
2 Is it of outstanding aesthetic importance?
3 Is it of outstanding significance for the study of some particular branch of art, learning, or history?

[288] In relation to forfeiture of illegally imported objects, see 4.06–4.07.

[289] See Arts 9 and 30–34 EC (prohibitions of quantitative restrictions on imports and exports and all measures having equivalent effect).

[290] Originally Art 36 of the Treaty of Rome 1957.

[291] *Commissioners of the EC v Italy* [1968] ECR 633 (ECJ).

[292] See the Import, Export and Customs Powers (Defence) Act 1939, now largely superseded by the Export Control Act 2002.

[293] *Report of the Committee on the Export of Works of Art, etc* (London, HMSO, 1952).

[294] The Quinquennial review set out a revised interpretation of the Waverley criteria by the Reviewing Committee on the Export of Works of Art on 8 December 2003: see guidance issued by the Department of Culture, Media and Sport in November 2005.

The Department for Culture, Media and Sport helpfully provided statutory guidance, *Export Controls on Objects of Cultural Interest*, in relation to the Waverley criteria in 2005. It was noted that, in relation to the first criterion, an object may be viewed as 'closely connected with our history and national life' despite the fact that it has been produced abroad. Examples are supplied in the guidance and include the deposit from the 'royal' ship burial at Sutton Hoo, the Royal Standard belonging to Sir Ernest Shackleton, and Captain Scott's sledging flag. As regards the second criterion, it was accepted that any judgement regarding an item's aesthetic importance would be subjective; examples included 'Venus and Adonis' by Titian, and a George III mahogany commode attributed to Thomas Chippendale. As regards the third criterion, the question of whether an object is significant for a branch of learning would be applied in a broad fashion to include anthropology, architecture and many other disciplines. The guidance provided examples such as mathematical instruments associated with Charles, Earl Stanhope, and a Hutton racing car.

An application for a Community Licence or an export licence under the Export of Objects of Cultural Interest (Control) Order 2003 may be referred to an expert adviser to consider whether it is of national importance according to the Waverley criteria set out above. The expert's views will be sent to the Reviewing Committee on the Export of Works of Art where an object is viewed as of national importance. If it is decided that the object satisfies one of these criteria, the application for an export licence will be temporarily deferred for a specified period in order to give public bodies time to raise the money to purchase it for a fair market price. The scheme is intended to be fair to an owner of a national treasure.[295] Consequently, if no offer is forthcoming at a fair market price, the export licence will eventually be granted. But, if an offer from a public body is made and refused, the export licence may be refused. If a museum or gallery is arranging a temporary loan, such as for the purposes of an exhibition, the application will not normally be referred to an expert adviser.[296]

3.57 Criminal Offences

The export licensing system can be said to contribute to reducing the illicit trade in cultural property in various ways. It provides a record of cultural objects which have been identified according to specified criteria, such as whether they are 'cultural goods' within the meaning of Regulation 116/2009. Furthermore, the system provides a check on the provenance of an object, making it more difficult for stolen objects to move in and out of the country freely. If an object is classified as a 'cultural good', within Regulation 116/2009, for example, a Community Licence can only be granted where the cultural object was 'lawfully and definitively located' within the territory of the Member State on 1 January 1993 or where it has been legally imported since that time.[297] A competent authority of a Member State will not issue a licence unless the object has a satisfactory provenance and will therefore ascertain whether, for example, there is evidence that the object was lawfully imported. A possessor

[295] In the context of an application to export Canova's marble statue, *The Three Graces, see R v Secretary of State for National Heritage, ex p J Paul Getty Trust* (CA, 27 October 1994). For further discussion, see J-F Canat and M Polonsky, 'The British and French Systems of Control of the Export of Works of Art' (1996) 45(3) *International and Comparative Law Quarterly* 557, 569–71.

[296] See UK Export Licensing for Cultural Goods: Procedures and Guidance for Exporters of Works of Art and other Cultural Goods (Museums, Libraries and Archives Council, 2009) [20].

[297] Council Regulation (EEC) No 116/2009.

of stolen cultural objects (and their agents[298]) will therefore be in some difficulty because, under article 2 of the Export of Objects of Cultural Interest (Control) Order 2003, it is prohibited to export an object without a licence where a Community Licence or other licence is needed.

In order to deter those tempted to make false statements about the provenance of an object in applying for a Community Licence, or a Licence under the Export of Objects of Cultural Interest (Control) Order 2003, the 2003 Order makes it an offence if the person has acted knowingly or recklessly in doing so.[299] A person will also commit an offence if he fails to comply with any condition attached to the licence.[300] For either offence, on summary conviction, the accused is liable to pay a fine of the prescribed sum; on conviction on indictment, the accused may be subject to a fine of any amount, or imprisonment for a term not exceeding two years, or to both penalties.

The Commissioners for Revenue and Customs have a duty to take such action as they consider appropriate to ensure the enforcement of the 2003 Order and of Council Regulation 116/2009 in respect of the export of cultural goods.[301] They may require, for example, information relating to the destination of cultural goods.[302] A failure to supply this information is an offence. On summary conviction, the accused is liable to pay a fine.[303] In practice, prosecutions are usually brought under section 68 of the Customs and Excise Management Act 1979, which provides more severe penalties. Under the 1979 Act, anyone knowingly involved (including agents) in exporting or shipping, or attempting to export or ship, goods in contravention of any legal prohibition or restriction, if convicted on indictment, will face a fine and/or imprisonment. The 1979 Act also provides for forfeiture of not only the goods but also the vehicle, ship or aircraft in specified circumstances.[304]

3.58 Forged Export Documents

In order to avoid export controls, a person in possession of a cultural object may choose to smuggle the object out (perhaps by disguising it as a tourist trinket) and hope to avoid detection in doing so. However, if an object is large or difficult to disguise, export documents may be forged instead.[305] In this situation, the government of the country of origin may be able to seek a declaration from an English court confirming that the export documents are forged, in order to avoid debasing the credibility of genuine documents.[306] If the cultural object has been exported from one member state in the European Union to another, its return can be sought by using the Return of Cultural Objects Regulations

[298] If a licence has not been issued, an agent must refuse to comply with instructions from his employer if they would involve him in committing an offence: *Garrett v Arthur Churchill (Glass) Ltd* [1970] 1 QB 92 (DC).

[299] SI 2003/2759, art 4. The licence is rendered void: art 4(2).

[300] ibid, art 5.

[301] ibid, art 7.

[302] 'Cultural goods' has the same meaning as that given in EC Regulation 116/2009 and the Export of Objects of Cultural Interest (Control) Order 2003, SI 2003/2759, art 1(2).

[303] SI 2003/2759, art 6.

[304] As regards forfeiture under the Customs and Management Excise Act 1979, see 4.06.

[305] See further, the Sevso Treasure, which involved forged Lebanese export documents, which is discussed in the ITAP Report (Report of the Ministerial Advisory Panel on Illicit Trade, Department for Culture, Media and Sport, December 2000) Annex A [41].

[306] In *Kingdom of Spain v Christie Manson and Woods* [1986] 1 WLR 1120, Sir Nicolas Browne-Wilkinson VC accepted that such an argument could be made, relying upon the decision in *Emperor of Austria v Day and Kossuth* (1861) 3 De GF & J 217.

1994.[307] In terms of the criminal law, the Export of Objects of Cultural Interest (Control) Order 2003 does not deal explicitly with forged documents. However, article 2 of the 2003 Order provides that: 'all objects are prohibited to be exported to any destination except under the authority of a licence in writing granted by the Secretary of State, and in accordance with all the conditions attached to the licence.' Article 7 adds that Customs and Excise Commissioners can take appropriate action under the Customs and Excise Management Act 1979 to secure the enforcement of the 2003 Order. Furthermore, if a person creates a forged licence, he is at risk of being prosecuted under the Fraud Act 2006, provided that it can be shown that he has acted dishonestly.

X Importing Cultural Objects

3.59 Import Duties

Smuggling goods will almost inevitably involve a criminal act. This is so even where the object being smuggled is an object of antiquity, where the source nation has not asserted ownership over such objects, and where the owner has given his consent. This is because there will usually be a violation of a tax law, such as customs duties and valued added tax. It is an offence to carry, harbour, deposit, keep, conceal, remove or deal in goods which are chargeable with duty which has not been paid with an intent to evade payment.[308] Goods which are improperly imported in breach of revenue laws are liable to forfeiture under section 49 of the Customs and Excise Management Act 1979.

Taxes, consisting of customs duties and value added tax, may be payable when goods are imported into the UK. Works of art are treated more generously in terms of tax when they are imported because it is recognised by the European Community that it is beneficial to support the international exchange of cultural and educational materials.[309] However, there is no general definition covering all types of cultural object in the relevant law; instead, there are sub-categories such as 'painting' or 'sculpture'. Even so, it is difficult to define in legal terms the intrinsic values contained within cultural objects. Courts understandably need guidance. This is particularly the case in relation to contemporary art, which embraces new artistic techniques. The decision of *Haunch of Venison Partners Ltd*[310] illustrates the importance of expert evidence in these circumstances. In the *Haunch of Venison* case, a commercial art gallery, Haunch of Venison, wished to import video installations (in a disassembled form) by Viola and a light sculpture by Flavin. The Inland Revenue argued that a video installation was not a sculpture, because it was not three-dimensional.[311] Haunch of Venison used expert witnesses to counter this argument: they suggested that the special way in which the digital equipment was customised, and Viola's precise installation instruc-

[307] See 5.08.
[308] Customs and Excise Management Act 1979, s 170(1)(b). See, for example, *R v White* [2010] EWCA Crim 978.
[309] See further, EC Council Regulation 918/83, OJ L105/1.
[310] *Haunch of Venison Partners Ltd*, Decision of the VAT and Duties Tribunal (London) of 8 December 2008.
[311] In *Reinhard Onnasch v Hauptzollamt Berlin-Packhof* C-155/84, sculptures had been referred to as three-dimensional. See further, *Brancusi v United States* [1928] TD 43063, US Customs Court, Third Division, 26 November 1928.

tions, demonstrated its three-dimensional qualities.[312] This expert evidence was accepted by the tribunal and it was held that, based on their objective characteristics, these objects were sculptures. The fact that they were disassembled for import did not affect this classification. Consequently, they could be imported into the UK as sculptures free of customs duty and subject to lower import value added tax.

The Inland Revenue had argued that there was a risk, if a generous approach was adopted in interpreting the law, that importers would be tempted to declare any object to be a work of art. The tribunal dismissed this fear as groundless. It was observed that importers would have to prove that the object was a work of art, relying upon the evidence of experts.[313] The case provides a useful illustration of the difficulty of defining cultural objects in legal terms and the administrative difficulties which may be created if there was an extensive system of import controls relating to cultural property.

3.60 The Dealing in Cultural Objects (Offences) Act 2003

In earlier times, there was no general criminal offence which covered smuggling goods that had been illegally exported from their source nation. The Return of Cultural Objects Regulations 1994,[314] which deal with imports of cultural objects that have been unlawfully removed from the territory of a Member State within the European Community, are concerned with civil recovery and do not create any criminal offences.[315]

In May 2000, the Secretary of State for the Department for Culture, Media and Sport (DCMS) established the Ministerial Advisory Panel on the Illicit Trade in Cultural Objects (ITAP) under the Chairmanship of Norman Palmer. ITAP was asked to consider the nature and extent of the illicit trade in art and antiquities and to advise upon how the UK could most effectively assist in preventing this trade. ITAP recommended the enactment of a statute which would make it an offence to dishonestly import, deal in or be in possession of any cultural object which had been stolen, or illegally excavated or removed, from any monument or wreck.[316] This recommendation led to the enactment of the Dealing in Cultural Objects (Offences) Act 2003, which is considered in detail below. However, it is important to note that it is not an offence under the 2003 Act to purchase an object where the sole objection is that it has been exported in contravention of the source nation's export legislation. The 2003 Act requires evidence that the object is 'tainted', in the sense that it has been unlawfully excavated or removed. The majority of the members of the ITAP panel baulked at extending the scope of criminal responsibility further, not least because certain source nations prohibit their citizens from exporting their own possessions if they are cultural items. It was thought that this type of legislative prohibition might be incompatible with Article 1 of the First Protocol, which guarantees a qualified right to enjoy one's own possessions, or might more broadly be too uncertain to be compatible with the rule of law.

[312] The Tate Modern erected similar installations by these artists for the benefit of the Tribunal. Haunch of Venison's witnesses included A Nairne, director of the National Portrait Gallery, M Caiger-Smith, programme leader at the Courtauld Institute of Art, and R Cumming, writer, lecturer and art critic: *Haunch of Venison Partners Ltd,* Decision of the VAT and Duties Tribunal (London) of 8 December 2008 [19].

[313] Decision of the VAT and Duties Tribunal (London) of 8 December 2008 [50].

[314] SI 1994/501.

[315] See 5.08 and 6.02.

[316] *Illicit Trade in Cultural Objects,* Report of the Ministerial Advisory Panel, London, December 2000 (hereafter ITAP Report) [67].

Furthermore, it is extremely difficult for dealers to obtain precise details of certain countries' export laws.[317]

3.61 No System of Inspection on Import

ITAP did not recommend the introduction of a system whereby all imported goods were inspected. This is sensible: most goods arrive in the UK in an anonymous form in a container. The work involved in attempting any inspection would be too immense to seriously contemplate. However, ITAP quite reasonably suggested that enforcement authorities could be given additional powers to search and seize objects which would be supported by additional resources.[318] This recommendation did not find its way into the new statute. However, enforcement authorities have been given wide powers in relation to serious crime in general. The Proceeds of Crime Act 2002 provided enforcement authorities with greater flexibility in prosecuting money laundering offences. HMRC was restructured: its Criminal Investigation Directorate was given greatly enhanced powers by the Serious Crime Act 2007.[319] It must also be borne in mind that there has been more scrutiny of imports in recent years because of concerns about serious organised crime and money laundering. One of the biggest challenges, however, is the lack of expertise amongst customs officers in relation to art and antiquities. There is no doubt that the fight against trafficking in cultural objects would have received a much-needed boost if ITAP's recommendation on powers and funding had been adopted.

XI Dealing in Cultural Objects (Offences) Act 2003

3.62 Background

The members of the Illicit Trade Advisory Panel (ITAP) recognised the importance of the criminal law in deterring the illicit trade in cultural property and accepted that ratification of the UNESCO Convention would not be enough by itself to deter this type of activity. There was concern that, where antiquities had been unlawfully excavated and removed, they could not necessarily be characterised as 'stolen', because they might not belong to anyone. If that was the case, anyone receiving those objects could not be accused of handling stolen goods. Yet this conduct needed to be stopped in order to protect vulnerable countries from being stripped of their antiquities. In order to tackle this problem, ITAP recommended that it should be a criminal offence to dishonestly import, deal in or be in possession of any cultural object which had been stolen, or illegally excavated or removed from any monument or wreck.[320] This recommendation was taken up, and the Dealing in Cultural Objects (Offences) Act 2003 was enacted.

[317] ibid [85].

[318] ibid [70].

[319] Serious Crime Act 2007, s 22 and Sch 12. See further, the Finance Act 2007, ss 82–86 and Sch 23, enabling customs officers to exercise the same powers as the police under the Police and Criminal Evidence Act 1984 (PACE).

[320] ITAP Report [67].

The members of ITAP were drawn from diverse backgrounds and included archaeologists who campaigned against the illicit trade in cultural objects, as well as dealers.[321] The ITAP Report in December 2000 might therefore be seen as representing a compromise between the various groups. For example, although the Report recommended accession to the UNESCO Convention on the Means of Prohibiting and Preventing the Illicit Import, Export and Transfer of Ownership of Cultural Property 1970, it rejected the proposal that the UK should ratify the UNIDROIT Convention, which was opposed by traders.[322]

The ITAP Report concluded that the UK could ratify the 1970 UNESCO Convention without the need for new legislation; however, the Report recommended that a criminal offence relating to trading in cultural objects should be created, which would complement the obligations contained in the UNESCO Convention. The Dealing in Cultural Objects (Offences) Act 2003 gave legislative effect to this recommendation.[323] The 2003 Act created the crime of dealing in a 'tainted' cultural object.[324]

3.63 Defining Cultural Objects

A cultural object is defined by section 2(1) of the Act as an object of historical, architectural or archaeological interest. It creates a single criminal offence and is designed to deter archaeological destruction. However, it does extend to cover theft of antiquities from museums and private properties. The definition of cultural object would cover works of art from earlier centuries, which may be of historical interest. According to DCMS Explanatory Notes on the Act, 'This is a wide definition and may cover a diversity of objects from structural, architectural and ornamental elements to portable artefacts of precious or base metal, ceramic, glass, stone or organic material.'[325] However, the Act is irrelevant if, for example, a contemporary work of art has been stolen, because objects of purely artistic interest do not fall within the scope of the Act. In addition to its Explanatory Notes, the DCMS also issued formal guidance in which they observe that: 'The new offence is likely to be of concern primarily to collectors, auctioneers and dealers in antiquities and architectural salvage rather than to fine art dealers.'[326]

3.64 Tainted Cultural Objects

A cultural object must be 'tainted' to fall within the scope of the Act. An object will be tainted in two sets of circumstances.[327] The first situation is where the object is excavated and this is illegal in the place where it occurred. The DCMS Explanatory Notes on the Act observe that, 'an excavation may refer to any site under archaeological investigation, including areas containing such artefact-rich deposits as votive offerings, cemeteries and graves, production sites, battlefields or encampments.'

[321] For critical discussion of whether dealers exerted too much influence, see S Mackenzie and P Green, 'Performative Regulation: A Case Study of How Powerful People Avoid Criminal Labels' (2008) *British Journal of Criminology* 138, 143.

[322] See 2.36.

[323] The Act took effect on 30 December 2003 and does not extend to Scotland.

[324] Proceedings may be instituted by the Commissioners of Customs and Excise: Dealing in Cultural Objects (Offences) Act 2003, s 4.

[325] DCMS Explanatory Notes on the 2003 Act [17].

[326] See the DCMS website: www.culture.gov.uk/cultural_property/illicit_trade.htm.

[327] Dealing in Cultural Objects (Offences) Act 2003, s 2(2) and (3).

The second situation where an object will be tainted is where it is removed either from 'a building or structure' or where it has 'at any time formed part of the building or structure' of historical, architectural or archaeological interest, or it is from a 'monument' of historical, architectural or archaeological interest.[328] It must also be shown that this removal is illegal in the place where it occurred. A monument is defined as:

(a) any work, cave or excavation;
(b) any site comprising the remains of any building or structure or of any work, cave or excavation;
(c) any site comprising, or comprising the remains of, any vehicle, vessel, aircraft or other movable structure, or part of any such thing.[329]

The notion of 'monument' is therefore very broad. Moreover, in the DCMS Explanatory Notes, it is suggested that 'A work, for example, may include surface traces or contours of structural remains, such as a prehistoric hill-fort, a burial cairn, field system or a deserted medieval village.'

The comments made in the DCMS guidance are particularly helpful in fleshing out section 2. It is stated:

> It should be noted that the illegal excavation or removal could take place within or outside the UK. Given that the legislation of each country will differ as to which offences are capable of rendering an object tainted, the Act does not identify particular provisions where the removal or excavation would constitute an offence. It is sufficient that the excavation or removal constitutes an offence (however defined) under the law of the UK or of some other country. English regulatory provisions which make excavation or removal unlawful are:
>
> – removing part of a vessel or objects from a vessel in a restricted area (section 1(3) Protection of Wrecks Act 1973);
> – works affecting a scheduled monument (section 2 Ancient Monuments and Archaeological Areas Act 1979 (AMAAA));
> – destroying or damaging a protected monument (section 28 AMAAA);
> – operations in an area of archaeological importance (section 35 AMAAA);
> – removal of an object discovered with a metal detector in a protected place (section 42(3) AMAAA);
> – removal of remains of military vessels or aircraft (section 2 Protection of Military Remains Act 1986);
> – demolition or alteration of a listed building (section 9 Planning (Listed Buildings and Conservation Areas) Act 1990);
> – removal of part of a wreck (section 246(3) Merchant Shipping Act 1995).
>
> So, for example, illegal removal of an object from a listed building in the UK, or illegal removal from a monument in China could trigger the offence. However, offences wholly unrelated to the process of excavation or removal – such as a breach of foreign export laws, a breach of local VAT regulations . . . would not taint the object. The tainting of the object is triggered by the excavation of the object or its removal from a building structure or monument. Thus offences such as theft or criminal damage would also taint the object if the theft or criminal damage occurred when it was removed or excavated. Where the theft occurred at a later stage, for example, by failing to report Treasure to the Coroner (and so stealing from the crown or a franchisee) it may be difficult to show that the theft occurred when the object was excavated rather than later when the holder decided not to report it. In such cases it may be preferable to prosecute for the offences of theft or handling stolen goods.

[328] ibid, s 2(4).
[329] ibid, s 2(5).

3.65 Dealing

The prosecution must establish that the accused is guilty of dealing with a tainted cultural object. Dealing includes acquiring, such as buying, hiring, borrowing and accepting. It embraces disposing, such as selling, letting on hire, lending or giving. It also covers importing or exporting a tainted cultural object.[330] The scope of the offence is widened further to include all those involved in arranging or agreeing with another to deal with a tainted object in this manner, regardless of where the act which was agreed or arranged took place. As a consequence, any museum, auctioneer or dealer runs a risk of committing an offence under this Act if the requisite mental state can be proven.

If a company has been involved in dealing in tainted cultural property, not only the company but also senior officers can be prosecuted under the Act. This may occur where the commission of the offence by the body corporate was attributable to the neglect of the relevant officer, or was committed with that officer's consent or connivance.[331] A relevant officer for this purpose is 'any director, manager, secretary or other similar officer of the body corporate or any person who was purporting to act in any such capacity.'

3.66 The Narrow Scope of the Act in Practice

The 2003 Act appears to cover a wide range of activities and to expose dealers, museums and others who deal in cultural objects to the risk of prosecution. Unfortunately, it is highly unlikely that there will be any prosecutions under this Act. It is very narrow in scope, because the prosecution will have difficulty in proving the mental element (*mens rea*). According to section 1(1) of the 2003 Act, 'A person is guilty of an offence if he dishonestly deals in a cultural object that is tainted, knowing or believing that the object is tainted.' As the mental element has been set at this high level, it will be difficult to prosecute traders for failing to enquire about the history of an object.[332]

Nevertheless, it might appear that the prosecution receives some assistance from section 1(2) of the Act, which provides that it is 'immaterial' whether the person 'knows or believes' that the object is a 'cultural object'. However, it is submitted that, although this provision is helpful, it does not assist the prosecution in any substantial way. The typical defendant will be a dealer or collector, and such people will be able to recognise whether an object is a cultural object or not. Surely a very real problem will be in establishing that the accused was dishonest? Like the offences of theft and deception, the prosecution must satisfy the *Ghosh* standard[333] by showing that the defendant was objectively dishonest by the ordinary standards of reasonable and honest people and that he should have realised that fact. The prosecution will therefore have a double hurdle of proving both that the defendant was dishonest, and that he knew or believed that the object was tainted. Furthermore, this is a new offence with which the prosecution will not be familiar. A prosecution may therefore be more willing to consider bringing charges for a more common offence, such as money laundering.

[330] ibid, s 3.

[331] ibid, s 5.

[332] For criticism, see Mackenzie and Green, 'Performative Regulation: A Case Study of How Powerful People Avoid Criminal Labels' (2008) *British Journal of Criminology* 138, 140.

[333] See 3.04.

3.67 Reflections on the Statute

The scope of the Dealing in Cultural Objects (Offences) Act 2003 is much wider than the offence of theft or handling, because it is concerned not only with stolen objects but also objects where, although the owner may have consented to their excavation or removal, the excavation or removal is illegal according to the domestic law of a state. It would also apply where the 'tainted' object was ownerless.[334] This is advantageous in a situation where soil samples or other evidence, such as shipping documents, indicate that an item was excavated from a source State which has not vested ownership in buried objects in the State.[335] Furthermore, an object which is 'tainted' remains tainted forever: the 2003 Act contains no provision equivalent to section 24(3) of the Theft Act 1968, whereby once the goods are returned to the owner or placed under his control, the goods cease to be stolen and the criminal offence of handling stolen goods can no longer be committed. However, it is unlikely that anyone dealing with the object would be dishonest in these circumstances, and so no charges will be brought.[336]

The Government's guidance states that the statute was intended to send out a 'strong signal' that it intended to put a stop to the illicit trade in cultural property. Unfortunately, prosecution under the statute is fraught with difficulty. One problem is that section 2(2) of the Act provides that a cultural object is only tainted if it is illegally excavated or removed 'after the commencement of this Act.' This means that the statute has no effect in relation to the large number of illicitly excavated or removed objects in circulation before the date when it came into force in December 2003. Article 7 Schedule 1 of the Human Rights Act 1998 provides that: 'No one shall be held guilty of any criminal offence on account of any act or omission which did not constitute a criminal offence under national or international law at the time when it was committed.' However, the 2003 statute would arguably have been Convention compliant if the main ingredient of dealing was committed after the statute took effect in December 2003. This restriction seems unnecessary, and in practice a prosecutor may find it impossible to precisely date when an object was removed from a source state.

The suspicion that the statute lacks teeth is borne out by the guidance issued in January 2004 by the DCMS. In the introduction, the DCMS expressly reassured traders that they had nothing to worry about in going about their ordinary business.

The Act does not necessarily oblige dealers to take steps to ascertain provenance or to exercise due diligence to avoid committing the offence. Knowledge or belief and dishonesty must be proved by the prosecution. Rather, the Act is designed to target irresponsible trading. It will inject greater transparency into the process of acquiring and disposing of cultural objects within the art market so that clear chains of ownership can be established in the event of suspected unlawful removal or excavation. In effect, the Act does not impose further costs in terms of due diligence checks but, rather, formalises them and encourages those not complying with industry-approved standards of good practice to come on board. The Act is designed to protect small business from the illicit trade, which threatens their

[334] Consequently, unlike the offence of handling stolen goods, there is no defence available based on the argument that the owner has ceased to have a right to restitution of the object: Theft Act 1968, s 24(3).

[335] See R Harwood, 'Dealing in Cultural Objects (Offences) Act 2003' (2003) VIII (4) *Art Antiquity and Law* 347, 349.

[336] A point made by A Parkhouse, 'The Illicit Trade in Cultural Objects: Recent Developments in the United Kingdom' in BT Hoffman (ed), *Art and Cultural Heritage: Law, Policy and Practice* (Cambridge, Cambridge University Press, 2006) 182.

commercial position through unfair competition. Any increase in costs to legitimate business, therefore, is likely to be minimal.

It has been argued that the requirement in the Act that there must be proof that the defendant knew or believed that the object was tainted makes it unworkable.[337] Critics have argued that the DCMS should be encouraging dealers to carry out due diligence checks rather than endorsing traditional market norms where there is an absence of stringent provenance investigation. A survey carried out suggests that little has changed since the Act was passed; dealers continue to turn a blind eye to an object's provenance.[338]

In practice, it will be a rare situation where it can easily be shown that the accused was dishonest and knew that the item had been illegally excavated or removed after 2003. The prosecution may prefer to bring charges for money laundering instead. Although the accused may face up to seven years' imprisonment or a fine (or both) upon conviction under the 2003 Act, he will face a maximum term of 14 years of imprisonment upon conviction for either handling stolen goods or a principal money laundering offence. Furthermore, the principal money laundering offences appear broader and more flexible, because they apply to all those who conceal, disguise, transfer or arrange to transfer or export criminal proceeds. Unless the suspect is caught importing goods which is not expressly covered by the Proceeds of Crime Act, a prosecutor may decide to prosecute for a money laundering offence because the burden of proof in relation to the mental element under the 2002 Act is the relatively low one of knowledge or suspicion.

XII The Iraq (United Nations Sanctions) Order 2003

3.68 Introduction

The trade in looted Iraqi antiquities became a matter of serious concern after the first Gulf War, when Iraq invaded Kuwait in 1990. An embargo on trade with Iraq was imposed in August 1990 by the United Nations Security Council[339] and looting became widespread after that time. It escalated in scale after Baghdad fell to the coalition forces led by the United States in 2003, when the Saddam regime was overthrown. The National Museum of Iraq in Baghdad was ravaged by looters.[340] The confusion caused by the outbreak of hostilities appeared to stimulate the looting of archaeological sites around the country. In a somewhat belated response, efforts have been made both at international and European level to curb the international trade in Iraqi cultural property.

[337] S Mackenzie and P Green, 'Criminalising the Market in Illicit Antiquities: an Evaluation of the Dealing in Cultural Objects (Offences) Act 2003 in England and Wales,' in S Mackenzie and P Green (eds), *Criminology and Archaeology: Studies in Looted Antiquities* (Oxford, Hart, 2009) 157.

[338] ibid, 149–50.

[339] UN Security Council Resolution 661. Brodie observes that this prompted auction houses to warn purchasers that they could not take bids from purchasers doing business in Iraq or Kuwait but that it was less clear that checks were being made in relation to the provenance of the items being sold: N Brodie, 'The Market Background to the April 2003 Plunder of the Iraq National Museum' in P Stone and J Farchakh Bajjaly (eds) *The Destruction of Cultural Heritage in Iraq* (Woodbridge, The Boydell Press, 2008) 41.

[340] See D G Youkhanna, 'The Looting of the Iraq National Museum' in Stone and Farchakh Bajjaly (eds) *The Destruction of Cultural Heritage in Iraq* 97.

3.69 Importing or Exporting Iraqi Cultural Property

Following the invasion of Iraq in March 2003, the European Community decided in July 2003 that the trade sanctions imposed upon Iraq[341] should be repealed. This was confirmed in Council Regulation 1210/2003.[342] However, certain restrictions on economic and financial relations with Iraq were set out in the Regulation. In particular, Article 3(1) prohibited the import and export of and dealing in Iraqi cultural property and 'other items of archaeological, historical, cultural, rare scientific and religious importance' if they had been illegally removed from Iraq on or after 6 August 1990, particularly if they formed part of a public collection listed in inventories of a museum or other public institution or there were reasonable grounds for suspicion that they had been stolen or unlawfully exported. The aim was to facilitate the safe return of Iraqi cultural objects. Unfortunately, recovery was hampered by the fact that some of the inventories were missing or had been destroyed. Even so, this restriction, taken in conjunction with the Dealing in Cultural Objects (Offences) Act 2003, and the Iraq (United Nations Sanctions) Order 2003, has encouraged those interested in acquiring objects from Iraq to make appropriate enquiries in relation to provenance and their import into the UK.

3.70 The Iraq (United Nations Sanctions) Order 2003

In response to the situation in Iraq, the United Nations Security Council adopted Resolution 1483 on 22 May 2003.[343] The Iraq (United Nations Sanctions) Order 2003 came into force on 14 June 2003 by way of statutory instrument.[344] The Order deals with various matters, but Article 8 creates two specific criminal offences in an attempt to curb the trade in looted antiquities from Iraq. Any British citizen or company may be guilty of an offence if they have either dealt with 'cultural property' which has been illegally removed from Iraq after 6 August 1990[345] or if, being in possession or control of such an object, there has been a failure to cause the transfer of the object to a constable.

Although the discussion below concentrates on the two main offences, it should be noted that there are restrictions on exporting Iraqi property from the UK. A licence is required and, if anyone knowingly or recklessly makes a false statement or provides false documents in obtaining a licence, the person will commit an offence.[346] The Commissioners for Revenue and Customs may require information relating to the destination of cultural goods to check whether it is an authorised destination; it is an offence to fail to disclose this information, although the accused may defend himself by showing that he did not consent to or connive at the goods reaching any destination other than their authorised destination.[347]

3.71 Mental Element (*Mens Rea*) and the Burden of Proof

The prosecution must establish two matters in particular. The criminal standard of proof beyond reasonable doubt will apply. First, it must be shown that the object is one of 'archae-

341 EC No 2465/96 of 17 December 1996.

342 7 July 2003 (2003 OJ L169/6). See (2003) VIII(3) *Art Antiquity and Law* 315.

343 See Resolution 1483, para 7, which imposes an obligation upon Member States to take appropriate steps to facilitate the return of cultural property removed since the adoption of Resolution 661 of 6 August 1990.

344 SI 2003/1519, as amended by SI 2004/1498.

345 This date was when the UN Security Council Resolution 661 was adopted.

346 SI 2003/1519, arts 5, 12. In relation to penalties, see ibid, art 20(3).

347 SI 2003/1519, art 11. In relation to penalties, see ibid, art 20(5). In relation to powers of search, see ibid, art 13. See further, ibid, arts 14–17.

ological, historical, cultural, rare scientific or religious importance' and that it has been illegally removed from Iraq after 6 August 1990.[348] Article 8(4) adds that the removal will be viewed as illegal if it violates English law or the law of some other country. Secondly, the prosecution must show that the defendant has either dealt with the object or failed to transfer it to a constable whilst in possession or control of it. Dealing is defined in similar manner to the equivalent concept in the Dealing in Cultural Objects (Offences) Act 2003.[349] The net is cast wide: it applies where a person acquires, disposes of, imports or exports the object; it also applies where a person agrees to do so, or makes arrangements to do so regardless of whether the agreement or arrangement takes place in the UK or elsewhere. The concept of acquiring is defined to mean buying, hiring, borrowing or accepting.[350] 'Disposing' is defined to mean selling, hiring, lending or giving. It would appear that anyone who happens to be in possession of an object illegally removed from Iraq after 6 August 1990 could be charged with an offence.

The prosecution is therefore based upon matters of fact, such as the conduct of the accused. However, the burden of proof shifts to the accused to prove what he did and did not know on a balance of probabilities. A prosecution will fail if the defendant can prove that, 'he did not know and had no reason to suppose that the item in question was illegally removed Iraqi cultural property'.[351] The reversal of the burden of proof can be seen as advantageous because this will deter traders from purchasing unprovenanced objects. If they fail to carry out any due diligence enquiries, such as by submitting information to the Art and Antiques Unit of Scotland Yard to check against its database and the Interpol database,[352] they may have great difficulty in discharging the burden of proof.[353]

Nevertheless, there is a risk that, if a person is prosecuted for one of these offences, the law will be challenged as being incompatible with Article 6(2) of the European Convention, as set out in the Human Right Act 1998.[354] Article 6(2) provides that 'Everyone charged with a criminal offence shall be presumed innocent until proved guilty according to law.' A defendant could argue that it should be a matter for the prosecution to show that he knew that the object was illegally removed Iraqi cultural property. Yet this right to a fair trial set out in Article 6(2) is not an absolute right. Some procedural modifications are acceptable if they are proportionate to public policy objectives.[355] The European Court does not demand, for example, that states all have the same procedural rules: they are given a wide discretion (a 'margin of appreciation'[356]). The European Court will not consider the fairness of the provisions of the substantive law but is simply concerned with the broad picture.[357] Thus,

[348] Thus, it can be argued that part of a statue of Saddam Hussein would be viewed as cultural property on the basis of its historical and cultural interest.

[349] SI 2003/1519, art 8(5).

[350] ibid, art 8(6).

[351] ibid, art 8(2),(3).

[352] See V Rapley, 'The Metropolitan Police's Art and Antiques Unit' in Stone and Farchakh Bajjaly (eds) *The Destruction of Cultural Heritage in Iraq* 56.

[353] PJ O'Keefe, *Commentary on the UNESCO 1970 Convention,* 2nd edn (Builth Wells, Institute of Art and Law, 2007) 17.

[354] See K Chamberlain, 'The Iraq (United Nations Sanctions) Order 2003 – is it Human Rights Act-Compatible?' (2003) XIII(4) *Art Antiquity and Law* 357; R Harwood 'Dealing in Cultural Objects (Offences) Act 2003' (2003) XIII (4) *Art Antiquity and Law* 347.

[355] *Brown v Stott* [2001] 2 All ER 97 (PC).

[356] As regards the margin of appreciation, see *James v United Kingdom* (1986) 8 EHRR 123 [46]. In relation to criminal trials, see *R v H; R v C* [2004] 1 All ER 1269 (HL) [13]; *A v Secretary of State for the Home Dept (No 2)* [2006] 2 AC 221 (HL) [26].

[357] *R v G (Secretary of State for the Home Office intervening)* [2008] UKHL 37, [2009] 1 AC 92 (HL) [4]–[6].

some interference with the burden of proof in criminal proceedings is tolerated provided that the interference is kept within reasonable limits.[358] Consequently, Article 6(2) does not prevent states from transferring the burden to the accused to establish a defence, provided the overall burden of proof remains on the prosecution. In the leading case of *Salabiaku v France*,[359] for example, the prosecution had the burden of establishing that a person had come through customs in possession of prohibited goods without declaring them; if this was shown, the presumption that he had smuggled those goods did not violate Article 6(2).

The law was reviewed by the House of Lords in *Sheldrake v DPP, Attorney-General's Reference (No 4 of 2002)*.[360] It was held that there was no obligation to create laws where every element of the burden of proof was placed entirely on the prosecution. Criminal offences cover a multitude of situations and some aspects of an offence may be impossible for a prosecutor to prove but easy for a defendant to rebut by way of a defence.[361] Consequently, as stated in *Salabiaku* above, presumptions of fact operate in every legal system and it is a matter of looking at the circumstances to decide whether the legislative response is proportionate. An offence which is drafted narrowly and where the court has the freedom to give the accused the benefit of the doubt is likely to be viewed as unobjectionable.[362] The test for proportionality in all cases, whether civil or criminal, will always involve looking at the substance of the matter and determining the basic but vital question of whether the defendant has received a fair trial.[363] In making this determination, various factors are taken into account: the more serious the crime, such as drug trafficking or terrorism, the more important it is to ensure that there are proper safeguards; furthermore, if the burden of proof was reversed in relation to a matter central to the wrongful conduct, this would almost certainly be in breach of Article 6(2).

It can therefore be argued that the Iraq (United Nations Sanctions) Order 2003 would be Convention compatible as the burden of proof remains upon the prosecution to prove the main elements of the offence and the facts of the defence are peculiarly within the knowledge of the suspect. Even so, a court might well decide to treat the burden of proof imposed on a defendant as no more than an evidential burden (rather than a legal one) in order to ensure compatibility with Article 6(2) of the European Convention. What this will mean in practice is that the prosecution will still bring forward evidence in relation to the mental state of the accused, and the accused will then attempt to rebut that evidence.[364]

3.72 Reflections

At first sight, the Iraq (United Nations Sanctions) Order 2003 appears to be a useful deterrent to the illicit trade in antiquities from Iraq. Legislation which requires the prosecution to prove that the accused was dishonest will not deter those who are prepared to turn a blind eye to suspicious circumstances in order to obtain a bargain. It can be argued that a dealer who is in

[358] *Salabiaku v France* (1988) 13 EHRR 379 [28]. See further *Spector Photo Group NV v Commissiee Voor Het Bank-, Financie- En Assurantiewezen (CBFA)* [2010] 2 CMLR 30 (ECtHR).

[359] *Salabiaku v France* (1988) 13 EHRR 379.

[360] *Sheldrake v DPP, Attorney-General's Reference (No 4 of 2002)* [2005] 1 AC 264 (HL).

[361] *X v UK* (1972) 42 CD 135; *R v Johnstone* [2003] 3 All ER 884 (HL); *R v Clarke* [2008] EWCA Crim 893 (CA).

[362] *H v UK* (Application No 15023/89) 4 April 1990; *AG v Malta* (Application No 16641/90) 10 December 1991; *Brown v UK* (Application No 44223/98) 2 July 2002; *Bates v UK* (Application No 26280/95) 16 January 1996.

[363] *R v Togher* [2001] 1 Cr App R 457 (CA) [30]; *Brown v Stott* [2001] 2 WLR 817 (PC) 836. See further, *Hoang v France* (1993) 16 EHRR 53 [33].

[364] In relation to the court's power to 'read down' a provision in this way, see *R v Lambert* [2002] 2 AC 545 (HL) [37]. See further, *R v Keogh* [2007] 3 All ER 789 (CA); *R v Hansen* [2008] 1 LRC 26.

possession of a stolen object should be put in a position where he has to explain how he came to acquire the object and what he knows about it.[365] Furthermore, the punishment is severe: by article 20(1), the offences of dealing and being in possession of Iraqi cultural objects are punishable on conviction on indictment by up to seven years' imprisonment and/or a fine. Where an offence is committed by a company, a prosecutor can bring charges against one of its officers if the commission of the offence was attributable to the neglect of that officer, or was committed with that officer's consent or connivance. By article 20(6), an officer is a 'director, manager, secretary or other similar officer' or 'any person who was purporting to act' in that capacity. A large number of people, including dealers, auction houses, museums, and private collectors, would appear to be exposed to the risk of prosecution if Iraqi material looted after 6 August 1990 falls into their possession.

Yet it is questionable whether the 2003 Order will be a particularly effective deterrent. One problem for the prosecution is the requirement that it must be shown that the cultural object has been illegally removed from Iraq since 6 August 1990. Although it may be possible to show that an item was removed from Iraq, it may be impossible to show precisely when it was exported. The difficulty lies with identification. As regards the Iraq Museum in Baghdad, part of the inventory had disappeared or been destroyed during the looting. Furthermore, the Museum housed objects belonging to other museums and these loans were not fully documented.[366] Although some objects bore a museum number making them instantly recognisable, others did not.

The position is worse in relation to antiquities excavated from archaeological sites. These objects will not have been documented and no signs may remain of their original context. After they have been transported abroad, all trace of their provenience may be obliterated (thereby damaging the historical, scientific and cultural record of the original site). Certain objects, such as cylindrical seals, were produced in their thousands over the centuries. These seals form a significant part of the archaeological record but, to the untrained eye, one may look much like another. Identification would be beyond the expertise of a police or customs officer. Indeed, even an expert may well not be able to determine the source of the object with any degree of precision. In these circumstances, the prosecution may face insurmountable problems in bringing charges.

The other factor which may deter prosecutors from bringing charges under this law is the consideration that this is a new and untested law. The defendant may well challenge any charge brought by arguing that the law violates Article 6(2) in relation to the reversed burden of proof. Furthermore, the criminal offences created by the Order could be characterised as retroactive and in violation of the European Convention. This is because it is not clear whether someone who acquired Iraqi cultural objects after 1990 but before the 2003 Order came into force, and who has then retained them, has committed an offence.[367] Although the 2003 Order may well be Convention compatible, the risk of lengthy litigation to establish a ruling on the matter might encourage prosecutors to bring charges for money laundering or some other well established offence with which they are familiar .

[365] P Gerstenblith, 'Controlling the International Market in Antiquities: Reducing the Harm, Preserving the Past' (2007) 8(1) *Chicago Journal of International Law* 169, 187.

[366] C Phuong, 'The Protection of Iraqi Cultural Property' (2004) 53(4) *International and Comparative Law Quarterly* 985, 995.

[367] PJ O'Keefe, *Commentary on the 1970 Convention,* 2nd edn (Builth Wells, Institute of Art and Law, 2007) 16.

XIII The Draft Cultural Property (Armed Conflict) Bill

3.73 The Hague Convention and its Protocols

Whilst the ethical argument for preventing destruction of cultural property is overwhelming, it is not easy to solve. The need for an international convention to encourage states to protect and preserve all cultural property became particularly pressing after the Second World War, as a response to the widespread looting and confiscation of private collections which had taken place and the damage caused by the Nazis to 427 museums., as well as other public buildings A key objective of the 1954 Hague Convention for the Protection of Cultural Property in the Event of Armed Conflict (the Hague Convention) was to safeguard cultural property during conflicts. The draft Cultural Property (Armed Conflict) Bill (Cm 7298) was designed to enable a UK Government to ratify the Hague Convention[368] and to accede to its two Protocols.[369] It was published in 2008 but has not yet been enacted.

The proposed legislation would be relevant where auctioneers, dealers, collectors and others have any form of control over a cultural object. There are a series of principal offences which would be created by section 3 and which address situations where a person, knowing or suspecting that the property in question is cultural property, intentionally endangers, steals, misappropriates or damages such property or extensively destroys or appropriates it, in serious violation of the Convention or the Second Protocol. It is irrelevant whether the act is committed in the UK or abroad; consequently, anyone who travels overseas to destroy a cultural item would commit an offence. Further ancillary offences (such as assisting, concealing, attempting and conspiring) would supplement the principal offences.[370]

A further offence would be created where an object has been unlawfully exported: by section 18 it would be an offence to deal in unlawfully exported cultural property where a person knows or has reason to suspect that it has been unlawfully exported.[371] Dealing is defined by section 18(3) to cover a wide range of conduct: acquiring, disposing, importing, exporting the object, or agreeing to do so, or making arrangements under which another person does such an act, or under which another agrees with a third person to do such an act.[372] One criticism made of this provision is that it covered items exported from occupied territories but failed to define occupied territories. A further objection made was that prosecutions could be brought too easily, because there was no need for the prosecutor to show

[368] See the Hague Convention, Arts 16–18. See further, K Chamberlain, *War and Cultural Heritage* (Powys, Institute of Art and Law, 2004) 205–16; S Von Schorlemer, 'Legal Changes in the Regime of the Protection of Cultural Property in Armed Conflict' [2004] IX (1) *Art Antiquity and Law* 43.

[369] The Second Protocol is helpfully included in the Bill as Sch 4.

[370] These ancillary offences are set out in s 4 and are extended to superior officers by s 5. By s 6, the scope of the main offences in s 3 and the further offences in s 4 are extended to company officers. In the Ninth Report of Session 2007–2008 of the CMS Committee (HC 693), it was acknowledged at [22] that the statutory wording relating to the ancillary offences would require further scrutiny.

[371] This provision is designed to satisfy Art 21 of the Second Protocol. Unlawfully exported property is liable to forfeiture if imported into the UK: Cultural Property (Armed Conflict) Bill, s 22. If such property is in the hands of a constable for the purposes of an investigation, an application can be made to retain it pending forfeiture or disposal under Sch 5: ibid, s 24. There are further provisions dealing with possession: by s 25, Customs and Excise can retain such property: by s 26, other persons in possession of such property must transfer it to a constable.

[372] This definition is precisely the same as that provided by s 3 of the Dealing in Cultural Objects (Offences) Act 2003.

that the accused was dishonest. This proposed offence has consequently caused anxiety amongst dealers and auction houses. There was concern that an offence might be committed where a dealer or auction house took an object into its possession in order to carry out due diligence checks to determine whether, for example, the object fell within the definition of cultural property set out in the Convention.[373] However, there is no requirement in the Hague Convention relating to dishonesty and the draft Bill is intended to mirror the terms of the Convention and its Protocols.[374] The Government's view has been that, if dealers carried out due diligence checks, such as the Code of Practice for the Control of International Trading in Works of Art, there should be no risk of prosecution. Moreover, the Government has suggested that, as the proposed offence would require the prosecution to show that the accused knew or had reason to suspect that cultural property had been unlawfully exported, prosecutions could not be made lightly and there was no reason to add a specific reference to dishonesty.[375] However, the dealers and auction houses have raised genuine concerns: proof that the accused had 'reason to suspect' is a less rigorous standard than dishonesty.

XIV The United States System

3.74 Cultural Property Implementation Act 1983

The Cultural Property Implementation Act (CPIA) brings the 1970 UNESCO Convention into effect; it deals with the import, export, and transfer of cultural objects which have been stolen or illegally exported. It was passed after much debate. Its only penalty is civil forfeiture: the authorities are enabled to seize, forfeit and return any stolen objects of cultural property.[376] The CPIA mirrors Article 7(b) of the Convention, which prohibits the import of stolen cultural objects which have been documented as part of the inventory of a museum, archaeological site or other public institution.[377] This aspect of the CPIA met with guarded approval from museums and collectors. It was limited in scope: it only applies to objects stolen after both the USA and the Contracting State from which it had originated had acceded to the Convention. It also provided clear bright lines in relation to liability: those acquiring cultural objects felt safe provided that they carried out checks to ensure that the object was not listed in an inventory.

Article 9 of the Convention calls for protection of cultural objects forming part of a State's cultural patrimony by the imposition of import controls. The US Government created a reservation, when ratifying the 1970 UNESCO Convention, which enables it to evaluate the requests for import controls by other Contracting States.[378] Although another state

[373] See the Ninth Report of Session 2007–2008 of the CMS Committee (HC 693) [33]–[34].

[374] ibid [36].

[375] DCMS: Government Response to the Culture, Media and Sport Committee Reports on the Draft Heritage Protection Bill and Draft Cultural Property (Armed Conflicts) Bill, October 2008, Cm 7472 [100].

[376] Cultural Property Implementation Act (CPIA) 1983, 19 USC s 2607, implementing Art 7(b) of the 1970 UNESCO Convention. See further, 2.18.

[377] CPIA 1983, 19 USC, s 308.

[378] ibid, ss 303–04. See further, WG Pearlstein, 'Cultural Property, Congress, the Courts, and Customs – The Decline and Fall of the Antiquities Market?' in K Fitzgibbon (ed), *Who Owns the Past? Cultural Policy, Cultural Property and the Law* (New Brunswick, New Jersey and London, Rutgers University Press, 2005) 9, 14–15.

can ask the United States to impose import restrictions on cultural objects that have been illegally exported, it must do so by submitting a request for a bilateral agreement to the US with documentation demonstrating that the Implementation Act's criteria are met. The requesting state cannot ask for an import ban on all cultural objects which have been removed from its jurisdiction; instead, it can only request restrictions in relation to significant archaeological or ethnological materials. The requesting state must produce evidence that it is suffering from pillage of these materials and that this endangers its cultural patrimony;[379] that it has taken steps in accordance with the UNESCO Convention to protect its heritage; that the application of import restrictions would be of substantial benefit to deter pillaging; that less severe remedies are not available; and that the application of import restrictions would be consistent with the general interest of the international community in promoting the international exchange of cultural materials for scientific, research and cultural purposes. The CPIA attempts to balance the policy concern to promote a healthy international market in cultural property with the need to prevent key cultural objects being smuggled out of vulnerable countries.

Once a request is submitted, it must be considered by the Cultural Property Advisory Committee, which is made up of representatives from the museum community, archaeologists and other stakeholders. The committee will decide whether to recommend that a bilateral agreement should be agreed. Where there is a case of emergency or crisis, the US can impose import restrictions without the immensely time-consuming negotiation process, provided that the source state has made a request for a bilateral agreement. The materials affected by any restrictions must be defined with precision and then published in the Federal Register so that importers and others will recognise them. The whole process is cumbersome; even so, once the restrictions are in place, the object can be seized by customs officials.

3.75 National Stolen Property Act

Like the Dealing in Cultural Objects (Offences) Act in the UK, the US Cultural Property Implementation Act is immensely important in terms of its symbolic value. It shows a Government commitment to combatting the illicit trade in cultural property. Yet, it is not intended to offer blanket protection to source nations; it attempts to strike a balance, reflecting an underlying concern to support international trade in cultural property.

The CPIA is not the only relevant law where there is trade in cultural property. For example, those who smuggle goods into the USA may falsify customs declarations. Equally, people who knowingly purchase stolen objects from a museum or private collection have always been vulnerable to prosecution for an offence under the National Stolen Property Act (NSPA).[380] This statute prohibits the transfer of goods or money which has been stolen, unlawfully converted or taken by fraud in interstate and foreign commerce.[381] It was established that it could be used against those who stole antiquities from source countries in

[379] It has been suggested that cultural 'patrimony' refers to more significant items than cultural property: J Cuno, 'Museums and the Acquisition of Antiquities' (2001) 19 *Cardozo Arts & Entertainment Law Journal* 83, 84–85.

[380] Cultural objects may be subject to forfeiture proceedings not only for falsifying customs declarations (see 18 USC) but also for violation of the NSPA: see the District Court's decision in the *Steinhardt* case: *United States v An Antique Platter of Gold* 900 F Supp 222 (SDNY 1997); 184 F 2d 131 (2d Cir 1999) cert denied, 528 US 1136 (2000). The case was discussed by the Court of Appeals for the second circuit in *United States v Schultz* 333 F 3d 393 (2d Cir 2003) 407. See P Gerstenblith, *Art, Cultural Heritage, and the Law*, 2nd edn (Durham, North Carolina, Carolina Academic Press, 2008) 636–43.

[381] CPIA 1983, ss 2314–15.

United States v Hollinshead.[382] Here, the accused participated in the removal of a Maya stela from Guatemala and its import into the USA. The stela had been well documented beforehand and it was therefore easy to prove that it had been stolen. The accused was successfully prosecuted for conspiracy to transport stolen property in violation of the NSPA.

The question of when an object might be considered to be 'stolen' has provoked heated debate. Wide-ranging patrimonial laws in some countries vest ownership of all cultural objects in the state; these claims are made despite the fact that the objects may be unknown if they are buried in the ground and will not be in the possession of the government of the state concerned. But, if the source state has a legitimate claim to ownership of undiscovered archaeological objects on the basis of its domestic law, the removal of these objects without permission will amount to theft. As a consequence, a dealer or other acquirer of such a cultural object can be prosecuted in the UK for handling stolen goods or money laundering. Similarly, in the USA, a dealer may be prosecuted for a general criminal offence under the NSPA. Unlike in the UK, this is seen as a controversial matter and some of the issues raised by the critics may present themselves for consideration in English courts in the future.

The first decision which analysed the issues in detail was *United States v McClain,*[383] in which the court distinguished unlawful export from theft. It was decided that cultural objects will be viewed as stolen if a state (in this case Mexico) has made a declaration of ownership, with a restriction on exportation, regardless of whether it had possession of the object before its removal.[384] In contrast, a law simply regulating the movement of antiquities, such as in the case of an export control law, would not suffice. However, it was stated in *McClain* that the source nation's domestic legislation must be clear so that people can understand that they risk being prosecuted for theft if they attempt to sneak excavated objects out of the country.[385]

These principles were endorsed approximately 20 years later in *United States v Schultz.*[386] Here, a successful dealer, Frederick Schultz, had worked with Jonathan Tokeley-Parry and had imported Egyptian antiquities, including the sculptured head of Pharaoh Amenhotep III. The domestic law of Egypt included a patrimonial law (Law 117) which vested ownership of all antiquities found after 1983 in the Egyptian Government, regardless of whether the Government had ever had prior possession of such objects. Schultz was convicted of conspiring to receive stolen objects in violation of the NSPA. He had argued that the objects which he had acquired were ownerless. He challenged the nature of the Egyptian Law 117, both at district court level and on appeal, arguing that it was concerned with licensing and export controls rather than being a national ownership law which vested title in the state. The Court of Appeals rejected this argument. It was decided that Law 117 was clear and unambiguous, vesting title, possession and right to transfer in the state.[387]

[382] *United States v Hollinshead* 495 F 2d 1154 (9th Cir 1974).

[383] *United States v McClain* 545 F 2d 988 (5th Cir, 1977).

[384] ibid, 1000–01.

[385] See *Peru v Jackson* 720 F Supp 810, 814 (CD Cal 1989), where the domestic law did not provide a sufficiently clear declaration of ownership. Moreover, it was not clear whether the antiquities were from Peru: see R Attwood, *Stealing History: Tomb Raiders, Smugglers and the Looting of the Ancient World* (New York, St Martin's Press, 2004) 88.

[386] *United States v Schultz* 333 F 3d 393 (2d Cir 2003), 178 F Supp 2d 445 (SDNY 2002). See M Lufkin, 'Criminal Liability For Receiving State-Claimed Antiquities in the United States: the "Schultz" case' (2003) VIII (4) *Art Antiquity and Law* 321.

[387] This was also the district court's view: 178 F Supp 2d 445, 447 (SDNY 2002).

The American taxpayer must pay the costs of any prosecution under the NSPA. It has been argued that source states should not be encouraged to take a lazy attitude in which they did not actively preserve their cultural property but merely enacted wide-ranging patrimonial laws instead, leaving it to US prosecutors to take action.[388] However, on the facts of *Schultz* itself, it was evident that the Egyptian Government had vigorously enforced Law 117 at every opportunity.

The decision in *Schultz* was seen as highly controversial by a number of dealers and collectors. The CPIA 1983 is narrow in scope, only offering protection to source nations in relation to known and inventoried objects which are stolen from an archaeological site or museum. The CPIA 1983 was passed after the decision in *McClain* but before the decision in *Schultz:* dealers and collectors had assumed that, if they took care to avoid inventoried objects, they were safe from prosecution. The conviction of Schultz caused consternation because dealers and others felt exposed to the risk of prosecution for a criminal offence based upon their possession of a cultural object which a foreign country had happened to declare was government property. It was argued unsuccessfully in *Schultz* that the CPIA pre-empted other legislation because it represented a delicate balancing act between the competing interests of dealers and collectors on the one hand and source nations on the other.[389] The district court, in rejecting this argument, stated that the statutes, although overlapping in their application, served different purposes. The CPIA was a civil law statute which was directed towards enhancing protection for foreign antiquities and represented a balancing act between foreign and domestic import and export laws. In contrast, the NSPA was concerned to deter criminal conduct. The Court of Appeals confirmed this view, stating that the CPIA was an import law whereas the NSPA was a criminal law.[390] The same conduct could therefore result in both a criminal prosecution and civil liability.

3.76 Reflections

There has been concern amongst dealers and collectors that a conviction under the NSPA may depend upon the interpretation of foreign 'patrimonial' laws, which might be sweeping in nature. These laws may be difficult to ascertain and tend to vary from country to country. For example, in England, there is a presumptive right of purchase of treasures by the state. In contrast, Mexican and Egyptian domestic law provides for the vesting of all cultural objects in the state. Critics suggested that it was highly unsatisfactory that the construction of a foreign country's domestic legislation would determine whether an American citizen was a thief or not. It was argued that the USA had abnegated its responsibilities and delegated any decision relating to whether certain cultural property should be banned to foreign governments.[391]

[388] JR McAlee, 'The *McClain* Case, Customs and Congress' (1982) 15 *NYU Journal of International Law and Politics* 813, 837.

[389] 333 F 3d 393, 408 (2d Cir 2003). The Federal Court of Appeals referred to a Senate Report which supported their view: ibid. This point was also made by the district court: 178 F Supp 2d 445, 449 (SDNY 2002). However, Cuno has observed that there was unsuccessful pressure to expressly modify the decision in *McClain* in Congress during the passage of the CPIA 1983: J Cuno, 'US Art Museums and Cultural Property' (2001) 16 *Connecticut Journal of International Law* 189, 193.

[390] 333 F 3d 393, 409 (2d Cir 2003).

[391] JR McAlee, 'From the Boston Raphael to Peruvian Pots: Limitations on the Importation of Art into the United States' (1981) 85 *Dickinson Law Review* 565–66; JM Podesta, 'Saving Culture, but Passing the Buck: How the UNESCO Convention Undermines its Goals by Unduly Targeting Market Nations' (2008) 16 *Cardozo Journal of International and Comparative Law* 457, 463.

One reason why the decision in *Schultz* caused alarm was because the standard of proof regarding the mental element appeared to be easier for the prosecution to satisfy than might have been anticipated. The District Court held that, although knowledge had to be established, Schultz's knowledge could be inferred by his 'conscious avoidance' of learning about the application of Egyptian law. The Court took account of Schultz's expertise and the knowledge of his contemporaries of foreign patrimonial laws.[392] Schultz was a prominent dealer and he had been the president of the National Association of Dealers in Ancient, Oriental and Primitive Art. Yet he had communicated in code with Tokeley-Parry and had concocted an entirely fictitious provenance when offering his antiquities for sale (asserting that they had come from the 'Thomas Alcock' collection[393]). The decision in *Schultz* cannot be characterised as one which penalised mere negligence.

In the UK, Tokeley-Parry's conviction for handling stolen goods has not been viewed as controversial.[394] But the variation in nations' patrimonial laws may become an issue at trial if a person is prosecuted for handling stolen goods in the future. There is a heavy burden of proof upon an English prosecutor to establish that the accused has been dishonest.[395] A jury would need to be convinced that the dealer knew perfectly well that a foreign state considered that the object belonged to a foreign government. This might be difficult to prove. Moreover, the relevant patrimonial law may need greater scrutiny in a different case. A conviction for handling will depend upon proof that the object was stolen and a conviction for money laundering will depend upon proof that a predicate offence, such as theft, has been committed. The patrimonial law will become all-important in establishing that an offence has been perpetrated: if it lacks clarity, it may be viewed as violating the rule of law and consequently incompatible with the European Convention.[396]

There is the risk of prosecution not only for violation of the NSPA but also for an offence under the Archaeological Resources Protection Act of 1979 (ARPA).[397] ARPA provides for civil fines and criminal penalties. It vests ownership of archaeological resources located in federally owned and controlled lands in the national government and prohibits their excavation, removal, damage or sale if this conflicts with state or local law. As state and local law prohibit theft, ARPA can be used as a basis for prosecuting people who have handled archaeological resources which can be viewed as having been stolen.

These two statutes were created to tackle domestic criminal activity. Critics have suggested that, by stretching these statutes to international trade in cultural objects, they erode the value and significance of the CPIA.[398] The CPIA has been praised for adopting a finely tuned approach to claims for the return of cultural objects so that, where a type of object is plentiful, a request for import restrictions will be rejected. It encourages source states to ratify the UNESCO Convention and to protect their cultural heritage, by designating

[392] 333 F 3d 393, 416 (2d Cir 2003).

[393] *United States v Schultz* 333 F 3d 393, 412 (2d Cir 2003). See 3.21, 3.75.

[394] *R v Tokeley-Parry* [1999] Crim LR 578. See further, *Government of the Islamic Republic of Iran v The Barakat Galleries Ltd* [2007] EWCA Civ 1374, [2009] QB 22 (CA) [150].

[395] See the *Ghosh* test: 3.04.

[396] The European Court has established that Art 6, which provides a guarantee of a fair trial, enshrines the fundamental principle of the rule of law: *Salabiaku v France* (1988) 13 EHRR 379 [28].

[397] 16 USC.

[398] JM Podesta, 'Saving Culture, but Passing the Buck: How the UNESCO Convention Undermines its Goals by Unduly Targeting Market Nations' (2008) 16 *Cardozo Journal of International and Comparative Law* 457; KD Vitale, 'The War on Antiquities: United States Law and Foreign Cultural Property' (2009) 84(4) *Notre Dame Law Review* 1835, 1869–71; G Green 'Evaluating the Application of the National Stolen Property Act to Art Trafficking Cases' (2007) 44 *Harvard Journal on Legislation* 251, 260–62.

certain types of object as part of its cultural patrimony. There is a strong internationalist argument in favour of permitting dispersal of objects to museums worldwide to benefit the public. It is feared that museum officials will be wary of acquiring new objects, because of fears of criminal prosecution.[399] There is the worry that private collectors will purchase these objects on the black market,[400] and they will be hidden away, rather than being traded openly in a healthy and vibrant international art market.

However, as soon as one views trafficking in art and antiquities in the same light as trafficking in drugs and humans, these objections to the extended application of general criminal legislation, such as the NSPA and ARPA, begin to lose their force. When a state is confronted with the challenges posed by serious organised criminal gangs, it should utilise a variety of strategies, provided that the principles are clear and well understood. Objections have been raised that dealers and officials will not necessarily know the patrimonial law of a particular source nation. But, in that case, they are unlikely to possess the requisite knowledge needed for conviction of an offence. Furthermore, although a prosecution can be brought against anyone dealing in stolen cultural objects of any sort under the NSPA and ARPA, it must not be overlooked that objects will only be viewed as stolen where the source nation has not only enacted legislation asserting ownership, but has also actively sought to enforce its patrimonial laws.

The general criminal law can be an effective way of deterring the illicit trade in cultural property by creating fear of detection and punishment. A drawback of relying solely upon statutes with a special focus upon cultural objects is that they may be too narrowly drawn and may have little impact as a consequence.[401] The CPIA, for example, does not offer protection in relation to all cultural property but only the most significant objects which form part of a state's archaeological or ethnological material. In contrast, the NSPA and ARPA deter criminal conduct in relation to all types of cultural property: their scope is much wider but needs to be triggered by criminal conduct and there needs to be proof of an effective patrimonial law. There is no doubt that the application of the criminal law, even if limited to a handful of cases, can have a significant social impact. American museum officials are aware that there is a risk of police raids if there is a suspicion that they have received looted objects.[402] The application of multiple strands of legislation puts pressure on possessors of objects with a doubtful history to return them to avoid any risk of legal action.[403] Attitudes in the United States towards cultural property whose provenance is obscure have changed.[404] This shift should be welcomed: a more responsible attitude towards collecting will mean a greater respect for the object concerned.

[399] Vitale, ibid, 1868.

[400] P Bator, 'An Essay on the International Trade in Art' (1981) 34 *Stanford Law Review* 275, 318.

[401] Attwood commented that illicit material continued to flow into the US after the enactment of the CPIA 1983: R Attwood, *Stealing History* (2004) at 90.

[402] J Felch, 'Raids Suggest a Deeper Network of Looted Art' (2008) *LA Times* 25 January; A Murr, 'Murky Provenance' (2008) *Newsweek* 25 January.

[403] See P Gerstenblich, '*Schultz* and *Barakat*: Universal Recognition of National Ownership of Antiquities' (2009) XIV (1) *Art Antiquity and Law* 21, 31–32.

[404] NC Wilkie, 'Public Opinion Regarding Cultural Property Policy' (2001) 19 *Cardozo Arts & Entertainment Law Journal* 97.

XV Conclusions

The criminal law presents a bewildering picture to anyone seeking advice, such as a museum director who wishes to acquire a cultural object by way of purchase or loan. Anyone who becomes involved with cultural objects, regardless of whether they are a dealer, collector, restorer or researcher, becomes vulnerable to prosecution for a number of offences, each with different core criteria and defences. These offences include not only cultural property offences under the Iraq (United Nations Sanctions) Order 2003 and the Dealing in Cultural Objects (Offences) Act 2003, but also under the general criminal law for handling stolen goods and money laundering. Some offences, such as theft, focus upon the mind of the accused and require dishonesty to be established; other offences, such as the Iraq Order 2003, place considerable emphasis upon conduct.

However, although there is a rather fragmentary and inconsistent treatment of the problem of the illicit trade in cultural property by the English criminal law, this does not necessarily mean that these offences are incompatible with the guarantee of a fair trial which is enshrined in Article 6 of the European Convention. It is of course vital that the details of each offence have been articulated with sufficient clarity to satisfy the rule of law. But the Government can defend any variations between offences on the basis that the offences may be intended to serve different policy objectives.

The Dealing in Cultural Objects (Offences) Act 2003 and the Iraq (United Nations Sanctions) Order 2003 have symbolic potency. They reinforce the notion that cultural objects are different from everyday items: they possess intrinsic values and consequently deserve special protection. These legislative measures act as a reminder to dealers and others that profit cannot be the only consideration. They may act as a deterrent: Brodie has suggested that the sale of unprovenanced cylindrical seals by auction dwindled to virtually nothing immediately after the Iraq (United Nations Sanctions) Order 2003 came into force.[405] However, enforcement authorities may well prefer to bring charges for offences with which they are familiar, such as handling and money laundering.

Money laundering measures will increasingly have an impact upon the trade in cultural property. The principal money laundering offences leave a wide range of accessories vulnerable to prosecution. The Money Laundering Regulations 2007 impose a heavy burden upon dealers and other professionals to establish a system to identify clients and those in control of goods. They are expected to report suspicious transactions, thereby heralding a shift towards greater transparency in commercial dealings. Traditional values of loyalty and confidentiality[406] are being eroded in the face of pressure to engage in active inquiry on matters of provenance.[407]

[405] N Brodie, 'The Plunder of Iraq's Cultural Heritage, 1991–2005, and the London Antiquities Trade' in N Brodie, MM Kersel, C Luke and KW Tubb (eds), *Archaeology, Cultural Heritage, and the Antiquities Trade* (Gainesville University Press of Florida, 2006) 206, 217.

[406] PM Bator, 'An Essay on the International Trade in Art' (1982) 34 *Stanford Law Review* 278, 360.

[407] NE Palmer, 'Adrift on a Sea of Troubles: Cross-Border Art Loans and the Spectre of Ulterior Title' (2005) 38 *Vanderbilt Journal of Transnational Law* 947; See further NE Palmer, 'Keeping the Score: the Rachmaninoff Claim and the Circumspection of Auction Houses' (2005) X(3) *Art Antiquity and Law* 317, discussing *Rachmaninoff v Sotheby's and Eva Teranyi* [2005] EWHC 258.

4

Recovery Through the Criminal and Civil Courts where Law Enforcement Agencies are Involved

IAN SMITH

I Introduction

4.01 Introduction

This chapter concerns recovery of art and antiquities in and by the English courts either in the course of criminal proceedings or in civil proceedings where a law enforcement agency is involved (rather than in private proceedings instigated by an individual victim[1]). In keeping with other chapters, a broad survey is provided, which includes money laundering and corruption.

The powers and proceedings considered in this chapter are divided into two categories: those available in respect of domestic investigations and proceedings, and those available to assist foreign courts and law enforcement agencies. The following is an outline of the powers discussed later in more detail in this chapter. This collection of powers and procedures can appear to be a confusing and even contradictory set of powers. The aim of this chapter is to outline their main features and provide a roadmap for those engaged in recovering art and antiquity objects, whether as owners or law enforcement agencies together with their lawyers.

Most of the powers and procedures set out in this chapter are intended to benefit the state (albeit that they may still benefit victims and third parties indirectly), whilst some powers are intended to benefit victims and third parties directly (such as restitution orders,[2] Police (Property) Act 1897 orders,[3] and orders under the Proceeds of Crime Act 2002, s 281[4]).

4.02 Powers and Procedures Available In Respect Of Domestic Investigations And Proceedings (Section II Below)

The following powers and procedures, dealt with in Section II below, are available in domestic proceedings in England and Wales, being proceedings which are not for the purpose of assisting foreign courts or law enforcement agencies:

[1] Private proceedings are the subject of Ch 5.
[2] See 4.09.
[3] See 4.13.
[4] See 4.22.

- *Seizure*: Police and Criminal Evidence Act 1984, Proceeds of Crime Act, sections 45 and 19, and Customs and Excise Management Act 1979.[5]
- *Restraint and Management receivership orders*: Proceeds of Crime Act 2002, sections 40–49.[6]
- *Property freezing orders and receivership orders*: Proceeds of Crime Act 2002, sections 245A–255.[7]
- *Restitution orders*: Powers of Criminal Courts (Sentencing) Act 2000, section 148.
- *Police (Property) Act 1897 orders*.[8]
- *Confiscation orders*: Proceeds of Crime Act 2002, Part 2.[9]
- *Civil recovery orders*: Proceeds of Crime Act 2002, Part 5.[10]
- *Deprivation orders*: Powers of Criminal Courts (Sentencing) Act 2000, section 143.[11]
- *Forfeiture orders*: Customs and Excise Management Act 1979, sections 49 and 53.[12]

4.03 Powers and Procedures available to Assist Foreign Courts and Law Enforcement Agencies (Section III Below)

The following powers and procedures, dealt with in Section III below, are available to law enforcement agencies when giving assistance to the courts and agencies of foreign jurisdictions:

- *Overseas external orders (both criminal and civil)*: Proceeds of Crime Act 2002 (External Requests and Orders) Order 2005.[13]
- *Overseas forfeiture orders*: Criminal Justice (International Co-operation) Act 1990 (Enforcement of Overseas Forfeiture Orders) Order 2005.[14]

It is important for foreign enforcement authorities (and the victims who rely upon them) to understand that property (or its equivalent in money) recovered at the request of a foreign authority and under a foreign confiscation, civil recovery or forfeiture order in the United Kingdom is not automatically transmitted to the foreign enforcement authority or state. Instead, property (or its equivalent in money) recovered is placed in the UK Government's Consolidated Fund.[15] There is no legal power to enable a court in the UK to order that property which has been recovered through confiscation or forfeiture powers be remitted to a foreign state or other recipient.

The United Kingdom's only firm multilateral obligation[16] to return items of art or antiquity confiscated by the state is to be found in the United Nations Convention against

[5] See 4.05–4.06.
[6] See 4.07.
[7] See 4.08.
[8] See 4.13.
[9] See 4.14–4.19.
[10] See 4.20–4.22.
[11] See 4.23–4.25.
[12] See 4.06.
[13] See 4.26–4.39.
[14] See 4.40–4.43.
[15] In the same way, where the United Kingdom seeks the assistance of a foreign state in enforcing a domestic confiscation order under POCA 2002, s 74, any property recovered in the foreign state falls to be dealt with under that state's law and is not automatically remitted to the UK: POCA 2002, s 74(3).
[16] In other international instruments, the United Kingdom has done no more than assume an obligation to consider returning confiscated property to requesting states. See for example, the (European Council's 1990) Convention on Laundering, Search, Seizure and Confiscation of the Proceeds of Crime (CETS No 141), Art 15 (which requires no more than disposal of confiscated property in accordance with domestic law of the requested

Corruption 2003, which the UK Government ratified in 2006.[17] Chapter V of the Convention concerns 'Asset Recovery'. It requires the United Kingdom to give assistance to other contracting states in the recovery of property which is the proceeds of a corruption offence.[18] As to disposal of confiscated property, the Convention requires the following action to be taken by states which confiscate property, 'taking into account the rights of bona fide third parties':[19]

- Return to the requesting state any property it confiscates as a result of an offence of embezzlement, misappropriation or diversion of property by a public official as referred to in Article 17 of the Convention or laundering as referred to in Article 23 of the Convention.[20]
- In the case of proceeds of any other corruption offence covered by the Convention, return the confiscated property to the requesting state when the requesting state 'reasonably establishes its prior ownership' of the confiscated property or when the requested state 'recognises damage to the requesting state as a basis for returning the confiscated property'.[21]
- In all other cases, give 'priority consideration' to returning confiscated property to the requesting state, 'returning such property to its prior legitimate owners or compensating the victims of the crime'.[22]

The United Kingdom has entered into bilateral agreements with a small number of countries, the earliest of which were with Canada[23] and the United States[24] to determine the ultimate destination of property or sums of money confiscated in England and Wales. These agreements require the United Kingdom to determine an appropriate share of the property (or an equivalent amount of money) recovered in the United Kingdom (net of the

state, 'unless otherwise agreed by the parties'); Harare Scheme Relating to Mutual Assistance in Criminal Matters within the Commonwealth, Art 30 (disposal of confiscated property in accordance with the domestic law of the requested state); UN Convention Against Transnational Organised Crime (A/55/383), Art 14 (disposal of confiscated property in accordance with the domestic law of the requested state but with 'priority consideration' to be given to returning property to the requesting state for the purposes of compensating victims or returning property to legitimate owners). The (Council of Europe's 2001) Second Additional Protocol to the European Convention on Mutual Assistance in Criminal Matters (CETS No 182), Art 12(1) merely requires that '[a]t the request of the requesting Party and without prejudice to the rights of bona fide third parties, the requested Party may place articles obtained by criminal means at the disposal of the requesting Party with a view to their return to their rightful owners.'

17 Convention against Corruption 2003 (A/RES/58/4). See also 2.42.

18 UN Convention against Corruption 2003, Art 55. See 2.42.

19 ibid, Art 57(2).

20 ibid, Art 57(3)(a).

21 ibid, Art 57(3)(b).

22 ibid, Art 57(3)(c).

23 Agreement between the Government of the United Kingdom and the Government of Canada Regarding the Sharing of Forfeited or Confiscated Assets or their Equivalent Funds, signed in London on 21 February 2001 (and extended to the Overseas Territories of Anguilla, British Virgin Islands, Cayman Islands, Gibraltar, Montserrat, and the Turks and Caicos Islands) (TS 028/2001, Cm 5180). The Agreement provides for the sharing of assets forfeited in Canada or confiscated in the United Kingdom. Forfeiture in Canada is equivalent to confiscation in the United Kingdom; both requiring a conviction of a person or at least a finding to the criminal standard of proof that property represents the proceeds of crime. For further detail of forfeiture under Canadian law, see the Canadian Criminal Code, ss 462.37 and 462.38. The Exchange of Notes between the United Kingdom and Canada to Extend the Agreement Regarding the Sharing of Forfeited or Confiscated Assets or their Equivalent Funds was signed on 21 January 2003.

24 Agreement between the Government of the United Kingdom and the Government of the United States of America Regarding the Sharing of Forfeited or Confiscated Assets or their Equivalent Funds, signed in Washington on 31 March 2003 and ratified by the Government of the United Kingdom on that date.

costs of recovery) to be shared with the requesting state. Obviously, if the property recovered in fact belongs to the other country (albeit that there may have been no court determination of this) then there would be a legitimate expectation that the whole of that property would be returned to the other state.

No asset-sharing agreements exist in relation to property recovered pursuant to a civil recovery order or forfeiture order made by an English court.

Where no asset-sharing agreement exists, a foreign state must request the remittance of property or sums of money on a diplomatic basis. If the property recovered in fact belongs to the other country (albeit that there may have been no court determination of this), then there would be a legitimate expectation that the whole of that property would be returned to the other state. In addition, if the requesting state is one which itself would remit property or sums of money, which it recovers in its own procedures this is likely to give rise to a diplomatic expectation of reciprocal remittance from the United Kingdom. Where it is the case that remittance is requested by a foreign state on the basis that the property and/or money, would, if remitted, be returned to a victim or paid as compensation to a victim of crime, the request for remittance has more force still. The Home Office deals with these requests and may agree to remit a portion of funds recovered (after itself obtaining the approval of the Treasury).

4.04 Law Enforcement Agencies Duties of Care When Holding Property and Duties to Return Property after the Expiration of Powers to Retain Such Property (Sections IV and V Below)

Sections IV and V of this chapter concern the duties owed by law enforcement agencies following seizure and retention of that property for a law enforcement purpose together with their duties to return property on the expiration of their powers.

II Domestic Powers and Proceedings

4.05 Seizure and Retention by Law Enforcement for Use in Criminal Investigations and Proceedings

As discussed in Chapter 3, an individual may be prosecuted for offences such as theft, handling stolen goods or under the Dealing in Cultural Objects (Offences) Act 2003 or the Iraq (United Nations Sanctions) Order 2003. In many cases the first step in the road to state-empowered recovery of an art item or antiquity will be its seizure by a law enforcement officer.[25]

Section 19 of the Police and Criminal Evidence Act 1984 (PACE) empowers an officer to seize anything where he has reasonable grounds for believing:

[25] The police owe a duty to take care in relation to objects which they have taken into their possession: see J Ulph, ch 35 in *Palmer on Bailment,* 3rd edn (London, Sweet and Maxwell, 2009) [35-054]. In relation to domestic powers and proceedings, see generally *Archbold: Criminal Pleading, Evidence & Practice* (London, Sweet & Maxwell, published annually) and *Smith Owen & Bodnar on Asset Recovery: Criminal Confiscation and Civil Recovery* (Oxford, Oxford University Press, Looseleaf).

(a) that it has been obtained in consequence of the commission of an offence if it is necessary to seize it to prevent its being concealed, lost damaged, altered or destroyed[26]; or
(b) that it is evidence in relation to an offence which he is investigating or any other offence if it is necessary to seize that evidence to prevent it being concealed, lost, altered or destroyed.[27]

Section 22 empowers an officer to retain a seized item:

(a) for use as evidence in a trial for an offence;[28] or
(b) for forensic examination or for investigation in connection with an offence[29] – but nothing may be retained under this power if a photograph or photocopy of the item would be sufficient for these purposes.[30]

Additional powers of seizure and retention on the grounds as those set out above are contained in the Criminal Justice and Police Act 2001 (CJPA), sections 50–57, which allow officers wider powers of seizure where it is not reasonably practicable for an officer conducting a search of premises to determine whilst searching the premises whether an item is something that he is entitled to seize.[31] The CJPA provides for the return of items which may no longer be retained. Significantly, the CJPA provides that where an officer is satisfied that another person has a better right to an item than the person from whom it was seized, the officer is duty-bound to return it to the person appearing to the officer to have the best right;[32] the officer may retain the item for as long as it is reasonably necessary for him to reach such a determination.[33]

4.06 Seizure and Retention by HM Revenue and Customs for Forfeiture Proceedings

Customs and Excise Management Act 1979 (CEMA), section 139, empowers an officer to seize and detain any item 'liable to forfeiture' under CEMA. If it later turns out that an item was liable to forfeiture, then the seizure is confirmed as lawful, whereas if it later turns out that the item was not liable to forfeiture, then the seizure will be viewed as unlawful.

Art or antiquities may be liable to forfeiture and therefore liable to seizure under section 139 CEMA if:

- they have been improperly imported within the meaning of section 49 CEMA, including being imported contrary to any prohibition or restriction in force under any enactment;[34] or
- they have been improperly exported (or attempted to be exported) within the meaning of sections 52 and 53 CEMA: importantly, that, as goods subject to export restrictions, they have not been properly declared to HM Revenue & Customs and HMRC's permission for export has not been obtained.[35]

[26] PACE, s 19(2).
[27] ibid, s 19(3).
[28] ibid, s 22(2)(a)(i).
[29] ibid, s 22(2)(a)(ii).
[30] ibid, s 22(4).
[31] CJPA, s 50.
[32] ibid, s 58(2). See also 5.03.
[33] ibid, s 58(3).
[34] CEMA, s 49. See also 3.54–3.58.
[35] ibid, ss 52 and 53.

For example, these forfeiture provisions will have effect in the case of illegally imported or exported tainted cultural objects under the Dealing in Cultural Objects Act 2003,[36] or in contravention of the Export of Objects of Cultural Interest (Control) Order 2003 or of the Customs and Excise Management Act 1979.[37]

4.07 Restraint Orders and Management Receiverships Pending Criminal Confiscation

Where a criminal investigation or criminal proceedings have been started in England and Wales[38] the Crown Court may make a restraint order prohibiting any specified person from dealing with any 'realisable property'[39] held by him.[40] 'Realisable property' would certainly include art and antiquities which are the subject matter of the criminal investigation or proceedings against an individual as well as any which are 'tainted gifts'[41] to other persons.[42] The restraint order freezes a persons right to deal with the restrained property. Third parties who know of a restraint order are not allowed to assist another to deal with or dispose of the restrained assets.

The rights of persons who have an interest in property are protected by POCA 2002. A person known to be affected by a restraint order must be served with a copy of the restraint order.[43] Persons who have an interest in property which is restrained clearly must be served with the order. Such persons then have the right to apply to the court to have the property in question released from the restraint.[44]

An object may be seized where confiscation proceedings are contemplated by a law enforcement agency and the agency obtains a restraint order. A law enforcement officer may seize any object which is 'realisable property' to which a restraint order applies.[45] An object so seized must be dealt with in accordance with the directions of the court which made the restraint order.[46]

Where the Crown Court makes a restraint order it also has the power to make a management receivership order, appointing a receiver to take possession of and manage objects pending future confiscation proceedings.[47] A management receiver is usually an accountant or licensed insolvency practitioner. His or her charges are met from the property under management.[48]

4.08 Property Freezing Orders and Interim Receiverships Pending Civil Recovery

Where a law enforcement agency may bring civil recovery proceedings for a civil recovery order in respect of an object, the High Court may make:

[36] See 3.63–3.65.
[37] See 3.57–3.58.
[38] POCA 2002, s 40.
[39] 'Realisable property' is defined by POCA 2002, s 83, and is all property held by the defendant and all property held by any recipient of a 'tainted gift'.
[40] POCA 2002, s 41.
[41] For the meaning of 'tainted gifts', see POCA 2002, ss 77–78.
[42] As the term includes all of a defendant's property (and any tainted gifts to third parties), property other than that the subject matter of a criminal investigation may also be restrained and indeed made the subject of a later confiscation order.
[43] Criminal Procedure Rules 2010, r 59.2(8)(b).
[44] ibid, s 42(3).
[45] ibid, s 45(1).
[46] ibid, s 45(2).
[47] ibid, ss 48 and 49.
[48] ibid, s 49(2)(d); *Hughes v Customs and Excise Commissioners* [2002] 4 All ER 633.

– a property freezing order in respect of the object, providing that there is a good arguable case that it is recoverable property,[49] and if it does so it may also make a receivership order appointing a receiver to take possession of and manage the object;[50]
– an interim receiving order[51] in respect of an object, providing that there is a good arguable case that it is recoverable property,[52] making provision for the detention, custody or preservation of the object and the appointment of an interim receiver in respect of the object.[53]

If property that is the subject of either a property freezing order or an interim receiving order is also the subject of another separate claim, the court dealing with that latter claim may, on being notified of the application, either stay those latter proceedings or allow them to continue on terms.[54] It would seem clearly appropriate that a private claim brought by an owner of an object the subject of civil recovery proceedings should be allowed to continue and should not be stayed and if successful would mean that the object would no longer be recoverable property.[55]

Restitution Orders

4.09 General Principles

The criminal courts[56] have powers to make restitution orders under sections 148 and 149 of Powers of Criminal Courts (Sentencing) Act 2000 (POCC(S)A).[57] A court may make a restitution order where it is satisfied that 'goods' (which would include art and antiquities) have been 'stolen' by a convicted person, whether stolen in England and Wales or overseas. Such orders are made entirely for the benefit of victims of crime.

The convicted person or any other person who has possession of the stolen goods may be ordered either to restore the stolen goods to their rightful owner or, where the goods have been disposed of, to transfer to the rightful owner the proceeds of that disposal or goods directly or indirectly representing those proceeds.

For the purposes of determining whether restitution orders may be made 'goods' and 'steal' have a very wide meaning:

– 'Goods' includes property of every description within the meaning of the Theft Act 1968, which includes personal property,[58] and also includes things severed from land by stealing.[59] The definition is clearly wide enough to include items of art and antiquity.
– 'Stealing' is to be interpreted in accordance with sections 1(1), 21(1) and 21(4) of the Theft Act 1968.[60] Restitution orders are available, both in the case of offences where theft

[49] ibid, s 245A.
[50] ibid, s 245E.
[51] ibid, s 246(4).
[52] ibid, s 246(5).
[53] ibid, s 246(2).
[54] ibid, ss 245D(1)(a), (2), 253(1)(a), (2).
[55] ibid, s 308(3)ff.
[56] Crown Courts and magistrates' courts.
[57] See generally *Smith Owen & Bodnar on Asset Recovery: Criminal Confiscation and Civil Recovery* (Oxford, Oxford University Press, Looseleaf).
[58] Theft Act 1968, s 4(1).
[59] POCC(S)A, s 143(10).
[60] ibid, s 143(8).

is a constituent element (burglary or robbery), and where goods are obtained by fraud or blackmail; a fraud being one in contravention of section 1 of the Fraud Act 2006 (being fraud by false representation, fraud by failing to disclose information and fraud by abuse of position).[61] Items are to be treated as stolen whether the stealing occurred in England and Wales or elsewhere, and whenever they were stolen, provided that the stealing amounted to an offence where and at the time when the goods were stolen.[62]

4.10 Return of a Stolen Item

The first and most important kind of restitution available is the return of a 'stolen' item.[63] Criminal courts may order anyone who possesses or controls a stolen item to restore it to the person entitled to recover it. The words 'possession' and 'control' are clearly intended to include persons other than the person who originally stole the item, and may include innocent third parties such as auctioneers, dealers and galleries. The 'person entitled to recover' an item would clearly include the owner of the item, but may also include a person with lawful possessory title.[64]

The statutory provisions for restitution of a stolen item make no mention of a defence of innocent purchase for value under a foreign law equivalent to that which is available under private law.[65] That said, there is at least scope for argument that the original owner of a stolen item is no longer a 'person entitled to recover' if, by reference to private international law, he is no longer to be regarded as having any interest in the item. Since the criminal courts have no jurisdiction to resolve disputes as to the title to the goods themselves, and have stated that such matters should be left to the civil courts,[66] it would probably be the case that the courts would decline to make a restitution order where there were competing ownership claims to a stolen item from its original owner and from an innocent purchaser who had obtained good title to the item.

Some statutory protection for an innocent third party purchaser of a stolen item is given. Although they may be ordered to restore a stolen item, a person who has bought a stolen item from a convicted person or lent money on the security of a stolen item from a convicted person may be awarded monetary compensation from the convicted person.[67] This is however limited to money from the convicted offender and 'money taken out of his possession on his apprehension'.[68] Under English law, since a purchaser (or lender) would not usually obtain any legal title to stolen property,[69] this is clearly necessary compensation for such innocent third parties.

[61] See 3.52.
[62] Theft Act 1968, s 24(1).
[63] POCC(S)A, s 148(2)(a).
[64] For discussion of a possessory title, see 5.02.
[65] See 5.33–5.51.
[66] *R v Ferguson* (1970) 54 Cr App R 410; *Calcutt* [1985] 7 Cr App R(S) 385, *Re Norris* [2001] UKHL 34, [2001] 1 WLR 1388.
[67] POCC(S)A, s 148(4).
[68] ibid, s 148(4). The term 'money taken out of his possession on his apprehension' has been interpreted to include money seized from a safety deposit box days after the initial arrest of the person later convicted: *R v Ferguson* (1970) 54 Cr App R 410.
[69] See 5.34–5.35. As regards any defence available, based upon the expiration of the limitation period, see 5.38–5.51.

4.11 Restitution of Substitute Property

The second kind of restitution available is the return of property which represents the original item that was stolen.[70] If the return of the stolen goods by the offender is not possible, then the court must trace into the proceeds of the sale of the stolen goods, for the purpose of ordering those proceeds to be paid to the person entitled to recover them.

4.12 Procedure

All of the evidence which the criminal court should consider in deciding whether to make a restitution order must be contained within the evidence and documents which were used or available for use in the criminal proceedings which have triggered the restitution power together with any admissions by any person in connection with the restitution proceedings,[71] and it has been held that evidence received after the conclusion of the trial will be inadmissible to found the basis for a restitution order.[72]

A third party may have a role to play in triggering the jurisdiction for the making of a restitution order. The statute is silent on the question of whether or not a person has the right to apply directly to the criminal court for the restoration of an item he is entitled to recover and so a person seeking restitution of a 'stolen' item should petition the prosecutor who brought the criminal case to seek such an order from the criminal court.[73] By contrast, in relation to restitution of substitute property power[74] is to be exercised 'on the application of' a person entitled to recover goods representing the stolen goods from the person convicted,[75] and extraordinary though it may seem, the power may not be available to the criminal court in the absence of an application by the person claiming the restitution. The person claiming the substitute property restitution should therefore make a direct application for such restitution to the relevant criminal court.

Is there a time limit within which restitution orders must be made? The statute under which restitution orders may be made[76] makes no reference to a time limit for the making of an order. Nor has any case dealt with this issue. There are two reasons to think that some limits must apply:

- To the extent that it is the case that the claim arises out of existing criminal proceedings, it must be right that the defendant to those proceedings has a right to their finality, whether the restitution proceedings are properly characterised as part of the criminal punishment or are civil proceedings. The Article 6 right to a fair trial would be engaged, including the right to the conclusion of proceedings within a 'reasonable time'.[77]

[70] POCC(S)A, s 148(2)(b).

[71] See ibid, s 148(6) for the exact statutory terms regarding material which was used or available for use in the criminal proceedings.

[72] *R v Church* (1970) 55 Cr App R 65.

[73] ie, silent in relation to the restitution power under s 148(2)(a).

[74] ie, under s 148(2)(b).

[75] POCC(S)A, s 148(2)(b).

[76] POCC(S)A.

[77] In relation to criminal proceedings see *R (on the application of Lloyd) v Bow Street Magistrates' Court* [2003] EWHC Admin 2294 [26] and [34]. In relation to civil proceedings, see *Hornsby v Greece* [1998] ELR 365 [40]; *Immobiliare Saffi v Italy* (Application No 22774/93) (1999) 30 EHRR 756 (ECtHR) [63]; *Bennett v Customs and Excise Commissioners (No 2)* [2001] STC 137 (HC) (Patten J, citing *Hornsby*); *St Brice v London Borough of Southwark* [2001] EWCA Civ 1138, [2002] 1 WLR 1537 (CA) (citing *Hornsby*); *Re D (Intractable Contact Dispute: Publicity)* [2004] EWHC 727 (Fam) (Munby J, citing *Hornsby* and *Immobiliare Saffi*).

– In relation to restitution orders for the recovery of a sum of money from a defendant, it is arguable that section 9 of the Limitation Act 1980 would apply. If applicable, section 9(1) would prohibit any restitution action from being brought more than six years from the date on which the cause of action accrued. That is most likely to be the date of the relevant conviction which triggered the power to make the restitution order.

Police (Property) Act 1897 Orders

4.13 General Principles

The Police (Property) Act 1897 (PPA)[78] enables a court of summary jurisdiction, on the application of a claimant of property, a police officer or an officer of the Serious Organised Crime Agency, to make:[79]

– an order for the delivery of the property to the person appearing to the court to be the owner of the property; or
– if the owner cannot be ascertained, such order with respect to the property as the court thinks appropriate.[80]

Although these powers and proceedings are clearly available to victims of crime, they are equally available to any person who can claim ownership of property which has come into the possession or control of the police.

The police (or other bailees) are not necessarily liable for failing to return the goods immediately an investigation ends if they have to determine the validity of a claim to possession and act with reasonable efficiency in doing so.[81] The PPA applies where personal property has come into possession of the police or the Serious Organised Crime Agency (SOCA)[82] in the course of investigating a suspected offence.

For law enforcement officers, returning an object to its apparent owner carries risk. If a police officer delivers the object to someone other than the person properly entitled, he will be liable for conversion of the object, unless he can show that he did not have notice of the third party's adverse claim.[83] Liability in conversion may result even where an officer returns an object to the person from whom he initially took the object.[84] Furthermore, the police are bailees, owe a duty of care to the person entitled to possession of the goods and must take reasonable steps to notify the apparent owner of any rival claim.[85] They must also be under a duty to notify the apparent owner of their possession of the object in question.

The PPA provides that a court of summary jurisdiction may make an order 'for the delivery of the property to the person appearing to the magistrate or court to be the owner

[78] For detailed discussion of the operation of the Police (Property) Act 1897, see J Ulph, ch 35 in *Palmer on Bailment*, 3rd edn (London, Sweet and Maxwell, 2009) [35-059], [35-061], [35-063], [35-065]. See also NE Palmer and J Ulph, 'Art in Police Custody: The Police (Property) Act 1897 in Context' (1997) II(1) *Art Antiquity and Law* 3.

[79] PPA, s 1(1).

[80] The authors of this work have given the statute what is considered to be its modern interpretation: the PPA uses the words 'as to the magistrate or court may seem meet'.

[81] *Clayton v Le Roy* [1911] 2 KB 1031 (CA). See also 5.03.

[82] Police (Property) Act 1897, s 2A, as amended by the Serious Organised Crime and Police Act 2005, s 59, Sch 4.

[83] *Marcq v Christie, Manson and Woods (t/a Christie's)* [2004] QB 286 (CA). See 5.10.

[84] *Winter v Bancks* (1901) 65 JP 468; *R v Uxbridge Justices, ex p Commissioner of Police of the Metropolis* [1981] QB 829 (CA) 834 (Lord Denning MR).

[85] *Ranson v Platt* [1911] 2 KB 291 (CA).

thereof.'[86] Section 1(2) of the PPA requires that any challenge to an order must be made within six months from the date of the order.[87] After this period of time, an order made will extinguish the title of third parties. If the statutory procedure is followed and an order is made, the police cannot be sued for conversion.[88] Any private individual must therefore act promptly in taking legal proceedings in the civil courts to prove that he is in fact the true owner of an object.[89]

The PPA provides a simple procedure. It is appropriate to use it where no complex issue of law or significant factual question needs to be resolved.[90] Reflecting this fact, costs are rarely awarded.[91] However, an application under the PPA is merely one option open to the owner of an object[92] and there may be good reasons why a claimant will wish to sue in the civil courts instead.[93]

The procedure available under the PPA is inappropriate in any case where there is difficulty regarding title.[94] If a litigant is not an owner but merely has a claim to possession,[95] he will not be able to obtain an order for delivery up under the PPA. The PPA provides that the claimant must demonstrate that he is the 'owner'.[96] It has therefore been held that the mere fact that the claimant was in possession of an object before it was seized by the police will not suffice.[97]

The court may refuse to make an order where, for example, there are concurrent civil proceedings, the case is complicated or large sums of money are at stake.[98] Conflicting claims to goods may raise difficult legal questions, such as where it is claimed that title has been acquired by way of one of the exceptions to the *nemo dat* rule set out in the Sale of Goods Act 1979.[99] There is the additional risk that the country of origin will make a claim to the property under its national laws, including its export laws.[100]

[86] PPA, s 1(1).

[87] *R (on the application of Simin) v Miksin, Cynon Valley and Merthyr Tydfil Magistrates' Court* [2001] EWHC Admin 710; *Rashid v Chief Constable of Northumbria Police* (CA, 17 December 1990).

[88] See the remarks of Lord Denning MR and Sir Stanley Rees in *R v Uxbridge Justices, ex p Commissioner of Police of the Metropolis* [1981] QB 829 (CA) 834, 846–47, followed in *Chief Constable of Merseyside v Parker* (CA, 13 June 1994) (McCowan J). See further, *Betts v Receiver for the Metropolitan Police District and Carter Paterson & Co Ltd* [1932] 2 KB 595, 604 (Du Parcq J).

[89] *Irving v National Provincial Bank Ltd* [1962] 2 QB 73 (CA) 78–79; *Stupple v Royal Insurance Co* [1971] 1 QB 50 (CA) 63.

[90] *Price v Dobson* [2006] EWHC 1017 [4]; *Gough v Chief Constable of the West Midlands Police* [2004] EWCA Civ 206 (CA) [18]–[19]; *Haley v Chief Constable of Northumbria Police* [2002] EWHC 1942 [17]; *Raymond Lyons & Co Ltd v Met Police Comr* [1975] 1 QB 321 (CA) 326. See further *R v Basildon Justices, ex p Holding & Barnes plc* (1994) *The Times*, 26 April; *Flynn v Commissioner of Police* (6 October 1993).

[91] *R v Uxbridge Justices, ex p Commissioner of Police of the Metropolis* [1981] QB 829 (CA) 847 (Sir Stanley Rees), followed in *Chief Constable of Merseyside v Parker* (CA, 13 June 1994) (where an appeal from an award of costs was successful).

[92] *McK v McD* [2005] IEHC 205.

[93] As regards the action in conversion, see 5.09–5.13. See also 5.03.

[94] *Raymond Lyons & Co Ltd v Met Police Comr* [1975] QB 321 (CA) 326; approved in *Flynn v Commissioner of Police* (CA, 6 October 1993); see further, *R v Calcutt and Varty* [1986] Crim LR 267 (DC).

[95] As regards the distinction between a legal title and a possessory title, see ch 5.

[96] This expression is given its ordinary meaning, so that a purchaser under a void contract would still be described as the owner: *Chief Constable of West Midlands v White* (3 March 1992).

[97] *Raymond Lyons & Co. Ltd v Metropolitan Police Commissioner* [1975] QB 321 (CA) 325 (Lord Widgery CJ). However, where the person in possession had a lien over the property, the owner will need to satisfy the debt and thereby discharge the lien in order to recover the property: *Marsh v Commissioner of Police* [1945] KB 43 (CA).

[98] *Vidail Ltd v Metropolitan Police Commissioner* (28 January 1993); *Rashid v Chief Constable of Northumbria Police* (CA, 17 December 1990); *Jackson v Chief Constable of the West Midlands Police* (22 October 1993) (Laws J).

[99] See 5.33–5.51.

[100] *Government of the Islamic Republic of Iran v Barakat Galleries Ltd* [2007] EWCA Civ 1374, [2009] QB 22 (CA); *A-G of New Zealand v Ortiz* [1984] AC 1 (HL); *United States v An Antique Platter of Gold, Known as a Gold*

Even where goods in police custody are not the subject matter of any criminal charge, if they are expected to be used in evidence in relation to other offences with which the accused has been charged, then no order should be made until the criminal proceedings have been completed or discharged.[101] However, where it turns out that an individual is not charged with or convicted of an offence relating to goods taken from him by the police in the course of their investigations, the ordinary procedure is for the court to order the return of the goods to the individual concerned. Each case will turn on its own facts, and will depend on the credibility of the parties and other relevant circumstances.[102] A court cannot refuse to return an item of property because it suspects that it is derived from criminal activity.[103]

Confiscation Orders

4.14 General Principles

The Proceeds of Crime Act 2002 provides the statutory scheme by which persons who are convicted of crimes and have benefited from those crimes may be ordered by a Crown Court to pay to the state a sum of money equivalent to that benefit, failing which they will be imprisoned for their failure to pay.[104] The property recovered under a confiscation order ordinarily accrues to the benefit of the state rather than to a victim or third party who may have an interest in the property concerned but who fails to protect his interests.[105]

'Confiscation' in this context is something of a misnomer, since a confiscation order is a debt owed to the state. It is an order *in personam* to pay the sum of money, rather than 'confiscating' particular assets. So if, for example, a person was convicted of handling a stolen antiquity valued at £100,000, this was assessed as his benefit from the crime, and the court made a confiscation order in the sum of £100,000, then the offender would (under confiscation laws) be free to pay that sum from another source of wealth and retain the stolen antiquity. That said, a number of features of the confiscation regime mean that an offender will often be required to hand possession of a stolen item to a receiver appointed to the court for the purpose of realising sums to satisfy the confiscation order against him, and so the item in question may be recovered by the state in this way.

4.15 'Benefit' From Criminal Conduct

According to section 6(4) of the Proceeds of Crime Act 2002, a court must decide whether, on the balance of probabilities, the criminal obtained a benefit 'as a result of or in connection

Phiale Mesomphalos, c. 400 BC, 900 F Supp 222 (SDNY 1997); 184 F 2d 131 (2d Cir 1999) cert denied, 528 US 1136 (2000); M Lufkin, 'Forfeiture of an Antiquity Claimed by Italy: the Steinhardt Case' (2000) V *Art Antiquity and Law* 57; *Schultz v US* 533 F 3d 393 (2003): US CA 2nd Circuit decision of 25 June 2003. M Lufkin, 'Criminal Liability for Receiving State-Claimed Antiquities in the United States: The 'Schultz' Case' (2003) VIII *Art Antiquity and Law* 321; see further *R v Tokeley-Parry* [1999] Crim LR 578 (CA); *Autocephalous Greek-Orthodox Church v Goldberg* 717 F Supp 1374 (SD Ind 1989) and 917 F 2d 278 (7th Cir, 1990).

[101] *R v Blackburn Magistrates Court, ex p The Chief Constable of Lancashire Constabulary* (12 February 1996).

[102] See *R v Bristol Magistrates' Court ex p Clarke* (16 May 1994).

[103] *R (on the application of Morgan) v Dyfed Powys Magistrates' Court* [2003] All ER (D) 226.

[104] See generally *Smith Owen & Bodnar on Asset Recovery: Criminal Confiscation and Civil Recovery* (Oxford, Oxford University Press, Looseleaf) and *Millington and Sutherland-Williams on the Proceeds of Crime*, 3rd edn (Oxford, Oxford University Press, 2010). For a survey of modern confiscation law, see J Ulph, 'Confiscation Orders, Human Rights, and Penal Measures' (2010) 126 *Law Quarterly Review* 251.

[105] See 4.22 for the right of victims and third parties to assert their interests in property which is the subject of confiscation enforcement proceedings

with the conduct'.[106] The benefit can include intangible as well as tangible property.[107] In the simplest terms, in the case of theft of an object, the benefit will be the market value of that object. However, whilst it may be a simple matter to determine the market value of, say, a print, the same cannot be said in relation to cultural objects and original artwork, given their uniqueness.

But what does 'obtains' mean in this context? In *Crown Prosecution Service v Jennings*,[108] the House of Lords was invited to consider the precise meaning of these terms. The committee of the House of Lords considered that the statutory provisions should be given their plain English meaning and, regardless of whether the word 'obtains' or 'received' was used, the court should consider whether the defendant had gained property:

> This must ordinarily mean that he has obtained property so as to *own* it, whether alone or jointly, which will ordinarily connote *a power of disposition or control*, as where a person directs a payment or conveyance of property to someone else.[109]

Even if an object has been recovered by a law enforcement agency, if the offender had obtained the object it will still be counted as a benefit to him, regardless of the fact that he did not ultimately retain the object.[110]

4.16 'Criminal Lifestyle'

If any offender falls within the 'criminal lifestyle' definition[111], it is assumed by sections 6(4) and 10 that any income gained, or property received, or expenditure incurred, *over a period of six years* prior to the commencement of proceedings has been derived from the defendant's 'general criminal conduct'.[112] The defendant can rebut these assumptions by establishing that the property in question did not stem from criminal conduct.[113]

4.17 'A Course of Criminal Activity'

A defendant may also be subject to the assumptions if his conduct forms 'part of a course of criminal activity'. By section 75(3), this is where the criminal has two convictions for the same offence within the last six years from each of which he has benefited, or where he has been convicted of four charges in the same proceedings from each of which he has benefited. Equally, the assumptions will be applied if the offence is one committed over a period of more than six months. Unless the total benefit is less than £5,000,[114] these provisions will apply.

[106] POCA 2002, s 76(4).
[107] See ibid, s 84(1). See further, CJA 1988, s 102(1).
[108] *Crown Prosecution Service v Jennings* [2008] UKHL 29, [2008] AC 1046.
[109] [2008] UKHL 29; [2008] AC 1046 [13] (emphasis added).
[110] *R v Wilkes (Gary John)* [2003] Crim LR 487 (CA) [32].
[111] Contained in POCA 2002, s 75. There are three ways in which a person will be deemed to have a criminal lifestyle under this provision. First, a person has a criminal lifestyle if he has committed an offence specified in Sch 2 to POCA 2002 (which includes money laundering offences under ss 327 and 328 POCA 2002). Secondly, a person has a criminal lifestyle if his offence(s) 'constitutes conduct forming part of a course of criminal activity' as further defined in the provision. Thirdly, a person has a criminal lifestyle if his offence(s) is/are committed over a period of at least six months and the defendant has benefited from the conduct which constitutes the offence.
[112] This distinction between particular and general criminal conduct is set out in POCA 2002, s 76(1)–(3).
[113] POCA 2002, s 4(6).
[114] ibid, s 75(4)-(5).

4.18 The 'Available Amount'

Once the value of an offender's benefit has been assessed by the court, it will go on to make a confiscation order in that amount[115] unless the offender can show that 'the available amount' is less than the value of his benefit.[116] The 'available amount' is essentially the total value of all property[117] held by the offender, together with any 'tainted gifts'[118] to other persons. It will certainly include any property which the offender has illegally obtained, including objects of art or antiquity. Suppose a burglar steals a painting from a museum but is arrested as he leaves. The painting is eventually returned to the museum by the police. It is worth one million pounds. If the burglar is wealthy, the confiscation order which will be made will be for the sum of one million pounds, and this is the amount which the burglar will be obliged to pay to the state if he wishes to avoid a further term of imprisonment. However, the burglar may be relatively poor. If he only has £300 in assets, these assets are the available amount. The burglar will be expected to transfer them to satisfy the confiscation order which will be made for this lesser sum.

4.19 Protection of Victims and Third Parties Rights at the Enforcement Stage

A person who has a legal and/or beneficial interest in property continues to hold such an interest even where the property has been taken into consideration at the time of making a confiscation order against a defendant. At the confiscation enforcement stage, such a person must be served with a copy of the application to court for the appointment of an enforcement receiver.[119] The court is not permitted to empower the receiver to manage or realise the property without first giving the person who appears to hold an interest an opportunity to make representations to the court.[120]

Civil Recovery Orders

4.20 Conditions for Recovery Orders to be Made

POCA 2002 Part 5, Chapter 2, empowers the High Court to make civil recovery orders.[121] These are essentially orders forfeiting specified property to the state. Proceedings under Part 5 of POCA directly concern the property that is the subject of the claim, rather than the conduct of the defendant. The property recovered in civil recovery proceedings ordinarily accrues to the benefit of the state rather than to a victim or third party who may have an interest in the property concerned but who fails to protect his interests.[122]

[115] ibid, s 7(1).

[116] ibid, s 7(2).

[117] See ibid, ss 82 and 84.

[118] For the meaning of 'tainted gifts' see ibid, ss 77 and 78. A gift is tainted if it satisfied one or more of a number of triggers set out in s 77, including that the gift was of property which was obtained as a result of criminal conduct, that the gift was made on or after the time of the offending, and that the gift was made in the period of six years before the offender was prosecuted.

[119] Criminal Procedure Rules 2010, r 60.1(6)(b) and (c).

[120] POCA 2002, s 51(8).

[121] See generally *Smith Owen & Bodnar on Asset Recovery: Criminal Confiscation and Civil Recovery* (Oxford, Oxford University Press, Looseleaf) and *Millington and Sutherland-Williams on the Proceeds of Crime* (Oxford, Oxford University Press, 2010).

[122] See 4.22 for the right of victims and third parties to assert their interests in property which is the subject of civil recovery proceedings.

There is no requirement that a person be convicted of any crime before civil recovery proceedings may be brought. In order to make a civil recovery order in respect of an object of art or antiquity, the court must be satisfied that the property in question is 'recoverable property'.[123] 'Recoverable property' is defined quite simply as 'property obtained through unlawful conduct'.[124] 'Unlawful conduct' is any conduct which is 'unlawful' under the criminal law of the part of the United Kingdom in which it occurs.[125] Additionally, conduct occurring in another country which is unlawful both under the criminal law of that country and the United Kingdom is also unlawful for this purpose.[126] However, no civil recovery proceedings may be brought for the recovery of property situated outside the UK.[127] It is not necessary for the law enforcement claimant to show that the unlawful conduct was of a particular kind if it is shown that the property was obtained through conduct of one of a number of kinds, each of them which would have been unlawful conduct.[128] It is not sufficient for the claimant law enforcement agency simply to show that a respondent had no identifiable lawful income to warrant his holding of the property in question[129] but an untruthful explanation or a failure to offer an explanation may add strength to the case for civil recovery.[130]

Property is obtained 'through unlawful conduct' if it is obtained 'by or in return for' that conduct.[131] For this to be the case:

- there must be a direct link between the unlawful conduct and the obtaining of the property;[132] and
- the unlawful conduct must have made a 'material contribution' to the acquisition of the property in question.[133]

4.21 Defences to Civil Recovery

A person will have a defence and no recovery order would be made in respect of an object where:[134]

- the respondent obtained the recoverable property in good faith;
- he took steps after obtaining the property which he would not have taken if he had not obtained it, or he took steps before obtaining the property which he would not have taken if he had not believed he was going to obtain it;
- when he took the steps he had no notice that the property was recoverable;
- if a recovery order were made in respect of the property, it would, by reason of the steps, be detrimental to him; and
- it would not be just and equitable to make the order for civil recovery.

[123] POCA 2002, s 266(1).
[124] ibid, s 304(1).
[125] ibid, s 241(1).
[126] ibid, s 241(2). See, for example, *Serious Organised Crime Agency v Perry* (2009) ACD 254(68), QBD.
[127] *Perry v Serious Organised Crime Agency* [2012] UK SC 35.
[128] ibid, s 242(2)(b).
[129] *Director of the Assets Recovery Agency v Szepietowski* [2007] EWCA Civ 766, [2008] Lloyd's Rep FC 10, *The Times*, 21 August 2007 [26]; *Director of the Assets Recovery Agency v Olupitan* [2008] EWCA Civ 104, [2008] CP Rep 24, [2008] Lloyd's Rep FC 253,.
[130] *Director of the Assets Recovery Agency v Szepietowski* cited above, [28]; *Director of the Assets Recovery Agency v Olupitan* [2008] CP Rep 24 [16].
[131] POCA 2002, s 242(1).
[132] *Director of the Assets Recovery Agency v Lord* [2007] EWHC 360 (QB) (Tugendhat J) [63ff].
[133] *R (Chief Constable of Greater Manchester) v Salford Magistrates' Court* [2008] EWHC 1651 (Admin).
[134] POCA 2002, s 266(3), (4) and (6).

It would appear that this defence is open to a person who:

– receives the property by way of a gift or having given value for it; or
– is a mere possessor of the property, rather than a beneficial owner,

and can otherwise satisfy the conditions of this defence.

The holder of an object sought in civil recovery proceedings may also have a defence where he was not the person to first obtain the object in question by unlawful conduct. A subsequent acquirer of property is able to defeat a civil recovery claim, where he obtained it:[135]

– in good faith;
– for value; and
– without notice that it was recoverable property.

So for example a purchaser who acts honestly in buying an object (at value) would have a defence to a civil recovery claim. It is likely that the courts would draw on established principles from common law case law in relation to the concepts of good faith, value and without notice.[136]

A person is entitled to invoke the rights contained in the European Convention on Human Rights (within the meaning of the Human Rights Act 1998).[137] Of particular significance is Article 1 of Protocol 1 to the European Convention on Human Rights, which entitles a person to peaceful enjoyment of his possessions. The right to peaceful enjoyment is a qualified right with the state permitted to deprive a person of property 'in the general interest and subject to the conditions provided for by law and by the general principles of international law.' An innocent acquirer of an object but who cannot show that he acquired the object for value and so would not have a defence under POCA may be able to challenge the order on the basis that there is a violation of Article 1 of Protocol 1, where he is able to show that he has obtained good title to the object in question pursuant to the law applicable to the transaction by which he obtained the object.[138]

Lastly, a person may defeat civil recovery proceedings and no civil recovery order may be made where a limitation defence applies. Civil recovery proceedings may not be brought after 20 years from the date on which a cause of action accrued,[139] the cause of action accruing when then the property was unlawfully obtained.[140]

4.22 Victims' Rights

A person to whom an object 'belongs' is entitled to apply to the High Court, where civil recovery proceedings are pending, for a declaration that the property belongs to that person and should not be made the subject of a recovery order in favour of the state.[141] Obviously, such an application is to be brought by, and if successful is entirely in favour of, the person applying for the declaration. The applicant must not only show that the object

[135] ibid, s 308(1).
[136] See 5.37. For a detailed analysis of these principles, see ch 17 'Good Faith and Due Diligence' in N E Palmer and E McKendrick (eds) *Interests in Goods,* 2nd edn (London, Lloyd's of London Press, 1998) 403–27.
[137] POCA 2002, s 266(3)(b)
[138] See 6.25–6.30 for further discussion of the applicable law to the disposal of property.
[139] Limitation Act 1980, s 27A(2).
[140] ibid, s 27A(4)(a).
[141] POCA 2002, s 281(1).

'belongs' to him but that he was deprived of the object by 'unlawful conduct'[142] and that the object was not already recoverable property when he was deprived of it.[143]

There has been no interpretation from the courts of the meaning of 'belongs'. This is mostly likely to be interpreted as meaning that the applicant beneficially owns the object in question. Broadly speaking, the protection afforded will not apply to persons who are deprived of an object after it has already been unlawfully obtained by another unless they can show that one of the defences to civil recovery applies.[144]

For an owner of property to assert his rights in the property under POCA 2002, s 281, he must of course be aware that it has become the subject of proceedings. This is likely to be the case as it is very likely that he will have been served with the claim either on the basis that he 'holds' the property in question[145] or because he holds so called 'associated property',[146] which in simplest terms is an interest in property which is partly said to be recoverable and partly which is not recoverable.

Clearly, an intervention seeking a declaration under POCA 2002, s 281 must be made whilst the recovery proceedings are ongoing.[147]

A declaration under POCA 2002, s 281 in respect of movable property would be enforceable under the EU Judgments Regulation[148] or Lugano[149] Conventions.[150] It would not however be enforceable under a bilateral convention between the United Kingdom and an overseas state, given that it is a judgment *in rem* rather than a money judgment.

Deprivation Orders

4.23 General Principles

Forfeiture of 'the instrumentalities of crime', meaning property used in committing the crime, by the criminal courts has been provided for under a number of statutes for many years.[151] There is a general power to forfeit property under s 143 of POCC(S)A 2000, which is triggered by conviction of a person for any offence. We refer to these orders as Deprivation Orders.[152]

[142] See 4.20 for the meaning of this term.

[143] POCA 2002, s 281(2) and (3).

[144] See 4.21.

[145] POCA 2002, s 243(1).

[146] ibid, s 243(2)(b) (unless the court dispenses with such service, and it is difficult to see in what circumstances it would).

[147] ibid, s 281(1) prefaces the right to seek such an order with the words 'In proceedings for a recovery order'.

[148] Council Regulation 44/2001/EC of 22 December 2000 on jurisdiction and the recognition and enforcement of judgments in civil and commercial matters, OJ L307/1.

[149] Lugano Convention on Jurisdiction and the Enforcement of Judgments in Civil and Commercial Matters, OJ L319/9.

[150] See Regulation 44/2001/EC, s 2 (Enforcement), mirrored by the Brussels and Lugano Conventions.

[151] For example, counterfeit coins and forged banknotes may be forfeited under s 24 of the Forgery and Counterfeiting Act 1981; controlled drugs under the Misuse of Drugs Act 1971, s 27.

[152] POCC(S)A does not name these orders. Deprivation Order is the term used by the leading criminal practitioners' text, *Archbold: Criminal Pleading, Evidence & Practice* (London, Sweet & Maxwell, Looseleaf). See generally *Smith Owen & Bodnar on Asset Recovery: Criminal Confiscation and Civil Recovery* (Oxford, Oxford University Press, Looseleaf).

4.24 What May be Forfeit under a Deprivation Order?

Following a person's conviction by a criminal court, any property used to commit or facilitate the commission of any offence,[153] or which was intended to be so used, may be ordered to be forfeit, as long as it was lawfully seized from him or if it was in the defendant's possession or control at the time of arrest or when a summons in respect of it was issued.[154]

This power is wide enough to enable the criminal courts to make deprivation orders in respect of stolen property, including art and antiquities, where the stolen item will be used by a defendant to commit or facilitate the commission of an offence, for example an offence of money laundering or fraud.[155] The use of the property does not need to relate to the offence of which the defendant has been convicted, but it should not relate to an offence committed by someone other than the defendant.[156]

Deprivation orders may be made in conjunction with any other sentence but when considering whether to make a deprivation order the court must have regard to the value of the property proposed to be forfeit and to the likely financial and other effects on the defendant.[157] A court must not excessively punish a defendant.[158] It is difficult to see how depriving an offender of stolen property would ever be considered excessive, even when combined with other punishments.

4.25 Effect of a Deprivation Order

The effect of a deprivation order is to deprive the relevant convicted person of his rights, if any, in the property in question. The property, if not already in the possession of the police, is taken into their possession.[159] Following a deprivation order, the police are required to deal with the property in accordance with the general law and in accordance with the PPA.[160] The PPA applies to items which are the subject of a deprivation order, subject to the following modifications to the ordinary application of the PPA:

- No application may be made for delivery up of property under section 1(1) of the PPA after the end of six months from the date of any deprivation order in respect of the property.[161]
- No application under the PPA shall succeed unless the claimant satisfies the court either that he has not consented to the offender having possession of the property, or that he did not know and had no reason to suspect that the property was likely to be used for the purpose of committing, or facilitating the commission of, any offence, or was intended by him to be used for that purpose.[162]

[153] POCC(S)A, s 143(8) provides: 'Facilitating the commission of an offence shall be taken for the purposes of subsection (1) above to include the taking of any steps after it has been committed for the purpose of disposing of any property to which it relates or of avoiding apprehension or detection.'

[154] POCC(S)A, s 143(1).

[155] Money laundering is a misnomer as the money laundering offences apply to acts concerning criminal property. See POCA 2002 ss 327–29 (read together with s 340).

[156] *R v Slater* [1986] 1 WLR 1340.

[157] POCC(S)A, s 143(4) and (5).

[158] In *R v Buddo* [1982] Crim LR 837 the Court of Appeal allowed an appeal against a forfeiture order in respect of a caravanette which the defendant had driven to a chemist's shop which he had then burgled. The defendant had been sentenced to two years in custody for assaults on police officers while resisting arrest. The Court of Appeal held that the forfeiture of the caravanette in addition to the custodial sentence was 'overdoing the punishment'.

[159] POCC(S)A, s 143(3)

[160] See 4.13.

[161] POCC(S)A, s 144(1)(a).

[162] ibid, s 144(1)(b).

Forfeiture Orders

4.26 Summary

As set out above,[163] objects which have been improperly imported or exported (or attempted to be improperly exported) are liable to be forfeited under CEMA.

III Powers and Procedures Available to Assist Foreign Courts and Law Enforcement Agencies

4.27 Introduction

This section deals with the assistance which the English and Welsh courts may give to overseas courts for the recovery of art and antiquities. For example, assistance would be available to recover an object stolen in a foreign state but which is located in England and Wales.

Cooperation is available under two regimes.

- *Overseas External Orders*: Proceeds of Crime Act 2002 (External Requests and Orders) Order 2005;[164]
- *Overseas Forfeiture Orders*: Criminal Justice (International Co-operation) Act 1990 (Enforcement of Overseas Forfeiture Orders) Order 2005.[165]

Overseas External Requests and Orders – in Respect of Foreign Criminal Proceedings

4.28 Introduction

Under the Proceeds of Crime Act 2002 (External Requests and Orders) Order 2005 (the POCA Order 2005), the United Kingdom can provide assistance in enforcing foreign forfeiture and confiscation orders in respect of assets held in the United Kingdom.[166] The United Kingdom is also able to restrain assets held in the United Kingdom at the request of foreign states. It is not able to restrain assets outside the United Kingdom in support of foreign proceedings.[167]

The POCA Order 2005 sets out a scheme for the enforcement of foreign confiscation orders and provision of assistance in obtaining restraint orders in all criminal cases. The powers to give assistance are triggered by the receipt by the Secretary of State of either an 'external request' or an 'external order' from an overseas authority.

[163] See 4.06.

[164] SI 2005/3181.

[165] SI 2005/3180.

[166] POCA Order 2005, art 6; *King v Serious Fraud Office* [2009] UKHL 17, [2009] 1 WLR 718, [2009] Lloyd's Rep FC 435 [34]–[38]. See generally *Smith Owen & Bodnar on Asset Recovery: Criminal Confiscation and Civil Recovery* (Oxford, Oxford University Press, Looseleaf).

[167] *King v Serious Fraud Office*, cited above, [34]–[38]

The POCA Order 2005 uses the following terms:

- 'external request': a request by an overseas authority to prohibit dealing with relevant property which is identified in the request;[168]
- 'external order': this is an order which is made by an overseas court where property is found or believed to have been obtained as a result of or in connection with criminal conduct, and is for the recovery of specified property or a specified sum of money;[169]
- 'relevant property': property is relevant property if there are reasonable grounds to believe that it may be needed to satisfy an external order which has been or which may be made.[170]

4.29 Restraint Orders

On an application by a prosecuting agency (it having been referred the case by the Secretary of State[171] who has received an 'external request' from an overseas authority); the court may make an order prohibiting a person from dealing with relevant property which is identified in the external request. A restraint order may be made where one of the following two conditions are satisfied.[172]

The first condition is that:[173]

- relevant property in England and Wales is identified in the external request;
- a criminal investigation has been started in the country from which the external request was made with regard to an offence; and
- there is reasonable cause to believe that the alleged offender named in the request has benefited from his criminal conduct.

The second condition is that:[174]

- relevant property in England and Wales is identified in the external request;
- proceedings for an offence have been started in the country from which the external request was made and not concluded; and
- there is reasonable cause to believe that the defendant named in the request has benefited from his criminal conduct.

If a restraint order is in force, a constable or a relevant officer of Revenue and Customs may seize any property which is specified in it to prevent its removal from England and Wales. Any property so seized must be dealt with in accordance with the court's directions.[175] The court may appoint a management receiver[176] who may then exercise specified powers of management in respect of the relevant property specified in the order.[177]

168 POCA 2002, s 447(1).
169 ibid, s 447(2).
170 ibid, s 447(4).
171 POCA Order 2005, art 6.
172 ibid, art 8(1).
173 ibid, art 7(2).
174 ibid, art 7(3).
175 ibid, art 12; see above in relation to equivalent seizure in domestic cases.
176 ibid, art 15.
177 ibid, art 16.

4.30 Enforcement of External Orders

The Crown Court's power to enforce an 'external order' is contained in Chapter 2 of Part 2 of the POCA Order 2005. There are three stages in the enforcement of such an order:

– reference to the head of the appropriate prosecution agency by the Secretary of State;[178]
– application by the relevant director to the Crown Court for the registration of the order;[179]
– enforcement by order of the Crown Court.

The Crown Court must give effect to the external order by registering it where all four of the following conditions are satisfied:[180]

– the the external order was made consequent on the conviction of the person named in the order and no appeal is outstanding in respect of that conviction;[181]
– the external order is in force and no appeal is outstanding in respect of it;[182]
– the external order would not be incompatible with the Convention rights (within the meaning of the Human Rights Act 1998 (HRA 1998)) of any person affected by it;[183]
– in respect of any external order which authorises the confiscation of property other than money that is specified in the order,[184] the specified property must not be subject to a charge under the legislation specified in art 21(6).[185]

Where the Crown Court decides to give effect to an external order, it must register the order in that court[186] and provide for the notice of the registration to be given to any person affected by it.[187] Clearly, this means that any person with a genuine interest in an object must be given notice.

Overseas External Requests and Orders – in Respect of Foreign Civil Proceedings

4.31 Introduction

Foreign enforcement authorities and other persons seeking the enforcement of civil recovery orders or provisional and protective measures in civil recovery proceedings[188] may use provisions in the Proceeds of Crime Act 2002 (External Requests and Orders) Order 2005[189]

[178] Except in cases of serious or complex fraud the Secretary of State may refer an external order arising from a criminal conviction in the country from which the order was sent and concerning relevant property in England and Wales to either the Director of Public Prosecutions or the Director of Revenue and Customs Prosecutions (POCA Order 2005, art 18(1)). Cases of serious or complex fraud may be referred to the Director of SFO (ibid, art 18(2)).

[179] The relevant prosecuting agency may apply to the Crown Court to give effect to the external order under ibid, art 20(1).

[180] ibid, art 21(1).

[181] ibid, art 21(2).

[182] ibid, art 21(3).

[183] ibid, art 21(4).

[184] ibid, art 21(5).

[185] ibid, art 21(6): namely orders under various confiscation enactments.

[186] ibid, art 22(1)(a).

[187] ibid, art 22(1)(b).

[188] See generally *Smith Owen & Bodnar on Asset Recovery: Criminal Confiscation and Civil Recovery* (Oxford, Oxford University Press, Looseleaf).

[189] The Proceeds of Crime Act 2002 (External Requests and Orders) Order 2005, SI 2005/3181; in particular ch 5 of the Order.

(POCA Order 2005) in the High Court for the recovery of property derived from criminal conduct (albeit that such conduct does not have to be proved to the criminal standard). The property recovered in such proceedings ordinarily accrues to the benefit of the state[190] rather than to a victim or third party who may have an interest in the property concerned but who fails to protect his interests.

Part 5 of the POCA Order 2005 enables (but does not require) the Secretary of State to forward an external order to the relevant enforcement authority.[191] The powers under the POCA Order 2005 apply whether or not proceedings have been brought, in the country from which the external order was sent, for criminal conduct in connection with the property.[192] Governmental responsibility for mutual assistance in crime-related matters lies with the Secretary of State for the Home Department, whose responsibilities are delegated to the section of the Home Office called the UK Central Authority.

4.32 Orders that will be Enforced

The relevant enforcement authority in the UK is empowered to bring proceedings to enforce any order, which it thinks constitutes an 'external order' by an overseas court when a request has been forwarded to it by the Secretary of State.[193]

An 'external order' is defined as an order which is made by an overseas court where property is found or believed to have been obtained as a result of criminal conduct and is for the recovery of specified property or a specified sum of money.[194] 'Criminal conduct' is defined as conduct which constitutes an offence in any part of the United Kingdom or would constitute an offence in any part of the United Kingdom if it occurred there.[195]

4.33 External Orders that do not Arise from Criminal Convictions

Part 5 of the POCA Order 2005 is concerned with the enforcement of foreign court orders which do not arise from criminal convictions in the country from which the order was sent. Although the provisions in Part 5 are not expressly limited to orders which do not arise from criminal convictions, this is the effective position for two reasons:

- The POCA Order 2005 contains a separate regime for giving effect to external orders arising from criminal convictions.[196]
- Internationally, it is important to retain a clear distinction in procedures as between (criminal) recovery of the proceeds of crime following conviction and (civil) recovery without conviction.[197]

[190] See 4.03 regarding asset sharing agreements

[191] POCA Order, art 142(2). For the meaning of 'enforcement authority' in this context, see ibid, art 213.

[192] ibid, art 142(3).

[193] ibid, art 143

[194] POCA, s 447(2); POCA Order, art 2.

[195] POCA 2002, s 447(8). This provision mirrors the definitions of 'criminal conduct' for the purposes of confiscation proceedings in England and Wales (ibid, s 76(1)), Scotland (ibid, s 143(1)) and Northern Ireland (ibid, s 224 (1)).

[196] See 4.26–4.28.

[197] See *Smith Owen & Bodnar on Asset Recovery: Criminal Confiscation and Civil Recovery* (Oxford, Oxford University Press, Looseleaf), Pt III, ch 2 in relation to the importance of the distinction. The distinction was blurred under the earlier Criminal Justice Act 1988 (CJA 1988) and DTA which provided for the enforcement of 'external confiscation orders'. For a detailed commentary, see I Smith and T Owen, *Asset Recovery* (London, LexisNexis Butterworths, 2003) paras 13.50–13.55 and the cases of *Re S-L (also known as Re Londono)* [1995] 4 All ER 159, [1995] 3 WLR 830; and *Government of the United States v Montgomery* [1999] 1 All ER 84 (CA) (Stuart-Smith LJ) [22].

4.34 Proceedings for Recovery Orders

The enforcement authority may bring proceedings in the High Court against any person it thinks holds recoverable property.[198] Property is 'recoverable property' if it is specified in an external order (within the meaning of s 447(2) of POCA 2002).[199]

4.35 Following Recoverable Property into the Hands of Others

As a general rule, property which was found or believed to have been obtained as a result of criminal conduct is recoverable whoever holds the property. However, in order to mitigate the harshness of this rule in respect of innocent persons who acquire recoverable property, POCA Order 2005 provides certain safeguards for:

(1) a person who obtains property in good faith, for value and without notice that it was recoverable property;[200]
(2) a person who satisfies the following conditions:[201]
    (a) a person obtains property in good faith;
    (b) without notice that it was recoverable property;
    (c) he took steps after obtaining the property which he would not have taken if he had not obtained it or took steps before obtaining the property which he would not have taken if he had not believed he was going to obtain it;
    (d) when he took the steps he had no notice that the property was recoverable; and
    (e) if a recovery order were made in respect of the property, it would, by reason of the steps be detrimental to him;
(3) victims of crime who receive the recoverable property from persons having brought a private law suit alleging criminal conduct which gave rise to the criminal property.[202]

4.36 External Orders may Predate POCA 2002 and the POCA Order 2005

Neither POCA 2002 nor the POCA Order 2005 place any restriction on the enforcement of an external order by reference to the time when the external order was made. Under previous legislation for the enforcement of foreign orders, the House of Lords held that the court was not confined to orders made after the enabling legislation became operational in respect of the country of the court making the external order.[203] It is highly likely that the courts will adopt the same approach in relation to external orders under POCA 2002 and the POCA Order 2005.

4.37 Limitation Periods

Although the fact that an external order or the relevant criminal conduct predates POCA 2002 and the POCA Order 2005, limitation periods do apply to time-bar actions for recov-

[198] POCA Order 2005, art 143. (The corresponding provision in POCA 2002 is s 243.)
[199] ibid, art 202. (The corresponding provision in POCA is s 304.)
[200] ibid, art 205(1). (The corresponding provision in POCA is s 308.)
[201] ibid, art 177(5). (The corresponding provision in POCA is s 266.)
[202] ibid, art 205(2). (The corresponding provision in POCA is s 308.)
[203] *Government of the United States v Montgomery* [2001] 1 All ER 815, [2001] 1 WLR 196 (Lord Hoffman) [24]–[30] (a case concerning CJA 1988 and the Criminal Justice Act 1988 (Designated Countries etc) Order 1991, SI 1991/2873, Sch 3 of which contains modified provisions of CJA 1988).

ery of property under an external order. The enforcement authority is not permitted to bring such proceedings after the expiration of 20 years from the date on which the enforcement authority's cause of action accrued.[204] In the case of proceedings for a recovery order in respect of property obtained, or believed to have been obtained, as a result of or in connection with criminal conduct, the action accrued when the property is so obtained.[205] The 20-year period is a lengthy one, when compared with statutory periods of limitation generally under the Limitation Act 1980.[206]

4.38 Provisional and Protective Orders

The provisional and protective orders which the UK courts may make in support of proceedings for a recovery order are to a large extent the same as those available in support of purely domestic proceedings for a recovery order under POCA 2002 and are dealt with in detail in Part II, Chapter 1. The following is a summary of the provisional and protective orders available and the differences between the orders available under POCA Order 2005 and in purely domestic proceedings:

- *Freezing order*: either a Property Freezing Order[207] (England and Wales and Northern Ireland) or a Prohibitory Property Order[208] (Scotland) prohibiting a person from dealing with, diminishing the value of, or disposing of property.[209]
- *Interim Receiving Order* for the detention, custody or preservation of the property and the appointment of an interim receiver whose powers are set out in POCA Order 2005, Sch 2.

An interim receiving order:

- must require the interim receiver to take any steps which the court thinks necessary to establish whether or not the property to which the order applies is recoverable property;[210] and
- may (in England and Wales and Northern Ireland) or must (in Scotland) require him to take any steps which the court thinks necessary to establish whether or not any other property is recoverable property and, if it is, who holds it.[211]

4.39 Recovery Orders

The High Court must make a recovery order in respect of property if it is satisfied that the foreign court which has made the order has 'found' or 'believed' that the property in question

[204] Limitation Act 1980, s 27B(2).

[205] ibid, s 27B(4).

[206] In relation to the Limitation Act 1980, see 5.39–5.43.

[207] POCA Order 2005, arts 147–50. These provisions are substantially the same as the provisions of POCA, ss 245A, 245B, 245C, and 245D, save that the POCA provisions contain the narrower definition of recoverable property under POCA, s 304.

[208] ibid, arts 161–66. (The corresponding provision in POCA are ss 255A–255F.)

[209] The grant of a Property Freezing Order or Prohibitory Property Order is not automatic. There must be a 'good arguable case' that the property to be frozen (or, as the case may be, prohibited) is recoverable or associated property. See arts 147(5) and 161(5). In accordance with applicable principle developed in the Restraint Order regimes, such an order should only be made where 'there is a reasonable apprehension that, without it, realisable property may be dissipated . . . if there is no such risk or the risk is merely fanciful, the order ought not to be made since, ex hypothesi, it would not be necessary for the achievement of its proper purpose': *Re AJ and DJ* (CA (Civ Div), 9 December 1992). See Pt II, ch1 and Pt III, ch 1.

[210] POCA Order 2005, art 152(2)(a) (England and Wales and Northern Ireland), art 168(2)(a). (The corresponding provisions in POCA are ss 247 and 257.)

[211] ibid, art 152(2)(b) (England and Wales and Northern Ireland), art 168(2)(a). (The corresponding provisions in POCA are ss 247 and 257.)

was obtained as a result of criminal conduct.[212] The terms 'found' or 'believed' are not defined either in the enabling provisions of POCA 2002 or POCA Order 2005. The order in which the two words are given suggests that 'found' is a higher threshold of proof than 'believed' and that determinations of foreign courts that property is merely suspected or even reasonably suspected to have been obtained as a result of criminal conduct will not suffice. In each case, the UK court will clearly be assisted by clear evidence as to the findings of the foreign court, in the form of certificates and transcripts of judicial decisions and any other court records.

4.40 Victims of Theft etc

In any proceedings for a recovery order, a person who claims property which is alleged to be recoverable property, or any part of such property, may apply for a declaration to this effect and the court will make such a declaration (and not make a recovery order in relation to the property in question) if:

(1) the person was deprived of the property he claims, or of the property which it represents, by unlawful conduct within the meaning of s 241 of POCA 2002;[213]
(2) the property he was deprived of was not recoverable property immediately before he was deprived of it; and
(3) the property he claims belongs to him.

4.41 Realisation and Application of Property Recovered

On making a recovery order, the court must appoint a trustee for civil recovery[214] whose function it is to give effect to the recovery order and who has a number of powers to secure and realise the value of the recoverable property.[215] Such sums of money realised by the trustee for civil recovery are applied in the following order:

- first, payments to any associated or joint owners ordered by the court under POCA Order 2005, art 183;
- next, any payment of legal expenses payable in accordance with POCA Order 2005, art 177(11);
- next, any payment of expenses incurred by a person acting as an insolvency practitioner which are payable by virtue of POCA Order 2005, art 3(10).

The enforcement authority is empowered to pay a trustee for civil recovery or an interim receiver from the sums received from the trustee.[216]

[212] ibid, art 177. (The corresponding provision in POCA is s 266.)

[213] This section reads: '241 "Unlawful conduct" (1) Conduct occurring in any part of the United Kingdom is unlawful conduct if it is unlawful under the criminal law of that part. (2) Conduct which – (a) occurs in a country outside the United Kingdom and is unlawful under the criminal law of that country, and (b) if it occurred in a part of the United Kingdom, would be unlawful under the criminal law of that part, is also unlawful conduct.'

[214] Usually an accountant or licensed insolvency practitioner on a panel of persons who have been approved for this role.

[215] POCA Order 2005, art 178 and Sch 3. (The corresponding provisions in POCA are s 267 and Sch 7.)

[216] ibid, art 191(3). (The corresponding provision in POCA is s 280.)

Overseas Forfeiture Orders

4.42 Introduction

Overseas forfeiture orders[217] are orders for the forfeiture, destruction, deprivation, or other disposal of property used (or intended to be used) in the commission of a criminal offence and are broadly analogous to deprivation orders.[218] The property the subject of such orders is often referred to as 'the instrumentalities of crime'. The property forfeited in such proceedings ordinarily accrues to the benefit of the state[219] rather than to a victim or third party who may have an interest in the property concerned but who fails to protect his interests.

The Criminal Justice (International Co-operation) Act 1990 (Enforcement of Overseas Forfeiture Orders) Order 2005[220] (the CJ Order) is a self-contained Order in Council made under The Criminal Justice (International Co-operation) Act 1990 (the CJ(IC)A), s 9(1),[221] which permits forfeiture orders made by a foreign court of a designated country[222] to be enforced in England and Wales. It also permits restraint orders to be made in support of forfeiture orders.

4.43 'External Forfeiture Order'

The CJ Order defines an 'external forfeiture order' as an order[223] made by a court in a designated country[224] for the forfeiture and destruction, or the forfeiture and other disposal, of anything in respect of which a 'relevant offence' has been committed or which was used or intended for use in connection with the commission of such an offence.[225] A 'relevant offence' means any offence that corresponds to or is similar to an offence under the law of England and Wales.[226] This definition is wide enough to include any object of art or antiquity used (or intended for use) in connection with a money laundering or fraud offence.

4.44 Restraint in Support of an External Forfeiture Order

The Crown Court has power to grant a restraint order in aid of an external forfeiture order that is yet to be made under the CJ Order. This is an order made by a court in a designated country for the forfeiture and destruction, or the forfeiture and other disposal, of anything in respect of which a relevant offence has been committed or which was used or intended for use in connection with the commission of such an offence.[227]

[217] See generally *Smith Owen & Bodnar on Asset Recovery: Criminal Confiscation and Civil Recovery* (Oxford, Oxford University Press, Looseleaf).

[218] See 4.22–4.25 regarding deprivation orders.

[219] See 4.03 regarding asset sharing agreements.

[220] SI 2005/3180.

[221] CJ(IC)A, s 9(1), as amended by the Serious Organised Crime and Police Act 2005 (SOCPA), s 95. Section 95 of SOCPA extended the offences to which s 9 applies to cover any offence that corresponds to, or is similar to, an offence under the law of any part of the United Kingdom. By providing assistance in a greater range of circumstances, the United Kingdom is able to fulfil requirements to confiscate instrumentalities of crime under various international agreements.

[222] A country must be one designated by the CJ Order, Sch 2. As at July 2010 the list of designated countries includes in excess of 175 countries.

[223] Which may include any order, decree, direction or judgment or part thereof: CJ Order, art 36(2)(b).

[224] ibid, art 36(1)(a).

[225] ibid, art 36(1)(b).

[226] ibid, art 36(2)(a).

[227] ibid, art 36(1).

On an application by a relevant prosecuting agency, the Crown Court may make a restraint order (together with such other order it believes appropriate for the purpose of ensuring that the restraint order is effective)[228] if all of the following conditions are satisfied:[229]

– 'relevant property' in England and Wales is identified in the request;[230]
– a criminal investigation or proceedings for an offence have been started in the country from which the request was made;[231] and
– it appears to the court that there are reasonable grounds for believing that as a result of that investigation or those proceedings an external forfeiture order may be made against the person named in the request.[232]

Property is 'relevant property' if there are reasonable grounds to believe that it may be needed to satisfy an external forfeiture order which has been made or which may be made.[233]

If a restraint order is in force, a constable or a relevant officer of Revenue and Customs may seize any property which is specified in it to prevent its removal from England and Wales[234] and a management receiver may be appointed in respect of any property which is specified in the restraint order.

4.45 Enforcement of an External Forfeiture Order

Part 3 of the CJ Order contains provisions allowing for the enforcement of external forfeiture orders.

The Crown Court, on the application of a relevant prosecuting agency,[235] must give effect to an external forfeiture order if it is satisfied that all four of the following conditions are met:[236]

– the external forfeiture order was made consequent on the conviction of the person named in the order and no appeal is outstanding in respect of that conviction;[237]
– the external forfeiture order is in force and no appeal is outstanding in respect of it;[238]
– giving effect to the external forfeiture order would not be incompatible with any of the Convention rights (within the meaning of the Human Rights Act 1998) of any person affected by it;[239] and
– the property whose confiscation is specified in the external forfeiture order must not be subject to a charge under specified provisions.[240]

Where the Crown Court decides to give effect to an external forfeiture order, it must register the order in that court[241] and provide for notice of the registration to be given to any person affected by it.[242]

[228] ibid, art 5(4).
[229] ibid, art 5(1).
[230] ibid, art 4(2)(a).
[231] ibid, art 4(2)(b).
[232] ibid, art 4(2)(c).
[233] ibid, art 38(3).
[234] ibid, art 9(1).
[235] ibid, art 17(1).
[236] ibid, art 18(1).
[237] ibid, art 18(2).
[238] ibid, art 18(3).
[239] ibid, art 18(4).
[240] ibid, art 18(5); the specified provisions being a collection of statutes dealing with confiscation and forfeiture.
[241] ibid, art 19(1)(a).
[242] ibid, art 19(1)(b).

Where necessary, the Crown Court may go on to appoint an enforcement receiver to take possession of and to dispose of the property that is the subject of the external forfeiture order which has been registered by the Court.[243]

IV Conclusions

4.46 Conclusions

The relatively recent proliferation of international conventions designed to combat money laundering, corruption and organised crime have led to many countries putting in place national legislation confiscating the proceeds of crime. Some countries, like the UK, have gone further, and have also made provision for civil recovery orders. This means that an individual's proprietary rights have gained a new significance, because they will need to be asserted if there is a risk that the cultural object will otherwise be swept up by enforcement authorities to satisfy a confiscation order or other court order.

[243] ibid, art 22.

5

Civil Liability Affecting the Trade in Art and Antiquities

JANET ULPH

I Introduction

5.01 Introduction

This chapter concentrates upon the civil liability of all those who buy, sell, borrow or otherwise deal with stolen or illicit cultural objects. Potential defendants include auction houses, dealers and collectors. There is the risk that they will be sued by a claimant who is intent upon recovering the object, or obtaining compensation in lieu of its return. Yet this risk may be more apparent than real in certain cases. Any claimant, even with the assistance of expert evidence, may have great difficulty in identifying an object. This is a particular problem in relation to antiquities, where the court may need to take account of evidence such as the length of time during which an object has been buried, its chemical composition, and whether it has shared characteristics with other similar objects.[1] More generally, there may be problems in relation to identification if the works of art or antiquities have been altered, damaged, or changed whilst in the hands of the thieves. Yet a key difference between a criminal prosecution for an offence and a civil claim relates to the standard of proof. In the criminal courts, the prosecution must prove that the accused is guilty beyond reasonable doubt, whereas in the civil courts the claimant ordinarily needs only to establish the facts on the balance of probabilities. It may therefore be possible to bring a civil claim to recover an object, even where the evidence relating to identification would not be sufficient to support a criminal prosecution.

A claimant will ordinarily be concerned to recover the work of art or antiquity from a possessor. If he fails, he may wish to bring an action for financial compensation against an accessory, such as an agent. The focus of this chapter is therefore upon the liability of all those who possess stolen or illicit art and antiquities or who become involved in their transfer.

[1] *Bumper Development Corp Ltd v Comr of Police* [1991] 1 WLR 1362 (CA) 1366 (illegally excavated bronze idol representing the Hindu god Siva).

II Possession, Ownership and Conversion

5.02 Possessory Title and Legal Title

A claimant will not succeed in an English court of law if he can only prove is that he has a moral right to a cultural object. Even if the claimants have a special relationship with the intrinsic cultural values represented by the object, such as where an indigenous group can prove that the object in question is a religious relic, this will not suffice by itself. The English common law focuses upon the material aspects of the object. The claimant must show that he had an immediate right to physical possession of it.

No action exists which would allow the owner of an object to directly assert his 'ownership' rights. Instead, the original owner must resort to the law of torts, which offers a range of actions to protect those complaining of injury to their property. If an owner is concerned to recover an object, he is best advised to bring an action in the tort of conversion, which is a tort against the person entitled to possession.[2] It imposes liability upon anyone who has wrongfully interfered with another's rights to possess the object in question.[3]

In order to sue in conversion, the claimant need not show that he is the 'owner': but he must show that he had actual possession or an immediate right to possession of the object before it was removed.[4] Possession does not depend on immediate physical custody;[5] it depends upon proof of an intention to control the object to the exclusion of others, coupled with acts designed to carry out that intention.[6] The claimant must therefore show that he had control of the object and that he was exercising the control on his own behalf and for his own benefit, and to the exclusion of others.[7]

In many cases, the position will be straightforward and the claimant will clearly have a legal title. For example, a private collector should be able to furnish the court with a receipt, from a legitimate source, describing the art or antiquity which he has purchased. Similarly, a museum would provide evidence that the object has been inventoried. Antiquities are more problematic. If the claimant is a government, the easiest way to prove ownership of an antiquity which has been illegally excavated is to bring forward evidence that establishes, on the balance of probabilities, that there was a law in existence which vested ownership in the state *and* that the antiquity was removed after that law entered into force. If this evidence exists, the government has a proprietary title to the object.

[2] *Smith (as Administrator of Cosslett (Contractors) Ltd) v Bridgend County BC* [2001] UKHL 58, [2002] 1 AC 336 (HL) 351–52.

[3] The common law tort of conversion has been amended and encapsulated in the Torts (Interference with Goods) Act 1977.

[4] *MCC Proceeds Inc v Lehman Bros International (Europe)* [1998] 4 All ER 675 (CA) 686. See generally, *Government of the Islamic Republic of Iran v The Barakat Galleries Ltd* [2007] EWCA Civ 1374, [2009] QB 22 (CA); *Mainline Private Hire Ltd v Anthony Nolan* [2011] EWCA Civ 189; *Winkworth v Christie Manson & Wood Ltd* [1980] Ch 496, 499; *Union Transport Finance Ltd v British Car Auctions Ltd* [1978] 2 All ER 385 (CA); *RH Willis & Son v British Car Auctions Ltd* [1978] 1 WLR 438 (CA); *The 'Stone Gemini'* [1999] 2 Lloyds LR 255, 262 (Fed Ct of NSW); *J Sargent (Garages) Ltd v Motor Auctions (West Bromwich) Ltd* [1977] RTR 121; *North West Securities v Alexander Breckon* [1981] RTR 518. Ordinarily the claimant must have a legal interest rather than an equitable one: *MCC Proceeds Inc v Lehman Brothers International (Europe)* [1998] 4 All ER 675 (CA) 686.

[5] *R v Purdy* [1975] QB 288 (CA).

[6] *JA Pye (Oxford) Ltd v Graham* [2002] UKHL 30, [2003] 1 AC 419 (HL) [70]; *Flack v Chairperson, National Crime Authority* (1998) 156 ALR 501 (Fed Ct of NSW).

[7] *Mainline Private Hire Ltd v Anthony Nolan* [2011] EWCA Civ 189 [2]; *JA Pye (Oxford) Ltd v Graham* [2003] 1 AC 419 (HL) [40]–[41].

A claimant can sue in conversion even if his title is a possessory one rather than a proprietary one.[8] In determining whether a claimant has a possessory title, the common law pays particular regard to physical control. This is so because, as the common law evolved, it was strongly influenced by procedure and the rules of evidence. If a person has physical control, it is presumed that he has the intention to hold the object for his own benefit and therefore has a possessory title as well; this presumption aids the resolution of evidential uncertainties. This is particularly relevant where a person finds an object which appears to have been abandoned and takes it into his possession.[9] If someone finds a cultural object lying beside the road and picks it up with an intention to possess it and to exclude others, he will obtain a possessory title. The finder will have a right to the object unless and until it is claimed by someone who can prove that they were the previous owner and that the object was taken from them.[10] Thus, when a painting, 'Children Under a Palm Tree' by Winslow Homer, was found apparently abandoned on a rubbish dump in County Cork in 1987, the finder obtained a possessory title.[11] Anyone claiming that they had prior possession of the painting and that it was stolen would have the burden of proving this.

A person may obtain a possessory title even if their conduct was wrongful.[12] For example, a wrongdoer will obtain a possessory title if he goes on to another's land without permission and removes buried items,[13] or steals an object from a museum or private collection. The wrongdoer will have a right to sue anyone who interferes with his possession, unless it is someone having title conferred by earlier possession, such as the landowner, museum, or the owner of the private collection.[14]

The tort of conversion is complex, because of its focus upon different degrees of possession. Yet, from a pragmatic perspective, this has distinct advantages. The principles which have been established govern any type of tangible property. By concentrating on possession, and not merely ownership, the law is sufficiently flexible to cover situations such as where objects are lent to others or taken into custody for transportation or storage.[15] They prevent disorder by giving certain rights to those in possession. It can be argued that they maintain a balance between the competing concerns to protect an owner's property rights and to provide a market environment where traders can buy and sell with confidence.

5.03 Seizure by the Police

The police have the power to seize property temporarily when they reasonably believe that it is needed in evidence for the prosecution of an offence.[16] In the case of items such as

[8] The Torts (Inteference with Goods) Act 1977 does not define either proprietary title or possessory title: *Government of the Islamic Republic of Iran v The Barakat Galleries Ltd* [2009] QB 22 (CA) [15].

[9] Abandonment requires a mental decision: Scottish Law Commission, Discussion Paper on *Prescription and Title to Moveable Property* (Scot Law Com No 144, 2010) [9.3]–[9.4].

[10] *Armory v Delamirie* (1722) 1 Strange 505, 93 ER 664. See further, *Parker v British Airways Board* [1982] QB 1004 (CA) 1018; *Costello v Chief Constable of Derbyshire* [2001] EWCA Civ 381, [2001] 1 WLR 1437.

[11] For details, see eg '£110k Winslow Homer Painting is "a Steal"' *The Sunday Times* (31 May 2009).

[12] For further discussion, see R Hickey, ch 6 in *Property and the Law of Finders* (Oxford, Hart Publishing, 2010) 125.

[13] It will be presumed that the items belong to the owner or occupier of the land: *Waverley BC v Fletcher* [1995] QB 334 (CA); *Elwes v Brigg Gas Co* (1886) 33 Ch D 562; *South Staffordshire Water Co v Sharman* [1896] 2 QB 44 (DC); *Parker v British Airways Board* [1982] QB 1004 (CA); *Webb v Ireland* [1988] IR 353 (Sup Ct). See 3.11.

[14] *Mainline Private Hire Ltd v Anthony Nolan* [2011] EWCA Civ 189 [32].

[15] See S Green and J Randall, *The Tort of Conversion* (Oxford, Hart Publishing, 2009) 51.

[16] Police and Criminal Evidence Act 1984, ss 19, 22, as supplemented by the Police Reform Act 2002, Sch 4, para 19 and the Criminal Justice Act 2003, Sch 1, para 4.

drugs and smuggled goods, the court may make an order of forfeiture.[17] However, the police do not have a right to continue to keep property indefinitely. Where the accused obtained an object by theft or blackmail or fraud, the criminal courts can make a restitution order directing its return to the victim of the crime.[18] If the police have taken custody of an object in the course of investigating a crime but there has been no conviction, it will be restored to the apparent owner once the investigation and any proceedings have been concluded.[19]

When the power of the police to retain the object comes to an end, the rights of previous possessors revive. Where the object is one of antiquity, it may be particularly difficult to determine rights to property because the facts may be uncertain. For example, even if it is suspected that an object was excavated and removed from Iraq, it may be impossible to determine whether it was excavated recently or many years ago. The only evidence available may simply establish that the object was smuggled out of another country in the Middle East and sent to the UK. Although antiquities are frequently moved from one country to another before being shipped abroad, there may well be no proof of their route in transit. Consequently, anyone who can prove that they had possession of the object from the country from which it was exported (or the government of that country relying upon patrimonial legislation) may be viewed as the apparent owner.[20] It may be the case that the only apparent owner is the person who was in possession of the property before it was seized, even if he is suspected of having stolen the property. This point is illustrated by *Costello v Chief Constable of Derbyshire*,[21] where police took possession of a Ford Escort car; its engine identification number had been rubbed off and its previous owner could not be found. The claimant, who had been in possession of the car before it was seized, demanded its return. The police refused, on the basis that they suspected that the car had been stolen. Yet the police could not prove that the claimant had stolen the car, and no one else stepped forward to claim it. It was held that the police had no right to retain the car and it must be returned to the claimant.

If a person is prosecuted for an economic crime, the Proceeds of Crime Act 2002 will now apply. Although powers of confiscation existed before the 2002 Act came into force,[22] a major change is that the courts are now routinely expected to make confiscation orders.[23] Consequently, where the police have seized property in the course of an investigation because it appeared to represent proceeds of crime, they would not necessarily be obliged

[17] See, for example, the Misuse of Drugs Act 1971, s 27, and the Customs and Excise Management Act 1979, s 139, Sch 3.

[18] Powers of the Criminal Courts (Sentencing) Act 2000, s 148. See 4.09–4.10. In relation to restoring substitute property, see 4.11. In relation to the procedure, see 4.12.

[19] The police may apply to the magistrates' court to make an order under the Police (Property) Act 1897: see 4.13. However, this procedure is not suitable for complex claims: see 4.13.

[20] See V Rapley, 'The Metropolitan Police's Art and Antiques Unit' in P Stone and J Farchakh Bajjaly (eds), *The Destruction of Cultural Heritage in Iraq* (Woodbridge, The Boydell Press, 2008) 57.

[21] *Costello v Chief Constable of Derbyshire* [2001] EWCA Civ 381, [2001] 1 WLR 1437 (CA); noted by D Fox [2002] 61 *Cambridge Law Journal* 27. See further, *Betts v Metropolitan Police District Receiver and Carter Paterson* [1932] 2 KB 595.

[22] See, for example, the Drug Trafficking Act 1994, ss 2–10.

[23] In relation to confiscation orders, see 4.14. See also *R v May* [2008] UKHL 28, [2008] AC 1028; *Smith Owen & Bodnar on Asset Recovery: Criminal Confiscation and Civil Recovery*, 2nd edn (Oxford, Oxford University Press, 2007); *Millington and Sutherland-Williams on the Proceeds of Crime*, 3rd edn (Oxford, Oxford University Press, 2010); J Ulph, 'Confiscation Orders, Human Rights, and Penal Measures' (2010) 126 *Law Quarterly Review* 251; J Ulph, ch 4 in *Commercial Fraud – Civil Liability, Human Rights, and Money Laundering* (Oxford, Oxford University Press, 2006).

to return that property.[24] Instead, upon conviction, any property belonging to the criminal may be taken to satisfy a confiscation order.

Even where an individual is not convicted, the Serious Organised Crime Agency (SOCA)[25] may bring a proprietary action for civil recovery of property which appears on the balance of probabilities to be derived from unlawful conduct.[26] SOCA can pursue not only the object itself (such as a work of art which has been stolen) but also any money or other property with which it is exchanged. A civil recovery order can be obtained against the object, or property with which it has been exchanged, in the hands of anyone; however, there are defences available where, for example, the possessor has acted in good faith in acquiring it.[27] The victim from whom the object has been stolen may also apply for its return.[28] Where the proceeds of crime, or property representing the proceeds of crime, are situated abroad, enforcement authorities can still seek a civil recovery order against that property, even if their powers may be more limited in foreign courts.[29] Thus, where cultural objects are suspected of being stolen but the evidence is not strong enough to secure a conviction, a civil recovery order may still be made so that they are taken into the possession of the UK Government. However, if such an order is not made then, despite the wide-ranging nature of the changes brought in by the Proceeds of Crime Act 2002, the default position is that the property must be returned to the previous possessor.[30]

5.04 Loans

English law recognises that it is possible to enjoy different interests in objects.[31] For example, an owner may agree to transfer a painting to a museum (such as for the purposes of a special exhibition) upon the understanding that possession will revert after the expiration of an agreed period of time. This loan, involving the separation of physical possession from ownership, upon the understanding that the painting will be returned, is otherwise known as a bailment. The museum (the bailee) will enjoy possession of the painting during the time agreed and may have a *possessory* title. The owner who has handed over the object (the bailor), will retain his proprietary title.[32]

It is common to lend art and antiquities to museums and other event organisers for major exhibitions. However, ensuring the safety of exhibits is a significant problem. The theft of an object on loan is a particular hazard: if a painting or antiquity is stolen, should

[24] See 4.14.

[25] See the Serious Crime Act 2007, s 74. In relation to SOCA's establishment and general functions, see the Serious Organised Crime and Police Act 2005. SOCA will be replaced by a National Crime Agency in a bid to combat organised crime more effectively.

[26] See POCA 2002, ss 240, 241 and 304. See further, *Serious Organised Crime Agency v Sahota* [2011] EWHC 1397; *Director of the ARA v Jackson* [2007] EWHC 2553; *Director of the ARA v John* [2007] EWHC; *Director of the ARA v Taher* [2006] EWHC 3406. See 4.20.

[27] For details, see 4.21.

[28] See 4.22.

[29] *Perry v Serious Organised Crime Agency* [2011] EWCA 578.

[30] *Webb v Chief Constable of Merseyside Police* [2000] QB 427 (CA) 448; cited with approval by Lord Hope of Craighead in *Jaroo v Attorney General of Trinidad and Tobago* [2002] 1 AC 871 (PC) 880. See also *Field v Sullivan* [1923] VLR 70, 84–87. For a detailed discussion of the position where the police are faced with conflicting claims, see J Ulph, ch 35 in *Palmer on Bailment*, 3rd edn (London, Sweet and Maxwell, 2009) [35–59]–[35–64]. See 4.13.

[31] Torts (Interference with Goods) Act 1977, s 7; *Government of the Islamic Republic of Iran v The Barakat Galleries Ltd* [2009] QB 22 (CA) [14]; *Yearworth v North Bristol NHS Trust* [2009] EWCA Civ 39, [2009] 2 All ER 986 [28].

[32] *Government of the Islamic Republic of Iran v The Barakat Galleries Ltd* [2009] QB 22 (CA) [16].

the owner bring an action in conversion, or should the museum do so? In order to determine who has an immediate right to possession, the terms of the agreement must be analysed.[33] For example, the agreement may provide the museum or event organiser with possession for a fixed period of time, such as four months;[34] if the museum or organiser has an intention to possess along with sufficient control to exclude others during this period, it will have a possessory title. Consequently, the museum will have an immediate right to possession and can sue a thief in conversion.[35] In contrast, the loan agreement may not provide the bailee, such as the museum, with sufficient control over the object to enable it to say that it has possession to the exclusion of others. If the contract (as is the case with some, but not all, types of storage contract) provides that the object is being held on behalf of the owner, in accordance with the owner's instructions, and that possession can be terminated at will, it is the owner who may take action. The owner may terminate the agreement and will have control (and therefore constructive possession) of the object in question; he can therefore sue in conversion.[36]

5.05 The Role of Insurers

If an object which is stolen has been insured against the risk of theft, the insured (the original owner) can claim compensation for the loss from his insurers. The insurance company will step into the shoes of the insured under its rights of subrogation, so that it can sue to recover the object if it is subsequently discovered. If the art or antiquity is recovered, it will belong to the insurers. However, the insured will often arrange to return the insurance monies in exchange for receipt of the object itself.

On rare occasions, the insured may arrange to buy back its proprietary rights (ownership) in the cultural object before it is found. This is a speculative venture, because the object may never be located. For example, in July 1994, two paintings by Turner were stolen whilst on loan from the London Tate Gallery to the Schein Kunsthalle in Frankfurt. The Tate received £24 million from its insurers but subsequently bought back its ownership rights from the insurers, hoping that eventually the paintings would be discovered. It was a gamble which paid off: having paid £8 million to the insurers for title to the paintings, and £3.5 million to lawyers in Germany for their recovery, the paintings were eventually taken back into the Tate's care.[37] There was a risk that the money may have gone to those involved in their misappropriation. If such circumstances were ever to recur, an owner would need to take particular care to ensure that in making any payment in exchange for information or the object itself, he did not commit a money laundering offence.[38] The dangers of offering a reward with 'no questions asked' or paying a ransom are well-known: the money may be used to support further criminal activity, including further art thefts.[39]

[33] ibid [26].

[34] *Gordon v Harper* (1796) 7 TR 9, 101 ER 828.

[35] *Brink's Mat v Noye* [1991] 1 Bank LR 68 (CA) [6]. See also, *JA Pye (Oxford) Ltd v Graham* [2003] 1 AC 419 [39]–[43]; *Mainline Private Hire Ltd v Anthony Nolan* [2011] EWCA Civ 189 [34]; *Government of the Islamic Republic of Iran v The Barakat Galleries Ltd* [2009] QB 22 (CA) [19].

[36] *MCC Proceeds Inc v Lehman Brothers International (Europe)* [1998] 4 All ER 675 (CA) 686. See also *Mainline Private Hire Ltd v Anthony Nolan* [2011] EWCA Civ 189 [38].

[37] Tate Press Release, 16 December 2005.

[38] See the Proceeds of Crime Act 2008, s 328; see 3.39.

[39] See M Durney, 'Understanding the Motivations Behind Art Crime and the Effects of an Institution's Response' (2009) 2(1) *The Journal of Art Crime* 83, 85.

5.06 Antiquities: *Government of the Islamic Republic of Iran v The Barakat Galleries Ltd*

In *Government of the Islamic Republic of Iran v The Barakat Galleries Ltd*,[40] the Court of Appeal was asked to consider whether the Iranian Government had title to certain antiquities, and whether English courts would enforce that title. The antiquities consisted of 18 carved jars, bowls and cups made from chlorite which were almost over 5,000 years old. The Government of Iran asserted that the objects were part of Iran's national heritage.

Where an English court is invited to consider a claim in relation to tangible objects, the first step is to examine the surrounding circumstances to determine whether the claimant has a proprietary or possessory title.[41] Under English principles of conflict of laws, the question of whether Iran had title to the antiquities needed to be determined by examining the law of Iran (the *lex situs*).[42] The Court consequently subjected the relevant Iranian legislation to close analysis. The Iranian Civil Code of 1928 provided that a finder obtained title to objects which appeared ownerless.[43] The National Heritage Protection Act 1930, which established a scheme for recording heritage objects of national importance, gave the Iranian Government significant rights to control the disposition of heritage objects of national importance, including imposing an obligation upon finders to share their discoveries with the Government. However, it did not vest ownership of the objects in the state.[44] But the Court of Appeal decided that the Legal Bill of 1979 went much further, overriding the Civil Code and conferring ownership in the state of antiquities (that is to say, objects removed after the Legal Bill came into force and which have been made or produced at least one hundred years ago).[45] This was so, regardless of whether a public official had ever taken physical possession of them. In this case, it was assumed that the antiquities had been recently excavated; consequently, the Legal Bill of 1979 applied, and it was held that the Iranian Government had legal title and an immediate right to possession of the antiquities sufficient to provide a basis for a claim in conversion.[46]

The decision in *Barakat* illustrates how important the precise wording of domestic legislation may be.[47] If ownership of an unexcavated antiquity is spelt out with precision in domestic legislation, it should be clear whether an exported antiquity is in fact stolen. If so, anyone in possession is exposed to the risk of a criminal prosecution.[48] A person in possession of stolen goods may also be sued in the civil law for conversion. A defendant may consider it unjust that liability may depend upon a court's interpretation of a foreign country's legislation. A defendant may have no idea of the contents of the legislation which applied in the country from which the antiquity originated. But the law of conversion is no harsher in the context of looted antiquities than it is in other situations; a possessor of any type of stolen goods is vulnerable and civil liability does not depend upon proof of fault.

[40] *Government of the Islamic Republic of Iran v The Barakat Galleries Ltd* [2009] QB 22 (CA).
[41] See *Gotha City v Sotheby's, The Times* (8 October 1998).
[42] For further discussion of this point, see 6.30.
[43] [2009] QB 22 (CA) [36], [57].
[44] ibid [37]–[39], [62].
[45] ibid [41], [82].
[46] ibid [84], [86].
[47] See P Rogerson, 'Public policy and cultural objects' (2008) 67 *Cambridge Law Journal* 246, 248.
[48] *R v Tokeley-Parry* [1999] Crim LR 578 (CA); see 3.21, 3.30.

III Export Laws

5.07 Export Laws and Public Policy

Foreign penal, revenue, or other public laws may not be enforced in the English courts on public policy grounds unless there is EU or UK legislation which prompts the courts to do so.[49] In *Government of the Islamic Republic of Iran v The Barakat Galleries Ltd,* the defendant argued that the Iranian Government was attempting to enforce an export law which was penal and public in nature. In considering this issue, the Court of Appeal drew a distinction between laws which vest title to antiquities in the state, and those which do not. Where the government of a country does not have patrimonial legislation which spells out that the government owns any undiscovered antiquity, so that it is forced to rely upon its confiscatory powers contained in export legislation, there is a risk that the export laws might be seen as akin to penal and revenue laws and might consequently be unenforceable.[50]

As regards public policy objections, the Court of Appeal in *Barakat* suggested that there were 'positive reasons of policy why a claim by a State to recover antiquities which form part of its national heritage and which otherwise complies with the requirements of private international law' should be supported rather than opposed on public policy grounds.[51] The Court observed that there was 'international recognition that states should assist one another to prevent the unlawful removal of cultural objects including antiquities'.[52] The Court referred to various international, European and domestic initiatives, noting in particular that both the UK and Iran had ratified the 1970 UNESCO Convention. It was stated that:

> None of these instruments directly affects the outcome of this appeal, but they do illustrate the international acceptance of the desirability of protection of the national heritage. A refusal to recognise the title of a foreign state, conferred by its law, to antiquities unless they had come into the possession of such state, would in most cases render it impossible for this country to recognise any claim by such a state to recover antiquities unlawfully exported to this country.[53]

However, where a source country does not have patrimonial legislation and is relying upon its export laws to recover the object, there is a further difficulty. The government may not be able to show that it had an immediate right to possession of the object, entitling it to sue in conversion.[54] Export laws normally provide that smuggled objects can be forfeited to the state; if this has occurred, the government will have acquired a possessory title. But, even if a government has a legal right to confiscate a smuggled object, if it has not in fact done so, it will not have a proprietary or possessory title. If this is the case, it will not have any legal basis for bringing an action subsequently to recover it.[55]

[49] See the fuller discussion on this issue in 6.34–6.35.

[50] [2009] QB 22 (CA) [128]–[129]. The two cases cited did not offer proper support for this argument and the issue awaits further judicial exploration: CA Whomersley, 'Foreign States and British Courts' (2009) 125 *Law Quarterly Review* 227, 230.

[51] [2009] QB 22 (CA) [154].

[52] ibid [155].

[53] ibid [163].

[54] It might be able to rely upon the Return of Cultural Objects Regulations 1994 instead: see 5.08.

[55] [2009] QB 22 (CA) [143]. See also 6.34.

On the facts of *Barakat*, the Court of Appeal found that the Iranian Government was asserting its rights of ownership. It was not attempting to enforce its export restrictions.[56] The Legal Bill of 1979 vested title in undiscovered antiquities in the Republic of Iran. The Court of Appeal did not consider this law to be penal in character because it did not have retrospective effect. There could be no public policy objections to recovering one's own property.[57] This conclusion was not altered by the fact that the Iranian Government never enjoyed physical possession of the antiquities before they were excavated and removed.[58] This reasoning would seem correct in principle. Where the domestic law clearly vests ownership of all undiscovered antiquities in the state, it could be said that the state enjoys constructive possession of these objects as they lie buried in the ground. A government will therefore have title to its antiquities under its patrimonial laws[59] and can sue anyone who wrongfully intereferes with its rights; furthermore, if those dealing with the antiquities are not acting in good faith, they are exposed to the risk of prosecution.[60]

5.08 Return of Cultural Objects Regulations 1994

Even if a claimant government cannot prove ownership, it may be able to rely upon the Return of Cultural Objects Regulations 1994.[61] The Regulations are based upon European Council Directive 93/7/EEC of 15 March 1993.[62] The Directive deals with the illegal export of cultural objects which have been unlawfully removed from an EC Member State. It is not concerned with ownership and stolen property: it is about an object's location.[63] The operation of the Directive is confined within the internal borders of the Community. It provides for arrangements to be introduced to permit a Member State to bring proceedings in the courts of another Member State with the aim of securing the return of cultural objects found to have been unlawfully removed from its national territory.

Directive 93/7/EEC is concerned with the return of 'national treasures' possessing artistic, historical or archaeological value under national legislation. Additionally, these treasures must either form part of an inventoried public collection or the inventories of an ecclesiastical institution or, in the alternative, fall into one of the categories listed in the Annex to the Directive. The categories of protected objects specified in the Annex are wide-ranging and include pictures and paintings executed entirely by hand, sculptures, books, maps, and manuscripts. However, some categories are restricted by age or value. For example, to be included, archaeological objects must be more than 100 years old, but no value is specified. In contrast, pictures and paintings may be of any age in general, but must have a

[56] ibid [131], [148]–[149]. The decision in *Att-Gen of New Zealand v Ortiz* [1984] AC 1 (CA) could therefore be distinguished on this basis. In *Ortiz*, it was evident that New Zealand legislation, which provided for the forfeiture of cultural property which was exported unlawfully, did not vest ownership of the property in the State unless and until it was confiscated: ibid [98]. For a full discussion, see 6.35.

[57] [2009] QB 22 [135]–[136]; *City of Gotha v Sotheby's* (9 September 1998); *King of Italy v De Medici Tornaquinci* (1918) 34 TLR 623.

[58] [2009] QB 22 (CA) [149].

[59] Iran's Legal Bill of 1979 was described as a patrimonial law: ibid [149].

[60] ibid [149]; *US v Schultz* 333 F 3d 393 (2d Cir 2003); *R v Tokeley-Parry* [1999] Crim LR 578 (CA).

[61] SI 1994/501 (as amended by SI 1997/1719 and SI 2001/3972), which came into force on 2 March 1994.

[62] European Council Directive 1993/7/EEC of 15 March 1993 on the Return of Cultural Objects Unlawfully Removed from the Territory of a Member State, OJ L74/74. See NE Palmer, 'Statutory, Forensic and Ethical Initiatives in the Recovery of Stolen Art and Antiquities' in NE Palmer (ed), *The Recovery of Stolen Art* (The Netherlands, Kluwer Law International, 1998) 1, 13–15.

[63] Scottish Law Commission, Discussion Paper on *Prescription and Title to Moveable Property* (Scot Law Com No 144, 2010) [4.5].

value of 150,000 euros or more. Governments of countries such as Sweden, Spain and and Austria have argued that the thresholds are set too high and that more cultural objects should be covered by the Directive. In contrast, the government of the United Kingdom, and others, would like to see the threshold set higher still, to reduce the number of objects affected by the Directive.[64]

The UK Government made regulations to implement Directive 93/7/EEC with effect from 2 March 1994. The Return of Cultural Objects Regulations 1994 apply where cultural objects have been unlawfully removed from the territory of a Member State on or after 1 January 1993. By regulation 6(1) of the 1994 Regulations, a Member State may take proceedings against the possessor for the return of a national treasure which has been unlawfully removed. Removal will be unlawful where an object is removed in breach of the national legislation in force in the country concerned, or where the object is not returned at the end of a period of lawful removal (such as for the purposes of a loan).

When the UK ratified the UNESCO Convention 1970, it added a reservation to ensure that, where a request is made by an EC Member State for the return of an unlawfully exported object, the request is regulated by EC law. Directive 93/7/EEC has been transposed into UK law by the Regulations which establish a procedure:[65] the requesting state must provide the information needed to enable the government in the Member State in which it is suspected that the object may be located to search for the object. Alternatively, a Member State may notify another Member State of the fact that it has found an object which appears to have been unlawfully removed from that Member State.[66] However, it is open to Member States to bypass the legal return procedure and to arrive at an amicable settlement. The UK Government has returned manuscripts in this informal manner to Portugal and the Netherlands, and also returned books to Sweden.[67]

A Member State is obliged to pay the possessor compensation if he can show that he exercised due care and attention in acquiring the object.[68] Article 9 of the Directive appears to demand an objective standard of due diligence, and it has been suggested that it is easier to satisfy this requirement than the comparable provision of due diligence in the UNIDROIT Convention.[69] It is left to Member States to allocate the burden of proof in their domestic legislation. When a request is made, the law of the Member State receiving the request will govern. The 1994 Regulations do not expressly state where the burden of proof will lie. However, although regulation 7 is studiedly neutral, like Article 9 of the Directive itself, it appears probable that the courts will expect the possessor to show that he has exercised due care and diligence if he wishes to claim compensation.

Limitation periods are specified within which a claim can be brought from the date of the unlawful removal of the object. In relation to an object from a public collection, or ecclesiastical goods subject to special protection, the limitation period is 75 years; for other cultural objects, it is a period of 30 years.[70] However, the requirement that proceedings

[64] Report from the Commission, Brussels COM (2005) 675 final [6.3]. The financial thresholds are set out in sterling in the Return of Cultural Objects Regulations 1994, extracted in the Annex to this text.

[65] As regards the powers provide to the Secretary of State to search and take possession of a cultural object, see 6.03.

[66] SI 1994/501 reg 3.

[67] Annex to the Report from the Commission, Brussels COM (2005) 675 final.

[68] As the Scottish Law Commission observe, a government may opt to bring an action in private law instead to avoid paying compensation to the possessor: Scot Law Com No 144, 2010 [4.7].

[69] M van Gaalen and A Verheij, 'The Consequences for the Netherlands of the UNIDROIT Convention' (1998) III(1) *Art Antiquity and Law* 3, 12. In relation to the UNIDROIT Convention, see 2.31.

[70] SI 1994/501 reg 6(6),(7),(8). See also 6.05.

must be brought within 'one year after the Member State became aware of the location of the cultural object and of the identity of its possessor or holder' has proved to be a major obstacle. In response to strong criticism by some governments of this requirement, the period for bringing proceedings is now being reviewed, with the idea that it may be extended to three years.[71]

The 1994 Regulations are useful where the government of a state cannot prove that it has legal title to an object but can show that it has been illegally exported. Even so, the Regulations and the European Directive on which they are based are narrow in scope. They are concerned with the illegal export (rather than theft) of certain categories of cultural objects listed in the Annex to the Directive. Secondly, the request can only be made by a Member State, and not a private legal or natural person. Thirdly, there is no mechanism for the return of objects which are exported outside the European Union, because the Directive only applies to EC Member States. Fourthly, it only applies to objects which have been exported on or after 1 January 1993.[72]

In the ITAP Report, the Directive was described as administratively cumbersome, and it was suggested that it may have produced few if any concrete results. It was observed that, as the Directive is only concerned with objects removed from EU countries, it does not tackle the problem of the trade within the European Union of cultural objects which have been stolen or illicitly excavated from other countries.[73] The European Commission has noted that the Directive has not been as successful as had been hoped. It has not been effective in promoting co-operation between Member States, and there have been problems in relation to traceability of items.[74] There is evidence that a number of European states prefer to bring legal actions other than the one offered by the Directive.[75]

IV Conversion

5.09 Wrongful Interference With Property Rights: Purchasers

The action in conversion is straightforward. There are two key matters which must be proved. First, the claimant must establish that he has an immediate right to possession of the work of art or antiquity, as discussed.[76] Secondly, the claimant must prove that the defendant has treated the object as his own. A purchaser will ordinarily be seen as someone who has wrongly interfered with the claimant's rights to the object.[77] The action does not require the claimant to bring forward evidence in relation to the defendant's motives. Proof of innocent receipt is irrelevant. A good faith purchaser will be liable in conversion unless

[71] Report from the Commission, Brussels COM (2005) 675 final [6.2].

[72] SI 1994/501 reg 1(3).

[73] *Illicit Trade in Cultural Objects,* Report of the Ministerial Advisory Panel, London, December 2000 (hereafter ITAP Report) [32], [35].

[74] Report from the Commission, Brussels 21.12.2005 COM (2005) 675 final at [3.1].The Commission has reviewed the operation of the Directive regularly over the years. See, for example, OJ L o74, 27/03/1993 P. 0074-0079.

[75] Report from the Commission, Brussels 21.12.2005 COM (2005) 675 final [5.2.2].

[76] See 5.02–5.06.

[77] *MCC Proceeds Inc v Lehman Brothers International (Europe)* [1998] 4 All ER 675 (CA) 686. See also *Hollins v Fowler* (1875) 7 LR 757 (HL)

he can rely upon a statutory defence, such as the expiration of the limitation period within which a claim can be made.[78]

5.10 Wrongful Interference: Dealers, Auction Houses and other Third Parties

The original owner may have a choice of remedies and defendants. He may be able to sue anyone in possession of the object for its return. He can choose instead to sue any intermediate purchasers and sellers, and anyone else who can be viewed as interfering with his property rights, in order to obtain financial compensation.[79] Each defendant must account for the benefits which he has received,[80] but may have a right of action against another potential defendant.[81]

It is reasonably easy to show that the person in possession has treated the stolen object in a manner which is inconsistent with the claimant's proprietary rights[82] However, the situation may be far more complex where other people, such as agents, are involved. For example, third parties will not be liable if they have merely transported or stored objects in accordance with another person's instructions.[83] This is because the third party will not have exercised any control over the object for his own benefit.[84] In *Kuwait Airways Corp v Iraqi Airways Co*,[85] Lord Nicholls observed that, as conversion could take place in such widely differing circumstances, it was difficult to formulate a precise test. He suggested that the defendant's conduct must be 'so extensive an encroachment on the rights of the owner as to exclude him from use and possession of the goods.'[86] Thus, if a third party has deliberately destroyed an object belonging to another without that person's permission, such as paintings stolen from a museum,[87] he will ordinarily be liable in conversion.[88]

If possessors of stolen items use agents, such as dealers or auction houses, to sell an item, they may be liable in conversion. If an auctioneer carries out his instructions and sells and delivers goods which are then found to be stolen, the true owner can sue the auctioneer.[89] In contrast, an auctioneer will not be liable if he merely introduces a purchaser to a seller because he has not encroached on anyone's proprietary rights. Fine lines have been drawn at times in determining whether auctioneers have interfered with another's right to

[78] See 5.39.

[79] *Wilson v Anderton* (1830) 1 B & Ad 450, 109 ER 855; *Batut v Hartley* (1872) LR QB 594.

[80] *Kuwait Airways Corp v Iraqi Airways Co* [2002] AC 883 (HL) [79].

[81] Where there is a chain of sales, a purchaser can sue his immediate seller for breach of the term implied by s 12 of the Sale of Goods Act 1979 that he had the right to sell the item in question; see *Rowland v Divall* [1923] 2 KB 500 (CA). *Quare* whether converters can seek contributions from each other under s 1 of the Civil Liability (Contribution) Act 1978: *Middle Temple v Lloyds Bank plc* [1999] All ER Comm 193; *Linklaters* v *HSBC Bank plc* [2003] EWHC 1113, [2003] 2 Lloyd's Rep 505.

[82] *MCC Proceeds Inc v Lehman Bros International (Europe)* [1998] 4 All ER 675 (CA) 685–86.

[83] See *Hollins v Fowler* (1875) LR 7 HL 757 (HL) 766–67; *Consolidated Co v Curtis* [1892] 1 QB 495, 498; *Marcq v Christie Manson & Woods Ltd* [2003] EWCA Civ 731, [2004] QB 286 (CA) [14].

[84] *White v Withers LLP and Dearle* [2009] EWCA Civ 1122 (CA) [53]. Contrast *Fouldes v Willoughby* (1841) 8 M & W 540.

[85] *Kuwait Airways Corp v Iraqi Airways Co* [2002] AC 883 (HL).

[86] ibid [39]. See P Cane [2002] 118 *Law Quarterly Review* 544.

[87] There are suggestions that the five paintings stolen from the Museum of Modern Art in Paris in May 2010 have been destroyed; see 1.08.

[88] *Robot Arenas Ltd v Waterfield* [2010] EWHC 115 [15]. See also the Torts (Interference with Goods) Act 1977, s 2(2).

[89] *Lee v Bayes* (1856) 18 CB 599, 608, 139 ER 1504; *J Sargent (Garages) Ltd v Motor Auctions (West Bromwich) Ltd* [1977] RTR 121. This point was conceded by Christie's in the case of *Marcq v Christie Manson & Woods Ltd* [2004] QB 286 (CA) [24].

possession.[90] In *Marcq v Christie Manson & Woods Ltd*,[91] the court was obliged to consider whether Christie's was liable to the true owner in conversion where it had innocently offered a stolen painting for sale in one of its auctions. The painting failed to sell and Christie's returned the painting to its client. The true owner sued in conversion. It was decided both at first instance and on appeal that Christie's was not liable.

In *Marcq v Christie Manson & Woods Ltd*, Tuckey LJ stated:

> I agree with the judges below that the authorities indicate that an auctioneer who receives goods from their apparent owner and simply redelivers them to him when they are unsold is not liable in conversion provided he has acted in good faith and without knowledge of any adverse claim to them . . . The auctioneer intends to sell and if he does so will incur liability if he delivers the goods to the buyer. But his intention does not make him liable; it is what he does in relation to the goods which determines liability. Mere receipt of the goods does not amount to conversion. In receiving the goods from and redelivering them to their apparent owner the auctioneer in such a case has only acted ministerially. He has in the event merely changed the position of the goods and not the property in them.[92]

Thus, it appears from the decision in *Marcq v Christie Manson* that an auctioneer or any other agent who is merely taking care of a stolen object will not be liable in conversion, even if the possession is for some duration, such as a period of five months as in the case itself.[93] It is therefore possible for an agent to escape liability if, having failed to sell the object, he returns it to the ostensible owner, provided he acts in good faith and without notice of any adverse claim.[94] Controversially, Jack J held at first instance that the agent is not obliged to search the Art Loss Register or other databases. The agent is safe unless he has actual knowledge of a third party claim. Thus, if the agent is not aware that the title is in dispute, he can return the object to his client.[95]

The decision in *Marcq v Christie Manson* provides significant protection to innocent intermediaries who offer the claimant's property for sale but fail to find a buyer. Yet the arguments put by the claimant had a great deal of force. Christie's had done far more than simply store the stolen painting: it had catalogued the painting and marketed it. Furthermore, the contract between Christie's and its client gave it extensive rights to assert control over the painting: it provided Christie's with the right to a lien, so that it could retain the painting as security in the event that payment was not made by its client. If Christie's had exercised this lien, it would have been liable, because this would have been an interference with ownership rights.[96]

[90] In *National Mercantile Bank v Rymill* (1881) 44 LT (NS) 767 (CA) a seller intended to sell horses by auction, but then sold them privately beforehand in the auctioneer's yard; although the seller was guilty of conversion, the auctioneer was held not liable. The decision was criticised by the Court of Appeal in *RH Willis and Son v British Car Auctions Ltd* [1978] 1 WLR 438 (CA) 443 (Lord Denning MR), 444 (Roskill LJ) as being too generous to the defendant; in *Willis*, the auctioneer had intervened in a more active way to effect a sale and was therefore held liable. See further, *Cochrane v Rymill* (1879) 40 LT 744 (CA).

[91] *Marcq v Christie Manson & Woods Ltd* [2004] QB 286 (CA).

[92] [2004] QB 286 (CA) [24]; see further, *Hollins v Fowler* (1875) LR 7 HL 757 (HL) 795.

[93] ibid [33].

[94] ibid [24]. See also *Heald v Carey* (1852) 11 CB 977, 138 ER 762; *Alexander v Southey* (1821) 5 B & Ald 247.

[95] Although if the agent has reason to be suspicious, he should report his suspicions to SOCA (or its expected replacement, the National Crime Agency) in order to avoid committing a money laundering offence.

[96] [2004] QB 286 (CA) [36]; *Loeschman v Machin* (1818) 2 Stark 311. See the Torts (Interference with Goods) Act 1977, s 11(2), which provides that 'Receipt of goods by way of pledge is conversion if the delivery of the goods is conversion.'

From a policy perspective, the decision can be defended on the basis that, if an agent was liable for conversion on every occasion when they included a contractual term which entitled them to retain possession of objects by way of a lien until they were paid or all liabilities were discharged, then many agents could be held liable. Yet, the decision can be described as unsatisfactory because it erodes the rights of the original owner and does not fit easily with past decisions.[97] Any particular sympathy towards auctioneers is arguably misplaced, because they will be insured against such claims in any event.[98] Imposing liability in borderline situations would encourage auctioneers to take great care before returning an object to its apparent owner. This is desirable because it is surely well known that, because of the high economic value of various works of art, criminals have become involved in stealing pieces or dealing with them as part of a money laundering process.[99]

5.11 Wrongful Interference: Conflicting Claims

What is the position where an agent, such as an auction house, dealer, or restorer, is in possession of an object, and the true owner makes himself known? Should the agent return the object to his customer, or to the person alleging that the object has been stolen from him? Auction houses are particularly likely to be confronted by this problem because the sales catalogue may have alerted the true owner to the existence of the item. Their position may be hazardous: to defiantly retain possession of another's goods may give rise to liability in conversion where that other has the better right of possession. The unlawful possessor will thereupon be obliged to return the property and/or pay damages in compensation.

If the person coming forward can prove beyond doubt that he is the true owner, the agent may be best advised to surrender the art or antiquity to him. The agent would ordinarily be liable in conversion if the true owner has asked for its return and the agent has refused to surrender it. This is because the agent will be viewed as denying the owner's rights and excluding him from his property.[100] The position would be the same where all of the parties who might have had a claim to the object agree that one of them is entitled to it: the agent should follow their decision, or risk being held liable in conversion.[101]

If ownership of the object is uncertain, the agent would have an excuse for retaining the object for a reasonable period of time if the purpose was to make further enquiries about its provenance.[102] Thus, in *Clayton v Le Roy*,[103] a jeweller realised that a watch which had been left in his custody to be valued was stolen. The jeweller contacted the original owner and his customer (who had purchased it in good faith), so that they could discuss the matter. He refused to hand the watch over immediately to the original owner and the Court of Appeal held that he had not been obliged to do so: he was entitled to have an adequate

[97] For detailed criticism on this point, see A Hudson, 'Auctions and Conversion' (2005) X(2) *Art Antiquity and Law* 201.

[98] Auctioneers are expected to take out insurance: *R H Willis & Son v British Car Auctions Ltd* [1978] 1 WLR 438 (CA) 443.

[99] *Rachmaninoff v Sotheby's* [2005] EWHC 258 [35].

[100] *Howard Perry & Co v British Railways Board* [1980] 1 WLR 1375, 1380. See S Douglas, 'The Nature of Conversion' (2009) *Cambridge Law Journal* 198, 206–08.

[101] *Pendragon plc v Walon Ltd* [2005] EWHC 1082.

[102] *Hollins v Fowler* (1875) LR 7 HL 757, 765. See also *Vaughan v Watt* (1860) 6 M & W 492, 151 ER 506; *Isaack v Clark* (1615) 2 Buls 306, 80 ER 1143. An auctioneer should withdraw an object if it is alleged that it has been stolen: see 'Sotheby's Halts Auction of their "Stolen" Painting from Fly Tip' *London Evening Standard* (22 May 2009).

[103] *Clayton v Le Roy* [1911] 2 KB 1031 (CA).

period of time in which to determine whether the original owner was entitled to the return of the watch.

5.12 Suspicious Circumstances

In *Spencer v S Franses Ltd*,[104] the claimant, who was a dealer, asked the defendant, an expert in the field, to investigate whether two embroideries had been created at an earlier point than the nineteenth century. The claimant supplied the defendant with a receipt to show that he had a right to the embroideries. It was only much later, after there was a disagreement relating to payment for work carried out, that the defendant noticed that the receipt contained oddities, and did not specifically mention the embroideries but merely referred to a house clearance of items of low value on the death of the American owner.[105] Normally, a bailee (a person in possession of goods belonging to another) should not question his bailor's title.[106] The defendant became concerned that he might be sued by the true owner in conversion, and therefore began to question the claimant and to make checks in the USA. Thirlwall J accepted that a person in possession can make certain enquiries, because 'a bailee should have a reasonable opportunity to protect himself from a claim by the rightful owner.'[107] This accords with section 8(1) of the Torts (Interference with Goods) Act 1977, which provides:

> The defendant in an action for wrongful interference shall be entitled to show . . . that a third party has a better right than the plaintiff as respects all or any part of the interest claimed by the plaintiff, or in right of which he sues.

However, Thirlwall J in *Spencer v S Franses Ltd* held that a person in possession of an object with a doubtful provenance is not expected to make extensive enquiries. It was further held that the defendant had not carried out his enquiries within a reasonable time.

It would appear therefore that the safest course of action for a bailee is to return the object to his client, the bailor. In *Spencer,* Thirlwall J considered that, unless the bailee has actual knowledge that his customer, the bailor, is not the owner, he is obliged to return the object to him, even if he suspects him of having stolen it.[108] This reflects the traditional position at common law, where even a thief will have a possessory title. From a policy perspective, this can be defended: in relation to ordinary commodities, commercial people have no time to engage in elaborate enquiries. But is this approach appropriate in relation to art and antiquities? I would suggest not. First, these objects may have enormous cultural value; their provenance is important, and it is arguably wrong to equate transactions involving cultural objects with the bustle of the markets involving oil and grain. Each cultural object may also possess a high financial value: it is not unreasonable to distinguish them from ordinary commercial goods and to treat them as similar to land, where a detailed investigation of title is the norm. Secondly, now that the UK Government has ratified the 1970 UNESCO Convention, common law principles should be adjusted to take account of

[104] *Spencer v S Franses Ltd* [2011] EWHC 1269 [21].

[105] Although the embroideries were taken in clearing the flat, if they were wrongly included this could be viewed as theft: *Merry v Green* (1841) 7 M & W 623, 151 ER 916, discussed in 3.08.

[106] *China Pacific SA v Food Corporation of India (The Winson)* [1982] AC 939 (HL); *Palmer on Bailment,* 3rd edn (London, Sweet and Maxwell, 2009) [1-085].

[107] [2011] EWHC 1269 [301]. As regards making enquiries within a reasonable time, see *Tavoulareas v Lau* [2007] EWCA Civ 474.

[108] ibid [295]. See also *Costello v Chief Constable of Derbyshire* [2001] 1 WLR 1437 (CA). See 5.03, 5.11.

the need to prevent the trade in stolen cultural property. Thieves find it easier to sell objects in an environment where valuers, restorers, auction houses and others are not expected to ask questions or search databases. Thirdly, any agent, such as a dealer or auction house, who suspects that an item has been stolen should make a report to SOCA (or its expected replacement, the National Crime Agency) in order to protect himself from prosecution for a money laundering offence, as a stolen object may represent the proceeds of crime.[109] Yet, if agents are not expected to act upon their suspicions, apart from filing a report, it places a heavy burden upon law enforcement agencies such as SOCA. On receipt of a disclosure by the bailee, SOCA has a 'notice period' of seven days within which to investigate and make a decision.[110] If the bailee has carried out searches and made enquiries, this will be of great assistance to SOCA. Yet, in *Spencer v S Franses Ltd*, Thirlwall J, in discussing the defendant's actions, makes no reference to the risk of money laundering despite acknowledging that the facts were suspicious.[111] This area of law surely deserves scrutiny at a higher level, taking account of modern money laundering measures.

5.13 Conversion: Strict Liability

A claimant can bring an action for conversion against a defendant without needing to show that the defendant was at fault in any way. A defendant may have acted honestly and reasonably and yet may still be held liable. There is no need to establish that the defendant was aware that the object had been misappropriated.[112] In *Kuwait Airways*, Lord Nicholls accepted that liability should be strict where a claimant was bringing an action against the current possessor of the object.[113]

However, the application of the law appears harsh in relation to innocent intermediaries. If a defendant interferes with a claimant's proprietary rights to the object (such as by selling and delivering it), he cannot free himself from liability by showing that he was acting upon the instructions of a person who appeared to be the owner of the property in question.[114] In *Kuwait Airways*, Lord Nicholls controversially suggested that where an action was brought against an innocent intermediary who did not retain the property, the imposition of strict liability might require reappraisal in the future.[115] This suggestion was not a novel one: the Law Reform Committee had considered the issue of strict liability in 1971 and discussed whether liability should be fault-based in relation to all those involved in converting the goods other than the one in possession. The Committee concluded that no change to the existing law should be made. One reason for this decision was that the owner might face insuperable difficulties in attempting to establish that a seller or dealer in the chain of disposals was guilty of bad faith or negligence. It was thought that a change in the law would encourage dishonesty.[116] Furthermore, the Committee argued that, as most handlers of

[109] See 3.41–3.45.
[110] See 3.41.
[111] [2011] EWHC 1269 [211]–[213].
[112] *White v Withers LLP and Dearle* [2009] EWCA Civ 1122 (CA) [52]; *Marfani & Co Ltd v Midland Bank Ltd* [1968] 1 WLR 956, 970-71; *OBG Ltd v Allan* [2007] UKHL 21, [2008] 1 AC 1 (HL) [95]. But, if the defendant has purchased land on which the owner has left an object and he destroys it, believing it to be abandoned, he will be liable if he fails to show that he was not aware and could not reasonably be expected to be aware of a third party's rights over an object: *Robot Arenas Ltd v Waterfield* [2010] EWHC 115.
[113] *Kuwait Airways Corp v Iraqi Airways Co* [2002] AC 883 (HL) [78], [80].
[114] *Hollins v Fowler* (1875) LR 7 HL 757 (HL); *Consolidated Co v Curtis & Son* (1892) 1 QB 495; *Cochrane v Rymill* (1879) 40 LT 744.
[115] *Kuwait Airways Corp v Iraqi Airways Co* [2002] AC 883 (HL) [79].
[116] Law Reform Committee, *Eighteenth Report on Conversion and Detinue* (Cmnd 4774, 1971) [14].

goods were professionals who were insured, the advantage of strict liability was that it was clear and certain, so that claims could be made on insurance policies without difficulty.[117]

The principle of strict liability can be further defended on the basis that not all those who handle goods will be liable: it is only those who consciously interfere with proprietary rights who are vulnerable. In these circumstances, it can be argued that the law has maintained the balance between protection of the owner's rights and the defendant's freedom of action.[118] Green and Randall observe that the essence of the tort of conversion is the fact that the claim being made is a loss of the ability to exercise superior possessory rights over an object because of the defendant's wrongful interference with that object; they maintain that the defendant's lack of fault is irrelevant to such a claim.[119]

The owner would be in a very weak position if he were obliged to bring forward evidence that a defendant was at fault. By imposing strict liability upon those who interfere with another's proprietary rights, the current law puts pressure upon those dealing in or buying objects to take care to protect themselves from the risk of a lawsuit. They are best advised to make appropriate enquiries regarding the object's provenance. In the context of the art and antiquities market, where purchasers have sufficient time to investigate an item's history if they wish, the imposition of strict liability upon converters is welcome. It acts as a deterrent to all those who wish to turn a blind eye to the illicit trade in art and antiquities and money laundering.

V Code of Practice

5.14 Codes of Ethics Governing Museums: ICOM

The approach which museum employees take towards the acquisition of objects, whether by receipt of donations or purchase, was transformed by the UNESCO Convention 1970. Until this time, curators were primarily concerned to obtain items which would stimulate public interest, and their provenance was not seen as a significant matter.[120] The Convention ushered in a new era of ethical codes. It came to be appreciated that museums, as charities, should avoid acquiring illicit objects: it is not in the public interest to support an unethical and illegal trade.

The International Council of Museums (ICOM) is an international body which has brought hundreds of museums together. ICOM establishes minimum standards for all museums. ICOM's 2004 revised Code of Ethics states that all museums are expected to exercise due diligence in checking the provenance of an object before acquiring it.[121] However, the Code also provides that there may be exceptional circumstances where an object is viewed as sufficiently important that it can be acquired despite concerns about its provenance.[122] It is difficult to know what is envisaged by this statement. If the provision is

[117] ibid, [48, n 2].

[118] See S Douglas, 'The Nature of Conversion' (2009) *Cambridge Law Journal* 198, 220.

[119] See S Green and J Randall, *The Tort of Conversion* (Oxford, Hart Publishing, 2009) 72.

[120] For discussion of the position in the 1970s and 1980s, see P Boylan, 'Illicit Trafficking in Antiquities and Museum Ethics' in KW Tubb (ed), *Antiquities Trade or Betrayed: Legal, Ethical and Conservation Issues* (London, Archetype Publications, 1995) 94.

[121] ICOM Code of Ethics for Museums [2.3].

[122] ibid [3.4].

intended to cover situations where a very significant object is on offer, which has documents recording its provenance back towards the early part of the twentieth century, it is not controversial. The Policy Statement on the Acquisition of Antiquities by the British Museum has observed that, although the trustees will abide by the spirit of the ICOM Code of Ethics, the museum recognises that minor items often have very little supporting documentation; in these circumstances, it will rely upon the skills, knowledge and experience of its staff to determine whether an object is legitimate or not.[123]

It is also stated in the Code that museums can act as lawful depositories of illicit objects taken from a territory over which it has lawful responsibility.[124] The Code further provides that museums should not display objects lacking in provenance, in order to avoid contributing to the illicit trade in cultural property;[125] however, it fails to explain what should be done with such objects if they are not to be made available for display.

ICOM's Code of Ethics provides that, where there is a suspicion that objects have been illegally or illicitly acquired, transferred, imported, or exported, museum staff should notify the appropriate authorities.[126] Readers are expected to interpret the Code in the light of the major conventions, including the 1970 UNESCO Convention and the 1995 UNIDROIT Convention.[127] Paragraph 8.5 states: 'Members of the museum profession should not support the illicit traffic or market in natural and cultural property, directly or indirectly.' Although museum employees owe a general duty of confidentiality, paragraph 8.8 adds that this duty should give way to any legal obligation to assist the police or other proper authorities in investigating possible stolen, illicitly acquired, or illegally transferred property. The Code therefore presses museums to avoid authenticating suspicious objects and to report their concerns. These principles reflect UK money laundering measures which protect those who report their suspicions to the authorities from being prosecuted for a money laundering offence.[128]

5.15 Codes of Ethics Governing Museums: the UK Perspective

There are a number of regional and local codes of ethics, which direct museums to establish due diligence procedures in order to avoid acquiring property which is the product of the illicit trade in art and antiquities.[129] The Museums Association represents museums in the UK. It has a Code of Ethics for Museums, the latest version of which was published in 2008. It is recommended that the provisions of the Code should form part of the contract of employment for all museum employees. This means that, although the Code of Ethics has no legal force, if it is annexed to a contract of employment, an employee is exposed to the risk of disciplinary proceedings if he ignores it.

Part 5 of the Code of Ethics for Museums provides guidance in relation to acquisitions. Museums are expected to frame their acquisitions policy in the light of their own objectives. However, their acquisition policies are subject to the principles set out in the Code,

[123] N Brodie, J Doole and P Watson, *Stealing History: The Illicit Trade in Cultural Material* (Cambridge, the McDonald Institute for Archaeological Research, 2000) 45.

[124] One example is the purchase of items from the Salisbury Hoard by the British Museum: ibid 46. See also 3.11.

[125] ICOM Code of Ethics for Museums [4.5].

[126] ibid [5.1].

[127] ibid [7.2].

[128] See 3.41. See also, 3.43.

[129] See, for example, the Ethics Guidelines of the Canadian Museums Association [C.2, E].

which include exercising due diligence in relation to any purchase, acquisition or inward loan, and verifying ownership. Museums are expected to refuse any object if there is any suspicion that it has been stolen, or illicitly traded.[130] The Code also warns against offering expertise in relation to an object which may have been illicitly traded.[131] Paragraph 5.14 of the Code adds that museums must report any suspicious or criminal activity to the police. Thus, although the Code makes no reference to money laundering offences, the principles set out should ensure that museum employees will avoid any risk of prosecution.

The Museums Association's Code of Ethics is not intended to merely reflect the law. Museums are charities and exist for the public benefit. The Code is therefore intended to create a relationship of trust between museums and the communities which they serve. It therefore has an ethical dimension in order to reflect the fact that museum trustees act as ethical guardians of cultural objects for the benefit of future generations. One strength of the Code is that it goes further than the law requires. For example, paragraph 5.14 goes on to provide that museums should report 'any other suspicions of illicit trade to other museums collecting in the same area and to organisations that aim to curtail the illicit trade.' Furthermore, the Code states that museums should avoid appearing to tolerate this trade by inappropriate involvement with dealers and auction houses. They should also refuse to lend objects to any exhibition which may include illicit objects.[132] This responsible approach must be applauded.

The Museums Association Code and the ICOM Code do not provide museums with detailed guidance in relation to due diligence checks which should be carried out when acquiring an object. However, this is provided by the Department for Culture Media and Sport, discussed below.

5.16 Guidance from the Department for Culture Media and Sport

Trustees of many local museums in the UK have created their own internal management policies but, in doing so, they will have had regard to the ethical guidelines published by the International Council of Museums (ICOM) and the Museums Association. In addition, the Department for Culture Media and Sport (DCMS) issued guidelines in 2005, entitled 'Combating Illicit Trade: Due Diligence Guidelines for Museums, Libraries and Archives on Collecting and Borrowing Cultural Material'. These guidelines are invaluable in providing specific information on the steps which museum staff should take in acting diligently in relation to the acquisition of a cultural object.

The guidelines refer to the UNESCO Convention and emphasise that the year of 1970 was a watershed in relation to acquisition policies. From 1970 onwards, museums were expected to act in an ethical manner. The basic principle, as set out in the DCMS guidance is as follows:

> Museums should acquire and borrow items only if they are legally and ethically sound. They should reject an item if there is any suspicion about it, or about the circumstances surrounding it, after undertaking due diligence.

If the object did not originate in the UK, museums must ascertain whether the item was in the UK before 1970 with no evidence that it was illegally exported from its country of

[130] Museum Association Code of Ethics [5.9].
[131] ibid [5.16].
[132] ibid [5.15].

origin, or that it was out of its country of origin before 1970 and it was legally exported from an intermediate country to the UK or, if it was in its country of origin after 1970, that it was legally exported to the UK.

The DCMS guidelines are particularly useful because of the level of detail which they provide. They encourage museums and other institutions to take a cautious approach and to seek advice where necessary. They rightly flag up the fact that documents relating to provenance may be forged. They also give practical examples of the process of due diligence, which include inspecting the frames, binding, mounting, labels, inscriptions, marks, repairs, and any dust or dirt on the objects in question. Employees are expected to be on their guard in relation to objects from areas where it is well known that there has been extensive looting, such as Afghanistan, South East Asia and Iraq. There are also certain types of cultural objects which are known to be at risk.[133] A particular strength of this set of guidelines is that it steers the reader away from a 'box-ticking' approach to due diligence and promotes instead a careful assessment of the evidence and a steady focus on the object, its description, and the reliability of the seller.

5.17 Codes of Due Diligence for Auction Houses and Dealers in the Twentieth Century

A high standard of conduct is expected of museum staff, because they work for charities which exist for the public benefit. In contrast, dealers and auction houses are ordinary participants in the art market. In the last part of the twentieth century, codes of conduct reflected this distinction. There were a number of codes encouraging professionals to take steps to avoid being involved in the transfer or acquisition of an illicit cultural object.[134] However, they typically contained vague terms and operated at the level of exhortation, encouraging professionals to do their subjective best.

The low standard set is illustrated by the 1984 Code of Practice for the Control of International Trading in Works of Art. This Code did not require title to be investigated. However, by clause 2, members were required to 'undertake, to the best of their ability, not to import, export or transfer the ownership' in illicit objects. It did not impose any sanctions upon auctioneers and dealers but merely stated that any matter would be rigorously investigated.[135] By clause 4, where the Code has been breached unintentionally, the dealer was merely expected to co-operate, subject to reimbursement, in the return of an illegally obtained object.[136] This Code was discussed in *Kingdom of Spain v Christie, Manson & Woods Ltd*,[137] where it was alleged that a picture had been exported from Spain with the use of forged documents. Browne-Wilkinson VC noted with some surprise that, although the defendant, Christie's, was a party to the Code, it still planned to go ahead and auction the picture. Christie's indicated that even if the court declared that the documents were forgeries, it would still sell the picture because the seller had acquired the picture innocently, not knowing of its illegal export. Christie's maintained that clause 4 governed as a consequence

[133] ICOM publishes on its website a 'red list' of certain cultural objects at risk from Africa (2000), Latin America (2003), Iraq (2003). Afghanistan (2006), Peru (2007) and Central America and Mexico (2009).

[134] See A Griffiths, 'Codes of Conduct' (1997) II(2) *Art Antiquity and Law* 173. In particular, there is the Code of Practice for the Control of International Trading in Works of Art 1984; the Code of Ethics adopted by the International Association of Dealers in Ancient Art 1993; and the Museums Association Code of Practice for Museum Authorities 1977, as amended in 1987.

[135] The Code of Practice for the Control of International Trading in Works of Art [5]. The Code is set out in full in (1997) II(1) *Art Antiquity and Law* 97.

[136] The Code of Practice for the Control of International Trading in Works of Art [4].

[137] [1986] 1 WLR 1120.

and that, as the claimant, the Spanish Government, had not offered satisfactory reimbursement, the sale would take place.

This low level of diligence can be seen as consistent with the civil law, and with decisions such as *Marcq v Christie Manson & Woods Ltd*[138] and *Spencer v S Franses Ltd.*[139] However, it clearly encourages rather than deters those intent on trafficking in illicit objects. Yet, if the picture was smuggled into this country with forged papers and an offence has been committed, the Serious Organised Crime Agency might now seek a civil recovery order on the basis that the picture represents the proceeds of crime.

5.18 Raising Standards: Modern Codes Regulating the Conduct of Dealers

The Council for the Prevention of Art Theft (CoPAT) introduced a much higher standard of conduct in its Code of Due Diligence for Dealers Trading in Fine Art, Antiques, Antiquarian Books, Manuscripts and Collectors' Items.[140] Although it was adopted in the United Kingdom in 1999, it was controversial because its rules go far beyond the demands of the common law.

The Code of Due Diligence recommends that dealers should endeavour to verify and document the name and address of vendors and to describe the items which are to be sold. This is reminiscent of the 'know your client' provisions contained in the Money Laundering Regulations, which were extended to 'high value' dealers[141] in 2003 and which require identification checks to be carried out.[142] There are other provisions which are in step with money laundering requirements: dealers undertake to contact the police and to make further enquiries if they believe that an item may be stolen, and senior employees within an organisation will be made responsible for receiving information where internal staff wish to report their suspicions. The Code also provides that dealers should be suspicious of an inexplicably low purchase price demanded for an item. They are encouraged to pay any money by cheque rather than cash in order to create an audit trail, and also to become familiar with money laundering regulations.

There are a number of codes of conduct aimed at specific professional groups within the art market. They vary in their terms. For example, the British Art Market Federation has 'Anti-Money Laundering and Financial Crime' guidelines. These warn members about money laundering measures and point out that, even if they are not 'high value' dealers, they should report suspicious transactions, to avoid committing a money laundering offence. The Antiquities Dealers Association appears to place a heavy emphasis upon ethics. It not only expects its members to verify the identity of their customers but also to check the Art Loss Register and to take photographs of the object prior to any repairs being made.

These codes do not give private individuals a right to sue dealers and others. They are intended to assist prospective buyers in identifying which dealers comply with legal and ethical standards in relation to the provenance of cultural objects. Furthermore, they will not necessarily assist any claimant suing in conversion because the key issue in such cases is normally whether the defendant has treated the property as his own. However, these codes are helpful in combatting the illicit trade in cultural property.

138 [2004] QB 286 (CA) discussed at 5.10.

139 [2011] EWHC 1269, discussed at 5.12.

140 CoPAT's Policy of Due Diligence for Dealers Trading in Fine Art, Antiques, Antiquarian Books, Manuscripts and Collectors' Items is set out in (1997) 2 *Art Antiquity and Law* 430. See further, J Ulph, 'Exercising Due Diligence in Art Transactions' (1998) III 4 *Art Antiquity and Law* 323.

141 Receiving cash payments of over 15,000 euros. See 3.45.

142 See 3.45.

5.19 The International Code of Ethics for Dealers in Cultural Property

The International Code of Ethics for Dealers in Cultural Property was launched by UNESCO in November 2000. It builds upon the principles which can be found in the 1970 UNESCO Convention and the 1995 UNIDROIT Convention. The drafters of the Code considered the codes of conduct which applied to dealers in a variety of jurisdictions, including the United Kingdom, France and Switzerland. The drafters were also guided by ICOM's Code of Ethics, article 1 of which provides:

> Professional traders in cultural property will not import, export or transfer the ownership of this property when they have reasonable cause to believe it has been stolen, illegally alienated, clandestinely excavated or illegally exported.

The notes which accompany the Code make it clear that the phrase 'reasonable cause to believe' is to be understood as 'requiring traders to investigate the provenance of the material they handle'. However, if dealers examine the background to a transaction properly, asking searching questions of the vendor, and everything appears to be above board, they may proceed. Article 1 therefore seems to be a clear and firm direction that dealers must avoid becoming involved in the illicit trade in cultural property. Further paragraphs build upon this principle. For example, Article 3 adds that:

> A trader who has reasonable cause to believe that an object has been the product of a clandestine excavation, or has been acquired illegally or dishonestly from an official excavation site or monument will not assist in any further transaction with that object, except with the agreement of the country where the site or monument exists. A trader who is in possession of the object, where that country seeks its return within a reasonable period of time, will take all legally permissible steps to co-operate in the return of that object to the country of origin.

The Code clearly marks a shift away from the traditional manner of trading in the art market where no questions are asked. The notes which accompany this Code suggest that its aims are even more ambitious. It is hoped that the Code will provide ethical dealers who adopt it with an advantage in transacting. Their adherence to the Code will indicate to members of the public that 'there is an ethical body of dealers who are not to be confused with those exposed by the media as instigating and commissioning thefts, clandestine excavations and illegal exports of cultural property.'

VI Remedies: Financial Compensation

5.20 The Action for Conversion

A dispossessed owner of a cultural object will normally wish to recover that object. If he has an immediate right to possession, he could attempt to physically retake the object and thereby avoid litigation. However, usually this is not feasible. The owner will therefore ordinarily bring an action in conversion alleging that the defendant is liable for wrongful interference with his property and will ask the court to exercise its discretion in favour of ordering its return.[143] However, there may be situations where the claimant is content with

[143] Torts (Interference with Goods) Act 1977 s 3(2)(a).

financial compensation instead. For example, if he has bought a signed print, it may be easy enough to purchase another print. If a substitute can easily be acquired, an order by the court that the defendant should pay damages in compensation will be appropriate.[144] Where the claimant is compensated for the whole of his interest in the goods, the effect of the payment will be to extinguish the claimant's title.[145]

5.21 Money Had and Received

A dispossessed owner may choose to bring a common law action for money had and received, rather than suing in conversion.[146] The action for money had and received is wide in scope and is regularly used to recover the value of intangible property, such as money circulating as currency.[147] It can be employed to obtain the value of tangible assets. However, it cannot be employed to recover the assets themselves).[148]

An advantage of bringing an action for money had and received is that, using the process of tracing,[149] the claimant can demand all of the benefit received by the defendant, which may be much greater than the value of the original item. Thus, if a thief has stolen and sold a work of art and invested the proceeds in other cultural objects, or shares, or land, a claim may be made for the value of those investments. Where the thief has kept a painting and hired it out, a claim may be based upon unjust enrichment in order to claim not only to the value of the painting but also the profits from the loans, as a reversal of the enrichment received by the thief.[150]

The defences available will vary according to the claim being made. If the claimant brings an action in conversion, which will be made to recover the works of art or antiquities themselves, the only defence will be good faith purchase combined with reliance upon the limitation periods.[151] In contrast, if a defendant elects to bring a claim based upon unjust enrichment, the defendant may wish to plead change of position as a defence.[152]

[144] ibid, s 3(2)(3). In relation to ordinary commodities, the measure of damages will reflect the loss which the claimant has sustained, which will usually be the market value of the goods: *Kuwait Airways Corpn v Iraqi Airways Co* [2002] AC 883 (HL) [67]. However, in the case of a cultural object, it may not be possible to ascertain the market price: see *Clerk & Lindsell on Torts,* 20th edn (London, Sweet and Maxwell London, 2010) [17-93, nn 28ff].

[145] ibid s 5. See *Kuwait Airways Corpn v Iraqi Airways Co.* [2002] AC 883 (HL) [77].

[146] *United Australia Ltd v Barclays Bank Ltd* [1941] AC 1.

[147] *M'Lachlan v Evans* (1827) 1 Y & J 380, 148 ER 718, 720. The parties should have treated these assets as having a monetary value: *Spratt v Hobhouse* (1827) 4 Bing 173, 178, 130 ER 734, 737; *Pickard v Bankes* (1810) 13 East 20, 104 ER 273.

[148] The action in conversion is concerned with goods, not intangible property: Torts (Interference with Goods) Act 1977, s 14(1); *OBG Ltd v Allan* [2008] 1 AC 1 (HL).

[149] In relation to tracing, see 5.29. On tracing at common law, see *Trustee of the Property of FC Jones & Sons v Jones* [1997] Ch 159 (CA).

[150] *Strand Electric and Engineering Co Ltd v Brisford Entertainment Ltd* [1952] 2 QB 246 (CA). For a discussion of the distinction between a claim for proprietary restitution, where the claimant retains legal title, and a claim based upon unjust enrichment, see *Armstrong DLW Gmbh v Winnington Networks Ltd* [2012] EWHC 10 [70]–[98].

[151] For a full discussion of possible defences, see 5.33–5.51.

[152] This defence is discretionary. In *Lipkin Gorman v Karpnale Ltd* [1991] 2 AC 548 (HL), Lord Goff explained that the defence of change of position is available to a person 'whose position has so changed that it would be inequitable in all the circumstances to require him to make restitution, or alternatively to make restitution in full'; ibid 580. A defendant cannot rely upon this defence if he has acted dishonestly or in a commercially unacceptable way: *Niru Battery Manufacturing Co v Milestone Trading Ltd* [2004] EWCA Civ 487, [2004] 2 Lloyd's Rep 319 (CA).

VII Return of the Work of Art or Antiquity

5.22 Delivery: at the Court's Discretion

Although some claimants may be satisfied with financial compensation, most dispossessed owners will desire the return of the object itself. This is because these objects have a cultural dimension and any financial compensation may never fully reflect their loss. In this situation, they will bring an action in conversion, seeking an order from the court for its return. This is possible because the action for conversion is not only a personal action. It has proprietary characteristics as well: it depends upon proof of a right to possession by the claimant and of beneficial receipt at some stage by the defendant.

However, the claimant has no automatic right of recovery of the property in issue. By section 3 of the Torts (Inteference with Goods) Act 1977, the court has a discretion to order the return of the property itself 'against a person who is in possession or in control' of the object. The claimant can apply for interim custody of the property pending a full court hearing and decision.[153] The court will normally refuse to exercise its discretion to order the object's return where it has been treated as an item of commerce by the claimant. This might be so where the claimant is a dealer who originally had possession of the object because he wanted to sell it; in this case, financial compensation should suffice to compensate the claimant.[154] In contrast, the court would be expected to exercise its discretion in favour of the return of an object where it is unique in some way,[155] or where it has great sentimental value.[156] The claimant must therefore establish that he has a special interest in it.[157]

The courts have proceeded pragmatically in exercising their discretion. There is no point in ordering the return of an article which can easily be replaced by going into the market place; financial compensation should ordinarily suffice. However, the courts are careful to take account of all the circumstances and to adopt a common sense approach. There may be a good reason for ordering up delivery of a commonplace item.[158] Consequently, there should be no risk of a refusal being challenged by a claimant on the basis that he is being deprived of his property in violation of Article 1 of the First Protocol, contained in the Human Rights Act 1998, which provides a qualified guarantee in relation to enjoyment of property. In summary, if an object is unique – and most cultural property will fall into this category – a claimant should be confident in requesting its return.

153 Torts (Inteference with Goods) Act 1977, s 4; see *Howard Perry & Co v British Railways Board* [1980] 1 WLR 1375, 1381–82.

154 *Whiteley Ltd v Hilt* [1918] 2 KB 808 (CA) 819, concerning an ordinary piano. See further, *Tanks and Vessels Industries Ltd v Devon Cider Co Ltd* [2009] EWHC 1360. Contrast *Societé des Industries Metallurgiques SA v Bronx Engineering Co Ltd* [1975] 1 Lloyd's Rep 465.

155 *Nicole de Préval v Adrian Alan Ltd* (24 January 1997).

156 Torts (Interference with Goods) Act 1977, s 3(2)(a). See *Somerset v Cookson* (1735) 3 P Wms 390, 24 ER 1114 (Roman altar); *Fells v Read* (1796) 3 Ves 70, 30 ER 70 (silver tobacco box); *Lady Arundell v Phipps* (1804) 13 Ves 95 (family pictures).

157 In exercising its discretion, the courts' general approach is similar to that adopted in awarding specific performance of a contract: see generally, *Falcke v Gray* (1859) 4 Drew 651 (unusual jars); *Thorn v Commrs of Her Majesty's Works and Public Buildings* (1863) 32 Beav 490 (stone from old Westminster Bridge); *Phillips v Lamdin* [1949] 2 KB 33 (Adam door, which matched the mantelpiece in the room).

158 *Pendragon plc v Walon Ltd* [2005] EWHC 1082 [24] (uncertainty relating to the disposal of Rover cars caused by the appointment of administrators); *Howard Perry & Co v British Railways Board* [1980] 1 WLR 1375, 1382–83 (steel which was impossible to obtain on the open market).

The position becomes complex where a cultural object has been altered or improved. Even worse it may be mixed with similar objects or permanently affixed to a building. The discussion which follows is concerned with whether the claimant can recover an object which has been altered in some way. However, even when the claimant can identify his property in its altered form, it is clear from the explanation above that he has the further hurdle of persuading the court to exercise its discretion to order its redelivery.

VIII Following

5.23 Following an Object of Art or Antiquity at Common Law

If a thief has taken a work of art or antiquity, he may keep it, destroy it, sell it or give it away. Normally, the owner will contact the police in an attempt to locate this object and to *follow* it into the hands of the thief or a third party to whom it has been transferred. The use of computer databases, such as the Art Loss Register and the Historic Art Theft Database, can be particularly useful in pursuing the object itself.[159] The dispossessed owner has the legal title to the object and, if it can be identified, he will sue in the tort of conversion to recover it.

5.24 Alterations to the Original Item

Looting from archaeological sites and museums may involve smashing up a large stone object into pieces so that it can be carried away more easily. It is obviously no defence to a claim in conversion that the claimant is only asking for the return *of part* of a stone frieze or other object. If an object belonging, for example, to a state, is smashed into four pieces, the state owns all four pieces. The biggest difficulty, when an object has been transformed in some way, is in identifying it. The most obvious situation where this will become an insurmountable problem in practice is where objects made of metals are excavated and are then melted down for their gold content. Fears have been expressed that this may have been the fate of some of the items looted from Iraq's National Museum in Baghdad.[160] Criminals may be tempted to do this in order to escape prosecution: they hope that, by destroying the identity of an object, they will have obliterated the evidence of their crime.

5.25 Improvements

If a bailee is asked to carry out work on an object in exchange for payment, he can refuse to relinquish possession of the object to his customer until he has received that payment. In *Spencer v SF Franses Ltd*,[161] the defendant was the owner of the world's largest academic research archive on figurative embroideries and textiles. He had agreed to investigate the provenance of two embroideries which were thought to date from the nineteenth century. He gathered evidence suggesting that they were of medieval origin. His hard work improved

[159] See PJ O'Keefe, 'The Use of Databases to Combat Theft of Cultural Heritage Material' (1997) 2 *Art Antiquity and Law* 357.

[160] B Barnes and K Mazurkewich, 'Experts Scramble to Identify Iraq's Plundered Treasures' *Wall Street Journal* (16 April 2003).

[161] [2011] EWHC 1269.

the cultural and material value of the embroideries. However, he was not paid by the claimant, and therefore refused to return the embroideries. It was held that he was entitled to retain them (thereby asserting a lien) until he was paid for his services. He was not liable in conversion if he did so.

A stolen object may be sold to a good faith purchaser who later carries out work to repair any damage. For example, a painting may need to be relined, restretchered and recanvassed. The fact that the painting has been improved does not prevent the original owner from bringing an action in conversion for the return of the object, but the court may order the claimant to make some payment to reflect this enhanced value.[162] Equally, the claimant may need to compensate a good faith purchaser for any improvement to the object made by a third party.[163]

5.26 Return of the Object Where it has been Mixed with Similar Items

Rogues are increasingly aware that a highly prized piece of art may be difficult to dispose of because of its notoriety and unique characteristics. From their perspective, it may be better to steal an item which is similar to others, such as a cylinder seal or a signed print. If a dealer buys stolen cylinder seals, the first difficulty for any claimant will be to prove that an object which he once owned is part of the resulting collection. But, if his cylinder seal can be picked out because of unusual markings then, despite the fact that it has been stored with similar objects, the owner will retain his legal title and can sue in conversion to seek its recovery.

The situation is more complicated where similar objects have become mixed, so that each is indistinguishable from another. In this situation, the original owner loses his legal title to the object. However, provided the owner or owners can prove that their objects form part of the mixture of objects, the general rule is that the contributors have equal but proportionate shares.[164] Any doubts relating to quantities will be resolved in favour of the innocent victims and against the interests of the wrongdoer (the thief or anyone claiming title through the thief).[165] Thus, if cylinder seals have been stolen from different countries of origin, each government may wish to assert its legal title and to lay claim to part of the mixture.

5.27 Return of the Object Where it has been Attached to Another Item

Where a stolen object has been added to another object, the first step is to consider whether it can simply be detached and returned. If so, the owner can sue in conversion and ask the court to grant an order for its return.[166] However, if it has been used in a way where it is permanently fixed to another object, it may be seen as a new product which is different in nature from its constituent parts. The question then arises as to who owns this new property. In this situation, modern persuasive authorities have drawn a clear distinction between

[162] Torts (Interference with Goods) Act 1977, s 6(1).

[163] This would be so, regardless of whether the improver acted in good faith or not: ibid, s 6(2).

[164] *Glencore v MTI* [2001] 1 Lloyd's Rep 284 [158]–[159], [193]. See generally, *Lupton v White* (1808) 15 Ves 342; *Armory v Delamirie* (1722) 1 Str 505; *Sandeman & Sons v Tyzack and Branfoot Steamship Co Ltd* [1913] AC 680 (HL); *Coleman v Harvey* [1989] 1 NZLR 723.

[165] *Glencore v MTI* [2001] 1 Lloyd's Rep 284 [193]. See further, *Indian Oil Corporation Ltd v Greenstone Shipping SA (Panama)* [1988] 1 QB 345, 362.

[166] *Hendy Lennox (Industrial Engines) Ltd v Grahame Puttick Ltd* [1984] 1 WLR 485.

innocent and wrongful manufacture. Someone who innocently uses stolen goods to create a new item (such as where Georgian handles which have been stolen are added to Georgian urns) may be presumed to own the new product.[167] In contrast, where a thief is attempting to conceal his crime by modifying an object to make a new creation, the court will be concerned with identifying the origin of the new creation,[168] and may favour the original owner if it is composed either wholly or substantially of his object, concluding that he has title in the new creation.[169]

If, however, the original owner's object contributed to the new creation in a very minor way, such as where it has been used to merely repair a much larger object, legal title may be lost. The claimant could seek damages but could not ask the court to order the return of the new object itself.[170] But this is not the favoured approach: courts will normally favour co-ownership or division where it is appropriate to do so.[171] In making any division of the asset, innocent victims will have equal standing and any evidential doubts will be resolved in their favour.[172]

5.28 Following the Object: No Defence of Good Faith Purchase at Common Law

Where an employee, for example, has stolen art or antiquities, the employer can follow the object into a third party's hands. The claimant will have a particular reason for suing at common law. As will be discussed, there is no general defence of good faith purchase if a tangible item is stolen.[173] The only defences to a common law claim are that the defendant acquired a good title in another country or that the limitation period within which a claim can be brought has expired.

IX Tracing the Value of Stolen Property into Substitute Assets

5.29 Tracing Assets with which the Cultural Object has been Exchanged

What is the position where art or antiquities have been stolen and sold and can no longer be located, but the proceeds of sale are identifiable?[174] Here, the owner (or his insurers) will wish to recover the proceeds of sale or any substitute property acquired with those proceeds. The process of identifying assets which represent the original stolen art and antiqui-

[167] *International Banking Corporation v Ferguson, Shaw & Sons* 1910 SC 182. See P Birks, 'Mixtures' in NE Palmer and E McKendrick (eds), *Interests in Goods,* 2nd edn (London, LLP, 1998) 227, 228.

[168] *Glencore v MTI* [2001] 1 Lloyd's Rep 284 [171]. See further, *Case of Leather* (1490) YB 5 Hen VII fol 15; a translation of the case is provided by the Supreme Court of Judicature of New York in *Silsbury & Calkins v McCoon* (1847) 4 Denio 332, 1847 NY, Lexis 128.

[169] *Glencore v MTI* [2001] 1 Lloyd's Rep 284 [179]; *McDonald v Provon (Scotland Street) Ltd* 1960 SLT 231. See further, *Jones v De Marchant* (1916) 28 DLR 561; *Silsbury & Calkins v McCoon & Sherman* (1850) 3 NY 379.

[170] *Glencore v MTI* [2001] 1 Lloyd's Rep 284 [179]; *Stock v Stock* (1594) Poph 37, 38; *Sandeman & Sons v Tyzack and Branfoot Steamship Co Ltd* [1913] AC 680, 695. The original owner would be relegated to a personal claim.

[171] *Glencore v MTI* [2001] 1 Lloyd's Rep 284 [185], [194].

[172] ibid [181], [194]. Any doubts would be resolved against the wrongdoer: ibid [182]; see also *Foskett v McKeown* [2001] 1 AC 102 (HL) 132–33.

[173] See 5.34. In contrast, a good faith seller who receives stolen money will obtain a good title to the money: *Miller v Race* (1758) 1 Burr 452.

[174] The claimant can no longer follow the object if it cannot be located. On the distinction between following and tracing, see *Foskett v McKeown* [2001] 1 AC 102 (HL) 127–28; *Armstrong DLW GmbH v Winnington Networks Ltd* [2012] EWHC 10 [65], [66].

ties is known as 'tracing'.[175] Earlier decisions by English courts have appeared to accept that, at common law, tracing is restricted to situations where money has not been mixed with other money.[176] In contrast, equity has flexible and certain tracing rules. Consequently, where the claimant wishes to bring a proprietary claim to recover the proceeds of sale with which the art or antiquity has been exchanged, he will wish to sue in equity. Yet, in order to trace the value of property in equity and to assert a claim, it appears that a fiduciary relationship must be established.[177]

5.30 Fiduciary Relationship

A claimant can bring an action in equity where the work of art or antiquity has been under the control of a fiduciary. A fiduciary is someone who has assumed a duty of loyalty towards the legal owner.[178] The basis for this duty is a relationship of trust and confidence, or one of influence, or of confidentiality.[179] A fiduciary relationship would exist, for example, between a trustee and a beneficiary, an executor and those beneficiaries entitled under the will, an agent and his principal, and an employee who is looking after the property of his employer. Thus a curator at a museum who steals art and antiquities from his employer,[180] or a housekeeper who spirits away a valuable item,[181] should be treated as being in breach of their duties of loyalty and good faith. If criminal gangs pay an employee of the owner to assist them in stealing cultural objects, the employee would be in breach of his fiduciary duties.[182] The same would be true of guards who were recruited to protect archaeological sites but who secretly assisted looters.[183]

Where a fiduciary is under a duty to receive assets on behalf of his principal (or employer), or to look after the assets of his principal (or employer), the fiduciary will become a constructive trustee of those assets if he attempts to appropriate them for his own benefit. A constructive trust is imposed because the fiduciary has secretly tried to enrich himself by depriving the principal (or employer) of the assets.[184] However, if a fiduciary enriches himself by doing a wrong, such as where an employee receives a payment from a gang of thieves in exchange for leaving premises unsecured, the employee will be personally liable to account for the money

[175] Tracing is neither a remedy nor a cause of action but can be called in aid to support a claim at common law or in equity: *Boscawen v Bajwa* [1996] 1 WLR 328 (CA) 334.

[176] *Taylor v Plumer* (1815) 3 M & S 562; *Banque Belge pour l'Etranger v Hambrouck* [1921] 1 KB 321 (CA); *Agip (Africa) v Jackson* [1990] Ch 265; *Bank Tejerat v Hong Kong and Shanghai Building Corp* [1995] 1 Lloyd's Rep 716.

[177] *Re Diplock* [1948] 1 Ch 465 (CA); *Agip (Africa) v Jackson* [1991] Ch 547; *Boscawen v Bajwa* [1996] 1 WLR 328 (CA). This requirement was strongly criticised by Lord Millett in *Foskett v McKeown* [2001] 1 AC 102 (HL) 128. Nevertheless, it remains the law until an appellate court decides otherwise: *Shalson v Russo* [2003] EWHC 1637, [2005] Ch 281 [104].

[178] *Bristol and West BS v Mothew* [1998] Ch 1 (CA) 18. Consequently, the relationship between a buyer and a seller can never ordinarily be a fiduciary one, because they will be negotiating at arm's length: *Re Goldcorp Exchange* [1995] 1 AC 74 (PC).

[179] PJ Millett, 'Equity's Place in the Law of Commerce' (1998) 114 *Law Quarterly Review* 214, 219–21.

[180] See A Dunee, 'The Curator did it' (1993) 92 *Art News* 56: a curator, piqued at not securing promotion, stole 36 items, including bundles of manuscripts which were broken up for resale on the open market.

[181] Forty-five of Chagall's paintings, worth millions of pounds, were taken by Chagall's housekeeper from his home after he died and sold: C Bremner, 'Chagall Art Dealers Quizzed – Marc Chagall' *The Times* (29 November 1994).

[182] See *Brinks Mat v Abu Saleh (No 3)* [1996] CLC 133, where a security guard at his employer's warehouse was held to be a fiduciary. In the past, there has been a suspicion that gangs have made arrangements with servants working in private houses to facilitate burglaries: C Lees, 'The fine art of stealth' *Sunday Times* (1 August 1993).

[183] See *Brinks Mat v Abu Saleh (No 3)* [1996] CLC 133; *Agip (Africa) Ltd v Jackson* [1990] 1 Ch 265, 269.

[184] The position is different where the fiduciary, such as dealer acting for a seller, has made a special agreement: *Accidia v Simon C Dickinson Ltd* [2010] EWHC 3058 [87].

received, but his employer may not be able to trace and claim the bribe. The employer will not have a proprietary claim if the money never belonged to the employer.[185]

Where a constructive trust is imposed, a claimant can choose between a personal or proprietary claim. For example, if an employee takes a painting belonging to his employer and sells it, the employer can sue the employee personally for equitable compensation. In the alternative, the employer could bring a proprietary claim against the employee in relation to the proceeds of sale. A proprietary claim is advantageous where the employee is insolvent and the employer wishes to gain priority over creditors, or where the employer wishes to ensure that the money is not swept up to satisfy a confiscation order by the state.[186]

What if a cultural object is stolen by a complete stranger? Has the stranger, by the act of stealing, assumed a duty of loyalty to his victim? It would be odd to think that a burglar or thief owed any fiduciary duties to the original owner. However, if there is no fiduciary relationship in these circumstances, an owner cannot bring a proprietary action in equity to recover the proceeds of sale from anyone to whom the thief has handed the money. If the object has disappeared, and the thief has transferred the proceeds to his wife and then become insolvent, the owner may have no remedy. This is because the tracing rules at common law have not been fully developed.[187] In the past, claimants have not been successful in tracing money at common law if that money has been paid into a bank account and become mixed with other money before being transferred to third parties.[188]

Due to the lack of clarity in relation to the common law tracing rules, claimants seeking the proceeds of sale or other traceable assets will usually argue that a fiduciary relationship existed. In *Westdeutsche Landesbank Girozentrale v Islington LBC*, Lord Browne-Wilkinson suggested that a constructive trust would be imposed where a thief steals money and obtains legal title to it by mixing it so that it can no longer be identified in specie: a constructive trust would be imposed enabling the victim to trace the money or exchanged assets in equity.[189] The basis of liability would be the unconscionable act of theft.

In *Shalson v Russo*, Rimer J was critical of Lord Browne-Wilkinson's analysis, observing that:

> a thief ordinarily acquires no property in what he steals and cannot give a title to it even to a good faith purchaser: both the thief and the purchaser are vulnerable to claims by the true owner to recover his property. If the thief has no title in the property, I cannot see how he can become a trustee of it for the true owner: the owner retains the legal and beneficial title.[190]

[185] *Sinclair Investments (UK) Ltd v Versailles Trade Finance Limited* [2011] EWCA Civ 347 [80], [88]–[89]. See also *Cadogan Petroleum plc v Tolley* [2011] EWHC 2286 [27]. For cogent criticism of the Court of Appeal's decision in *Versailles*, in which it was decided that there was only personal liability to account for a bribe, see DJ Hayton, 'No Proprietary Liability for Bribes and Other Secret Profits?' (2011) *Trust Law International* 3; R Nolan, 'Bribes: a Reprise' (2011) *Law Quarterly Review* 19.

[186] In relation to confiscation orders, see 4.14.

[187] For a discussion of the difficulties in tracing proceeds of sale at common law, see J Ulph, 'Tracing at Common Law and the Significance of Possession' [2007] *Restitution Law Review* 76.

[188] *Agip (Africa) v Jackson* [1990] Ch 265; *Bank Tejerat v Hong Kong and Shanghai Building Corp* [1995] 1 Lloyd's Rep 716.

[189] *Westdeutsche Landesbank Girozentrale v Islington LBC* [1996] AC 669 (HL) 715–16. See also, *Black v Freedman* (1910) 12 CLR 105 (High Ct of Australia). In *Armstrong DLW GmbH v Winnington Networks Ltd* [2012] EWHC 10 [128]–[129], this position was accepted without further discussion by S Morris QC, sitting as a Deputy High Court judge. In *Sinclair Investment Holdings SA v Versailles Trade Finance Ltd* [2005] EWCA Civ 722, [2006] 1 BCLC 60 (CA) [53], Lord Justice Buxton suggested that Lord Browne-Wilkinson's comments were directed at the theoretical explanation of tracing in equity and noted that it was not directly applicable on the facts before him.

[190] *Shalson v Russo* [2003] EWHC 1637, [2005] Ch 281 [110].

Barkehall Thomas has argued in support of Rimer J's view that a trust is not possible if the thief does not have legal title.[191]

This issue calls for a precise analysis of title and property rights. A thief, in taking possession of money or an object, does not immediately acquire the owner's legal title to it; instead, the thief obtains a right of possession (and therefore a possessory title) which is good against the whole world apart from the true owner.[192] It is only a good faith purchaser who, in taking stolen money as currency, will obtain a good title to it.[193] Tarrant had argued that the thief will hold his possessory right to the money on trust for the true owner.[194] Chambers has added that:

> A possessory title has market value, it can be sold or given away, and there is nothing to prevent it being held in trust. If it were otherwise, the consequences would be alarming. Defects in title and the possibility that we might not have the best possible title are risks we all face, including trustees. The suggestion that such defects might prevent those assets from being held in trust would certainly surprise settlors, trustees and beneficiaries around the world.[195]

The argument that a thief holds his possessory rights to a stolen object, such as a painting, upon trust for the true owner has persuasive force. It is supported by the Court of Appeal's analysis of property rights in *Islamic Republic of Iran v Barakat Galleries Ltd* in which it was accepted that multiple rights to objects can co-exist.[196] If a trust is imposed upon the thief, the owner can trace in equity and claim the proceeds of sale. But normally there will be no need to seek the proceeds of sale because the claimant has an effective action at common law to recover the object itself: namely, the tort of conversion. It is only where the thief has sold the painting or other object and has later become insolvent that the imposition of a constructive trust in relation to the proceeds of sale becomes significant.

A decision to impose a trust in relation to a thief's possessory rights to property in order to permit the claimant to trace the value of his property in equity may be seen as entirely pragmatic.[197] The two levels of property rights, legal and equitable, afford maximum protection to the owner, the victim of theft.[198] If an owner may use equity's powerful identification rules to assert proprietary rights in the proceeds of sale of an object dishonestly sold by his employee or agent, it may seem harsh to deny such assistance where it is a stranger who has taken it. Yet, rather than stretching the concept of a fiduciary relationship to encompass thieves and their victims,[199] the answer must surely be to allow the common law tracing rules to become uniform with equitable rules. In *Foskett v McKeown,* Lord Millett suggested that the law should be reformed so that there would be one set of tracing rules available for

[191] S Barkehall Thomas, 'Thieves as Trustees: The Enduring Legacy of *Black v S Freedman & Co Ltd*' (2009) 3 *Journal of Equity* 52.

[192] J Tarrant, 'Thieves as Trustees: In Defence of the Theft Principle' (2009) 3 *Journal of Equity* 170. For a case illustrating a thief's possessory title, see *Costello v Derbyshire Constabulary* [2001] EWCA Civ 381, [2001] 1 WLR 1437 (CA).

[193] *Miller v Race* (1758) 1 Burr 452.

[194] J Tarrant, 'Property Rights to Stolen Money' (2005) *University of Western Australia Law Review* 234. Tarrant argues that the trust created may be better analysed as a resulting trust: ibid, at 246–48.

[195] R Chambers, 'Trust and Theft' in E Bant and M Harding (eds), *Exploring Private Law* (Cambridge, Cambridge University Press, 2010) 223, 229.

[196] [2009] QB 22, at [15]–[16].

[197] J Tarrant, 'Thieves as Trustees' (2009) *Journal of Equity* 170, 179. See D Fox, *Property Rights in Money* (Oxford, Oxford University Press, 2008) 140 [4.93].

[198] For further discussion, see J Tarrant, 'Theft Principle in Private Law' (2006) 80 *ALJ* 531.

[199] Robert Chambers argues that a better analysis is that the proceeds of sale can be claimed on the basis of a purchase money resulting trust, in Bant and Harding, *Exploring Private Law* 223, 237.

both common law and equitable claims.[200] If the courts took this step, it would mean that where cultural objects had been sold, the claimant could sue at common law for the value of the proceeds of sale and could track this value through bank accounts before making a claim. There is judicial movement towards clarification and perfecting of the common law in this regard already.[201] In *BMP Global Distribution Inc v Bank of Nova Scotia*, the Supreme Court of Canada noted the decision in *Glencore* and ruled that 'it is possible at common law to trace funds into bank accounts if it is possible to identify the funds'.[202] At the moment, English law needs further elucidation. Nevertheless, it is to be hoped that an appellate court will soon accept that any owner of stolen objects can pursue the proceeds of sale from one bank account to another using the same tracing rules as those employed for equitable claims, without any need to resort to equity.[203]

5.31 Seeking Property: Equity's Tracing Rules

Once the claimant has established that a fiduciary relationship exists, he will seek a declaration that the defendant holds identified goods or money on trust for him.[204] In equity, it is possible to pursue the value of money (such as the proceeds of sale from a painting) as it is transferred from one bank account to another, regardless of any mixing with other money which may have occurred.[205] The claimant is not obliged to identify physical exchanges of property;[206] he merely needs to point to some evidence linking transactions between one bank account and another.[207]

Equity has a series of evidential rules which makes the process of tracing flexible and effective. The rules distinguish between innocent parties and wrongdoers.[208] In *Foskett v McKeown,* Lord Millett stated that the interests of wrongdoers (and anyone claiming through them) must be subordinated to those of innocent contributors.[209] This principle is reflected in various evidential rules. Everything is presumed against the wrongdoer who caused the evidential confusion by mixing the claimant's assets with his own. If, for example, the thief had paid the proceeds of sale from stolen art into his bank account, mixing it with his own money and then withdrawn £100 to spend on food, it will be presumed that the thief has used £100 of his own money. If the thief has moved the proceeds of sale rapidly from one account to another in order to attempt to launder the money by concealing

[200] *Foskett v McKeown* [2001] 1 AC 102 (HL) 128. See also, *Bristol and West Building Society v Mothew* [1998] Ch 1 (CA) 23; P Birks, 'The Necessity of a Unitary Law of Tracing' in *Making Commercial Law: Essays in Honour of Roy Goode* (1997) 239.

[201] *Glencore International AG v Metro Trading International Inc* [2001] 1 Lloyd's Rep 284. See J Ulph 'Retaining Proprietary Rights at Common Law through Mixtures and Changes' [2001] *Lloyd's Maritime and Commercial Law Quarterly* 449.

[202] *BMP Global Distribution Inc v Bank of Nova Scotia* [2009] 5 LRC 307 (Sup Ct of Canada).

[203] If the owner is in a position to recover his stolen asset or the proceeds of sale, he may be required to choose between them: *Creak v James Moore & Sons Pty Ltd* (1912) 15 CLR 426.

[204] P Birks, *Unjust Enrichment*, 2nd edn (Oxford, Clarendon Law Series, 2005), 64.

[205] *Boscawen v Bajwa* [1996] 1 WLR 328 (CA) 336; *El Ajou v Dollar Land Holdings Plc* [1993] 3 All ER 717, 736; *Campden Hill Ltd v Chakrani* [2005] EWHC 911 [78]. This basic principle underpins equitable tracing: *Re Diplock* [1948] Ch 465, 518–23.

[206] *Re Hallett's Estate* (1879–1880) LR 13 Ch D 696, 717; *Re Spectrum Plus Ltd* [2005] UKHL 41, [2005] 2 AC 680 [95]. See further *Holroyd v Marshall* (1862) 10 HLC 191.

[207] *El Ajou v Dollar Land Holdings Plc* [1993] 3 All ER 717; D Hayton, 'Equity's Identification Rules' in P Birks (ed), *Laundering and Tracing* (Oxford, Oxford University Press,1995) .

[208] *Foskett v McKeown* [2001] 1 AC 102, 132. See further *Re Hallett's Estate* (1879–1880) LR 13 Ch D 696*; Re Oatway* [1903] 2 Ch 356.

[209] *Foskett v McKeown* [2001] 1 AC 102 (HL) 132; LD Smith, *The Law of Tracing* (Oxford, Clarendon Press, 1997) 77–85.

its origins, this will not necessarily prevent the money being traced. In *Sinclair Investments (UK) Ltd v Versailles Trade Finance Ltd*,[210] Lord Neuberger stated that, where there has been a rapid cross-firing of cheques, so that a 'maelstrom' has been created, the burden will be on the wrongdoer to show that the money has in fact disappeared, because otherwise a link from one account to another will be presumed to enable the claimant to trace the value of his money.[211]

If the claimant brought a proprietary claim in equity, his claim for its return would fail if it is in the possession of a good faith purchaser for value of a legal estate without notice. It is a complete defence. The reason is that 'equity follows the law'. Where you have two innocent parties, the equities are equal; as a consequence, the common law prevails and the legal ownership of the good faith purchaser is given pre-eminence. Thus, supposing a dishonest employee sells a painting and pays for a car with the proceeds of sale. The seller of the car is in the position of a good faith purchaser: honestly receiving the money in exchange for the car. But the claimant can trace the value of his painting through to the proceeds of sale and then to the car itself.

5.32 Personal Liability of Third Parties

In the context of theft, a claimant will normally pursue a proprietary claim in order to recover his property: the stolen work of art or antiquity or the traceable proceeds of sale. There are advantages in bringing a proprietary claim: the claimant can thereby gain priority over unsecured creditors if the defendant is insolvent. Furthermore, he can claim the asset even if its value has risen in the meantime and, perhaps most importantly, the asset is then removed from the reach of the Crown, which may be seeking to confiscate the property under the Proceeds of Crime Act 2002.[212]

Where the stolen art or antiquities have been destroyed or have disappeared and the thief is not worth suing, claimants may wish to sue third parties to obtain compensation. In equity, anyone who has dishonestly assisted in a breach of a fiduciary relationship will be personally liable. For example, if a curator of a museum steals a work of art from his museum, this is a breach of fiduciary duty. If the curator asks a friend to make arrangements for its sale, the friend is at risk of being sued in equity for dishonest assistance. The test for dishonesty in equity is not as stringent as the *Ghosh* test which is used in a criminal prosecution for theft or handling stolen goods.[213] In *Barlow Clowes International Ltd v Eurotrust International Ltd*,[214] the Privy Council held that the standard is an objective one but taking account of subjective factors, such as the defendant's expertise and the circumstances.[215] As a result, a defendant will be liable if he consciously refrains from making enquiries, where the circumstances are obviously suspicious, in order to avoid discovering the truth.[216]

[210] *Sinclair Investments (UK) Ltd v Versailles Trade Finance Ltd* [2011] EWCA 347 (CA).

[211] ibid [135]–[138].

[212] *Director of the Serious Fraud Office v Lexi Holdings plc* [2009] QB 376 (CA). For more detail on confiscation orders, see 4.14–4.19.

[213] *R v Ghosh* [1982] QB 1053 (CA). See 3.03.

[214] *Barlow Clowes International v Eurotrust International* [2005] UKPC 37, [2006] 1 All ER 333 (PC).

[215] The second strand of the *Ghosh* test was rejected as a test for civil liability in equity for dishonest assistance: ibid. See also *Royal Brunei Airlines Sdn Bhd v Tan* [1995] 2 AC 378 (PC) 391; *Abouh-Ramah v Abacha* [2006] EWCA 1492 (CA). In *Barlow Clowes*, ibid, the decision in *Twinsectra Ltd v Yardley* [2002] 2 AC 164 (HL) on this issue was interpreted and explained.

[216] See eg *Glen Dimplex Home Appliances Ltd v Smith* [2011] EWHC 3392 [48].

If the defendant appears to have been involved in assisting in a breach of trust or fiduciary relationship with dishonest intentions, he is at risk of being prosecuted for a money laundering offence, where suspicion is enough. The test for suspicion for this type of offence is a subjective one, and suspicion can include situations where the defendant engages in wilful blindness, by deliberately refraining from enquiry.[217]

Recipients of property which represents the stolen art and antiquities (such as proceeds of sale) may also be held liable in equity for unconscionable receipt. The claimant must show that the recipient's state of knowledge was such as to make it unconscionable for him to retain the benefit of the receipt (such as the proceeds of sale).[218] As a result of money laundering measures and the civil law, agents such as solicitors, auction houses and dealers should take great care to enquire further where the circumstances are suspicious.

X Conversion, Defences and the 'Nemo Dat' Rule

5.33 Policy Issues

In English law, there is a tension between two policy concerns. The common law has long recognised the need for transactional security. Most types of portable property are unlikely to last for ever and can be expected to change hands quickly. Bargaining is the lifeblood of commerce, and purchasers must feel confident to buy without the need to make a detailed investigation of the life history of an object. Yet, on the other hand, the property interest of the true owner should receive some protection, and theft and fraud should not be facilitated by providing an environment where misappropriated property can be easily disposed of.

As regards art and antiquities, it has been argued above that there is no reason why purchasers should not be expected to make enquiries about their provenance.[219] Unlike ordinary commodities, cultural objects are expected to be preserved indefinitely. Their cultural value gives extra force to the argument that the original owner (which may be the source state) should be protected. Nevertheless, although there are a number of international conventions specifically dealing with the return of cultural objects, no distinction is usually made in a country's domestic law between cultural objects and other types of tangible property where there are disputes over title. This is true of English law; the same approach is taken for all types of goods.

A compromise between the competing policy concerns outlined in the first paragraph above is offered by English law. The basic principle which applies is that no one can transfer a better title to an object than the one which he possesses (the principle of *nemo dat quod non habet*). This principle is reflected in section 21(1) of the Sale of Goods Act 1979, which provides:

> where goods are sold by a person who is not their owner, and who does not sell them under the authority or with the consent of the owner, the buyer acquires no better title to the goods than the seller had unless the owner of the goods is by his conduct precluded from denying the seller`s authority to sell.

[217] *R v Saik* [2007] 1 AC 18 (HL) [62]. See 3.37.

[218] *BCCI v Akindele* [2001] Ch 437 (CA) 455; *Law Society v Isaac & Isaac International* [2010] EWHC 1670. Lord Browne-Wilkinson emphasised that conscience has a pivotal role to play in equity in relation to personal liability: *Westdeutsche Landesbank Girozentrale v Islington LBC* [1996] AC 669 (HL) 705, 709.

[219] See 5.12.

In essence, in a battle between these innocent parties, the law favours the original owner. A person in possession may be liable in conversion unless he falls within some narrowly defined exceptions. A plea that one has purchased the goods in good faith (whether sacks of grain or more valuable items, such as art and antiquities) is not sufficient by itself: but it may be pleaded as an ingredient of a defence to combat a claim by the true owner for wrongful interference with his goods. However, none of these exceptions assist where goods are stolen; they are therefore discussed relatively briefly below.

5.34 Sales in Market Overt: the UK Position

If someone has found an object then, unless it had been deliberately abandoned, the finder only obtains a possessory title: if the true owner claims it, the finder will be obliged to return it or to pay compensation. The same is true of a thief: he merely has a possessory title. However, there was once a rule that, if someone with a possessory title, such as a finder or a thief, sold the object openly in a traditional market, the purchaser obtained a legal title which was good against the whole world, including the previous owner. This exception to the general *nemo dat* principle was known as the 'market overt' exception. It was eventually scrapped by the UK Government in order to offer better protection to owners.

Before its repeal by the Sale of Goods (Amendment) Act 1994, section 22(1) of the Sale of Goods Act 1979 provided:

> Where goods are sold in market overt, according to the usage of the market, the buyer acquires a good title to the goods, provided he buys them in good faith and without notice of any defect or want of title on the part of the seller.[220]

'Market overt' literally meant an 'open market,' and referred to markets long established by custom, statute or charter.[221] An example is Bermondsey market in South East London, which specialises in antiques, and was established by statute. It also included all shops in the City of London where goods were on display and sales were visible to passers-by.[222]

The market overt exception developed in the Middle Ages and was based on the idea that, if goods were stolen, the original owner could reclaim them by visiting his local market or fair.[223] The exception consequently had limitations: the sale had to be open rather than secretive, so that the goods were on display and people could pass by and see them,[224] and the sale had to take place between sunrise and sunset.[225] The sale had to be above board in every respect, and so it had to be in accordance with the custom of the market.[226] Although this exception favoured the innocent purchaser more than any other, it developed at a time when the original owner could be said to have a reasonable chance of recovering his goods if he was

[220] This exception did not apply to Scotland.

[221] 'Market overt' meant an 'open, public and legally constituted market': *Lee v Bayes* (1856) 18 CB 599, 601.

[222] *Hargreave v Spink* [1892] 1 QB 25. It was suggested by Wills J that the exception applied to a sale *by* a shopkeeper but not *to* a shopkeeper; the distinction is based upon the fact that there is a degree of permanence about a shop, and enquiries can be made of the shopkeeper's reputation. See further, *Wilkinson v King* (1809) 2 Camp 335, where a sale from a wharf was not treated as the same as a sale from a shop; the sale consequently fell outside this exception.

[223] Consultation Paper, *Transfer of Title: ss 21–26 of the Sale of Goods Act 1979* [1.4].

[224] *Clayton v Le Roy* [1911] 2 QB 1031.

[225] *Reid v Commissioner of Police of the Metropolis* [1973] 1 QB 551 (CA).

[226] *Bishopsgate Motor Finance Corporation v Transport Brakes Ltd* [1949] 1 KB 322 (CA). See further, *Market-Overt Case* (1596) 5 Rep 83b, where it was held that a scrivener's shop was not a usual place for the sale of a silver basin and ewer.

diligent.[227] By the late twentieth century, when thieves could move goods to another part of the country or abroad within a day, the exception appeared archaic.

Writing in 1966, the Law Reform Committee, considered that the rule was 'of comparatively little practical importance':[228] it was noted that the exception had never applied in Wales, did not apply to privately owned markets but only to public markets, and did not affect the law relating to the sale of horses.[229] The Committee recommended that the exception should be abolished. However, the Committee went on to suggest that in its place there should be a more coherent and wide-ranging exception to cover all retail sales at trade premises or at a public auction.[230] The Committee acknowledged that this would be at the expense of the protection of property rights but the majority favoured protecting innocent purchasers and were content to leave the original owner to his common law right to sue the thief in conversion.[231] Lord Donovan delivered a powerful dissent. In his view, such a reform could encourage purchasers to suppress any lurking suspicions they might have about the provenance of the goods and this could have the effect of facilitating traffic in stolen goods.

In 1989, Professor Diamond in his review of security interests in property proposed amending the law to give an innocent purchaser greater protection: he suggested that where an owner allowed another to have possession of his or her goods and the goods were sold in the ordinary course of business, then good title in those goods could be passed to a good faith purchaser.[232] However, as concern to curb the growth in fraud and theft increased, the tide began to turn. There was little enthusiasm for the Committee's idea of an extension of the exception to all retail sales; it was feared that this would encourage crime. In 1994, the Government issued a Consultation Document which recommended the abolition of the market overt exception.[233]

By 1994, the Government had become acutely conscious of the striking growth in the illicit trade of art and antiquities. There was strong pressure from the fine art industry, loss adjusters and the theft publication *Trace*[234] to abolish the exception in market overt. The market overt exception had been the oldest of the small number of exceptions to the *nemo dat* rule. But, in modern times, it had been exploited by professional thieves, enabling them to provide good faith purchasers with a good title.[235] This exception was therefore repealed by the Sale of Goods (Amendment) Act 1994 with effect from 3 January 1995. The original owner's position is strengthened as a result, as it was only this exception and the general rules regarding stolen money which favoured free trade by protecting the good faith purchaser.[236]

227 If the thief was convicted, then proprietary rights acquired under this exception would revest in the owner: Hale, *Pleas of the Crown* (ed. of 1800) 1543; RST Chorley 'The Conflict of Law and Commerce' (1932) 48 *Law Quarterly Review* 51, 65.

228 Law Reform Committee, Twelfth Report (*Transfer of Title to Chattels*) Cmnd 2958 [30].

229 ibid [30].

230 ibid [14], [33], [40(2)]. 'Trade premises' would include shops but not street markets: ibid [33].

231 ibid [32].

232 Professor AL Diamond, *A Review of Security Interests in Property* (London, HMSO, 1989) (The Diamond Report).

233 Consultation Paper, *Transfer of Title: ss 21–26 of the Sale of Goods Act 1979* (1994) [6.2].

234 This publication has now merged with the Art Loss Register.

235 In introducing the Sale of Goods (Amendment) Bill, Lord Renton described the market overt exception as a 'thieves' charter' and referred to the theft of paintings by Gainsborough and Reynolds from Lincoln's Inn two years earlier, which had been sold in Bermondsey market in London for less than £150 to a purchaser who relied upon this exception: *Hansard* (HL) *Deb 12 January 1994 vol 551 cc 209–23.*

236 A good faith purchaser who takes stolen money will obtain a good title to it: see *Miller v Race* (1758) 1 Burr 452. For discussion, see D Fox, 'Bona Fide Purchase and the Currency of Money' (1996) 55 *Cambridge Law Journal* 547.

The abolition of the market overt exception means that, if anyone sues to recover a stolen cultural object using the action for conversion in the English courts, there are only two defences available to a purchaser: he can provide evidence that he purchased the art or antiquity in circumstances where title has been acquired in another jurisdiction, such as Italy or Switzerland; alternatively, he must show that the limitation period within which claims must be made has expired.

5.35 Gaining Title Overseas

The market overt exception can still be found as part of the existing law of a few Commonwealth jurisdictions.[237] New Zealand has abolished the exception.[238] It may be found in the sales legislation of countries which have no market which could be regarded as coming within the market overt exception. The Law Reform Commission of Western Australia remarked in its Report that,

> It is highly doubtful whether there is any market or other place in Australia which constitutes market overt, and it is regrettable that the rule was copied into the Western Australian Sale of Goods Act 1895.[239]

The Report continued by noting that some states have never adopted this rule and that Victoria has repealed it: the Report concluded that it should be repealed in Western Australia as well.[240]

As regards Canada, British Columbia has been the only province to adopt the market overt rule.[241] As a consequence, the British Columbia Supreme Court has been obliged to consider the application of the rule from time to time. It has been invoked unsuccessfully in some cases, where it was not clear that there was an established market.[242] In *Manning v Algarde Estate*, involving the recovery of stolen Swedish antique coins purchased in good faith in a garage sale, the Supreme Court of British Columbia noted that the market overt rule had no application on the facts, and indeed had never been applied by any Canadian court.[243] Even so, it remains on the statute books of British Columbia and may be called into play as a defence in the future.

The extent to which the national law of each country offers protection to good faith purchasers differs considerably.[244] Some countries, such as the USA, have very limited

[237] See, for example, Tasmania: Sale of Goods Act 1896, s 29.

[238] Sale of Goods Amendment Act 1961 (NZ) s 2, repealing the Sale of Goods Act 1908 (NZ) s 24.

[239] See Law Reform Commission of Western Australia, *Report on the Sale of Goods Act 1895* (Project No 89) 1998 [3.4]. See further, Sale of Goods Act 1895, s 22.

[240] ibid [3.5].

[241] Sale of Goods Act, Revised Statutes of BC (RSBC), 1996, c 410, s 27(1). For further discussion, see Ontario Law Reform Commission, *Report on Sale of Goods* 1979 Vol II Ch. 12 [1], 284.

[242] *Director of Trade Practices v Stewart* (1987) 22 BCLR (2d) 51 (BC Co Ct) 57. See the discussion by B MacDougall, 'The Market Overt Exception to Obtain Ownership of Lost or Stolen Goods: Comment on *Manning v Algarde Estate*, [2008] BCSC 1129' (2009) 16 *International Journal of Cultural Property* 85, 90–91.

[243] *Manning v Algarde Estate* [2008] BCSC 1129. See further, *Westcoast Leasing Ltd v Westcoast Communications Ltd* (1980) 22 BCLR 285 (BCSC).

[244] See KT Burke, 'International Transfers of Stolen Cultural Property: Should Thieves Continue to Benefit from Domestic Laws Favoring Bona Fide Purchasers?' [1990] 13 *Loyola of Los Angeles International and Comparative Law Journal* 427, 448–49; ES Myerowitz, 'Protecting Cultural Property during a Time of War: Why Russia Should Return Nazi-Looted Art' (1998) III(2) *Art Antiquity and Law* 137. See further, *Winkworth v Christie Manson & Woods Ltd* [1980] 2 WLR 937.

exceptions to the *nemo dat* principle, which do not include a market overt exception.[245] In France, acquisition of an object in good faith may be sufficient to obtain a good title in accordance with article 2279 of the Code Civil of 1804.[246] The limitation period within which a claim can be made may also vary from one country to another. This may lead to conflicting claims to a work of art or antiquity, with international litigation leading to results which are not necessarily predictable. For example, in *Government of the Islamic Republic of Iran v The Barakat Galleries Ltd*[247] discussed above, it would appear that the Iranian Government was successful: the English courts recognised that it had proprietary rights in buried antiquities. But the court's decision was not the end of the matter. As the Court of Appeal acknowledged, the defendant trader has also asserted that it had purchased these antiquities in France, Germany and Switzerland, under laws which had provided it with a good title.[248]

5.36 Further Exceptions to the Nemo Dat Rule

Although there are other statutory defences, which are exceptions to the *nemo dat* rule and which offer protection to good faith purchasers, none of them assist where objects are stolen. An exception mentioned in the Sale of Goods Act 1979 is estoppel; it is relevant where the true owner has held out another person (a rogue) as either his agent or as the owner of the item: a good faith purchaser can obtain a good title, relying upon the owner's representation that the rogue has the power to sell the item. However, there does need to be a representation: if an owner has accidentally left an object in a public place or has been careless in some other way, the defence of estoppel cannot be used.[249] The relative fault of the original owner and the purchaser is not weighed in the balance. If a work of art or antiquity has been stolen, it must be returned. It does not matter that a museum or a private individual was negligent and did not take sufficient precautions to protect their property from theft; nor does it matter that the good faith purchaser took every precaution possible in attempting to check an object's provenance.[250]

There are further exceptions to the principle that a seller cannot transfer a better title than the one he enjoys. Although each exception is hedged with restrictions, they offer some protection to good faith purchasers. One example is a purchase from a mercantile agent, such as an art dealer, who is in possession of another's property.[251] Other exceptions include purchasing from those who have possession but not legal title to an object which they had agreed to buy, or purchasing from someone who, having sold the object once, either carelessly or dishonestly sells the same object again.[252] None of these exceptions assist a good faith purchaser of stolen art or antiquities.

[245] An exception is available where there has been fraud leading to the entrustment of goods to another: UCC s 2-403(2). See P Gerstenblith, 'The Kanakariá Mosaics and United States Law' in KW Tubb (ed) *Antiquities, Trade or Betrayed* (London, Archetype Publications, 1995) 105, 108; G Gilmore, 'The Commercial Doctrine of Good Faith Purchase' (1954) 53 *Yale Law Journal* 1057.

[246] See further, *The Islamic Republic of Iran v Berend* [2007] EWHC 132.

[247] *Government of the Islamic Republic of Iran v The Barakat Galleries Ltd* [2009] QB 22 CA.

[248] ibid [5]. See further, *The Islamic Republic of Iran v Berend* [2007] EWHC 132.

[249] *Farquharson v King* (1902) AC 325; *Heap v Motorists' Advisory Agency Ltd* [1923] 1 KB 577; *Jerome v Bentley & Co* [1952] 2 All ER 114; *Central Newbury Car Auctions Ltd v Unity Finance Ltd* [1957] 1 QB 371; *Moorgate Mercantile Co Ltd v Twitchings* [1977] AC 890.

[250] Contributory negligence is not a defence to an action in conversion: Torts (Interference with Goods) Act 1977, s 11(1).

[251] Factors Act 1889, s 2(1).

[252] Factors Act 1889, ss 8 and 9, which are largely but not entirely reproduced in the Sale of Goods Act 1979, ss 24 and 25. A further exception exists where the seller has only a voidable title because, for example, he has tricked

5.37 Good Faith

The concept of the 'good faith' purchaser is relevant in a number of contexts[253] and therefore deserves elaboration. The definition, which codifies the common law,[254] is currently set out in section 61(3) of the Sale of Goods Act 1979, and provides:

> A thing is deemed to be done in good faith within the meaning of this Act when it is in fact done honestly, whether it is done negligently or not.

From this definition, it appears that a good faith purchaser must be subjectively honest; if this is evident, then the fact that he has been foolish will not matter. Other statutes typically remain silent on this issue.[255]

A defendant purchaser is expected to act in accordance with the norms of the particular market. If everything appears above board, the defendant is not expected to enquire further. It is only if the circumstances are suspicious that the court will consider whether the defendant deliberately refrained from making enquiries because he was afraid that he would discover fraud if he did so. What factors should prompt further enquiries? If the price paid was substantially less than the goods are worth, this may suggest bad faith.[256] However, there may be a good reason for the low price. In sales of ordinary commodities, a low price might also be explained away on the basis that it relates to a sale of second hand goods where the price is known to fluctuate.[257] In general, the courts will take account of factors such as whether the purchase was a hasty one,[258] whether the purchaser was experienced in the trade or business,[259] whether the purchaser appeared suspicious of his seller, and whether there was a gross disparity between the price paid and the obvious value of the object.[260] In the context of antiquities, a court should take account of the country from which the object has been exported. It is known that some countries are more at risk than others, and some of these are identified on the Red List published by ICOM. Objects derived from countries under military occupation, such as Cyprus, should also excite suspicion. In the case of the sale of the Kanakariá mosaics, which were removed from a church in Cyprus, there were other suspicious circumstances as well. The mosaics were unique and highly valuable, and had clearly been attached to a building, and had religious significance. The defendant had paid $1.08 million in cash for all of the mosaics but was attempting to sell them for $20 million. She knew nothing of the background of her seller, who was described as a Turkish archaeologist.[261] For these and other reasons, it was decided that the purchaser had not acted in good faith.

the true owner into giving him possession: Sale of Goods Act 1979, s 23. See MG Bridge (ed), *Benjamin's Sale of Goods*, 8th edn (London, Sweet and Maxwell, 2010) Pt 2, ch 7; NE Palmer, 'Conversion, Trespass and Title to Art Works' ch 2 in *The Recovery of Stolen Art* (The Netherlands, Kluwer Law International, 1998) 54–60.

[253] In relation to civil recovery orders, see 4.21.

[254] For a more detailed study of this topic in relation to both sale and charging of goods, see JS Ulph, 'Good Faith and Due Diligence' in Palmer and McKendrick (eds) *Interests in Goods.*

[255] For example, although the Torts (Interference with Goods) Act 1977, s 6(2) provides that, where goods have been improved, an allowance to reflect this can be made to a purchaser in good faith, there is no definition of good faith. See NE Palmer and A Hudson, 'Improving Stolen Art', ch 6 in *The Recovery of Stolen Art* (The Netherlands, Kluwer Law International, 1998).

[256] *Re Gomersall* (1875) 1 Ch D 137, 150; aff'd by the House of Lords in *Jones v Gordon* [1877] 2 App Cas 616.

[257] *Newtons of Wembley Ltd v Williams* [1965] 1 QB 560 (CA) 576.

[258] See *Central Newbury Car Auctions Ltd v Unity Finance Ltd* [1957] 1 QB 371 (CA).

[259] *Moody v Pall Mall Deposit and Forwarding Co Ltd* (1917) 33 TLR 306; *Henderson v Prosser* (25 May 1982) .

[260] eg *Heap v Motorists' Advisory Agency Ltd* [1922] 1 KB 577.

[261] See *Autocephalous Greek-Orthodox Church of Cyprus and the Republic of Cyprus v Goldberg & Feldman Fine Arts, Inc* (1989) 717 E Supp 1374, US District Ct, Southern District of Indiana, which involved the looting of Kanakariá mosaics; the case is extracted and discussed in P Gerstenblith, *Art, Cultural Heritage, and the Law* 2nd

In English law, the burden is generally on the purchaser to prove that he acted in good faith and without notice.[262] It is submitted that, even where there are no suspicious circumstances, any purchaser of art and antiquities, whether a trader or private collector, should check the provenance thoroughly (such as auction receipts, photographs and markings on the object), and consult experts. If there are any oddities at all, the purchaser should do much more in order to demonstrate that that he has investigated every avenue and has been reassured that any suspicions are groundless. The further measures that will need to be taken will depend upon the circumstances. For example, the purchaser could search the Art Loss Register, the Interpol database, and the International Foundation for Art Research (IFAR). A purchaser could also contact a government department in the country concerned. If, after all of these efforts, there is still cause for concern, the prospective purchaser should decline to go ahead with the transaction and should report his suspicions to the relevant authority, such as SOCA.

XI Defences: Limitation Periods

5.38 Policy Issues

Limitation periods vary from one country to another. If a country's laws state that a good faith acquirer of stolen property may obtain legal title after a short period of time, it is harsh upon the dispossessed owner. The process 'takes away property rights without compensation'[263] and makes it easier for the thief or intermediaries to sell looted property, which can lead to increased insurance costs. Yet, where the original owner can recover his property, the effect is hard on an innocent purchaser, who may well be as much a victim of dishonest or reckless people as the claimant. The innocent purchaser may be able to sue his seller, but his seller may have sold in good faith too. Furthermore, taking a stolen item away from a good faith purchaser may seem particularly unjust where the original owner has not taken steps to publicise the theft.

These policy issues are relevant in relation to any objects which are stolen. However, where cultural objects have been removed, there are other considerations. Limitation periods should be lengthy for various reasons. First, if the objects have been stripped from a country during a period of armed conflict, their return may be particularly important because they may help to give people a sense of group identity.[264] Secondly, it is common for cultural objects to be stored for years, to appear 30 or 50 years later. The obvious example would be art confiscated by the Nazis during the Holocaust, some of which is only now being located. However, the diligence of owners is also significant. There are various databases, such as the Art Loss Register, where a dispossessed owner can register his loss; it is

edn (Durham, North Carolina, Carolina Academic Press, 2008) 482–84. See also *Cyprus v Turkey* App No 25781/94 (1997) 23 EHRR 244, 262

[262] *Heap v Motorists' Advisory Agency Ltd* [1922] 1 KB 577, 590; *Mobil Oil Company Ltd v St Pier* (CA, 6 November 1986). An isolated exception is to this principle is where the contract of sale is voidable, where a seller, having avoided the contract, must demonstrate that any sub-purchaser acquired the object in bad faith: *Whitehorn Brothers v Davison* [1911] 1 KB 463.

[263] Scottish Law Commission, Discussion Paper on *Prescription and Title to Moveable Property* (Scot Law Com No 144, 2010) [1.10].

[264] See 1.13.

not unreasonable to expect dispossessed owners, and their insurers, to be diligent in their search for missing objects.

5.39 Limitation Act 1980

Where a person is sued in England for the return of works of art and antiquities, the most important defence available to a good faith purchaser is likely to be that the claimant's action is time-barred due to delay: although good title can never be acquired in stolen goods under one of the exceptions to the *nemo dat* rule, it is possible under the Limitation Act 1980. In the context of the illicit trade in cultural property, this is a particularly important defence, because it is common for cultural property to disappear for a long period before re-emerging on the market.[265]

There are various policy issues which have been identified as underlying the Limitation Act 1980. It is in the interests of litigants and the state to impose a limitation on the period within which a claimant can bring a legal action because it may be difficult for either party to produce accurate evidence after a lengthy delay.[266] The recollection of witnesses is likely to have been affected by the passage of time and the defendant may no longer have any written records relating to the matter in dispute. These considerations are important because trials must be fair; indeed, the defendant is expressly guaranteed a fair trial by Article 6 of the European Convention on Human Rights. Furthermore, there must come a time when the defendant can feel that the matter is closed and that he is free to dispose of his records. There is also the need to promote certainty in transacting.[267] On the other hand, the time period cannot be too short because parties need time to negotiate with a view to settlement.[268] Yet whatever time periods are laid down, an exception needs to be made where a defendant has deliberately concealed matters from the claimant: a claimant deserves a reasonable opportunity to bring an action.[269]

It is usually the case that, where the limitation period is pleaded as a defence, the court is confronted with two unfortunate innocent parties: the dispossessed owner and the good faith purchaser. A successful plea by the defendant will have a dramatic effect: it will extinguish the claimant's rights to his property entirely.[270] This means that, if the claimant subsequently was presented with an opportunity to physically seize the object, he would be liable for conversion (and perhaps also guilty of theft) if he did so.

5.40 Action for Conversion: Six-Year Period

In order to recover his property, the claimant will bring an action in the tort of conversion. The general rule is that an action in tort cannot be brought after a period of six years has

[265] Boylan refers to the fact that illicit objects possess a 'hope' value, where dealers and collectors retain illicit objects for many years in the expectation that their increased rarity will drive up market prices: P Boylan, 'Illicit Trafficking in Antiquities and Museum Ethics' in K Tubb (ed), *Antiquities: Trade or Betrayed* (London, Archetype Publications, 1995) 94, 99.

[266] *Cave v Robinson Jarvis & Rolf* [2003] 1 AC 384 (HL) [6]; *Donovan v Gwentoys Ltd* [1990] 2 WLR 472 (HL) 479; *Birkett v James* [1978] AC 297 (HL) 327; *A'Court v Cross* (1825) 3 Bing 329, 332–33; Law Commission Consultation Paper, *Limitation of Actions* (Law Com No 151, 1998) [1.23], [1.26]; Law Commission Report, *Limitation of Actions* (Law Com No 270, 2001) [1.6].

[267] Law Com No 151 [1.27], [1.31].

[268] Law Com No 151 [1.32].

[269] See the Limitation Act 1980, ss 21(1), 32.

[270] Limitation Act 1980, s 3(2). The current law does not contravene Art 1 of the First Protocol: *JA Pye (Oxford) Ltd v UK* (2008) 46 EHRR 45 (ECtHR, GC).

elapsed from the date when 'the cause of action accrued'.[271] This means the date on which the object was converted. For example, if there is a dispute between a warehouse-keeper and his customer over storage costs, and the warehouse-keeper unjustifiably refuses to return his customer's property, six years will begin to run from the time of refusal. What if the warehouse-keeper later sells the customer's property? Although the sale would be a further conversion, the owner cannot argue that time starts running afresh.[272]

Although a six-year limitation period normally runs from the date on which the object was converted, there are exceptions.[273] For example, an exception is made where a defendent, such as a museum employee, has concealed his fraudulent actions, such as where he secretly pockets a museum item from the storeroom and conceals the fact that it has disappeared. In this situation, section 32(1) of the Limitation Act 1980 applies and the six-year limitation period does not begin to run until the fraud is discovered or could with diligence have been discovered. However, this exception does not affect good faith purchasers.

5.41 Action for Conversion against the Thief

Special rules apply where assets are stolen. By section 4 of the Limitation Act 1980, the six-year limitation period does not apply where the thief remains in possession. The reference to 'theft' in the Limitation Act includes blackmail and fraud (within the meaning of the Fraud Act 2006).[274] Significantly, the definition of theft includes any conduct outside of England and Wales which would be viewed as theft if committed within England and Wales.[275] If a person dishonestly removed an antiquity from someone's land in England, he would be guilty of theft. Consequently, anyone who dishonestly excavates objects of antiquity in another country will be classified as a thief for the purposes of the limitation period and time will not run whilst the object remains in the hands of the thief.[276]

Thieves may choose to retain the property for a long period of time, rather than selling immediately. This is particularly common where the property is unique in some respect, such as a well-known painting or a composer's manuscript. The previous owner never loses the right to recover the object from the thief. Furthermore, no protection is offered to a donee or bad faith purchaser from the thief.[277] Various consequences follow. The true owner can sue the thief and any other person to whom he has transferred the object (unless the defendant is a good faith purchaser). Auction houses run the risk of being sued in conversion if, many

[271] ibid, s 2. An action founded on a simple contract cannot be brought after six years; time begins to run from the date when the breach occurs: ibid, s 5. Although one notable gap in the legislation is that there is no special provision made for claims in unjust enrichment, a claim for money had and received will be treated as falling within s 5: *Kleinwort Benson Ltd v Sandwell BC* [1994] 4 All ER 890.

[272] ibid, s 3. What if the warehouse-keeper concealed the fact of the sale? Ordinarily the warehouse-keeper will not be a fiduciary and consequently the claimant cannot rely upon s 21(1) of the Limitation Act 1980 to argue that the action is not time-barred; however, the claimant can rely upon s 32 of the Act in arguing that time will only run from when the owner discovered the truth or should have discovered it. See further, *Sheldon v R H M Outhwaite (Underwriting Agencies) Ltd* [1996] AC 102 (HL).

[273] See R Redmond-Cooper, 'Time Limits in Art and Antiquity Claims' (2000) IV(4) *Art Antiquity and Law* 323, 326.

[274] Limitation Act 1980, s 4.

[275] ibid, s 4(5), as amended.

[276] *Bumper Development Corp Ltd v Commr of Police* [1991] 1 WLR 1362, where it was held that a secretly excavated idol representing the Hindu god Siva would be viewed in English law as stolen. For further discussion, see R Redmond-Cooper, 'Limitation of Actions in Art and Antiquities Claims' (2000) V(2) *Art Antiquity and Law* 185, 189.

[277] The position is the same in Scotland in relation to thieves and those who are privy to the theft: see the Prescription and Limitation (Scotland) Act 1973, Sch 3.

years later, they put stolen property up for sale by auction.[278] If a thief (or handler of stolen goods) is prosecuted for criminal offences, the claimant can assert his proprietary rights to the object, so that it is not swept up in a confiscation order for the benefit of the state.[279]

5.42 Theft and the Good Faith Purchaser

Where an object is stolen, section 4 of the Limitation Act 1980 provides that a good faith purchaser can acquire a legal title in the object if more than six years have elapsed since the date of its purchase.[280] Any conversion subsequent to the theft (such as a purchase) is presumed to be related to the theft: consequently, any purchaser must prove that his purchase of the object was innocently made. This requirement will present problems for any good faith purchaser who has bought the object in question less than six years ago. In these circumstances, the good faith purchaser must prove that his seller also purchased the object in good faith so that time can run from that earlier purchase.[281]

Even with these statutory modifications in the case of theft, so that the owner's legal title is not automatically lost six years after the object is stolen, the Limitation Act can still be viewed as unsympathetic to the original owner. When an item is first stolen, the owner will not know the identity of thief or the whereabouts of his lost possession. Yet these considerations are irrelevant.[282] It may take many years before the item openly re-emerges on the market. By the time it does so, it may be too late for the owner to sue because the purchaser may have innocently bought it more than six years before.[283]

5.43 The Notion of 'Good Faith'

The issue of 'good faith' in the context of the limitation periods was considered for the first time in *Nicole de Préval v Adrian Alan Ltd.*[284] In this case, the claimant sued to recover two nineteenth-century Barye candelabra, which had been stolen from her home in France in 1986. The defendant company disputed whether the candelabra had been correctly identified: it was asserted that the company had purchased the candelabra in 1984, long before the theft from the claimant's home in 1986. Unfortunately, much of the evidence which related to the alleged purchase in 1984, and which might have assisted the defendant in establishing its version of events, no longer existed. The few documents which survived were vague and unhelpful. The candelabra in the defendant's possession were almost certainly unique: they possessed the insignia of the *Légion d'Honneur*, and they also featured the initials 'EM' which would suggest that they were made by Barye for Emil Martine. Arden J found on the balance of probabilities that these candelabra were the ones which had been stolen from the claimant.

[278] An interim injunction may be sought whilst the facts are investigated: *Rachmaninoff v Sotheby's* [2005] EWHC 258.

[279] See 4.19.

[280] Limitation Act 1980, s 4(2); *City of Gotha v Sotheby's (No 2), The Times* (8 October 1998). In Scotland, a dispossessed owner will lose his right to claim the property – by way of negative prescription – after a period of 20 years in accordance with s 8 of the Prescription and Limitation (Scotland) Act 1973. See Discussion Paper on *Prescription and Title to Moveable Property* (Scot Law Com No 144, 2010) [2.5]–[2.7]; DC Miller, 'Positive Prescription of Corporeal Moveables?' (2011) 15(3) *Edinburgh Law Review* 452.

[281] Limitation Act 1980, s 4 (4). See *Bumper Development Corp Ltd v Commr of Police* [1991] 1 WLR 1362.

[282] *RB Policies at Lloyd's v Butler* [1950] 1 KB 76.

[283] If 20 years have elapsed, it will also be too late for an enforcement authority to bring a civil recovery order: see the Limitation Act 1980, s 27A(2), discussed at 4.21.

[284] *Nicole de Préval v Adrian Alan Ltd* (24 January 1997) (Arden J). See also *Kurtha v Marks* [2008] EWHC 336.

The defendant company also relied upon section 4 of the Limitation Act 1980, arguing that the claim was statute-barred. Arden J accepted that the director of the defendant company, Adrian Alan, had purchased the candelabra from a reputable dealer, and that he had twice attempted to sell them by public auction at Sotheby's. However, Arden J considered that Adrian Alan, who was a highly experienced dealer, should have recognised the most unusual characteristics of these candelabra and made further enquiries. There was no evidence that he had consulted the Art Loss Register or the International Foundation for Art Research. On the other hand, there was no evidence that the claimant had taken steps to publicise her loss, such as by contacting the Art Loss Register, or by advertising in *The Art Newspaper*. However, the burden of proof was upon the defendant to prove good faith. Arden J ruled that the defendant had not discharged this burden, because there was no evidence that Adrian Alan had taken sufficient steps to check the provenance of the candelabra.

Redmond-Cooper observes that, 'The *De Préval* judgment has been criticized by dealers as imposing unreasonably high standards on them in relation to identifying "suspicious" goods, whilst leaving the victim of theft free to sit idly back and wait until the goods surface on the market, possibly many years after the theft.'[285] In response, it could be argued that, if dealers carry out due diligence enquiries properly, and search the relevant databases, they can then sit back safe in the knowledge that everyone would accept that they have acted in good faith.

It has been questioned whether, if the defendant had been a private buyer, the outcome in *De Préval* might have been different.[286] It is submitted that the court will look at all of the circumstances, and the status of the buyer would be merely one factor which could be taken into account. Arguably, the most important factor will be the value and unique nature of an object. If it is of high value, then one would expect any private buyer to seek advice from experts in the field. Professionals should advise the buyer to carry out all proper checks in relation to provenance, including checking the Art Loss Register and any other relevant databases of stolen or missing art. If a private buyer ignores such advice, he risks being unable to discharge the burden of proof that he acquired the object in good faith.

To what extent does the approach taken by Arden J in *Préval v Adrian Alan* towards the concept of good faith appear surprising? Is it markedly different from the approach taken in relation to the exceptions to the *nemo dat* rule discussed above?[287] At common law, there is no need to make enquiries if everything appears above board. However, if the circumstances are unusual, the buyer is expected to enquire further. These candelabra were sufficiently unusual that the circumstances surrounding their acquisition were suspicious: consequently, checks relating to their provenance were necessary. Arguably, it would be different if the defendant had purchased a fairly common and relatively low value antique, such as a Victorian card table, valued at a few hundred pounds. Even so, the decision by Arden J puts pressure upon buyers of cultural objects to exercise due diligence in transacting, which should include making detailed enquiries regarding their provenance.

Yet there is no doubt that an expectation that buyers should search electronic databases for information in order to demonstrate good faith involves raising standards which do not apply in other contexts. For example, in *Marcq v Christie Manson*,[288] Jack J made it clear that

[285] See R Redmond-Cooper, 'Time Limits in Actions to Recover Stolen Art' in NE Palmer (ed), *The Recovery of Stolen Art* (The Netherlands, Kluwer Law International, 1998) 145, 151.

[286] R Redmond-Cooper, 'Good Faith Acquisition of Stolen Art' (1997) II(1) *Art Antiquity and Law* 55, 58.

[287] See 5.37.

[288] *Marcq v Christie Manson* [2002] EWHC 2148; this issue was not explored further at Court of Appeal level: [2004] QB 286 (CA).

the auction house could be viewed as having acted in good faith, even though it had not checked databases before returning an unsold painting to a customer. However, it is submitted that, in the light of the Money Laundering Regulations 2007 and the Proceeds of Crime Act 2002, the decision in *Préval v Adrian Alan* seems to be the best way forward. One can hardly have a situation where an auctioneer is successfully prosecuted for failing to report a suspicious transaction, whilst he is found to have acted in good faith in the civil courts. Dealers and auction houses should inspect databases and make enquiries about provenance if they wish to protect themselves. Indeed, one could go further and argue that, as all countries are expected to establish a legislative regime to combat money laundering, all countries should encourage purchasers of cultural property to inspect any relevant electronic registers.[289]

Arden J has therefore extended the notion of good faith by establishing a principle that a dealer could not claim to be a good faith purchaser if he has not searched certain cultural databases, such as the Art Loss Register. This is not the general position in the commercial field. For example, Lindley LJ observed, in *Manchester Trust v Furness,* that:

> In dealing with estates in land title is everything, and it can be leisurely investigated; in commercial transactions possession is everything, and there is no time to investigate title; and if we were to extend the doctrine of constructive notice to commercial transactions we should be doing infinite mischief and paralysing the trade of the country.[290]

Although those who participate in the art market may see themselves as commercial people, they are dealing with cultural objects which possess special values, such as social and historical information about the past. In these circumstances, it is surely not unreasonable to expect all purchasers to respect the object which they wish to buy and to take time to investigate its provenance.

5.44 The Doctrine of Laches

There are certain situations where the Limitation Act 1980 does not apply, such as where a claimant is seeking an equitable remedy such as specific performance or an injunction. There is also no statutory limitation period where a fiduciary (such as a curator or an agent) retains property with which he has been entrusted.[291] However, if the claimant has delayed in making any claim, the defendant will plead the equitable doctrine of laches as a defence. The court will be invited to consider the delay and the reasons for it, and its consequences, and whether it would be inequitable or unconscionable to enforce the claimant's rights because of the delay.[292] Two factors are therefore particularly important in carrying out a balancing exercise between the parties: the length of the delay and the conduct of the

[289] It would be desirable to have one global computerised registry for cultural property. For further discussion, see KT Burke, 'International Transfers of Stolen Cultural Property: Should Thieves Continue to Benefit from Domestic Laws Favoring Bona Fide Purchasers?' [1990] 13 *Loyola LA International & Competition Law Journal* 427, 465.

[290] *Manchester Trust v Furness* [1895] 2 QB 539 (CA) 545. Lindley LJ's views were strongly endorsed by the other two judges in the Court of Appeal: 547 (Lopes LJ), 549 (Rigby LJ). See also, *Feuer Leather Corpn v Frank Johnstone & Sons* [1981] Com LR 251; *Miramar Maritime Corp v Holborn Oil Trading Ltd* [1984] 1 AC 676 (HL); *Ceval Alimentos SA v Agrimpex Trading Co Ltd* [1996] 2 Lloyd's Rep 319.

[291] Limitation Act 1980, s 21(1). In *Central Bank of Nigeria v Louis Emovbira Williams* [2012] EWCA Civ 415, the Court of Appeal held that there is no statutory limitation period bacause of the application of the Limitation Act 1980, s 21(1), not only in relation to claims trustees and fidiciaries who retain property in breach of trust but also to claims against those who dishonestly assist them in doing so.

[292] *Edwin M Hughes v La Baia Ltd* [2011] UKPC 9 [36]; *P&O Nedlloyd BV v Arab Metals Co (No 2)* [2007] 1 WLR 2288 [55]; *Garcia v De Aldama* [2002] EWHC 2087 [253].

parties.[293] If the claimant has done his best to find the object which has been taken from him and acts promptly to recover it once he finds where it is located, a plea of laches is unlikely to be successful.

5.45 United States: Limitation Periods

In the United States, limitation periods are governed by the individual laws of states, rather than by federal law. Whereas there is a uniform rule that a thief cannot obtain a good title, there has not been the same consenus over limitation periods in relation to purchasers. The law leans in favour of the original owner, but details vary. In California and a number of other states, the law provides that time only begins to run from when the owner knew or should have known the location of the stolen property. This is called 'the disclosure rule' or 'discovery rule', and it is based upon the diligence of the owner in attempting to recover his property.[294] In contrast, New York law provides that there must be a 'demand and refusal' once the object is found, and a three-year limitation period runs from this point.[295]

It can be argued that the discovery rule is the better rule because it encourages the dispossessed owner to search for his property. In contrast, the 'demand and refusal' rule allows the dispossessed owner to wait until, for example, it is put up for auction. However, some modification of this rule is provided by the doctrine of laches.[296] For example, when a Chagall painting was stolen from the Guggenheim Museum, the administrators did not report it to the police, but claimed it when it was later put up for sale. They were not time-barred under the 'demand and refusal' rule, but the court ruled that, because the museum administrators had not informed anyone of the theft or made an active attempt to find the painting, they were time-barred under the equitable doctrine of laches. Due to the claimant's unreasonable delay, to the prejudice of the defendant, it would be unconscionable to allow the claimant to recover the painting.[297]

5.46 Conflict of Laws and the Lex Situs

The limitation periods in different jurisdictions differ remarkably from each other. Common law jurisdictions generally offer more protection to the dispossessed owner than civil law jurisdictions. Criminals may exploit these differences by moving cultural objects to a country which offers better protection to possessors. These variations in national laws become significant where a claim is brought before an English court which determines that the law of a different jurisdiction should be applied and, by that law, a possessor acquires a good title after the expiration of a short period of time. In this situation, the owner no longer has an immediate right to possession and cannot sue in conversion.[298]

[293] *Lindsay Petroleum Co v Hurd* (1874) LR 5 PC 221, 239–40; approved in *Erlanger v New Sombrero Phosphate Co* (1878) 3 App Cas 1218 (HL) 1279. See also *Cheltenham & Gloucester plc v Appleyard* [2004] EWCA Civ 291; *Jones v Stones* [1999] 1 WLR 1739 (CA). The equitable doctrine was expressly preserved by s 36(2) of the Limitation Act 1980.

[294] *O'Keeffe v Snyder* 170 NJ Super 83 NJ 478, 416 A 2d 862 (1980); *Kunstsammlungen zu Weimar v Elicofon* 536 F Supp 829 (1981), aff'd 678 F 2d 1150 (1982); *Autocephalous Greek-Orthodox Church of Cyprus and the Republic of Cyprus v Goldberg & Feldman Fine Arts, Inc* (1989) 717 F Supp 1374.

[295] *Menzel v List* 24 NY 91, 246 NE 2d 742, aff'd 298 NYS 2d 979, 6 UCC Rep Serv 330 (1969).

[296] See P Gerstenblith, 'The Kanakariá Mosaics and United States Law' in KW Tubb (ed), *Antiquities, Trade or Betrayed* (London, Archetype Publications 1995) 105, 110–11.

[297] *Solomon R Guggenheim Foundation v Lubell* 153 AD 2d 143, 550 NYS 2d 618 (1990), aff'd 77 NYS 2d 311, 569 NE 2d 426, 567 NYS 2d 623 (1991).

[298] ITAP Report [25].

The governing law where there are disputes over ownership of portable objects is the law of the place where the cultural object was located each time it changed hands: the *lex situs.* Section 1 of the Foreign Limitation Periods Act 1984 provides:

> where in any action or proceedings in a court in England and Wales the law of any other country falls . . . to be taken into account in the determination of any matter –
>
> (a) the law of that other country relating to limitation shall apply in respect of that matter for the purposes of the action or proceedings.

Consequently, if an object is stolen, smuggled out of the United Kingdom and sold in a country in circumstances which give the purchaser a good title, the law of that country will be applied as the *lex situs* to the exclusion of the limitation laws of England and Wales.[299]

In *City of Gotha v Sotheby's,*[300] Joachim Wtewael's painting of 1603, 'Holy Family with Saints John and Elizabeth', was taken from the East German City of Gotha in 1946 at the end of World War II to Russia, possibly by Soviet Trophy Brigades. The painting was given to an agent to smuggle out of Russia to West Berlin in the 1980s. The agent misappropriated it and it disappeared. After the painting re-emerged, Cobert Finance purchased it and later put it up for sale at Sotheby's in London in 1992. The German Government sued Cobert Finance to recover it. Cobert Finance admitted that it had not acquired the painting in good faith. Moses J considered the relevant principles of German law which existed in 1946 as the *lex situs* in deciding whether the German government could recover the painting, and decided that the German Government had title to the painting. German legal provisions which protected good faith purchasers who bought at a public auction were irrelevant, as the defendant was a bad faith purchaser. However, German law prescribed a 30-year limitation period in relation to theft and bad faith purchase. The next question before the court was when, according to German law, did this 30-year period begin to run? Moses J held that time did not run until 1987 when, after the painting was smuggled into West Berlin by the agent as a bailee, it was misappropriated. The claim was therefore not time-barred under German law.

In *Gotha,* Moses J also considered section 2(1) of the 1984 Act, which provides that if the application of a foreign law relating to limitation periods conflicts with public policy, English law should prevail. Moses J suggested that the foreign law should only be disapplied in exceptional circumstances,[301] such as where there is a conflict with a fundamental principle of justice. He considered that foreign laws were not objectionable on public policy grounds simply because they afforded less protection to the dispossessed owner than English law. Moses J then proceeded to consider whether the 30-year period prescribed by German law, which would run from the date of the theft or misappropriation regardless of whether the owner knew of the location of the object or not, was contrary to public policy. English law relating to limitation periods does not reward thieves and bad faith transferees for their misconduct: time will not run whilst an object remains in their possession. Moses J decided that German law was contrary to public policy on this point. Orton and Lomas are critical of this aspect of the judgment. In their opinion, it should be accepted that German law takes a different approach in dealing with typical policy concerns (such as the

[299] *Garcia v De Aldama* [2002] EWHC 2087; *Winkworth v Christie Manson and Woods Ltd* [1980] Ch 496.

[300] *City of Gotha v Sotheby's (No 2), The Times* (8 October 1998), noted by A Mair, 'Misappropriation and Skulduggery in Germany and Russia: the Case of Wtewael's *The Holy Family*' (1998) III(4) *Art Antiquity and Law* 413.

[301] See also *Arab Monetary Fund v Hashim (No 9)* [1993] 1 Lloyd's Rep 543.

increasing unreliability of witnesses) in providing a long stop of 30 years.[302] On the other hand, it should be noted that it is common for valuable cultural objects to disappear for many years, and these long stop periods favoured by civil law systems encourage dealers to buy stolen objects and to store them away with the intention of selling them in their old age.

5.47 Limitation Periods: Thieves and Bad Faith Acquirers

Some countries offer generous protection not only to good faith purchasers but also to the thieves themselves. In civil law systems, the general principle which applies is that possession equates with title, so that a possessor of an item is presumed to be the owner thereof. As a result, a thief or bad faith acquirer will eventually obtain a good title. By way of contrast, in English law, the thief and any bad faith acquirer will never be able to rely on the passage of time to defeat a claim by the dispossessed owner for recovery: they are always at risk of being sued in conversion.

From a policy perspective, it is particularly unsatisfactory where a state's laws are generous to thieves and dishonest acquirers. There seems little point in creating measures to combat money laundering if certain countries have domestic laws which provide thieves with legal title after a relatively short period of time. Yet, a number of civil law countries permit it. In Italian law, those acting in bad faith can obtain title to a stolen object after 20 years. In French law, where the object is in the possession of thieves and bad faith acquirers, there is a 30-year limitation period. In the Netherlands, thieves may obtain legal title after 20 years. Criminals may be tempted to store cultural items in these countries as a consequence. In the past, the south of the Netherlands near the border with Belgium has been a popular transit route for stolen art from northern and eastern Europe, before being smuggled to the UK or the US.

5.48 Good Faith Purchase

The domestic laws of a number of countries make a general distinction between the thief and bad faith acquirer on the one hand, and the good faith purchaser on the other. Good faith purchasers of tangible objects are seen as deserving protection in order to promote purchaser confidence in buying goods and to encourage the owner to be diligent in attempting to track the object which he has lost.

In Italian law, objects in the public domain receive special protection.[303] However, objects from private collections are dealt with in accordance with the general law. If there is no documentation evidencing a transaction, title to an object can only be acquired by a good faith purchaser after possession for ten years. But a purchaser can obtain a good title immediately if the transaction is of a type which is typical for the market, and therefore falls within the scope of articles 1153 and 1154 of the Italian Civil Code. If the purchaser acted in good faith and took possession of an object with a document which was capable of transferring title and which was appropriate for the transaction concerned, the purchaser is completely protected from the time of purchase. The concept of 'good faith' is therefore significant: it is strictly defined by article 1147 so that, if the circumstances are suspicious,

[302] S Orton and P Lomas, 'Potential repercussions from the City of Gotha decision' (1999) IV(2) *Art Antiquity and Law* 159–65.

[303] See 5.48.

the purchaser is expected to enquire further. If the purchaser is a dealer, his expertise will be taken into account in determining whether he has been grossly negligent and has therefore not acted in good faith. Nevertheless, the protection offered to good faith purchasers must make Italy an attractive transit country for objects stolen from private collections. For example, in *Winkworth v Christie, Manson and Woods Ltd*,[304] the claimant's cultural objects were stolen, taken to Italy and sold to an innocent purchaser. The objects were then imported into the UK and offered up for sale at Christie's. Slade J applied Italian law as the law where the transaction took place (the *lex situs*); consequently title passed immediately to the good faith purchaser. The claimant therefore failed to obtain their return.

In France, where the object is not an inventoried object belonging to a museum and was acquired in good faith, the limitation period is peaceful possession for three years from the date of the theft.[305] The law favours the purchaser at the expense of the owner of a private collection. If the object is secretly stolen from a warehouse, the owner may not even be aware that it is missing until it is too late. The burden is upon the claimant to establish that the purchaser did not acquire in good faith. Furthermore, even where the owner can recover the object within that three-year period, he must compensate the possessor for the value of the item, if it had been acquired in a public manner, such as from a shop or market or established dealer in goods of that nature.[306]

The protection which the Netherlands offers to good faith purchasers is similar to French law: good faith purchasers obtain a good title after three years when purchasing from professionals. Switzerland has been a popular transit point for the illicit trade in cultural objects for many years. The limitation period prescribed by the Swiss Civil Code of 1907 provides that a good faith purchaser will acquire legal title after five years of possession.[307]

5.49 Longer Limitation Periods for Works of Art and Antiquities?

Certain countries make a distinction between objects in public hands, such as museum collections, and those in private hands. For example, in Italy, it is not possible to acquire a good title to a stolen 'public domain' object. This property consists of objects owned by public authorities, which have been held for the benefit of the public. Equally, in France, it is not possible to obtain a good title to inventoried material stolen from museums.[308] There are drawbacks in providing lengthy limitation periods within which a claim can be made in relation to an object from a museum collection, whilst providing a short limitation period for other types of portable object. For example, if legislation only protects inventoried museum objects, it will not assist governments which are attempting to recover recently excavated antiquities. A further difficulty is that, in some countries such as the USA, museums are privately owned and this distinction in domestic law between publicly owned and privately owned property would not be appropriate. Even so, any strategy which provides a longer limitation period for cultural objects in civil law jurisdictions should be welcomed. The current position is particularly unsatisfactory because cases may arise where a government in a civil law jurisdiction will wish to avoid the rigour of its own national laws by

304 *Winkworth v Christie, Manson and Woods Ltd* [1980] Ch 496.

305 Code Civil, art 2279.

306 Code Civil, art 2280.

307 Swiss Civil Code, art 728. However, recent legislation now makes an exception in relation to objects falling within the 1970 UNESCO Convention: see 5.49.

308 Code du patrimoine 2004. In relation to the Netherlands, see Dutch Civil Code (BW) art 3:99(3).

suing to recover an object in a common law jurisdiction in order to take advantage of less generous protection offered to good faith purchasers.[309]

Although there are sound policy reasons for the establishment of limitation periods, it can be argued that cultural objects are a special case because of the information which they contain and because they are part of national, and perhaps also, international heritage. If a distinction is to be made between cultural items and everyday objects, it is surely better to provide a wide definition of cultural property, rather than confine it to inventoried museum items. For example, in the past, criminals have used Switzerland to either sell or store illicit cultural objects.[310] However, a special regime in relation to cultural property has been created in recent Swiss legislation: the limitation period is now 30 years from when the cultural property was stolen.[311] Interestingly, the objects falling within the scope of this regime are defined by reference to the 1970 UNESCO Convention.

The Draft Common Frame of Reference (DCFR), which distinguishes cultural objects from other commodities, takes a different approach from the domestic laws discussed above. There is a limitation period for everyday items of 10 years for good faith possessors (who remain in good faith throughout that period), and 30 years for thieves and those who are not good faith possessors. However, separate provisions apply in relation to cultural objects and there would be extended periods of 30 and 50 years, depending upon whether the possession was in continuous good faith or not. In the DCFR, for the purpose of defining cultural objects, reference is made to the European Council Directive 93/7/EEC of 15 March 1993 on the return of cultural objects unlawfully removed from the territory of a Member State.[312] In its Report, the Scottish Law Commission noted that the list of categories of objects in Directive 93/7/EC had attracted a number of criticisms: it was thought that the list was subjective and lacking in clarity.[313] The Scottish Law Commission concluded that, given the difficulty of defining cultural property, it was better to propose new legislation with a lengthy period of prescription of twenty years which did not distinguish between cultural property and other types of objects.[314] The Scottish Law Commission's Report is a further reminder of how difficult it may be to create effective legislation to deter the illicit trade in art and antiquities: if the focus of the legislation is exclusively upon cultural property, there is a danger that its scope will become a source of numerous legal battles to be fought in the courts.

5.50 UNIDROIT Convention

The relatively small number of states which have ratified the UNIDROIT Convention can be largely explained by its approach to issues relating to title and the limitation periods. Article 3 begins by asserting a general principle that a stolen object should be returned. Although it provides for a limitation period of only three years,[315] that period does not run

[309] *City of Gotha v Sotheby's (No 2), The Times* (8 October1998).

[310] D Gill and C Chippindale, 'From Malibu to Rome: Further Developments on the Return of Antiquities' (2007) 14 *International Journal of Cultural Property* 205.

[311] A Parkhouse, 'Hot Art' (2006) *European Lawyer* 70; Discussion Paper on *Prescription and Title to Moveable Property* (Scot Law Com No 144, 2010) [5.15].

[312] See 5.08.

[313] Scottish Law Commission, Report on *Prescription and Title to Moveable Property* (Scot Law Com No 228, 2012) at 3.18–3.19.

[314] Ibid, at 3.20, See further (Scot Law Com No 144, 2010) [10.4], [10.7].

[315] The period of three years was agreed because a claimant might need that length of time to collect the evidence where an object was located abroad.

from the date of the theft but only from the date when the owner had actual knowledge of the location of his property and the identity of its possessor. It is no defence that, if the dispossessed owner had been diligent, he could and should have discovered the object years before. There is a 50-year long stop for a claim (with the exception of objects forming an integral part of any monument or archaeological site or belonging to a public collection).[316]

The members of the UNIDROIT Study Group were influenced by one policy concern in particular: what was the best rule which deters the illicit trade in cultural property?[317] Article 3 of the Convention puts pressure upon purchasers to check the provenance of the object thoroughly in order to avoid exposing themselves to claims by dispossessed owners. Yet Article 3 is not as strict as it might have been: it had been suggested by Chatelain that, in order to deter the illicit trade in cultural property, there should be no protection of good faith purchasers and no compensation.[318] From this perspective, the provision in the UNIDROIT Convention to compensate good faith purchasers who have exercised due diligence seems generous.

The provisions in the UNIDROIT Convention dealing with limitation periods are contentious because they differ from the domestic law of a number of countries.[319] In the UK, the ITAP Panel considered that Article 3(2) of the UNIDROIT Convention should have permitted the three-year time period to run from when the owner had constructive knowledge of where the object was to be found and who was in possession of it. It was thought that this would encourage owners to be diligent.[320] The drafters of the UNIDROIT Convention had considered this issue. As the Explanatory Note to the Convention observes, constructive knowledge can be a vague notion. In other words, would the dispossessed owner have constructive knowledge of the whereabouts of the object once it is offered for sale at public auction, given that this auction could be taking place in any city in the world? The drafters thought that it was best if this question was left to domestic courts to resolve.[321]

Some governments might also find the lengthy 50-year long stop period objectionable. In response, it might be observed that the paintings and other objects stolen during World War II are only recently beginning to appear on world markets. In the context of particularly important cultural objects, there is much to be said for Chatelain's view that a purchaser should never be protected. The current position is that the domestic law of most countries will encourage possessors to keep objects out of the public eye for a sufficiently long period that they can argue that any claim is time-barred.

5.51 Forfeiture by Enforcement Authorities in the US

A claimant may be in a much better position to recover their cultural property if the enforcement authorities in the country in which the object is located are prepared to use their enforcement powers. For example, in *United States v Davis*,[322] a Pissaro artwork, 'Le

[316] See 2.30.

[317] LV Prott, 'The Preliminary Draft UNIDROIT Convention on Stolen or Illegally Exported Cultural Objects' (1992) *International and Comparative Law Quarterly* 160, 162.

[318] J Chatelain, *Means of Combating the Theft of and Illegal Traffic in Works of Art in the Nine Countries of the EEC* (Commission of the European Communities, Doc XII/757/76-E (1976)) 114.

[319] See the Explanatory Report prepared by the UNIDROIT Secretariat (2001–2003) *Uniform Law Review* 476, 506.

[320] See 2.36.

[321] See 2.30, n 138. It is clear from the Explanatory Report prepared by the UNIDROIT Secretariat (2001–2003) *Uniform Law Review* 476, 508, that owners were expected to show that they had been diligent in making a claim.

[322] *United States v Davis* No 10-300-cv, F 3d, 2011 WL 2162897.

Marché', was stolen from the Musée Faure in Aix-les-Bains in France in 1981. The painting was sold to a dealer in the US, who resold it to a good faith purchaser. When she later consigned it for sale to Sotheby's, the French National Police intervened and the artwork was withdrawn from the auction. The artwork was subject to civil forfeiture because it contravened US customs law, which prohibited the import of objects which had been 'stolen, smuggled, or clandestinely imported or introduced contrary to law';[323] in this case, as a stolen object, it was 'contrary to law', because it contravened the National Stolen Property Act.[324] The US Court of Appeals for the Second Circuit ruled that no defence of good faith purchase was available.[325] The decision demonstrates that a US purchaser may be better able to resist a civil claim than forfeiture by enforcement agencies. In relation to a civil law suit, a purchaser may plead that he has purchased in good faith and the limitation period has expired. In contrast, if enforcement authorities seek forfeiture of the item, then a US purchaser must show that the object in their possession is not stolen. The case illustrates the fact that a purchaser of stolen cultural property is not necessarily protected even where a limitation period has expired: the weapons of the criminal law, such as forfeiture, can be called into play to obtain the delivery up of illicitly traded cultural objects.

XII Loans: Immunity From Seizure

5.52 Background

There is a risk that, if a possessor of a cultural object lends it to a museum in a different country for the purposes of an exhibition, it may be seized. For example, an earlier owner may take advantage of the fact that an object has been moved to a country which offers less protection to purchasers of stolen property and may bring a law suit to recover it. Another possibility is that a creditor may seek to enforce a judgment debt owed by the possessor of the cultural object. If a crime has been committed and the object represents the proceeds of crime, the object may be taken into custody by enforcement authorities. The risk of damage to objects during the process of seizure and the difficulty of obtaining their return will discourage possessors of iconic items from lending them to museums for the purposes of a special exhibition.

In 2005, it was widely reported that a number of works by Picasso, Monet and Van Gogh, which were insured for $1 billion, were seized in Switzerland at the instigation of a Swiss company called Noga. The works belonged to Russia's Pushkin Fine Arts Museum. Noga alleged that it was owed money by the Russian Government. In effect, the works were being held hostage in an attempt to force the Russian Government to pay its debts. Eventually, the works were released. However, the Russian Government stated that it would no longer lend works to museums in countries which did not grant immunity from seizure. This announcement prompted governments in a number of countries to change their laws to protect cultural objects from being seized whilst on temporary loan to museums.[326] The

[323] 19 USC [1595].

[324] For discussion of the National Stolen Property Act, see 3.75.

[325] No 10-300-cv, F 3d, 2011 WL 2162897. For discussion of this case, which was decided on 3 June 2011, see M Hamblett, '"Innocent Buyer" of Stolen Art Loses Out to French Museum' *New York Journal* (6 June 2011).

[326] DCMS Consultation Paper on Anti-Seizure Legislation [1.3].

UK Government eventually followed suit, although the relevant legislative provisions, which can be found in the Tribunals, Courts and Enforcement Act 2007, differ from the laws of other countries in various respects.[327]

5.53 Tribunals, Courts and Enforcement Act 2007

The immunity from seizure provisions can be found in Part 6 of the 2007 Act. They only apply where the object is usually kept outside the UK, the owner is not ordinarily resident in the UK, its import is legal, and it has have been brought to the UK for the purposes of a temporary exhibition at a museum or gallery.[328] These provisions protect private individuals, as well as governments, who lend cultural objects to approved museums and galleries in the UK. The statutory protection offered only lasts for 12 months, as it is only concerned with temporary loans (although this period can be extended if an object was damaged during this period and repairs or restoration is needed).[329]

In order to take advantage of the immunity from seizure provisions, museums and galleries must take two steps in turn. They must first apply to be registered as an approved institution. The application must be made to the body specified in the legislation and, for museums based in England, this would be the Secretary of State. In order to succeed, the applicant must establish that it has proper due diligence procedures in place.[330] In practice, this will mean that the applicant museum will need to demonstrate that its acquisition team is familiar with DCMS guidance and the Museums Association's Code of Ethics, carrying out checks on title to works of art or antiquities and details of their provenance. In order to do this, an applicant will ordinarily provide some examples of when its team has carried out due diligence procedures.

Once a museum or gallery has been registered as an approved body, it must publish information on its website if it wishes to borrow an item and take advantage of the anti-seizure protection. This information will describe the object, and identify its owner (or his agent), detail its provenance, and provide information about the exhibition.[331] This information must be published at least four weeks before the opening of the exhibition and must continue to be advertised for a further 12 weeks or until the close of the exhibition, if this is shorter. For example, in 2011, the National Gallery advertised the fact that it had borrowed various paintings from museums and art galleries from around the world. There was a description supplied alongside each painting and, in particular, it was stated whether or not there were details of its provenance during the period between 1933 and 1945. Similarly, the Courtauld Gallery provided information regarding objects which it had borrowed from

[327] For details of the background to this legislation, see the DCMS Consultation Paper on Anti-Seizure Legislation and A O'Connell, 'The United Kingdom's Immunity from Seizure Legislation' (2009) 72 *Modern Law Review* 783. In relation to a review of immunity legislation in other jurisdictions, see the Annex to the Consultation Paper, which was prepared by A O'Connell.

[328] Tribunals, Courts and Enforcement Act 2007, Pt 6, 'Protection of Cultural Objects on Loan' s 134. For specific guidance on particular terms, such as 'resident,' see ibid, s 137. As regards co-ownership, see ibid, s 134(3). Pt 6 came into force in England on 31 December 2007: Tribunals, Courts and Enforcement Act 2007 (Commencement No 2) Order 2007, SI 2007/3613; in relation to Scotland on 21 April 2008: Tribunals, Courts and Enforcement Act 2007 (Commencement) (Scotland) Order 2008, SSI 2008/150; in relation to Wales and Northern Ireland on 22 April 2008, see Tribunals, Courts and Enforcement Act 2007 (Commencement No 4) Order 2008, SI 2008/1158.

[329] Tribunals, Courts and Enforcement Act 2007, s 134(4)(5). See also 6.07.

[330] ibid, s 136.

[331] A copy of this information should be sent to the Acquisitions Export and Loans Unit of the Museums, Libraries and Archives Council (MLA). There will be links to the DCMS's cultural property advice website.

various museums and galleries for an exhibition in the summer of 2011 of the work of Toulouse-Lautrec. A number of paintings had an incomplete provenance for the years 1933–45 but, in these cases, it was noted that a search had been made of the Art Loss Register.

5.54 Effect of the Tribunals, Courts and Enforcement Act 2007

The UK Government had become concerned that, if it did not act, UK museums would be at a competitive disadvantage with museums in other countries. Governments and private collectors had become increasingly reluctant to lend items for exhibitions in countries which did not provide immunity from seizure.[332] The UK Government hoped that the change in the law would allow UK museums to organise outstanding international exhibitions. The change in the law has generally been welcomed. Although the legislation requires a degree of advance planning in terms of seeking approved status, the procedure itself for publicising loans is relatively straightforward. The legislation was therefore seen as providing a workable solution in the context of complex and often delicate loan negotiations in advance of an exhibition. Moreover, the legislation is seen as enabling museums to realise a public value in privately owned collections by bringing them into the public domain for the purposes of the exhibition.[333]

One advantage of the publicity provided in relation to these loans is that anyone with a claim to the object may see it. They can request more information about, for example, the provenance of the object. The museum must respond to any reasonable query[334] but, in doing so, the museum has the opportunity to carry out further due diligence checks and can review its decision to borrow the object for the purposes of the planned exhibition. Even so, the change in the law must be frustrating to those families who are unable to recover objects which they once owned.[335] It bolsters the position of bad faith recipients who can enhance the prestige of an object by lending it to an exhibition, whilst having the satisfaction of knowing that it cannot be seized.

There is a risk that an owner could challenge this legislative provision on the basis that it is in breach of his human rights. As an owner, the claimant could argue that these provisions violate his right to peaceful enjoyment of his possessions, in contravention of Article 1 of the First Protocol. Yet this guarantee is not absolute. Article 1 states that a government can deprive a person of the enjoyment of his property, subject to certain conditions, if it is in the public interest.[336] It is doubtful whether a legal challenge would be successful because the Government could argue that the protection offered to these items serves a legitimate public policy objective, which is to promote an exchange of cultural information between countries whilst preserving the sustainability of museums. There must be a reasonable relationship of proportionality between the policy behind the law and its effect upon the individual.[337] The immunity from seizure legislation is arguably a proportionate response in

[332] DCMS Consultation Paper on Anti-Seizure Legislation [1.3]–[1.5].

[333] See the positive views of both the Museums Association and the Museums, Libraries and Archives Council in response to the DCMS Consultation Paper.

[334] O'Connell is critical of the fact that, if information about the object has already been sought in another jurisdiction, the query will not be viewed as reasonable: O'Connell, (2009) 72 *Modern Law Review* 783.

[335] NE Palmer, *Museums and the Holocaust* (Leicester, Institute of Art and Law, 2000) 47.

[336] *Sporrong and Lönnroth v Sweden* (1982) 5 EHRR 35 [61]; *James v UK* (1986) 8 EHRR 123 (ECtHR) 139 [37],

[337] *JA Pye (Oxford) Ltd v UK* (2008) 46 EHRR 45 (ECtHR GC) [55]; *Gabric v Croatia* [2009] ECtHR 9702/04, Decision of 5 February 2009 [35]; *Allgemeine Gold- und Silverscheideanstalt AG v UK* (1986) 9 EHRR 1 (ECtHR) [52]; *James v UK* (1986) 8 EHRR 123 (ECtHR) [50]; *R v DPP, ex p Kebilene* [2000] 2 AC 326 (HL) 380.

that the protection is limited in time and also limited in scope, in the sense that it is only concerned with temporary loans to museums and galleries.

The anti-seizure legislation assures the lender that the object will not be seized to satisfy a claim in conversion by an earlier owner, or a proprietary claim by a creditor. In these circumstances, a potential claimant might argue that he is being deprived of the right to a fair trial, which includes access to the courts, in contravention of Article 6 of the European Convention on Human Rights.[338] In response, it can be observed that, although the overall requirement of a right to a fair trial cannot be compromised, specific rules on constituent rights comprised within Article 6, such as the burden of proof or the remedies available, are not absolute.[339] States enjoy considerable discretion in relation to the precise form which legislation may take (known as a 'margin of appreciation') because they are in a better position to make a judgment regarding social and economic factors within their jurisdiction.[340] The legislature's judgment is respected 'unless that judgment is manifestly without reasonable foundation'.[341] The UK Government's rationale is to preserve the high standing of its museums and to promote cultural awareness.[342] Furthermore, the protection offered appears to be limited to protection of the object itself from physical seizure.

Can a dispossessed owner therefore sue the lender or museum in conversion for financial compensation if the object which has been lent has been stolen from him? The answer, although not free from doubt, appears to be in the affirmative. The Government's Consultation Paper stated that its aim would be 'to suspend the claimant's ability to be granted a particular form of relief for a strictly limited period of time'.[343] When the Bill was introduced in the House of Lords, Lord Howarth of Newport stated:

> We should note that while the Bill precludes seizure of the work of art, it does not preclude suit. It would still be possible to bring an action for damages against, for example, the museum, or for restitution for unjust enrichment, conversion or declaration of title. The only remedy precluded under the Government's proposals is physical seizure.[344]

This statement is reinforced by section 135 of the 2007 Act, which makes it clear that the lender of a cultural object is not protected from every type of claim. In particular, no protection is offered where a government requests the return of an object under the Return of Cultural Objects Regulations 1994 or under the UNESCO Convention 1970 and a court order is made to seize the object in question.

Section 135(d) of the 2007 Act prevents enforcement agencies from seizing an object which appears to represent the proceeds of crime. The police will still be able to examine the object but cannot take it into custody. However, no protection is offered in relation to prosecution for a criminal offence, such as where the lender or another imports a cultural object contrary to the Customs and Management Excise Act 1979,[345] or appears to have

[338] See J Ulph, *Commercial Fraud – Civil Liability, Human Rights, and Money Laundering* (Oxford, Oxford University Press, 2006) at [2.05]–[2.23].

[339] *Salabiaku v France* (1988) 13 EHRR 379. See further, ibid [2.24] et seq.

[340] *JA Pye (Oxford) Ltd v UK* (2008) 46 EHRR 45 (ECtHR GC) [55], [71], [75]; *Allgemeine Gold- und Silverscheideanstalt AG v UK* (1986) 9 EHRR 1 [48].

[341] *Kozacioğlu v Turkey* (2009) ECHR 2334/03, Decision of 19 February 2009 (ECtHR GC) [53]; *JA Pye (Oxford) Ltd v UK* (2008) 46 EHRR 45 (ECtHR GC) [71].

[342] DCMS Consultation Paper on Anti-Seizure Legislation [1.18].

[343] ibid [1.16].

[344] *Hansard*, HL Deb 29 November 2006, c 781.

[345] See 3.59.

contravened the Dealing in Cultural Objects (Offences) Act 2003,[346] or the Iraq (United Nations) Sanctions Order 2003.[347] Equally, the 2007 Act will not offer protection where there is a charge of money laundering[348] or handling stolen goods.[349] This aspect of the law has been criticised and it has been suggested that it is unacceptable to strip enforcement authorities of the power to confiscate property.[350] However, it is highly unlikely that property which is suspected of being stolen will be borrowed; as discussed, museum staff risk civil suits and, depending upon their state of knowledge, criminal charges: they have every incentive to be scrupulous in carrying out due diligence checks beforehand.

XIII Action Against the Seller

5.55 The Seller must have the Right to Sell the Object

If a person sells a work of art or antiquity which has been stolen or looted without disclosing this, he will be in breach of contract. This is so even if the seller had no idea that it was looted and had made checks in relation to its provenance. Section 12 of the Sale of Goods Act 1979 provides that:

> In a contract of sale . . . there is an implied [term] on the part of the seller that in the case of a sale he has a right to sell the goods, and in the case of an agreement to sell he will have such a right at the time when the property is to pass.

The section is carefully phrased: the seller must either own the goods himself or be in a position to cause the owner to transfer his rights in the goods to the purchaser.[351] Commercial dealings are frequently complex and a seller may promise to sell a cultural object which he does not own but which, on agreeing a sale, he plans to acquire from an associate and then deliver, with title passing on delivery. This section is flexible enough to deal with various arrangements under which title will pass to the purchaser at an agreed point in time, such as upon delivery.

The seller must have the 'right to sell'. This means that the seller must transfer his whole interest in the goods (and not some limited right to hire the goods, which would be a bailment rather than a sale) and he must also have the right to give his buyer undisturbed possession.[352] If a seller transfers works of art or antiquities which have been stolen, the seller will not have a 'right to sell' them because there is a risk that the true owner may step forward to claim them and thereby disturb the buyer's enjoyment of these purchases.

The common law never developed a sophisticated system of rules to govern portable property. Where there are conflicting claims of ownership relating to the same object, the

[346] See 3.60, 3.62–3.67.

[347] See 3.68–3.72.

[348] See 3.32.

[349] See 3.22.

[350] LM Kaye, 'Art Loans and Immunity from Seizure in the United States and the United Kingdom' (2010) 17 *International Journal of Cultural Property* 335, 351.

[351] *Karlshamns Oljefabriker v Eastport Navigation Corpn (The Elafi)* [1981] 2 Lloyd's Rep 679, 685.

[352] *Niblett v Confectioners' Materials Co* [1921] 3 KB 387 (CA) 398, 402. See further, *Mason v Burningham* [1949] 2 KB 545, 562; *Egekvist Bakeries Inc v Tizel & Blinick* [1950] 1 DLR 585, 590–91. (affd by Ontario Court of Appeal [1950] 2 DLR 592); *J Barry Winsor & Associates Ltd v Belgo Canadian Mfg Co Ltd* (1976) 76 DLR (3d) 685, 687.

common law protected the one who had the better right to possession. It was never concerned with discovering who had the best title of all. However, despite the fact that the Sale of Goods Act does not expressly state that the seller must provide a perfect title, free from any possible third party claim, the courts have interpreted section 12(1) as requiring the seller to provide absolute ownership rights which are good against the whole world.

5.56 Treating the Contract as at an End

The courts have always seen the transfer of title to an object as fundamental to the contract of sale. A breach of the term implied by section 12(1) of the Sale of Goods Act 1979 will mean that the contract can be brought to an end.[353] In *Rowland v Divall*, Atkin LJ suggested that, if the seller has no right to sell an object, then no sale of it can be said to have taken place.[354] There will be a total failure of consideration on the seller's part.[355] The buyer is entitled to recover the purchase price suing at common law for money had and received. The buyer can choose, however, to seek damages by way of compensation instead.[356]

Ordinarily, if the purchaser wishes to bring a contract to an end, he must return his purchase to the seller. However, this may not be possible where the object has been stolen, because the police may have taken it into custody for the purposes of a prosecution. Furthermore, the true owner may have insisted upon its return. The true owner has a choice of courses of action, and can sue the thief, intermediaries, or the current possessor in conversion.[357] In practice, the true owner will normally contact the possessor, and this is particularly likely where the object is a work of art or antiquity. In *Rowland v Divall*,[358] it was held that the purchaser could recover the purchase price even though he could not return the stolen car because the true owner had recovered it. It was thought that the seller could hardly complain about the failure to return the car when the purchaser's inability to do so was entirely due to the fact that the seller had no title to the car in the first place.[359]

If the purchaser rescinds the contract, the seller cannot argue that he should have been given time to remedy the defect in title, by attempting to persuade the original owner to drop his claim. It may be a different matter if the seller manages to cure the defect before the buyer discovers that the object was stolen; if, for example, the seller has compensated the original owner before the purchaser learns of the true state of affairs, it may be too late to rescind the contract: the purchaser will have acquired the legal title to the object and arguably has no cause for complaint.[360]

5.57 The Position of Intermediaries

The law is severe on sellers who have no right to sell. For example, suppose a painting is stolen and sold by the thief to A, who resells to B, who resells C, who resells to D. If the

[353] Sale of Goods Act 1979, s 12(5A) provides that s 12(1) is a condition. If there is an express term relating to title, it will also be treated as a condition: *Barber v NWS Bank Plc* [1996] 1 WLR 641, 646.

[354] *Rowland v Divall* [1923] 2 KB 500 (CA) 506–07.

[355] ibid, 504 (Bankes LJ), 504–05 (Scrutton LJ), 506 (Atkin LJ).

[356] *Warman v Southern Counties Car Finance Ltd* [1949] 2 KB 576.

[357] Torts (Interference with Goods) Act 1977, s 3(2)(c).

[358] *Rowland v Divall* [1923] 2 KB 500 (CA).

[359] *Rowland v Divall* [1923] 2 KB 500 (CA) 505 (Scrutton LJ), 507 (Atkin LJ).

[360] *Lucas v Smith* [1926] VLR 400, 403–04; *Patten v Thomas Motors Pty Ltd* [1965] NSWLR 1457; *Whitehorn Bros v Davison* [1911] 1 KB 463 (CA) 475, 481; *Blundell-Leigh v Attenborough* [1921] 3 KB 235 (CA) 240, 242. See also *Butterworth v Kingsway Motor Ltd* [1954] 1 WLR 1286 1295, where Pearson J suggested that it would be extraordinary if a purchaser could rescind the contract when the title had been cured.

owner recovers the painting from D who is in possession of it, D can sue C for the price because of the breach of section 12. C can sue B, and B can sue A. Each can recover his purchase price together with any consequential loss, such as legal costs, if it is within the contemplation of the parties.[361] Liability can be transferred back up the chain of sales until it rests with the person who originally sold with a defective title.

A purchaser can recover the whole of the purchase price even where he has been in possession of the object for a lengthy period of time.[362] This principle operates harshly on dealers, who like the certainty of feeling that they have closed the book on a particular transaction. However, a seller may be able to plead that the purchaser's claim for the recovery of the purchase price or damages is time-barred after the expiration of six years from the date of the contract.[363]

5.58 Section 12(2): Warranties of Freedom from Quiet Possession

In any contract to sell goods, two warranties will be implied.[364] By section 12(2)(a), there is a warranty that the goods will be free of any proprietary right which has not been disclosed. By section 12(2)(b), a continuing warranty of quiet possession is implied. These warranties are separate and independent from the term implied by section 12(1) that the seller must have the right to sell;[365] however, a seller may be in breach of both section 12(1) and section 12(2) if he sells stolen goods.

The warranty of quiet possession implied by section 12(2)(b) is very wide, in that it is a continuing warranty which may be broken years after the transaction has been completed.[366] The warranty offers continuing protection to the purchaser against being disturbed not only by the seller[367] but also by the lawful acts of any third party, such as an earlier owner.[368] The seller would therefore be in breach of section 12(2) if he sold stolen goods which were then later confiscated by the police and returned to their rightful owner. If there is a breach of the warranty, then the claimant can seek damages in compensation.

5.59 Extinction of Title Due to the Expiration of the Limitation Period

The original owner of a work of art or object of antiquity which has been stolen may be too late to bring a legal action because the limitation period may have expired. If so, his title will be extinguished. The purchaser will have acquired a good title and has the right to sell

[361] *Butterworth v Kingsway Motors Ltd* [1954] 1 WLR 1286; *Bowmaker (Commercial) Ltd v Day* [1965] 1 WLR 1396. On costs, see further, *Bankamerica Finance Ltd v Nock* [1988] 1 AC 1002 (HL).

[362] s 11(4) of the Sale of Goods Act 1979 has no application: *Rowland v Divall* [1923] 2 KB 500 (CA) 506–07. See, for example, *Butterworth v Kingsway Motors Ltd* [1954] 1 WLR 1286 (use of a car for almost a year); *Warman v Southern Counties Car Finance Corp Ltd* [1949] 2 KB 576 (use of a car for seven months); *Barber v NWS Bank Plc* [1996] 1 WLR 641 (CA) (almost two years of use).

[363] For the purposes of the limitation periods, the claim for money had and received falls within the Limitation Act 1980, s 5.

[364] Sale of Goods Act 1979, s 12(5A).

[365] *Microbeads AG v Vinhurst Road Markings Ltd* [1975] 1 WLR 218 (CA) 226; *Empresa Exportadora de Azucar v Industria Azucarera Nacional SA, The Playa Larga* [1983] 2 Lloyd's Rep 171 (CA) 180.

[366] *Quare* whether the purchaser's action would nevertheless be time-barred under the Limitation Act 1980 if quiet possession is disturbed more than six years after the sale took place.

[367] *Empresa Exportadora de Azucar v Industria Azucarera Nacional SA, The Playa Larga* [1983] 2 Lloyd's Rep 171 (CA) 180; *Gatoil International Inc v Tradax Petroleum Ltd, The Rio Sun* [1985] 1 Lloyd's Rep 350, 360; *Healing (Sales) Pty Ltd v English Electrix Pty Ltd* (1968) 121 CLR 584.

[368] *Microbeads AG v Vinhurst Markings Ltd* [1975] 1 WLR 218 (CA) 222; *Niblett v Confectioners' Materials Co Ltd* [1921] 3 KB 387 (CA) 403. See further *Lloyds and Scottish Finance Ltd v Modern Cars and Caravans (Kingston) Ltd* [1966] 1 QB 764, 781.

the object; consequently, he would have the right to sell the object and a subsequent buyer would not be able to argue that there has been a breach of section 12(1). Even so, can the purchaser argue that his seller is in breach of contract because he did not have the right to sell the object? The position is unclear.

One approach is to concentrate on the question of whether the purchaser can resell the goods without himself being in breach of section 12. It could be argued that, if the purchaser can resell, then his seller should not be in breach. Some tenuous support for this approach is provided by Atkin LJ in *Niblett v Confectioners' Materials Co Ltd.*[369] Furthermore, in *R v Wheeler,*[370] Stuart-Smith L.J. suggested that a purchaser could not reject the goods (either on the basis of a breach of section 12 or on the basis of misrepresentation) where stolen goods were sold in market overt because the purchaser had acquired a good title and had suffered no loss.[371] Yet this approach is inappropriate in relation to important works of art or antiquity. A dispossessed owner may well make a complaint to any organiser of an exhibition at which the cultural object is displayed subsequently. It also ignores the fact that, in practice, it may be difficult to resell illicit cultural objects even where the seller has a good title.[372] Later purchasers would require information about the provenance of a work and may be wary of purchasing it once its true history is revealed. In the light of these considerations, it is submitted that the purchaser should be entitled to the return of his purchase price on the basis that his seller had no right to sell the object; the fact that the purchaser has acquired a good title by the operation of a statutory mechanism is irrelevant to this complaint.

5.60 Illegally Exported Objects and Section 12

What if a purchaser discovers that the object which he has purchased has been illegally exported from its country of origin? This will be a cause of anguish for museums in particular, because its officials will have gone to great lengths to avoid this situation. But forgers can create very accurate and convincing documents, and no moral blame can be attached to a purchaser who has acted diligently but has been duped by false materials. In this situation, if the work of art or antiquity has not been stolen but has only been illegally exported, a purchaser may nonetheless face a demand to surrender it where the Return of Cultural Objects Regulations 1994 apply because the object has been illegally exported from another Member State within the European Union. Equally, a government may make a request for its return in accordance with the 1970 UNESCO Convention. If the purchaser is pressed to return the object to a government, he can sue his seller for breach of section 12 (or, in relation to the 1994 Regulations, could seek compensation from the government of the EC Member State concerned).[373]

[369] In *Niblett v Confectioners' Materials Co Ltd* [1921] 3 KB 387 (CA) 401 his Lordship suggested that 'It may be that the implied condition is not broken if the seller is able to pass to the purchaser a right to sell notwithstanding his own inability; but that is not so here'.

[370] *R v Wheeler* (1991) 92 Cr App R 279.

[371] ibid, 283.

[372] See I Brown, 'The Scope of Section 12 of the Sale of Goods Act' (1992) 108 LQR 221, 223. However, a purchaser could not sue for mental anguish in these circumstances: MG Bridge, 'The Title Obligations of the Seller of Goods' in McKendrick and Palmer (eds), *Interests in Goods* 303, 308; *Bliss v South East Thames Regional Health Authority* [1987] ICR 700; *W v Egdell* [1900] Ch 359; *Hayes v James & Charles Dodd* [1990] 2 All ER 815 (CA); *Watts v Morrow* [1991] 4 All ER 937.

[373] See 5.08.

If the work of art or antiquity is not subject to a claim from a foreign government under the 1970 Convention or the 1994 Regulations, can the purchaser nevertheless argue that the seller had no right to sell the object and is therefore in breach of section 12(1)? A painting or antiquity is likely to be worth much less if it has been illegally exported.[374] Any purchaser who planned to resell the object would need to reveal that it had been illegally exported. As a consequence, it could never be sold to a museum. More broadly, the reputation of the object would be tarnished. A foreign government could, for example, seek a court declaration that it has been illegally exported: its justification for doing so would be that it wished to avoid debasing the credibility of the nation's genuine export documents.[375] Purchasers may also have a fear, whether well founded or not, that the object could be confiscated. Moreover, an auction house may refuse to sell an illegally exported object. For example, Christie's had planned to sell a rediscovered bronze by Adriaen de Vries (d.1626) on 7 July 2011, but it was withdrawn from sale when it became clear that the validity of its export licence was questionable.[376] Nevertheless, the legal principle to be applied where the purchaser of an illegally exported object wishes to terminate the contract and obtain reimbursement cannot be stated with confidence. This is because it can be argued that, if no one is making any attempt to seize the object itself, it cannot be said that the purchaser's possession has been disturbed.[377]

5.61 Statements Which Attempt to Modify or Exclude the Seller's Obligations

The terms implied by section 12(1) and (2) that the seller has the right to sell the object and that the purchaser will enjoy quiet possession of it may be modified by express or implied agreement. According to section 12(3) of the Sale of Goods Act 1979, the parties should be free to agree that the seller should transfer only such title as he or a third party possesses. Even in these circumstances, there is a warranty implied by section 12(4) that the seller must disclose all charges and encumbrances of which he is aware and, by section 12(5), there is a further warranty that the purchaser should enjoy quiet undisturbed possession of the goods save for the charges or encumbrances disclosed.

In *Kingdom of Spain v Christie, Manson & Woods*,[378] Christie's proposed to sell a painting with a statement in its catalogue that 'The seller will transfer to the buyer only such title as the seller may have in the lot. The seller is Overseas Art Investments Ltd . . . Claims have been made by the Government of Spain concerning the circumstances in which the painting left Spain, and in particular they have alleged illegal export. Christie's give no independent warranties.' It was also stated that, 'Purchasers should note that this lot is not being sold on Christie's Standard Conditions of Sale and that the seller is selling only such title as it has to the picture'. Christie's was therefore quite frank in its disclosure and, if challenged, would no doubt have argued that it was acting in accordance with section 12(3) to (5). Even so, this attempt to sell the painting with a limited title appears surprising by modern standards. The case was heard in 1986 and Christie's voluntarily decided to withdraw the painting. The UK Government became party to the 1970 UNESCO Convention in 2002. It may well be that, in the light of the Convention and money laundering measures, an auction house would swiftly withdraw an illegally exported object from sale whilst it investigated

374 *Kingdom of Spain v Christie, Manson & Woods Ltd* [1986] 1 WLR 1120, 1125.
375 ibid, 1131. It was assumed for the purposes of argument that the documents were forged.
376 *Antique Trade Gazette* (15 August 2011).
377 *Niblett v Confectioners' Materials Co Ltd* [1921] 3 KB 387 (CA) 403.
378 *Kingdom of Spain v Christie, Manson & Woods* [1986] 1 WLR 1120.

the matter further. Although some modification of the obligations implied by section 12(1) and (2) is permitted by section 12(3), it is not possible to exclude liability for breach of section 12 entirely. According to section 6(1)(a) of the Unfair Contract Terms Act 1977, the term implied by section 12 relating to title cannot be restricted or excluded, regardless of whether the purchaser is a consumer or not.[379] Consequently, anyone purchasing a cultural object should carry out due diligence checks in order to protect themselves; if they do not, they may find that they cannot hurriedly sell the object and avoid all risk of adverse consequences by doing so,

[379] This statutory provision is reinforced by the existence of the Unfair Terms in Consumer Contracts Regulations 1999, SI 1999/2083, as amended by SI 2001/1186. Reg 5(1) provides that any term 'which has not been individually negotiated shall be regarded as unfair if, contrary to the requirement of good faith, it causes a significant imbalance in the parties' rights and obligations arising under the contract, to the detriment of the consumer.' According to reg 6(1), in assessing whether a term is unfair, the circumstances at the time of contracting must be considered.

6

Private Recovery Through The Civil Courts

IAN SMITH

I Introduction

6.01 Introduction

This chapter concerns recovery of art and antiquities in private civil proceedings not involving law enforcement agencies.[1] It is intended to deal with some key legal issues concerning the recovery of art and antiquities by either private individuals or foreign governments; it includes an explanation of the defences available which may prevent such recovery.

The contents of this chapter are as follows:

Statutory claims and defences: a discussion of the Return of Cultural Objects Regulations 1994 where a government which is a member of the EC is seeking the return of cultural property. The statutory defence available against claims by governments or private litigants where an object is on loan in Part 6 of the Tribunals, Courts and Enforcement Act 2007 is also considered.

Jurisdiction: whether the English Court can and should try a case for the recovery of art or antiquities.

Applicable law: which law must be applied to determine whether objects are recoverable.

Enforcement of foreign judgments.

Provisional measures in support of domestic and foreign claims: the procedures available in recovery proceedings, including search orders, interim delivery-up orders and injunctions; freezing and receivership orders.

II Statutory Claims and Defences

Where the Claimant is a Government Within the EC: the Return of Cultural Objects Regulations 1994

6.02 Introduction

The Return of Cultural Objects Regulations 1994 (the 1994 Regulations) came into force on 2 March 1994, giving effect to the 1993 Council Directive on the return of cultural

[1] See Chapter 4 for recovery involving law enforcement agencies in civil and criminal courts.

objects unlawfully removed from the territory of a Member State (the 1993 Directive).[2] These Regulations require Member States of the European Union to take actions in respect of specified cultural property which has been unlawfully removed from another Member State. These Regulations are therefore important to governments, but provide no direct assistance to a private claimant.

6.03 Action by the Secretary of State

The 1994 Regulations require the Secretary of State to search for[3] and identify any possessor or holder[4] of a specified cultural object;

The 1994 Regulations also require the Secretary of State to take steps (including legal proceedings[5]) and enable the competent court[6] to make orders to enable the competent authority of the requesting Member State to check that the object in question is a specified cultural object[7] and to preserve the object[8] and to prevent any steps being taken by any person to evade the return procedure within the 1994 Regulations.[9]

A court making such orders has the power to authorise the Secretary of State's officer to take possession of the object[10] and to hand it over to the custody of a person or institution specified in the order.[11]

In addition the court has additional powers if there are reasonable grounds for believing:

- that a cultural object which has been unlawfully removed from the territory of a Member State;[12]
- that it is on premises specified in the application;[13] and
- either that admission to the premises has been refused, or the case is one of urgency or that an application for admission to the premises would defeat the object of the entry.[14]

In these circumstances, the court is empowered to make an order authorising an officer of the Secretary of State (and other accompanying persons) to enter and search the specified premises.[15]

[2] Council Directive 93/7/EEC of 15 March 1993 on the return of cultural objects unlawfully removed from the territory of a Member State (*L074/74) as amended by Council Directive 96/100/EC and Directive 2001/38/EC of the European Parliament and of the Council. See 5.08.*

[3] 1994 Regulations, reg 3(1)(a).

[4] ibid, reg 3(1)(b).

[5] Court applications under the 1994 Regulations may be made without Notice to respondents: ibid, reg 4(2)(a).

[6] The 'competent court' in England, Wales and Northern Ireland is the High Court; in Scotland it is the Court of Session: ibid, reg 2(4).

[7] ibid, regs 3(4)(a) and 4(1)(a); CPR 25.1(1)(c)(ii) also gives power to order inspection of relevant property; CPR 25.1(1)(c)(iii) enable the court to make an order the taking of a sample of relevant property and CPR 25.1(1)(d)(iv) enables the order to make an order for the carrying out of an experiment on or with relevant property.

[8] ibid, regs 3(4)(b) and 4(1)(b); CPR 25.1(1)(c)(i) also gives the court power to order detention, custody or preservation of relevant property.

[9] ibid, regs 3(4)(c) and 4(1)(c).

[10] ibid, reg 4(3)(a).

[11] ibid, reg 4(3)(b).

[12] ibid, reg 5(1)(a)(i).

[13] ibid, reg 5(1)(a)(ii).

[14] ibid, reg 5(1)(b) and 5(2).

[15] ibid, reg 5(2).

6.04 Member State's Right to Take Proceedings

A Member State may bring proceedings under the 1994 Regulations, against a possessor or holder of a cultural object which has been unlawfully removed from its territory.[16] However, proceedings cannot be brought if at the time of their intended commencement the removal of the cultural object is no longer unlawful.[17]

6.05 Limitation Periods

Subject to provisions relating to limitation periods, the court must order the return of a cultural object where it finds that:

– it is the cultural object covered by the Member State's request for its return;[18] and
– it was unlawfully removed from the national territory of the Member State.[19]

The 1994 Regulations prescribe limitation periods. If they have expired the court cannot order the return of a cultural object. The court cannot order return where proceedings were brought more than one year after the Member State became aware of the location of the cultural object and the of the identity of its possessor or holder.[20]

The regulations make special provision for objects which have been taken from a museum or other public collection in providing further limitation periods. A court is unable to order the return of a cultural object after the expiry of the 'special limitation period'.[21]

The 'special limitation period' is:

– 75 years from the date of unlawful removal of objects forming part of 'public collections' (as referred to in Article 1(1) of the 1993 Directive)[22] or of ecclesiastical goods subject to special protection arrangements under the national law of the Member State;[23]
– 30 years from the date of unlawful removal in any other case.[24]

6.06 Compensation for those in Possession of a Cultural Object Ordered to be Returned

Subject to two limitations, upon ordering the return of a cultural object, the court must order the requesting Member State to pay such compensation as the court deems fair according to the circumstances of the case.[25]

The limitations on such compensation are:

– The court shall not order compensation unless it is satisfied that the possessor exercised due care and attention in acquiring the object.[26]
– A court shall not order compensation to a possessor who was gifted or bequeathed the object unless the donor or testator had exercised due care and attention in acquiring the object.[27]

16 ibid, reg 6(1).
17 ibid, reg 6(2).
18 ibid, reg 6(5)(a).
19 ibid, reg 6(5)(b).
20 ibid, reg 6(6)(a).
21 ibid, reg 6(6)(b).
22 ibid, reg 6(7)(a).
23 ibid, reg 6(7)(b).
24 ibid, reg 6(8).
25 ibid, reg 7(1).
26 ibid, reg 7(2). The notion of 'due care' is discussed in 5.08.
27 ibid, reg 7(3).

Statutory Defence where an Object Is on Loan: Part VI of the Tribunals, Courts and Enforcement Act 2007

6.07 General Principles

Part VI of the Tribunals, Courts and Enforcement Act 2007 (TCEA) provides certain protection to owners of any objects which they lend to an approved 'museum or gallery'[28] in the United Kingdom. The Protection of Cultural Objects on Loan (Publication and Provision of Information) Regulations 2008 (2008 Regulations) proscribes information which must be published and provided by museums and galleries who borrow protected objects. The information which must be published by the borrowing institution on its website, at least four weeks before the object enters the UK,[29] includes:[30]

- the name and address of the lender and any person authorised to act on behalf of the lender;
- a detailed description of the object that is sufficient to identify it;
- details of provenance of the object;
- the location where the object is to be on public display and the duration of that display.

6.08 Protected Objects at Time of Entry to the United Kingdom

An object is protected under the TCEA if all of the following conditions are met at the time that it enters the United Kingdom:[31]

- The object is usually kept outside the United Kingdom.[32]
- It is not owned[33] by a person resident[34] in the United Kingdom.[35]
- Its import does not contravene a prohibition or restriction on the import of goods, imposed by or under any enactment, that applies to the object, a part of it or anything it conceals.[36]
- It is brought to the United Kingdom for public display[37] in a temporary exhibition[38] at a museum or gallery.[39]

[28] The museum or gallery must be one approved under s 136 of TCEA. Museums and galleries may be approved by the Secretary of State in England, by the Welsh Ministers in Wales, by the Scottish Ministers in Scotland, and the Department for Culture, Art and Leisure in Northern Ireland. See further, 5.52–5.53.

[29] At least four weeks ending on the day before the object enters the UK: 2008 Regulation, reg 4.

[30] ibid, reg 3.

[31] TCEA, s 134(1). 'The United Kingdom' includes the territorial sea adjacent to the United Kingdom (within the meaning given by s 1 of the Territorial Sea Act 1987): ibid, s 137(10).

[32] ibid, s 134(2)(a).

[33] Ownership can be beneficial or not and alone or with others: ibid, s 134(3). Accordingly, the protection will be lost if a part-owner of an object is resident in the United Kingdom.

[34] An individual is resident in the United Kingdom if he is ordinarily resident in the United Kingdom for the purposes of income tax, or would be if he were receiving income on which tax is payable: ibid, s 137(6). A partnership (including a limited partnership) or unincorporated association is resident in the United Kingdom if it is established under the law of any part of the United Kingdom: ibid, s 137(8). A body corporate is resident in the United Kingdom if it is incorporated under the law of any part of the United Kingdom.

[35] ibid, s 134(2)(b).

[36] ibid, s 134(2)(c). For further discussion, see 5.53. In relation to or the Customs and Excise Management Act 1979, the Iraq (United Nations) Sanctions Order 2003 and the Dealing in Cultural Objects (Offences) Act 2003, see 3.59–3.72.

[37] 'Public display' means display to which the public are admitted, on payment or not, but does not include display with a view to sale: TCEA, s 137(3).

[38] 'Temporary Exhibition' means an exhibition of one or more objects which is open to the public for a period of less than 12 months, whether at a single location or at a succession of locations: ibid, s 137(4).

[39] ibid, s 134(2)(d); the museum or gallery must be one approved under ibid, s 136.

– The museum or gallery has complied with any requirements prescribed by regulations made by the Secretary of State under this paragraph about the publication of specified information about the object.[40]

6.09 Duration and Conditions of Continued Protection

Protection continues only so long as the object is in the United Kingdom for any of the following purposes:[41]

– public display in a temporary exhibition at a museum or gallery;[42]
– going to or returning from public display in a temporary exhibition at a museum or gallery;[43]
– related[44] repair, conservation or restoration;[45]
– going to or returning from related repair, conservation or restoration;[46]
– leaving the United Kingdom.[47]

6.10 The Protection Given

While an object is protected, it may not be seized or forfeited unless:

– it is seized or forfeited under or by virtue of an order made by the court in the United Kingdom; and
– the court is required to make the order under, or under provision giving effect to, a Community obligation or any international treaty.

For these purposes, a relevant Community obligation must include an obligation to order the return of a cultural object under the Return of Cultural Objects Regulations 1994.[48]

The types of seizure and forfeiture prohibited includes (but is not limited to):

– taking control of the object under Schedule 12 to the TCEA (in England and Wales);[49]
– execution or distress (in England and Wales);[50]
– diligence or sequestration (in Scotland);[51]
– seizure, confiscation or forfeiture, or any other measure relating to the custody or control of the object, in the course of a criminal investigation or criminal proceedings (against the owner, the museum or gallery or any other person);[52]
– the making or enforcement of an order relating to the custody and control of the object in civil proceedings (against the owner, the museum or gallery or any other person).[53]

[40] ibid, s 134(2)(e).
[41] ibid, s 134(4)(a).
[42] ibid, s 134(7)(a).
[43] ibid, s 134(7)(b).
[44] Repair, conservation or restoration is 'related' if it is carried out in the United Kingdom and is done either to prepare the object for public display in a temporary exhibition at a museum or gallery or because of damage suffered in the course of any of the purposes set out in s 134(7): ibid, s 134(8).
[45] ibid, s 134(7)(c).
[46] ibid, s 134(7)(d).
[47] ibid, s 134(7)(e).
[48] See 6.01–6.08.
[49] TCEA, s 135(3)(a).
[50] ibid, s 135(3)(b).
[51] ibid, s 135(3)(c).
[52] ibid, s 135(3)(d).
[53] ibid, s 135(3)(e).

6.11 Protection Not Given

The TCEA does not protect those who bring objects to the United Kingdom generally from civil or criminal proceedings. It only prevents enforcement against the protected objects. Accordingly, there is nothing to prevent, for example, a victim from bringing a claim in the United Kingdom seeking damages. The TCEA explicitly states that the protection given does not affect liability for an offence of importing, exporting or otherwise dealing with the object.[54]

III Jurisdiction

Introduction

6.12 Conflict of Laws

When can a person sue in England and Wales to recover an object? What can he do to avoid a lawsuit in this jurisdiction? These are the issues addressed by this section. They are determined by reference to English conflict of laws.

English[55] conflict of laws relating to jurisdiction comprises a mixture of traditional common law rules (hereafter 'the traditional rules'), the 'Judgments Regulation' (EU Regulation)[56] and the application of the 'Lugano Convention'[57] (hereafter the Judgments Regulation and Lugano Convention are referred to together as the European rules).[58] Not surprisingly, the result is a set of principles that do not always sit easily together and are not always clear.

In jurisdiction matters, the question of whether the English court applies either its traditional rules or the European rules is determined by the European rules. The traditional rules apply only if the European rules do not.[59] When the European rules apply, the English court has no jurisdiction to disapply them. When applying the Judgments Regulation, the English courts must follow the interpretations of the European Court of Justice (ECJ).[60]

[54] ibid, s 135(2).

[55] This text considers English law (more particularly, that which applies to the jurisdiction of England and Wales). Similar laws apply in relation to the other parts of the United Kingdom, being Scotland and Northern Ireland.

[56] Council Regulation (EC) No 44/2001 of 22 December 2000 on jurisdiction and the recognition and enforcement of judgments in civil and commercial matters, as amended from time to time and as applied by the Agreement made on 19 October 2005 between the European Community and the Kingdom of Denmark on jurisdiction and the recognition and enforcement judgments in civil and commercial matters (OJ L299/62). These Regulations are frequently referred to by commentators as the 'Brussels I Regulation'. We have followed the terminology used in the Civil Procedure Rules 1998, r 6.31(d).

[57] Convention on jurisdiction and the recognition and enforcement of judgments in civil and commercial matters, between the European Community and the Republic of Iceland, the Kingdom of Norway, the Swiss Confederation and the Kingdom of Denmark signed on behalf of the European Community on 30 October 2007 (OJ L147/5). It currently applies to Denmark, Iceland, Norway and Switzerland.

[58] For a detailed exposition of the relevant principles, see *Dicey, Morris & Collins: The Conflict of Laws*, 14th edn (London, Sweet & Maxwell, 2006); J Hill and A Chong *International Commercial Disputes, Commercial Conflict of Laws in the English Courts*, 4th edn (Oxford, Hart, 2010) and *Cheshire and North's Private International Law*, 14th edn (Oxford, Oxford University Press, 2008).

[59] Arts 3(1) and 4(1) of each of the Judgments Regulation and Lugano Convention; CPR 6.36.

[60] Civil Jurisdiction and Judgments Act 1982, s 3(1).

As a rule of thumb, one can be fairly sure that if a target defendant is domiciled[61] within an EU Member State, Iceland, Switzerland or Norway, then the European rules will have effect. If a defendant is outside the EU, the European rules may still apply; it is only if and to the extent that the European rules do not apply that the traditional rules then apply.

Both under the European rules and traditional rules, the English courts will not have jurisdiction to try any claim, nor enforce any foreign judgment, which is based on foreign penal, public or revenue law. This is considered in detail in section VI below.

The English courts have jurisdiction, under the traditional rules, to try claims under the Return of Cultural Objects Regulations 1994.[62]

The European Rules as Applied by the English Courts

6.13 The Hierarchical Scheme

Where a claimant considers that the English court has jurisdiction under the European rules, it simply certifies this to be the case and serves its claim on the defendant(s).[63] Although the onus is then on a defendant to dispute the court's jurisdiction, the burden remains on the claimant to show that it has a 'good arguable case' that the English court has jurisdiction.[64]

The European rules are hierarchical. Some cases – known as exclusive jurisdiction cases – must be heard in the courts local to an issue, whatever the wishes of the parties.[65] Next, the scheme accords jurisdiction wherever both parties submit to the jurisdiction of the English courts.[66] The court will then examine any prior agreements of contracting parties (not necessarily the litigants) where one of those parties was, at the time of contracting, domiciled in an EU state. When considering whether parties have chosen a forum, the court must apply strict criteria.[67] Next, if not yet afforded jurisdiction, the English court

[61] In brief, Art 60 of the EU Regulation provides that a company is domiciled at the place where it has its '(a) statutory seat, or (b) its central administration, or (c) its principal place of business' (ie it may have more than one domicile). The Regulation leaves the determination of individuals' domiciles to be determined by Member States' national laws. Under English law a person is domiciled in the UK if (a) he is resident in the UK; and (b) the nature and circumstances of his residence indicate that he has a substantial connection with the United Kingdom (which is presumed to be the case if the individual has been so resident for three months or more). Civil Jurisdiction and Judgments Act 1982, s 41. In relation to 'central administration' see the recent case of *889457 Alberta Inc v Katanga Mining Ltd* [2008] EWHC 2679 (Comm), [2009] 1 BCLC 189, [2008] All ER (D) 61 (Nov) (HC), in particular [22] and [23].

[62] See 6.24 below.

[63] CPR, rr 6.32–6.34.

[64] The burden is on claimants to be able to justify European rules jurisdiction to the standard of a good arguable case: *Canada Trust Co v Stolzenberg (No 2)* [1998] 1 AC 1; *Bols Distilleries BV v Superior Yacht Services Ltd* [2007] 1 WLR 12 (PC); *Kolden Holdings Limited v Rodette Commerce Limited and anor* [2008] EWCA Civ 10 (CA). The burden remains upon the claimant if and when the defendant challenges jurisdiction. *Carnoustie Universal SA v International Transport Workers' Federation* [2002] 2 All ER (Com) 657 (HC).

[65] Art 22 of each of the Judgments Regulation and the Lugano Convention.

[66] Art 24 of each of the Judgments Regulation and the Lugano Convention.

[67] Art 23 of each of the Judgments Regulation and the Lugano Convention. Art 23 applies even if the defendant is not domiciled in a Member State, so long as the claimant is domiciled in a Member State; it has no application, however, to cases where the parties have chosen the courts of a non-Member State: Case C-387/98 *Coreck Maritime GmbH v Handelsveen BV* [2000] ECR I-9337 (ECJ). It is the domicile of the original contracting parties which is relevant rather than the domicile of the litigants: *Coreck Maritime*. Even if neither party is domiciled in a Member State, a jurisdiction clause which satisfies the other requirements of Art 23 (including the requirement that the jurisdiction of a member state was chosen) prevents any member state court, other than the courts chosen by the parties, from exercising jurisdiction unless the chosen courts have declined jurisdiction: Art 23(3). So, for exam-

will have jurisdiction if the defendant is domiciled in England and Wales, irrespective of the defendant's nationality.[68] Lastly, by way of derogation from the principle that a defendant should be sued where he is domiciled, the European rules provide that defendants may be sued in England if certain criteria are met, depending on the cause(s) of action alleged by the claimant. These are known as 'special jurisdiction' alternatives and exist for contract cases as well as other types of claims. These alternatives to the defendant's domicile often offer choices of forum to claimants.

6.14 Exclusive Jurisdiction in Cases Regarding Rights *in Rem* in Land

Under the European rules, all 'proceedings which have as their object rights *in rem* in immovable property' located in another Member State (or in the case of the Lugano Convention, another Contracting State) must be brought in the state where that property is located.[69] It is obviously important to understand whether an item of art or antiquity is so-called 'immovable property' for these purposes, and if it is, whether or not a particular kind of claim comes within this exclusive jurisdiction rule.

Whether cultural property is movable or immovable, is not an issue on which the (European) Court of Justice has yet pronounced judgment and so it is open to argument. Commentators on this area of law[70] have not focused on the issue of whether particular items of cultural property should be classified as immovable or movable. There has however been some discussion (in English law) of the nature of fixtures to land and how these should be treated if severed from the land to which they were originally fixed. That discussion appears to suggest that the items which have been severed from land should be treated as immovables, given that the alternative would be to allow severed items of land to become movables for the purposes of the conflict of laws, which may have the effect of rewarding the severance with a more advantageous classification for the purposes of conflict of laws.[71] Whether this is the correct approach is, it is considered, a highly contentious point.[72] If it is the case that fragments of land remain, for the purpose of private international law, immovable property rather than movable property, then the courts of the country from which the fragment was originally removed will continue to have exclusive jurisdiction over questions of rights *in rem* to the fragment.[73]

What then are the kinds of case which amount to proceedings 'which have as their objects rights *in rem*'? The existing (European) law shows that:[74]

ple, where parties who are both domiciled outside the EU have agreed on the jurisdiction of Greece the English court would be unable to exercise its jurisdiction under the traditional rules unless the Greek courts decline jurisdiction. An Art 23 agreement will be superseded when a defendant submits to the jurisdiction of another court under Art 24. *Case 150/80 Elefanten Schuh GmbH v Jacqmain* [1981] ECR 1671 (ECJ).

[68] Art 2 of each of the Judgments Regulation and the Lugano Convention.

[69] Art 22(1) of both the Judgments Regulation and Lugano Convention.

[70] See Caruthers, *The Transfer of Property in the Conflict of Laws, Choice of Law Rules Concerning Inter Vivos Transfers of Property* (Oxford, Oxford University Press, 2005), ch 1.

[71] See ibid, 14–15.

[72] The issue was not argued in the case of *The Islamic Republic of Iran v Berend* [2007] EWHC 132 (QB), where the claimant itself argued the question of title to a fragment of a national monument excavated from the ruins of the ancient city of Persepolis. The argument may not have been available to the Government of Iran, as the fragment may have been lawfully severed from the archaeological site in question – and so lawfully becoming a movable – before being sold on. The law report does not contain sufficient facts for us to know.

[73] Similarly, the law of the country from which the fragment was unlawfully excavated from land would remain the law which governs all subsequent dealings with the fragment even though it may be the subject of a number of transactions in a number of different countries.

[74] *Webb v Webb* (Case C-294/92) [1994] QB 696, [1994] 3 WLR 801.

– A claim for a declaration of ownership (*in rem*, as against the rest of world) of immovable property must be brought where that property is located.
– However, a claim for a declaration that another person holds the immovable property on trust for the claimant does not have to be brought where that property is located.

6.15 The Tort Special Jurisdiction Alternative

The European rules allow a defendant to be sued in a matter relating to tort in another Member State. Under this special alternative a person may be sued 'in the courts for the place where the harmful event occurred or may occur'.[75] Where proceedings are brought in England, the English court must apply English law to determine whether a harmful event has taken place.[76] The harmful event occurs either:

– at the place where the damage occurs; or
– at the place of the event giving rise to it,

and if these are in different jurisdictions the claimant can chose between them.[77]

Assuming that conversion claims fall within this alternative head of jurisdiction,[78] the question to be determined in each case is where 'the harmful event occurred or may occur'. In the case of conversion of an object of art or antiquity, one must consider the conduct of the defendant in question. It is considered that there will broadly speaking be two different scenarios, with two different legal results:

– If the current holder of the object was the person who wrongfully appropriated the object from its original owner, then the 'harmful event' is likely to be that wrongful taking of the object, and the place of that event judged accordingly, as this will be the focus of any case by the original owner against the original wrongdoer.[79] Accordingly, if an object is stolen in Italy, that is likely to be place of the harmful event as between the original owner and the thief.
– If the current holder is not the same person who wrongfully took the object from its original owner, then the focus of the conversion claim is not on the original misappropriation of the object but on the continued (wrongful) retention of the object by the current holder against the demand of the original owner for its return.[80] Accordingly, if an object is stolen in Italy but then transferred by the thief to another person who holds the object in England, England is likely to be the place where the 'harmful event' takes place in the case where the holder refuses to return the object to its original owner.[81]

[75] Art 5(3) of both the Judgments Regulation and the Lugano Convention.

[76] C-68/93 *Shevill v Presse Alliance SA* [1995] ECR I-415, 464 [41].

[77] Case 21/76 *Handelskwekrig GJ Bier BV v Mines de Potasse d'Alsace SA* [1976] ECR 1735.

[78] It is considered that it would. It appeared to be assumed to be the case in *Mazur Media Ltd and another v Mazur Media GmbH and others* [2004] EWHC 1566 (Ch). It is, however, considered arguable that the strict liability nature of the tort of conversion means that it cannot be considered to be a 'matter relating to tort' as interpreted by European law. For the law regarding classification generally see J Hill and A Chong, *International Commercial Disputes, Commercial Conflict of Laws in English Courts,* 4th edn (Oxford, Hart, 2010) 159–60.

[79] It is theoretically possible than an original owner would chose to sue the thief in conversion not on the basis of the original theft but simply on the basis that, following a demand for the return of the object, the thief wrongfully retains the object. This would, however, be rather contrived and limiting.

[80] For detail on the tort of conversion, see ch 5.02–5.06, 5.09–5.13.

[81] *Mazur Media Ltd and another v Mazur Media GmbH and others* [2004] EWHC 1566 (Ch), at [30]

6.16 Co-defendants

The fact that one defendant is domiciled in England may ground jurisdiction against co-defendants.[82] This is widely known as the 'anchoring' provision in the European rules, avoiding the need for claimants to bring proceedings against different defendants in different jurisdictions. However, a claimant must be able to show that claims against the different defendants are 'so closely connected that it is expedient to hear and determine them together to avoid irreconcilable judgments resulting from separate proceedings'. According to the English court, 'courts must look at the substance of the claims against the different defendants and assess the risk giving due weight to the possibility of conflicting determinations of factual and other issues common to each of the claims',[83] and the relevant risk of irreconcilable judgements extends to findings of law as well as fact.[84] This anchoring provision will provide jurisdiction over other defendants even where they are sued under different heads of claim to the English domiciled defendant.[85]

6.17 Parallel and Related Cases in Different Jurisdictions

Whatever the basis of jurisdiction, once it is founded under the European rules, other courts of the EU are prevented from trying the same cause of action between the same parties.[86] Jurisdiction is therefore taken on a 'first come, first served' principle and parallel proceedings in different EU Member States are barred. The prohibition applies where 'the claims are so closely connected that it is expedient to hear and determine them together in order to avoid the risk of irreconcilable judgments', and applies even if one of the parties

[82] Art 6(1) of both the Judgments Regulation and the Lugano Convention. A claimant must have issued proceedings against a defendant but need not have served those proceedings to commence proceedings against other defendants under Art 6(1): *Canada Trust Co v Stolzenberg (No 2)* [2002] 1 AC 1 (CA). The claimant must show that there was a 'good arguable case' at the time at which proceedings were issued against the original defendant and not at a later date when seeking to join other defendants to the action: *Petrotrade Inc v Smith and others* [1998] 2 All ER 346 (HC).

[83] [1994] ILPr 82 (CA).

[84] *Casio Computer Co Ltd v Sayo and others* [2001] EWCA Civ 661, [2001] ILPr 43 (CA).

[85] *Freeport Plc v Arnoldsson* (Case C-98/06) [2007] ECR I-8319. Prior to this case the position had been in doubt. In *Réunion Européene SA v Spliethoff's Bevrachtingskantoor BV* (C-51/97) [1998] I-6511 [50] the ECJ stated: 'It follows that two claims in one action for compensation, directed against different defendants and based in one instance on contractual liability and in the other on liability in tort or delict, cannot be regarded as connected.' The Court of Appeal, in *Watson v First Choice Holidays and Flights Ltd* [2001] EWCA Civ 972, [2001] 2 Lloyd's Rep 339 (CA), took the view that Art 6(1) should not be interpreted so restrictively, doubted if this has been the real intention of the ECJ and referred the matter to the ECJ for a preliminary ruling. However, the case was subsequently settled and so the reference was withdrawn. Cooke J refused to follow such a restriction in the case of *Andrew Weir Shipping Ltd v Wartsila UK Ltd* [2004] EWHC 1284 (Comm), [2004] 2 Lloyd's Rep 377 (HC), following the reasoning of the Court of Appeal in *Watson* that identical causes of action were not required. The Irish High Court, in *Daly v Irish Travel Group Ltd t/a 'Crystal Holidays'* [2003] ILPr 623 found that the crucial passage of *Réunion Européene SA* was *obiter dicta.*

[86] Art 27 of both the Judgments Regulation and the Lugano Convention. The English language version of Art 27 refers only to the 'same cause of action . . . between the parties'; however, Art 27 has been interpreted by the ECJ, with regard to other language versions, as requiring the same subject matter (or the same object) as well as and distinct from the requirement that there be the same cause of action and the same parties: Case 144/86 *Gubisch Maschinenfabrik KG v Palumbo* [1987] ECR 4861 (ECJ); Case C-406/92 *The Tatry* [1994] ECR I-5439, [1995] All ER (EC) 229 (ECJ). Parallel proceedings are to be regarded as involving the same cause of action where each is based on the same facts and rule of law: Case 144/86 *Gubisch Maschinenfabrik KG v Palumbo* [1987] ECR 4861 (ECJ). The issue is whether the two cases as presented by the claimants (and not as defended by the defendants) involve the same cause of action: Case C-111/01 *Gantner Electronic GmbH v Basch Exploitatie Maatschappij BV* [2003] ECR I-4207 (ECJ).

begins proceedings in another EU state in bad faith.[87] A court which is second-seised[88] of such parallel proceedings must stay its proceedings unless and until the first court declines jurisdiction. This prohibition on parallel proceedings takes priority over a jurisdiction agreement (exclusive or non-exclusive).[89] The first come, first served principle applies whether it is a victim who has a brought a lawsuit claiming compensation, or whether it is an alleged wrongdoer who has brought the suit to obtain a negative declaration of non-liability.[90] The European rules contain a more flexible approach with regard to 'related' proceedings.[91]

The first come, first served approach in the European rules, available to both victims (bringing a typical claim) and wrongdoers (who may seek a declaration of non-liability), together with some flexibility in grounding jurisdiction and no need for initial court permission to serve proceedings, offers great scope to all parties to determine the forum for a case. Parties who fail to spot and use this to their advantage miss great opportunities. A party who is served with proceedings under the European scheme may of course challenge the court's jurisdiction, but unless and until this has successfully been done, there is no opportunity to bring the case in another EU Member State.

The Traditional Rules

6.18 General Principles

Before examining the traditional rules it is important to note that, in two situations, the European rules predominate and apply even where a target defendant is domiciled outside the European rules. The European rules will apply to exclusive jurisdiction cases, which importantly include cases which involve 'proceedings which have as their object rights in rem in immovable property' located in another Member State (or in the case of the Lugano Convention, another contracting state); and, secondly, where the parties have previously entered into a jurisdiction agreement in favour of courts of another Member State (or in the case of the Lugano Convention, another contracting state). In all other cases, the traditional rules apply wherever an intended defendant is domiciled outside the EU.

The traditional approach of the English rules is quite distinct from the European rules. First, a claimant wishing to serve a claim against a defendant overseas must obtain permission from the court to this course of action on the basis of an ex parte finding by the court

[87] Case C-159/02 *Turner v Grovit* [2004] 2 All ER (Comm) 381 (ECJ).

[88] Art 30 of both the Judgments Regulation and the Lugano Convention provides that a court is deemed to be seised 'at the time when the document instituting the proceedings or an equivalent document is lodged with the court, provided that the plaintiff has not subsequently failed to take the steps he was required to take to have service effected on the defendant'. The editors of *Dicey, Morris & Collins* (at p 497) and *Hill & Chong* (at p 272) are of the view that this means that the English court is seised at the time proceedings are issued in the court registry so long as the claimant does not subsequently fail to serve the claim form. See *WPP Holdings Italy Srl v Benatti* [2007] 1 WLR 2316.

[89] Case C-116/02 *Erich Gasser GmbH v MISAT Srl* [2004] ILPr 132 (ECJ). (The contrary position previously adopted by the Court of Appeal in *Continental Bank NA v Aekos Compania Naviera SA* [1994] 1 WLR 588 (CA) should no longer be considered good law.)

[90] Case C-406/92 *The Tatry* [1994] ECR I-5439, [1995] All ER (EC) 229 (ECJ).

[91] See Art 28 of both the Judgments Regulation and the Lugano Convention (providing for permissive stay of 'related' actions, ie, actions that 'are so closely connected that it is expedient to hear and determine them together to avoid the risk of irreconcilable judgments resulting from separate proceedings').

that it has jurisdiction.[92] Secondly, the English court exercises discretion as to whether to exercise any jurisdiction it has. Thirdly, there is no 'first come, first served' principle at play. Before exercising its discretion as to whether or not to exercise discretion, the English court first has to decide whether it has jurisdiction. What are the rules which determine this issue?

The traditional rules of the English courts on jurisdiction are now largely codified in the Civil Procedure Rules. The CPR set out the circumstances in which an English court will grant permission to a claimant to serve proceedings on a defendant overseas and not domiciled within the EU. The rules are split between general ones applicable to all cases, and specific ones applicable to particular types of case, whether tort or property etc. In each case, the claimant must show that it has a 'good arguable case' that it can ground jurisdiction under the relevant rule, otherwise commonly referred to as a 'gateway'.[93]

6.19 General Gateways to Jurisdiction

The general rules of the English courts provide that a court may exercise its discretion and permit service overseas where the claimant can satisfy one of the following general 'gateways': (1) the defendant is domiciled[94] within the jurisdiction;[95] (2) a claim is made for an injunction ordering the defendant to do or refrain from doing an act within the jurisdiction – which may include ordering a defendant to deliver-up an object;[96] or (3) a claim is made against someone on whom the claim form has been or will be served and the claimant wishes to serve the claim on another person who is a 'necessary or proper party' to that claim.[97]

6.20 The Property Gateway

A claim satisfies this gateway if 'the whole subject matter of [the] claim relates to property located within the jurisdiction'.[98] This simple rule replaced more convoluted rules dealing with both land and personal property.[99]

[92] No such permission is necessary where the defendant is present in England or where the defendant submits to the jurisdiction of the English court. Corporate presence in England is determined by a combination of procedural service rules and company law.

[93] *Seaconsar Far East Ltd v Bank Markazi Jomhouri Islam Iran* [1994] 1 AC 438 (HL). This is higher than the 'serious issue to be tried' (merits) test: *Carvill America Inc v Camperdown UK Ltd* (QBD, 2 September 2004), para 39, but a less stringent test than requiring proof on the balance of probabilities: *MRG (Japan) Ltd v Engelhard Metals Japan Ltd* [2003] EWHC 3428 (Comm), [2004] 1 Lloyd's Rep 731 (HC).

[94] This test is largely a European one. See 6.12 for the meaning of domicile.

[95] CPR 6.36 and PD6B 3.1(1).

[96] CPR 6.36 and PD6B 3.1(2). Permission will not be granted unless an injunction is a genuine part of the substantive relief sought and has not been claimed merely to bring the case within this rule (*Rosler v Hilbery* [1925] 1 Ch 250 (CA)) and there is a reasonable prospect of an injunction being granted (*Watson v Daily Record* [1907] 1 KB 853 (CA)). An application for an injunction to restrain a person outside the jurisdiction will not come within this ground: *Amoco (UK) Exploration Co v British American Offshore Ltd* [1999] 2 All ER (Comm) 201, [1999] 2 Lloyd's Rep 772 (HC).

[97] CPR 6.36 and PD6B 3.1(3). Where a claim is made against someone on whom the claim form has been or will be served (other than in reliance on this provision) and: (i) there is a real issue which is reasonable for the court to try; and (ii) the claimant wishes to serve the claim form on another person who is a necessary or proper party to that claim. Generally, any person who may be joined as a party in accordance with the courts general joinder rules is a 'proper' party: *Massey v Heynes* [1881] 21 QBD 330 (CA); *889457 Alberta Inc v Katanga Mining Ltd* [2008] EWHC 2679 (Comm), [2009] 1 BCLC 189, [2008] All ER (D) 61 (Nov) (HC).

[98] CPR 6.36 and PD6B, 3.1(11). This gateway is the obverse of the common law refusal of courts to adjudicate on issues relating to title to foreign land: *British South Africa Co v Companhia de Moçambique* [1893] AC 602; *Deschamps v Miller* [1908] 1 Ch 856; *Hesperides Hotels Ltd v Muftizade* [1979] AC 508, [1978] 2 All ER 1168.

[99] For the earlier rules see RSC Order 11, r 1(g), (h) and (i).

As to its application, it has been said by the High Court that:

> [O]n its proper construction the rule cannot be construed as confined to claims relating to the ownership or possession of property. It extends to any claim for relief (whether for damages or otherwise) so long as it is related to property within the jurisdiction.[100]

Although clearly open to some argument, this gateway is a very helpful one where the relevant object of art or antiquity is physically located in England at the time proceedings are commenced. It must, however, be read subject to the prohibition on enforcement of foreign penal, public or revenue law[101] and the prohibition on enforcement of a foreign confiscation law.[102]

6.21 The Tort Gateway

The tort gateway allows a claim in England where:[103]

– damage was sustained within the jurisdiction; or
– the damage sustained resulted from an act committed within the jurisdiction.

As in the European scheme,[104] 'damage sustained' means the direct damage rather than any reflective or ultimate financial loss felt elsewhere[105] although it is enough that 'significant' damage is suffered in the jurisdiction.[106] A court deciding whether a case comes within this rule must look at the alleged tort in a 'common sense way' and ask whether damage has resulted from 'substantial and efficacious acts committed within the jurisdiction.'[107]

The tort we are principally concerned with here is conversion.[108] It is considered that, as set out above in relation to the European rules,[109] where the conversion takes place is likely to be determined by whether the case is one against the original thief of an item, or against a subsequent possessor whose wrongdoing is a failure to relinquish the object on the demand of the original owner.

6.22 Serious Issue to be Tried and the Court's Discretion

Assuming that a claimant is able to satisfy the English court that it has a 'good arguable case' on one of the above traditional grounds of jurisdiction, the court must still be satisfied of two other general matters. The claimant must demonstrate, first, that the case generally raises a 'serious issue to be tried', and secondly that England is the proper place in which to bring the claim.[110] The first of these issues – although wider than a jurisdictional gateway

[100] *Banca Carige Spa v Banco Nacionale de Cuba* [2001] 2 Lloyd's Rep 147, 157.
[101] See 6.32 and 6.34.
[102] See 6.35.
[103] CPR 6.36 and PD6B, 3.1(9).
[104] See 6.15
[105] *Beecham Group Plc v Norton Healthcare Ltd* [1997] FSR 81; *Bastone & Firminger Ltd v Nasima Enterprises (Nigeria) Ltd* [1996] CLC 1902.
[106] *Metall und Rohstoff AG v Donaldson Lufkin & Jenrette Inc* [1990] 1 QB 391 (CA) 437
[107] ibid.
[108] It is highly likely to be a tort within the meaning of the rule, given that it is most likely that the courts must apply English law to classify the claim for the purposes of determining whether it falls within the rule, as the courts were bound to do under the predecessor tort gateway rule: *Metall und Rohstoff AG v Donaldson Lufkin & Jenrette Inc* [1990] 1 QB 391 (CA) 443. For a discussion of conversion, see 5.02–5.06, 5.09–5.13.
[109] See 6.15.
[110] *Seaconsar Far East Ltd v Bank Markazi Jomhouri Islam Iran* [1994] 1 AC 438; [1993] 4 All ER 456 (HL).

issue – is usually easily satisfied by a claimant.[111] The second, now codified,[112] is the traditional requirement that the claimant bears the burden of persuading the court to exercise its jurisdiction over the defendant, a matter of discretion for the court.

Courts are required to exercise their discretion to exercise jurisdiction based upon a balancing of a number of factors, with the aim of ensuring that each case is brought and pursued by a claimant in the 'natural forum' for the case, whether that is in England or elsewhere. The 'natural forum' is that with which the case has the 'most real and substantial connection' and connecting factors include convenience or expense (witness availability, etc), governing law, the places where the respective parties reside or carry on their business, the nature of the dispute and questions of local knowledge.[113]

It is possible to argue, under English law, that even though a case's most real and substantial connection is with a foreign jurisdiction, justice would not be done in the foreign forum, and that for this reason the English court should exercise its jurisdiction rather than stay the case. This principle has been successfully invoked by reference to the US legal system and costs, on the basis that the claimant's inability to obtain costs before a US court would have prevented that party from obtaining 'justice'.[114]

6.23 Parallel and Related Proceedings in Different Jurisdictions

What is the position if overseas proceedings are commenced before or subsequent to the commencement of English proceedings? Unlike the European rules, under traditional rules, there is no first come, first served prohibition on parallel proceedings. However, if genuine proceedings have already been commenced outside England, the parties already incurred expense and the non-English proceedings have already had some impact on the dispute between the parties (particularly if the impact will continue to have effect) then this will favour a stay of the English proceedings.[115]

The fact that there is no equivalent of the European first come, first served principle means that obtaining and keeping jurisdiction in the English courts is a more nuanced affair under the traditional rules. As a result a defendant to English proceedings has greater opportunities to dispute jurisdiction. Not only can the defendant dispute the fact of jurisdiction but it can also challenge the court's discretionary exercise of jurisdiction and in

[111] The serious issue to be tried must be in respect of each and every alleged cause of action. The test has been equated to the prospects of success required to successfully resist an application under CPR Pt 24 (reverse summary judgment against a claimant), ie a 'real prospect' of succeeding (real meaning better than merely arguable): *De Molestina v Ponton* [2002] 1 All ER (Comm) 587, [2002] 1 Lloyd's Rep 271 (HC); *Swiss Reinsurance v United India* [2002] EWHC 741 (Comm), [2004] ILPr 4 (HC). The test is the same as a 'reasonable prospect of success': *BAS Capital Funding Corp v Medfinco Ltd* [2003] EWHC 1798, [2004] 1 Lloyd's Rep 652 (HC).

[112] CPR 6.37(3).

[113] *Spiliada Maritime Corp v Cansulex Ltd (The Spiliada)* [1987] AC 460, [1986] 3 WLR 972 (HL). With regard to the factor of applicable law, this factor has differing weight according to the circumstances of the case. Factors in favour of an English forum would include the fact that issues of English public policy may be involved, or that the foreign forum may not apply English law despite the existence of a clear choice by the contracting parties that English law should apply. See *Novus Aviation Ltd v Onur Air Tasimacilik AS* [2009] EWCA Civ 122 (CA) 77, 78, in which Lawrence Collins LJ (as he then was) reviewed relevant authorities.

[114] Costs would not be awarded to the claimant if successful: *Roneleigh Ltd v MII Exports Inc* [1989] 1 WLR 619 (CA).

[115] See *The Abidin Daver* [1984] AC 398 (HL); *Cleveland Museum of Art v Capricorn International SA* [1990] 2 Lloyd's Rep 437 (CA); *Meadows Indemnity Co Ltd v Insurance Corp of Ireland Plc* [1989] 2 Lloyd's Rep 298 (CA).

each case the claimant will continue to have the burden of showing that the English court has and should exercise jurisdiction.[116]

6.24 The Return of Cultural Objects Regulations 2004

The English courts have jurisdiction to try a claim under the 2004 Regulations. This jurisdiction is derived from CPR 6.36 together with 6BPD 3.1(20).[117] The latter provides for jurisdiction where a claim is made under an enactment and which is not covered by the other traditional gateways in 6BPD 3.1. The 2004 Regulations are such an enactment.

IV The Applicable Law

6.25 General Principles

This section considers which law will apply to a claim brought before the English courts. Although related to the issue of jurisdiction to try a claim, the issue of what law or laws will apply for the purposes of determining a case must be considered separately from any jurisdiction issue. English private international law determines which laws shall apply to particular aspects of a claim before the English courts. If, however, no point is taken by the party entitled to put (or defend) his case on the basis of a foreign law, English law applies by default,[118] as the English court has no choice but to apply English law.[119]

A claim involving an object of art and antiquity is likely to have a number of international features. An object may, for example, be stolen in Iran, sold by the thief to a dealer in Iran, shipped through a number of countries, sold to a collector in France who makes a gift of the object to a trust which subsequently brings the object to an auction house in and for sale in England. Although an English court may have jurisdiction to try a claim by the original (Iranian) owner of the object, questions about the effect of the sale of the object in Iran and then in France are likely to have to be determined by applying Iranian and French laws.

The 'Rome II Regulation'[120] now applies to the determination of 'non-contractual obligations' in 'civil and commercial matters' and explicitly excludes from its scope 'revenue, customs or administrative matters'.[121] It applies to events which occurred after 20 July 2007.[122]

[116] The advantage of challenging jurisdiction (including the requirement that the claimant show that England is the 'proper place in which to bring the claim' is that the burden then remains on the claimant/applicant: *Carnoustie Universal SA v International Transport Workers' Federation* [2002] EWHC 1624 (Comm), [2002] 2 All ER (Comm) 657 (HC); *ISC Technologies Ltd v James Howard Guerin* [1992] 2 Lloyd's Rep 430 (HC); *Hindocha v Gheewala* [2003] UKPC 77 (PC) (the unanimous judgment of the court commented on this tactical advantage, which the defendant in that case had failed to avail himself of); and *Konkola Copper Mines Plc v Coromin Ltd* [2006] EWCA Civ 5 (CA). If the defendant merely challenges the court's decision to exercise its jurisdiction, then the burden of establishing that England is not the appropriate forum for the case shifts to the defendant.

[117] Practice Direction 6B – Service out of the Jurisdiction.

[118] *Dynamit AG v Rio Tinto Co* [1918] AC 260; *Guarantee Trust Co of New York v Hannay & Co* [1918] 2 KB 623; *Callwood v Callwood* [1960] AC 659.

[119] *Global Multimedia International Ltd v ARA Media Services* [2007] 1 All ER (Comm) 1160 [38].

[120] Regulation (EC) No 864/2007 of the European Parliament and of the Council of 11 July 2007 on the law applicable to non-contractual obligations (Rome II) (OJ L199/40).

[121] For the meaning and scope of this Regulation, reference must be had to the meaning and scope of the same phrases in the Judgments Regulation. See 6.33.

[122] Rome II Regulation, Arts 31 and 32. For the applicable law to tort claims which fall outside the Rome II Regulation, including those based on events before 20 July 2007, see Dicey, Morris & Collins, *The Conflict of Laws*, 14th edn (London, Sweet & Maxwell, 2010).

(Tort) Conversion Claims

6.26 Classification for the Purposes of Determining the Applicable Law

Conversion claims, the main form of claim available before the English courts for the recovery of objects, are, according to English law, classified as torts.[123] Whether they also fall within the scope of the Rome II Regulation is a question ultimately to be determined by the (European) Court of Justice applying a European autonomous meaning.[124] It is considered likely that a conversion claim would be accepted by the ECJ as a 'non-contractual obligation' for the purpose of the Rome II Regulation.

6.27 Applying the Rome II Regulation

The 'general rule' in the Rome II Regulation[125] is worth repeating in full:

1. Unless otherwise provided for the law applicable to a non-contractual obligation arising out of a tort/delict shall be the law of the country in which the damage occurs irrespective of the country in which the event giving rise to the damage occurred and irrespective of the country or countries in which the indirect consequences of that event occur.
2. However, where the person claimed to be liable and the person sustaining damage both have their habitual residence in the same country at the time when the damage occurs, the law of that country shall apply.
3. Where it is clear from all the circumstances of the case that the tort/delict is manifestly more closely connected with a country other than that indicated in paragraphs 1 or 2, the law of that other country shall apply. A manifestly closer connection with another country might be based in particular on a pre-existing relationship between the parties, such as a contract, that is closely connected with the tort/delict in question.

Accordingly, a person wishing to rely on a conversion claim in the English courts should be able to show that it suffered damage in this jurisdiction or that both the claimant and defendant had their 'habitual residence'[126] in this jurisdiction or finally that the tort is manifestly more closely connected with this jurisdiction than the alternatives provided for by paragraphs 1 and 2 of the general rule.

If one takes the example of an object of art or antiquity stolen outside England, the starting point is that the law of the country where the theft took place would apply to determine liability of the alleged thief.[127] If, however, the English courts are asked to determine whether or not a person who has acquired the property from the thief should be liable for wrongfully refusing to hand over an object in this jurisdiction to its original owner, then it is likely that damage will have occurred in this jurisdiction,[128] leading to the application of English law under paragraph 1 above (unless the application of rules 2 or 3 leads to a different result).

[123] See 5.02.

[124] Rome II Regulation, Recital 11.

[125] ibid, Art 4.

[126] Defined by ibid, Art 23.

[127] ibid, Art 24, excludes any application of *renvoi*. Accordingly, even if the application of the private international foreign law of the state in question would lead to a result that another state's law would be applied to the issue of the theft, this would not be permitted. Instead it is the foreign domestic law which must be applied to the alleged theft to determine whether this occurred and its effect on title to the object in question. This is consistent with the common law position in relation to moveables. See 6.29.

[128] *Mazur Media Ltd and another v Mazur Media GmbH and others* [2004] 1 WLR 2966 (Ch) [50].

It is important to note that even though Rome II may apply to determine the law applicable to the wrongdoing itself (and therefore whether or not the English tort of conversion is available as a head of claim), whether or not a claimant has sufficient title to sue in conversion is likely to be determined by reference to private international law relating to property.

Property Title Issues

6.28 Introduction

The distinction between immovable property and moveable property (discussed above)[129] applies here in the context of determining the applicable law to determine title to an object of art or antiquity.

6.29 Immovable Property

It is a fundamental general rule of private international law that issues as to rights in and in relation to the transfer of land must be determined in accordance with the law of the country where that land is situated (the *lex situs*).[130]

6.30 Movable Property

Questions of creation of ownership of tangible movable property and the proprietary effects of all subsequent transfers of that property, whether by way of sale, gift, mortgage or otherwise, are to be determined by the *lex situs* of the property at the relevant time, namely the law of the country where the property was sited at the time of the relevant event.[131] It is the domestic law of that country rather than its private international law which is to be applied.[132] This principle applies even where property has been stolen in one country and sold in another country whose laws give title to an innocent purchaser of the property.[133]

A governmental act of expropriation (compulsory acquisition) from a private owner of property is effective in giving the relevant foreign state title to property and will be recognised and enforced by the English courts as long as the expropriation was valid and effective under the foreign law where the object was situated when the expropriation took effect[134] and the foreign state has taken the property into its possession.[135] The proclaimed

[129] See 6.14.

[130] *Nelson v Bridport* (1846) 8 Beav 547; *Re Duke of Wellington* [1947] Ch 506; affd [1948] Ch 118.

[131] *Cammell v Sewell* (1858) 3 H & N 728, at 744 is considered to be the source of this modern formulation of choice of law rules, which has been the subject of subsequent elaboration by the English courts. See Caruthers, *The Transfer of Property in the Conflict of Laws*, 79–85. For a recent affirmation and application of this principle, see *Islamic Republic of Iran v Barakat Galleries Ltd* [2007] EWCA Civ 1374 [132].

[132] Although the position is not beyond doubt, and the cases rejecting *renvoi* are first instance decisions. They are *Macmillan Inc v Bishopsgate Investment Trust plc (No 3)* [1995] 1 WLR 978 (HC) 1008; *The Islamic Republic of Iran v Berend* [2007] EWHC 132 (QB) [31]; *Blue Sky One Ltd v Mahan Air; PK Airfinance US Inc v Blue Sky Two Ltd* [2010] EWHC 631 (Comm) [157]–[185].

[133] *Winkworth v Christie, Manson & Woods Ltd* [1980] Ch 496, 509 and 512.

[134] *Dicey, Morris & Collins* (14th edn), Rule 128 and the cases cited thereunder. See in particular *Aksionairenoye Obschestvo AM Luther v James Sagor & Co* [1921] 3 KB 532; *Princess Paley Olga v Weisz* [1929] 1 KB 718; and *Williams & Humbert Ltd v W & H Trade Marks (Jersey) Ltd* [1986] AC 368, 431.

[135] *Islamic Republic of Iran v Barakat Galleries Ltd* [2007] EWCA Civ 1374 and the cases cited therein at [143]–[148]. See also 5.06–5.07.

right of any foreign state to interfere with property outside that foreign state is not recognised in English law.[136]

If on the other hand a foreign state's title to an object was not acquired through expropriation from a private owner, the foreign state's right to ownership and possession of the object will not depend on the state actually having taken possession of the object in question.[137] Consequently, a state may sue to recover an object of antiquity which has been illegally excavated and will not necessarily be obliged to show that it once had possession of the object.

V Enforcement Of Foreign Judgments

6.31 European Rules

When enforcing orders for the return of objects of art and antiquity, only the European rules can be used.[138] The Judgments Regulation and Lugano Convention each contain a self-contained regime for the recognition and enforcement of judgments of the courts of other EU Member States. The opportunities to resist enforcement of a judgment are deliberately very limited.[139] Of particular note is that judgments are not recognisable if they contravene the exclusive jurisdiction provisions in relation to immovable land.[140]

VI Prohibition Against Enforcement of Foreign Penal, Public or Revenue Laws

6.32 The General Principle

The English courts will not directly or indirectly permit any claim or enforce any judgment which would amount to the enforcement of foreign penal, revenue or public law (although in this last category, the Court of Appeal has held that there is no rule that all foreign public laws are unenforceable[141]) unless this has been specifically permitted by statute.[142] The lack of jurisdiction on the part of the English courts is said to be the result of the fact that a foreign state has no right to enforce its law outside its own jurisdiction and so the English

[136] *Peer International Corp v Termidor Music Publishers* [2003] EWCA Civ 1156, [2004] Ch 212.

[137] *Islamic Republic of Iran v Barakat Galleries Ltd* [2007] EWCA Civ 1374 [149].

[138] Common law enforcement, enforcement under the Administration of Justice Act 1920 and under the Foreign Judgments (Reciprocal Enforcement) 1933 are not available in respect of judgments for the return of objects as they only permit enforcement of money judgments.

[139] See Arts 34–36 of both the Judgments Regulation and the Lugano Convention.

[140] Art 35(1) of both the Judgments Regulation and the Lugano Convention.

[141] *Government of the Islamic Republic of Iran v The Barakat Galleries Ltd* [2007] EWCA Civ 1374, [2009] QB 22 [125]. For further discussion, particularly on the issue of whether export laws are penal or public laws, see 5.07.

[142] For the English and common law prohibition on enforcement of penal and revenue laws see *Dicey, Morris & Collins* (14th edn), [5-027] to [5-031]. Some doubt had existed as to whether the prohibition included public laws but that is no longer the case. See the Privy Council decision in *The President of the State of Equatorial Guinea and Another v The Royal Bank of Scotland International and Others* [2006] UKPC 7, [2006] 3 LRC 676 and *Mbasogo and another v Logo Ltd and others* [2006] EWCA Civ 1370, [2007] 2 WLR 1062.

courts will not exercise their jurisdiction in aid of such an attempt[143] and that a claim for enforcement is not justiciable in England.[144]

6.33 The Position under the European Rules

The Judgments Regulation[145] and Lugano Convention[146] apply only to 'civil and commercial' judgments; both stipulate that they do not extend to 'revenue, customs or administrative matters'. The ECJ has held that cases involving judgments pursuant to the exercise of public functions by a public authority are outside the scope of their *ratione materiae*.[147] Nor are interim remedies available in such cases under the European scheme.[148]

An action would not fall within the meaning of a civil and commercial matter unless the basis and the detailed rules relating to the bringing of that action are governed by the rules of the ordinary law applicable and available to all persons. By contrast, where the claim in question is founded on legal provisions giving a public body a prerogative of its own not available to ordinary persons, that action cannot be regarded as being brought within the meaning of 'civil and commercial' matter.[149] Although foreign criminal law claims clearly cannot be brought or enforced in the English courts, awards of compensation made within criminal proceedings are permitted.[150] It is considered that orders of restitution of property to victims would also be permitted.

6.34 The Position under the Traditional Rules

Whether or not a claim in fact amounts to the enforcement of foreign penal, revenue or public law is to be determined by the court deciding on the case in question (the *lex forum*).[151]

The English courts examine the substance of what is being claimed, looking beyond the mere form of proceedings themselves but at what is being sought and what would be the substantive result of any judgment and enforcement of that judgment.[152] The crucial question is whether or not the claimant's claim is of a sovereign character or is done by virtue of sovereign authority, and whether it amounts to the exercise of a sovereign right.[153]

143 This was suggested by the editors of the (1987) 11th edition of *Dicey & Morris* (as it was then called), substantially adopted by the House of Lords in *Re State of Norway's Application (Nos 1 and 2)* [1990] 1 AC 723, 808.

144 This term is used throughout the judgement of the Court of Appeal in *Government of the Islamic Republic of Iran v The Barakat Galleries Ltd* [2007] EWCA Civ 1374, [2009] QB 22.

145 See 6.14.

146 See 6.14.

147 Case 814/79 *Netherlands State v Rüffer* [1980] ECR 3807; Case 271/00 *Gemeente Steenbergen v Luc Baten* [2002] ECR I-10527.

148 See the EU Judgments Regulation, Art 31; Lugano Convention, Art 24. In Case C-391/95 *Van Uden Maritime BV, trading as Van Uden Africa Line v Kommanditgesellschaft in Firma Deco-Line* [1998] ECR I-7091, the ECJ held that the lack of jurisdiction to try a substantive cause of action would not affect the ability of the requesting state to assist with provisional or protective measures available under its own national laws, but if a case did not fall within the 'scope ratione materiae' of the Brussels Convention (the predecessor to the EU Judgments Regulation), then the Convention and its provisional and protective measures would not be available.

149 Case 271/00 *Gemeente Steenbergen v Luc Baten* [2002] ECR I-10527 [37].

150 *Sonntag v Waidmann* (Case C-172/91) [1993] ECR I-1963.

151 See the analysis of and cases cited by the Court of Appeal in *Government of the Islamic Republic of Iran v The Barakat Galleries Ltd* [2007] EWCA Civ 1374, [2009] QB 22 [104]–[109] and [119]

152 See *Schemmer v Property Resources Ltd* [1975] 1 Ch 273, 288; *Evans (of Robb Associates) v European Bank Ltd* [2004] NSWCA 82 [89] approved and adopted by the Court of Appeal in *Islamic Republic of Iran v Barakat Galleries Ltd* [2007] EWCA Civ 1374, [2009] QB 22 [124] and [125]; *United States Securities and Exchange Commission v Manterfield* [2009] EWCA Civ 27, [2010] 1 WLR 172 [24].

153 *Mbasogo v Logo Ltd* [2007] QB 846 [50].

In the case of objects of art and antiquity, claims may be made by foreign governments and public authorities as long as, in substance, the claims are based on patrimonial title rights acquired by those governments.[154] In addition, in *Islamic Republic of Iran v Barakat Galleries Ltd*, the Court of Appeal has declared that claims for the return of cultural property should not be prohibited by reason of the prohibition on enforcement of public law:

> In our judgment, there are positive reasons of policy why a claim by a state to recover antiquities which form part of its national heritage and which otherwise complies with the requirements of private international law should not be shut out by the general principle [prohibiting enforcement of foreign public law]. Conversely, in our judgment it is certainly contrary to public policy for such claims to be shut out.[155]

The above decision of course refers to the necessity that a claim must otherwise comply with the requirements of private international law. This means that it must not for example amount to a claim for enforcement of extra-territorial confiscation of an object, which has not yet been reduced into the state's possession.[156]

VII Prohibition Against Enforcement of Foreign Confiscation Laws

6.35 General Principles and their Application

English conflict of laws prohibits the recognition and enforcement of some (but not all) foreign confiscation laws. In *Williams and Humbert Ltd v W & H Trade Marks (Jersey) Ltd*,[157] Nourse J set out a number of propositions,[158] not the subject of argument in the Court of Appeal, which are worth repeating in full:

> I am not concerned with penal or revenue laws simpliciter. I confine myself to expropriatory laws of duly recognised states, principally to confiscatory laws, that is to say, expropriatory laws which do not provide for payment of any or any proper compensation. In this regard the existing authorities appear to me to support the following propositions.
>
> (1A) English law will not recognise foreign confiscatory laws which, by reason of their being discriminatory on grounds of race, religion or the like, constitute so grave an infringement of human rights that they ought not to be recognised as laws at all: see *Oppenheimer* v. *Cattermole* [1976] A.C. 249. These are class I laws.
>
> (1B) English law will not recognise foreign laws which discriminate against nationals of this country in time of war by purporting to confiscate their movable property situated in the foreign state: see *Wolff v. Oxholm* (1817) 6 M. & S. 92; *In re Fried Krupp Actien-Gesellschaft* [1917] 2 Ch. 188 and *In re Claim by Helbert Wagg & Co. Ltd.* [1956] Ch. 323, 345. These are also class I laws.
>
> (2A) English law, while recognising foreign laws not falling within class I which confiscate property situated in the foreign state – see (3) below – will not directly or indirectly enforce them here if they are also penal: see *Banco de Vizcaya v. Don Alfonso de Borbon y Austria* [1935]

[154] See 6.35.
[155] *Islamic Republic of Iran v Barakat Galleries Ltd* [2007] EWCA Civ 1374, [2009] QB 22 [154].
[156] See 6.35.
[157] *Williams and Humbert Ltd v W & H Trade Marks (Jersey) Ltd* [1986] 1 AC 368.
[158] ibid 379.

1 K.B. 140, in some respects a puzzling case which has sometimes been misunderstood. These are class II laws.

(2B) English law will not enforce foreign laws which purport to confiscate property situated in this country: see *Frankfurther v. W. L. Exner Ltd.* [1947] Ch. 629 and *Novello & Co. Ltd.* v. *Hinrichsen Edition Ltd.* [1951] Ch. 595. This can now be seen to be an application of the wider rule that English law will not enforce foreign laws which purport to have extra-territorial effect: see *Bank voor Handel en Scheepvaart N.V.* v. *Slatford* [1953] 1 Q.B. 248. Thus the rule would just as much apply to expropriatory laws which provided for payment of proper compensation: see *Oppenheimer* v. *Cattermole* [1976] A.C. 249, 276, *per* Lord Cross of Chelsea. All these are class II laws, although the first two cases cited might now be decided on the ground that the laws there in question were class I laws falling within category (1A).

(3) English law will recognise foreign laws not falling within class I which confiscate property situated in the foreign state and, where title is perfected there, will enforce its incidents in this country: see P *Aksionairnoye Obschestvo A. M. Luther v. James Sagor & Co.* [1921] 3 K.B. 532; *Princess Paley Olga v. Weisz* [1929] 1 K.B. 718 and *Frankfurther* v. *W. L. Exner Ltd.* [1947] Ch. 629, 644. The nationality of the owner is immaterial: see *In re Claim by Helbert Wagg & Co. Ltd.* [1956] Ch. 323, 348–349.

In the application of these principles, a crucial question is whether a state had some kind of pre-existing proprietary right over the property in question, as distinct from seeking to enforce an order to effect such an outcome. In some English cases the overseas states claimed interest in the property in question has been considered to be effective.[159] In a number of cases, the English courts have refused to enforce foreign states' claims over property forfeited, confiscated, or expropriated at a time when the property was not located within the territory of the foreign state.[160]

If a state can show that it has, by the operation of its law, gained a proprietary right to (even possessory title to) property then, under English principles of conflict of law it would be able to have those rights enforced in England and Wales. As Lord Denning MR said in *Brokaw v Seatrain UK Ltd*[161] (in respect of a US government levy claiming possession of goods on the ground that their owners owed the US government money for revenue due):

If this notice of levy had been effective to reduce the goods into the possession of the United States Government, it would, I think, have been enforced by these courts, because we would then be enforcing an actual possessory title. There would be no need for the United States Government to have recourse to their revenue law. I would apply to this situation some words of the United States Supreme Court in *Compania Espanola de Navegacion Maritima, SA v The Navemar* (1938) 303 U.S. 68, 75 in an analogous case: '. . . since the decree was in invitum, actual possession by some act of physical dominion or control on behalf of the Spanish Government was needful'.

[159] *Princess Paley Olga v Weisz* [1929] 1 KB 718, 725, in which Scrutton LJ said: 'Our Government has recognised the present Russian Government as the de jure Government of Russia, and our courts are bound to give effect to the laws and acts of that Government so far as they relate to property within that jurisdiction when it was affected by those laws and acts'; *Bank voor Handel en Scheepvaart, NV v Administrator of Hungarian Property* [1954] AC 584, [1954] 1 All ER 969; *Williams and Humbert Ltd v W & H Trade Marks (Jersey) Ltd* [1986] AC 368, [1986] 1 All ER 129.

[160] *Don Alonso de Velasco v Corneros* (1611) Hob 212, 2 Brownl 29; *Banco de Vizcaya v Don Alfonso de Borbon y Austria* [1935] 1 KB 140; *King of Italy v de Medici Tornaquinci* (1918) 34 TLR 623; *Brokaw v Seatrain UK Ltd* [1971] 2 QB 476; *A-G of New Zealand v Ortiz* [1984] AC 1, [1983] 2 All ER 93; *Government of the Islamic Republic of Iran v Barakat Galleries Ltd* [2007] EWHC 705 (QB).

[161] *Brokaw v Seatrain UK Ltd* [1971] 2 QB 476, 482.

The timing of any expropriation or forfeiture and the establishment of a state's proprietary right to an object will often be an important issue. The case of *Attorney-General of New Zealand v Ortiz*, heard by both the Court of Appeal and House of Lords, concerned the prohibition against enforcement of foreign confiscation laws over property outside the confiscating country. The case concerned a claim by the state of New Zealand that an unlawfully exported rare artifact was deemed forfeited to the New Zealand government at the time of its unlawful exportation, even before the New Zealand authorities became aware of this unlawful act. In the Court of Appeal proceedings,[162] Lord Denning MR examined a number of statutory forfeiture provisions and English cases concerning those provisions. He concluded:[163]

> So far as England is concerned, whenever there is legislation providing that goods are to be forfeited for one cause or another, the law has always said that the forfeiture does not take effect until the goods are seized and that the title then relates back to the cause of forfeiture. If the owner or anyone else disputes the forfeiture, there are proceedings for condemnation. After condemnation, the title is perfected and can no longer be disputed by anyone.

The House of Lords made the same finding. Lord Brightman found:[164]

- Forfeiture depended on a finding under New Zealand law that the article was 'knowingly' unlawfully exported.
- It also depended on actual seizure by the New Zealand authorities and could not take place before such seizure had taken place, following which the forfeiture would be deemed to have taken place at the time of the unlawful export.
- If so forfeited, the article would be forfeited *in rem*.
- The forfeiture would amount to a 'penalty'.
- Accordingly, the New Zealand law rendered unlawfully exported articles 'liable to forfeiture' rather than automatically forfeited at the time of the unlawful forfeiture.

Lord Brightman went on to identify a method by which a state could circumvent the kinds of arguments against it in *Attorney-General of New Zealand v Ortiz*: 'I am disposed to agree, that the recovery of unlawfully exported historic articles would be best ensured if title thereto were to vest in the Crown independently of seizure.'[165]

VIII Provisional Measures in Support of Domestic and Foreign Claims

6.36 Introduction

The English courts have the power to grant interim relief in support of domestic claims brought before them. They may also grant interim relief in support of any foreign claims, whether these are proceedings under the Judgments Regulation or the Lugano Convention[166]

[162] *A-G of New Zealand v Ortiz* [1982] 3 All ER 432.
[163] ibid, 452.
[164] *A-G of New Zealand v Ortiz* [1984] 1 AC 1, 48–49, [1983] 2 All ER 93.
[165] ibid, 49.
[166] Civil Jurisdiction and Judgments Act 1982, s 25(1).

or otherwise,[167] including in relation to proceedings which fall outside the scope of the Judgments Regulation or Lugano Convention.[168]

6.37 Search Orders and Interim Delivery-Up Orders

The following criteria must be established by an applicant for a search order in respect of premises.[169]

– First, there must be an extremely strong prima facie case.
– Secondly, the damage, potential or actual, must be very serious for the applicant.
– Thirdly, there must be clear evidence that the defendants have in their possession incriminating documents or things, and that there is a real possibility that they may destroy such material before any application on notice can be made.

The court may also order that an object which is the subject of a claim should be delivered-up by the person holding it so that it can be safely detained and preserved pending the determination of the claim.[170]

Practice Direction 25A to Part 25 of the CPR contains a specimen form of search order. It contains terms for the search for delivery-up and detention of items.

6.38 Proprietary Injunctions, Freezing and Management Receivership Orders

An injunction can be obtained to prohibit a defendant from disposing of or dealing with an object which is the subject of a proprietary claim.[171] Given that a conversion claim can (and in the case of art and antiquities) if successful would usually involve an order for delivery-up of the object in question, the court has, it is considered, jurisdiction to order a proprietary injunction in respect of the object the subject matter of a claim.

Even if not the subject of a proprietary claim, an object can also be made the subject of a freezing order prohibiting its holder from dealing with or disposing of the object[172] if the claimant has a good arguable case that he will succeed in his claim[173] and there is a real risk that without the freezing order his judgment would go unsatisfied.[174]

Lastly, the court has the power to appoint a receiver over an object to manage that object pending the resolution of the claim over the object.[175] They should in general be appointed only when a freezing order would provide insufficient protection,[176] which is likely to be the

[167] Civil Jurisdiction and Judgments Act 1982 (Interim Relief) Order, para 2(a).

[168] ibid, para 2(a). See generally S Gee QC, *Commercial Injunctions*, 5th edn (London, Sweet & Maxwell, 2004) and P Magrath, *Commercial Fraud in Civil Practice* (Oxford, Oxford University Press, 2008).

[169] The statutory jurisdictional basis for a search order is s 7 of the Civil Procedure Act 1997 and CPR 25.1(1)(h). The core principles applied by a court when deciding whether or not to grant such an order remain those set out in *Anton Piller KG v Manufacturing Processes* [1976] Ch 55, 62A-B and are the first to third principles set out in paragraph 6.37 above. The fourth principle is derived from *Lock International Plc v Beswick* [1989] 1 WLR 1268. All principles are summarised in *Indicii Salus Ltd (in receivership) v Chandrasekaran* [2007] EWHC 406 (Ch) [11] and are discussed in McGrath, *Commercial Fraud in Civil Practice*, 575.

[170] CPR 25.1(1)(c)(i).

[171] *Bankers Trust Co v Shapira* [1980] 1 WLR 1274, 1280H–1281D.

[172] s 37(1) of the Senior Courts Act 1981; CPR 25.1(1)(f).

[173] *Rasu Maritima SA v Perusahaan* [1978] QB 644.

[174] *Nimenia Maritime Corporation v Trave Schiffahrtgesellschaft mbH und Co KG* [1983] 1 WLR 1412, 1422E-H (CA).

[175] s 37(1) Senior Courts Act 1981; CPR 69.2(1)(b); *Derby & Co Ltd and Others v Weldon and Others (Nos 3 and 4)* [1990] 1 Ch 65.

[176] *Don King Productions Inc v Warren and Others* [1999] 2 Lloyd's Rep 392 (ChD) 400, Col 1.

case is the holder of the object in question cannot be trusted to comply with a freezing order or cannot be trusted to properly care for the object.

6.39 Enforcement of Foreign Provisional Measures

Interim judgements, including provisional measures, of the courts of the European countries subject to the Judgments Regulation[177] or Lugano Convention[178] may be enforced in England.[179] However, a provisional measure can only be enforced if it was ordered on notice to the respondent concerned and a without notice order cannot be enforced.[180]

177 See 6.12.

178 See 6.12.

179 The enforcement provisions in Ch III of the Judgments Regulation and Title III of the Lugano Convention do not distinguish between final and provisional orders. In the case of the Judgments Regulation on this point see *de Cavel v de Cavel* (Case 143/78) [1979] ECR 1055 [8]–[9].

180 *Denilauler v Snr Couchet Frères* [1980] ECR 1533 [18].

7

Conclusions: Identification, Ownership and Changing Market Norms

JANET ULPH

I Introduction

7.01 Challenges

Cultural objects deserve special protection because of the information which they contain and the sense of belonging which they may create. Yet the illicit trade in cultural objects is rooted in damage and destruction. Works of art are stolen each year and, even if some are eventually recovered, many will have disappeared either into private collections or, even worse, will have been abandoned because they are too well known to be sellable. When objects of antiquity are looted, valuable insights into our past are lost for ever. The profits generated from the unlawful removal and sale of these objects may well become a revenue stream for other criminal activity. In Iraq, after the invasion in 2003, it was not uncommon to find that smugglers and terrorists were involved in both taking ancient tablets and figurines out of the country and importing weapons, such as rocket propelled grenades, into the country.[1]

One of the biggest challenges is combatting opportunism. International gangs will often exploit a breakdown in social order in vulnerable states. Some local people may also be tempted to make money by stealing from museum collections or looting objects of antiquity from archaeological sites. This occurred in Afghanistan (1994–2001), in Iraq (2003), and in Egypt (2011). However, it is estimated that it is the middlemen who take 98 per cent of the profits from the final market price,[2] and yet will not have the spectre of starvation to explain their conduct.

The route along which looted items are taken will depend upon market demand for particular types of object and their original location. Transit countries, such as Lebanon and Jordan, may be chosen because they are thought to have relatively low levels of security, before arriving at a free port such as Dubai or Geneva. Looted objects may then be passed between dealers before being purchased by private collectors. If one of these dealers has created fake provenance documents, the collector may act in good faith in making the acquisition. There is therefore no simple solution to tackling this trade because it is global in character.

[1] M Bogdanos, 'Illegal antiquities trade funds terrorism' CNN World (7 July 2011).

[2] UNESCO, Information Kit, *The Fight Against the Illicit Trafficking of Cultural Objects, The 1970 Convention: Past, Present and Future* (2011) CLT/2011/CONF.207/6.

As the UK has a thriving market in art and antiquities, it might be thought that its laws would need to be enhanced even further to ensure that the trade in illicit material is repressed as far as possible. There is no doubt that it would be beneficial if the UK Government were to ratify the UNIDROIT Convention on Stolen or Illegally Exported Cultural Objects 1995 (the UNIDROIT Convention) and the Convention for the Protection of Cultural Property in the Event of Armed Conflict 1954 (the Hague Convention).[3] However, apart from any legislation needed to implement these conventions, UK laws appear to be robust.[4] What is needed is greater practical support for the laws which already exist. Indeed, the Preamble to the UNIDROIT Convention acknowledges that the Convention should be accompanied by other effective measures for the protection of cultural objects, 'such as the development and use of registers, the physical protection of archaeological sites and technical co-operation.'

The law cannot be viewed in isolation. To prevent the plunder of antiquities from vulnerable countries, and to deter the theft of cultural property, a number of different strategies are needed. All of these measures require global co-operation because international criminal gangs will inevitably take advantage of jurisdictional disparities. There are practical steps which can be taken to support the law, particularly in relation to identifying objects, establishing ownership and changing market norms. These issues and possible solutions are explored in this concluding chapter.

II Identification

7.02 Identification

A major reason why an owner may not be able to recover cultural property which has been taken from him is that he may not be able to identify it with sufficient confidence according to the civil law standard of the balance of probabilities. A stolen object may be disguised, or repaired, or accidentally damaged. In a civil action, the defendant may argue that the object is similar but not the same as the one which the claimant has lost.[5] Consequently, apart from taking appropriate security measures, owners should always record details of their property.

If the owner can identify his property, it will make the task of the prosecutor considerably easier. In order to secure a conviction for theft or handling stolen goods, the prosecutor must establish beyond reasonable doubt that that a particular object belonged to another. In order to prosecute for a money laundering offence, evidence must exist that the accused has dealt with property which represents the proceeds of crime. The police do not have

[3] See the *Illicit Trade in Cultural Objects,* Report of the Ministerial Advisory Panel, London, December 2000 (hereafter ITAP Report), The ITAP Report had recommended that the UK Government should give serious consideration to accession to the Hague Convention and the Second Protocol [41], fn 18. Although the Report did not recommend accession to the UNIDROIT Convention, this appeared to stem from a misunderstanding about what the drafters intended; see 2.30, 5.50.

[4] Although the Scottish Parliament did not enact the equivalent to the Dealing in Cultural Objects (Offences) Act 2003, the Proceeds of Crime Act 2002 does apply in Scotland and may well be sufficient to deal with any cases involving the illicit import of cultural property.

[5] See the defendant's unsuccessful argument to that effect in *Nicole de Préval v Adrian Alan Ltd* (24 January 1997).

infinite resources or manpower and the more information which is available, the more likely it will be that charges will be brought successfully.

7.03 Object ID

Enforcement authorities, museums, and other public bodies in every country are encouraged to use the Object ID system. This was created under the leadership of the Getty Information Institute, and is concerned with standardising the descriptive information relating to a cultural object. The Council for the Protection of Art Theft (CoPAT) has also been involved with this system from an early stage; details of Object ID can be found on its website. One great advantage of Object ID is that it largely solves the problems associated with the mismatch between police reports and information supplied by museums. If an item is stolen from a museum, the information supplied will focus upon the title of the work and its creator; in contrast, police reports have a tendency to provide a simplistic description of what the object looks like.[6] Another virtue of Object ID is that it prompts the supply of a minimum standard of information, such as details about the material from which an object has been created.

7.04 Databases Identifying Objects

Electronic databases are a valuable weapon against the illicit trade in cultural property because they restrict a criminal's access to the legitimate market. They may act as a deterrent. Thieves normally wish to dispose of stolen items quickly. If they are aware that details, including photographs, of cultural objects are likely to have been registered on a database, and that an auction house or potential buyer may carry out checks, they will be less likely to steal such objects. Yet, where a thief steals a cultural object on the spur of the moment, its registration on an electronic database to which the public have ready access may mean that the thief will keep the object hidden for many years. There is therefore much to be said for having a system where people are required to formally register before they can carry out a search.

Ideally, there should be one database detailing all unlawfully removed cultural objects from any place in the world, whether in the UK or overseas, which enforcement authorities, auction houses, dealers, insurers and acquirers could search. This is precisely what was recommended by the Ministerial Advisory Panel.[7] It was suggested that this database should be run by a government department.[8] The Panel proposed that access to the database would be regulated by means of a system of security codes: the amount of information supplied in response to an enquiry would vary according to whether, for example, the search was being carried out by a private individual or an enforcement authority.[9] The Panel also considered the conundrum of identifying buried objects. No photograph or other record would exist before their unlawful removal. However, the Panel suggested that a system of classification could be created instead.[10] This recommendation is workable. For example, a database could provide details (such as size, material, identifying features) of objects which are

[6] See K Hamma, 'Finding Cultural Property Online' (2001) 19 *Cardozo Arts & Entertainments Law Journal* 125, 130–31.

[7] Report of the Ministerial Advisory Panel on Illicit Trade, December 2000 [90].

[8] ibid, [94].

[9] ibid, [95].

[10] ibid, [92].

typically looted and could specify the source countries: this information would assist purchasers by putting them on their guard so that they checked the provenance of such objects with particular care. At present, the most useful guide is ICOM's Emergency Red List, which classifies endangered cultural objects in the most vulnerable areas of the world.[11] Rapley has observed that this resource is invaluable because it provides a 'simplistic, generic guide to the sort of objects of which law enforcement officers should be suspicious'.[12]

The Ministerial Advisory Panel emphasised in its Progress Report of 2001 that its recommendations in relation to a database of unlawfully removed cultural property, together with a database of relevant cultural property legislation, were of the utmost importance. The authority and viability of the UK Government's accession to the UNESCO Convention and the Dealing in Cultural Objects (Offences) Act 2003 were seen as resting on effective access to information via these two databases.[13] It was also recommended that information relating to all thefts of cultural property reported to the police should be included on the database of unlawfully removed cultural property.[14] Disappointingly, these recommendations have not borne fruit. Part of the problem has been that the police have wanted a database for their purposes which would be separate from any database used by the art trade and collectors.[15] The current position is that there are a number of different databases in existence. Furthermore, as discussed in Chapter 5, English courts have been slow to accept that dealers, auctioneers and collectors should routinely check them before acquiring a cultural object.[16]

The Art Loss Register is a significant international database of lost and stolen works of art, antiques, and other cultural items. It was created in 1991 by a private consortium of auction houses, insurers, art trade associations and the International Foundation of Art Research. It is essentially a commercial concern: charges are levied if an object is registered or a search is made; it may be agreed that a commission will be paid to the Art Loss Register if it recovers a stolen item. These charges help to meet the running costs of the Art Loss Register. As it is not possible to search the database before registering, this significantly reduces the risk of thieves and their accessories accessing the database. It has been instrumental in the recovery of numerous items worth millions of pounds.[17] It has played an important role in assisting Jewish families to recover works of art which had been misappropriated during the Nazi era.

The Art Loss Register recently merged with Trace in order to consolidate the two databases into one. The aim of the merger was to create a central database where victims of theft and insurers could register their loss. Auction houses and dealers would be expected

[11] See http://icom.museum/redlist. The Oriental Institute of the University of Chicago has published details of objects missing from the National Museum of Iraq: www-oi.uchicago.edu/OI/IRAQ/categories.htm.

[12] V Rapley, 'The Metropolitan Police's Art and Antiques Unit' in P Stone and J Farchakh Bajjaly (eds), *The Destruction of Cultural Heritage in Iraq* (Woodbridge, The Boydell Press, 2008) 61.

[13] Ministerial Advisory Panel on the Illicit Trade in Cultural Objects, Progress Report 2001, chaired by Norman Palmer, [40]. For further discussion, see GM Prescott, 'Much Ado About Cultural Object Databases' (2005) X(2) *Art Antiquity and Law* 371.

[14] ibid, [74], [91].

[15] Select Committee of Culture Media and Sport, First Report of 2003–2004, *Cultural objects: developments since 2000,* [33]. www.publications.parliament.uk/pa/cm200304/cmselect/cmcumeds/59/5905.htm.

[16] There is no positive duty on a bailee, such as an auction house, to investigate its bailor's title: *Marcq v Christie Manson & Woods Ltd* [2003] EWCA Civ 731, [2004] QB 286 (CA), discussed at 5.10. See further, F Meisel, 'Return is no Conversion' (2004) *Conveyancer and Property Lawyer* 145.

[17] See, for example, Julian Radcliffe's role in the recovery of a valuable Cézanne painting: *Bakwin v Sotheby's* (22 November 2005); AH Hudson, 'Duress, Arbitration and Contractual Illegality' (2006) XI(3) *Art Antiquity and Law* 297.

to check the Register before they could say that they had acted with due diligence, in order to avoid criminal charges or a civil suit. However, those administering the Art Loss Register – like the Interpol database, discussed below – are heavily dependent upon being supplied with information about stolen items. If they have not been notified that something is stolen – perhaps because it was taken hundreds of years ago – its due diligence check on behalf of a seller or intermediary will not reveal anything untoward.[18]

Enforcement authorities may also have databases. In the UK, the only specialist law enforcement agency dealing with the illicit trade in cultural property is the Metropolitan Police's Art and Antiques Unit at Scotland Yard. It is a small unit, and the few staff employed cannot necessarily devote all of their time to working with this unit.[19] However, it does have a database (the London Stolen Arts Database), which currently stores approximately 54,000 images of stolen cultural objects. Other countries, such as Italy and France, also have specialist forces with their own databases.

Interpol has a database and it draws its information from national Interpol bureaux and UNESCO. In 2009, it put its stolen art database online and allowed the public access to it. A meeting of experts of Interpol in April 2011 encouraged Member States to ensure that they provided information to the database.[20] It was estimated in October 2011 that Interpol's database on stolen works of art contained approximately 38,000 records contributed by 123 countries.[21]

Of all the reforms which could be made to combat the illicit trade, the most effective would be in relation to databases. It is vital to establish a norm throughout the world that no one can claim to be acting in 'good faith' in relation to a purchase of a cultural object if they have not searched relevant databases. Unfortunately, the current situation is complex, with too many databases. There have been calls for a single online portal, available globally, for linked access to databases which contained information about objects which had been stolen or misappropriated from around the world, together with databases which detailed relevant legislation and national inventories of cultural property.[22] This would be the best solution. If a number of databases exist, there needs to be an effective exchange of information between them. Victims of art thefts will in all probability report their loss to the police, and insurers should contact the Art Loss Register. What is needed is a system which guarantees that information on art theft is transferred between the various databases so that they are all kept up to date and correlate with each other.

[18] See, for example, the claim in November 2011 by the French Government to a Nicolas Tournier painting which was allegedly stolen in 1818; this painting had been sold in 2010 and 2011 at the European Fine Art Fair in Maastricht after due diligence checks with the Art Loss Register.

[19] See V Rapley, 'The Metropolitan Police's Art and Antiques Unit' in P Stone and J Farchakh Bajjaly (eds), *The Destruction of Cultural Heritage in Iraq* (Woodbridge, The Boydell Press, 2008) 55.

[20] Eighth Meeting of the INTERPOL Expert Group (IEG) on Stolen Cultural Property, Lyons, 5–6 April 2011.

[21] See the INTERPOL press release of 22 October 2011: http://interpolnoticeremoval.com/tag/interpol%E2%80%99s-stolen-works-of-art-database/.

[22] See *Protection Against Trafficking in Cultural Property* UNODC/CCPCJ/EG.1/2009/CRP.1 [44].

III Ownership

7.05 Defining Cultural Property

It is common for countries to have legislation in place to protect cultural property and to regulate its transfer. The details of domestic legislation will vary according to the history, economy and social context of each country. A particular problem is defining the property which deserves special protection because of its intrinsic value. There are some who might argue that the list provided in the UNESCO Convention does not go far enough because, although its list is extensive, it is confined by the fact that the objects must be of importance and must have been classified as such by the government.[23] There is no doubt that there will be items which are seen as significant by a particular interest group or community, but which fall outside the scope of the Convention.

Yet the definition of cultural property in the UNESCO Convention appears broad in comparison with English law, where there is considerable variation on this issue. Great care must be taken to examine a particular legislative measure to determine its reach. For example, the scope of the Return of Cultural Objects Regulations 1994 is confined to the objects listed in Directive 93/7/EEC.[24] This list could be described as unsatisfactory in allowing the financial value of certain types of object to be a key criterion in determining whether they receive protection or not. As regards the criminal law, the Dealing in Cultural Objects (Offences) Act 2003 is narrower still in excluding fine art entirely. However, the main civil law mechanism for obtaining the return of tangible property is conversion, which is not limited in its scope to particular types of cultural item; equally, in the criminal law, the offences of handling stolen goods and money laundering will apply to any type of item.

7.06 Clarifying Ownership

In order to deter the illicit trade in cultural property, all states should have laws which expressly identify the owner of unexcavated antiquities. Without such laws, it may be extremely difficult for any government to recover objects which are seen as part of its national heritage. It may also be impossible to prosecute those who have misappropriated or handled antiquities which have been removed from the state in which they were located. The law in the UK satisfies these requirements. Under the Treasure Act 1996,[25] the UK Government requires finders to report their finds, but they are rewarded if the Government elects to take over the object as a treasure for the benefit of a national museum.[26] As the illicit trade in cultural property presents global challenges, other countries also need to have laws in place dealing with ownership, so that criminals cannot target vulnerable countries which are rich in cultural items, taking advantage of any uncertainties in the laws.

[23] See 2.14.

[24] The list in Directive 93/7/EEC is set out in the Annex to this text.

[25] For discussion of the Treasure Act 1996, see 3.13.

[26] JM Podesta, 'Saving Culture, but Passing the Buck: How the UNESCO Convention Undermines its Goals by Unduly Targeting Market Nations' (2008) 16 *Cardozo Journal of International and Comparative Law* 457, 458–59.

7.07 The Scope of Domestic Legislation: Export Embargoes

The UNESCO handbook on *Legal and Practical Measures Against Illicit Trafficking in Cultural Property* suggests that, apart from regulating ownership, a legal regime should be established in each country which would provide answers to issues such as:

(i) what categories of cultural objects can be traded (if any), and whether a preliminary authorization by national authorities (Ministry of Culture etc.) is required; and
(ii) what categories of cultural objects may leave and/or enter the national territory, as well as the conditions (authorization, purpose, storage conditions, insurance, etc.) and the time period (temporary or permanent export or import) under which this may take place.

Import and export laws may be controversial. Some governments have passed wide-ranging laws which not only claim ownership of buried cultural items, but also place a complete embargo upon their export and provide that no one can ever obtain a good title to them. These sweeping laws have attracted fierce criticism from those who favour a free international market in cultural property; in turn, they have been defended by those who argue that cultural objects should be returned to their source nations.[27] This division of opinion has led to further discussion of what constitutes a 'source' nation, as many buried antiquities may have little connection with modern states. It is questioned whether any government should have the right to claim ownership of objects based upon modern geographical boundaries. Some argue that these objects should belong to the world.[28]

One difficulty with creating laws which impose an embargo on the export of a wide range of cultural items is that the state may not have the resources to guard and pay for the preservation of these objects. It may also prove impossible to police such an embargo effectively. There will no doubt be objects in circulation before the embargo was imposed, and it may be impossible to say whether the object was exported before the embargo or not. Podesta has criticised source nations which enact laws which impose severe restrictions on exporting such property and has suggested that:

> As many source countries do not have the resources to prevent the occurrence of these exchanges, either by offering market value for the item or by effectively policing underground art smuggling rings, they turn to the few market countries to essentially do their work for them. Instead of targeting those who neglect to report their cultural discoveries and those who illegally ship them to other countries, source countries simply wait for those possibly innocent *buyers* to be punished in another country.[29]

Bator has expressed concern that wide-ranging embargoes may have the unfortunate effect of fuelling demand by collectors for a particular type of object, thereby pushing up the price and ensuring a thriving black market for the benefit of criminals.[30] However, these arguments all relate to the content of the law and focus upon the links between culture, communities and humankind. The basic proposition in the UNESCO handbook that legislators should strive for clarity in drafting legal principles is not contentious in itself.

[27] P Gerstenblith, 'Controlling the International Market in Antiquities: Reducing the Harm, Preserving the Past' (2007) 8 *Chicago Journal of International Law* 169, 174, fn 14. See also JH Merryman, 'The Free International Movement of Cultural Property' (1998) 31 *NYU Journal of International Law and Politics* 1, 4.

[28] See the contributions of writers in J Cuno (ed), *Whose Culture? The Promise of Museums and the Debate over Antiquities* (Princeton NJ, Princeton University Press, 2009).

[29] JM Podesta, 'Saving Culture, but Passing the Buck: How the UNESCO Convention Undermines its Goals by Unduly Targeting Market Nations' (2008) 16 *Cardozo Journal of International and Competition Law* 457, 463.

[30] PM Bator, 'An Essay on the International Trade in Art' (1982) 34 *Stanford Law Review* 275, 315, 318.

7.08 Database of Cultural Property Laws

One of the difficulties in prosecuting a dealer for handling stolen goods or other offences is proving that the object in question was removed without the permission of its owner. In relation to antiquities, it may be vital to determine the precise date when a patrimonial law came into force in order to determine whether a government can recover an antiquity which has been exported abroad. The laws of a particular country may well have changed over the years, from a situation where finders obtained title to buried antiquities, to one where these are deemed to belong to the state.[31] The laws of each country will vary on this matter.[32]

Information relating to dates when legislation entered into force is important to those wishing to carry out due diligence checks on an object of antiquity. For example, a purchaser of an Egyptian artefact should know that the date of the Egyptian patrimonial law vesting ownership in the state was 1971. However, it is also important for prosecutors wishing to prove the relevant state of mind of a person charged with handling stolen goods. If, for example, it can be shown that any dealer in Egyptian objects would know the date of the patrimonial law, it may be easier to prove that a dealer has acted dishonestly in handling a recently excavated antiquity.

Any database containing laws relating to cultural property is likely to be imperfect because the domestic laws of each country will vary in terms of their scope. The database will be at its best in storing information about legislation with a narrow focus upon, for example, objects of antiquity illegally removed from one or more designated countries. But there will be some laws relating to portable property in general which may be relevant and which may be more problematic to record. Even so, the recommendation by the Ministerial Advisory Panel that there should be 'a comprehensive and universally accessible database of international legislative information' was eminently sound.[33] It was proposed that the database should include not only past and present legislation, but also judicial decisions. Although this recommendation was not taken forward by the Government, the United Nations launched an international database in 2005 and invited governments to provide electronic copies of their cultural legislation.[34] This is a welcome initiative which will aid prosecutions of dealers. There may still be evidential difficulties, however. For example, enforcement authorities will need to prove that a particular object of antiquity was unlawfully excavated after the patrimonial law was brought into force.

7.09 Limitation Periods and an International Tribunal

When works of art are stolen, they may remain hidden for many years. Wrongdoers hope that they will be forgotten. In the meantime, these works may be stored in a bank vault, or used by crooks as security for debts owed to other criminals. It is so well known that dealers in art and also antiquities may keep them in storage for long periods that it should be obvious that every country should restrict the protection offered to good faith purchasers of cultural items: limitation periods should be lengthy. Yet this issue is contentious, and

[31] In relation to Iraq and the story of how a change in the law led to the magnificent collection of artefacts in its national museum, see L Al-Gailani Werr, 'The Story of the Iraq Museum' in P Stone and J Farchakh Bajjaly (eds), *The Destruction of Cultural Heritage in Iraq* (Woodbridge, The Boydell Press, 2008) 25.

[32] In relation to the changes in domestic law in Iran, see *Government of the Islamic Republic of Iran v The Barakat Galleries Ltd* [2007] EWCA Civ 1374, [2009] QB 22 (CA).

[33] Report of the Ministerial Advisory Panel on Illicit Trade, December 2000, [89].

[34] www.unesco.org/culture/natlaws.

domestic laws on limitation periods are likely to have been created in response to a particular social, economic and historical context. As a result, governments have been slow to ratify the UNIDROIT Convention. Yet the current position, where the domestic law relating to limitation periods varies from country to country, is chaotic and can produce injustice.[35]

It is in these circumstances that the question of whether domestic courts, which are hamstrung by their laws relating to limitation periods, are the best forum for settling disputes in relation to the recovery of cultural property. Tompkins has called for an international tribunal to decide art-related disputes.[36] This is a controversial proposal, because there is a risk that some governments will make wide-ranging claims to objects in other countries where the links are quite tenuous; much would depend upon the composition of the tribunal as to whether such claims would be successful. However, Tompkins envisages that the tribunal will act as a forum for mediation, rather than imposing a decision upon the parties. This proposal is therefore worthy of consideration, as civil litigation is expensive and time-consuming and a claimant cannot necessarily be confident about recovery. It might be useful in dealing with claims related to Nazi-confiscated and looted art, wherever it may be located.[37] The creation of such a tribunal would immediately depress prices for looted items from Iraq and other countries and would act as a deterrent. No collector would be willing to pay substantial amounts of money for an item which, however long he stores it, is at risk of being reclaimed once it is sent for auction. In short, if one can create a situation where collectors cannot easily acquire title in a work of art or antiquity which has been unlawfully removed, intermediaries will be less interested in dealing with these items. Unfortunately, these sorts of people may then be tempted to deal in other illicit material, such as drugs. This is precisely why governments need flexible laws to deal with all types of economic crime, including trafficking in drugs, cultural items or weapons.

IV Money Laundering Measures

7.10 A Culture of Secrecy

A market culture of secrecy and intimacy has helped to support the trade in illicit material.[38] However, in the UK, since 2003, Money Laundering Regulations have chipped away at this norm by requiring 'high value' dealers and auctioneers to carry out checks on the identity of their customers, to establish a written trail in relation to transactions, and to notify

[35] See eg, *Winkworth v Christie, Manson and Woods Ltd* [1980] Ch 496, discussed at 5.48 and 6.30. For general discussion, see P Reyhan, 'A Chaotic Palette: Conflict of Laws in Litigation between Original Owners and Good-Faith Purchasers of Stolen Art' (2001) *Duke Law Journal* 955; MI Turner, 'The Innocent Buyer of Art Looted During World War II' (1995) 32(5) *Vanderbilt Journal of Transnational Law* 1511.

[36] A Tompkins J, 'A Permanent International Art Crime Tribunal?' (2009) 2(1) *The Journal of Art Crime* 35. Tompkins J suggests that it should extend to all 'stolen, looted, or misappropriated works of art, and items of cultural, heritage or historical significance': ibid, 38. The proposed tribunal could be supported by the Intergovernmental Committee for Promoting the Return of Cultural Property to its Countries of Origin or its Restitution in Case of Illicit Appropriation: see Meeting of the Expert Group on Protection Against Trafficking in Cultural Property, 2009, UNODC/CCPCJ/EG1/2009/CRP1, [42].

[37] The Spoliation Advisory Panel deals with claims to spoliated art which is now part of national collections in the UK.

[38] *Rachmaninoff v Sotheby's and Eva Teranyi* [2005] EWHC 258 [35].

the authorities when appropriate of any issues which arouse suspicion.[39] The offences created by these Regulations mesh with the provisions of the Proceeds of Crime Act 2002, which provide that high value dealers and auction houses will commit an offence if they negligently fail to report suspicious transactions.[40] Money laundering measures fit with the digital age: the secretive manner in which dealers and auction houses have traditionally operated seems antiquated in a world where so much information is readily available.

7.11 Analysing the Impact of Money Laundering Measures

The Proceeds of Crime Act creates money laundering offences which are wide in scope and which catch those dealing with property knowing or suspecting that it represents the proceeds of crime.[41] There is no need to prove dishonesty and there is no need to prove that the objects were stolen. It is enough to show that the accused was involved in dealing either with assets obtained by criminal activity or assets with which they had been exchanged. Those who become involved in hurried purchases for large sums of cash therefore risk prosecution. Furthermore, if they are convicted, they may be bankrupted as a result of a confiscation order: this is a personal debt which becomes payable to the state and which reflects the value of the criminal assets which they have received.[42]

The provenance of an object has become important due to money laundering measures. Along with revenue laws, they help to satisfy the expectation in Article 10 of the UNESCO Convention that signatory states should monitor the movement of cultural property which has been illegally removed from another signatory state and should impose obligations upon 'antique' dealers to maintain a register which records 'the origin of each item of cultural property, names and addresses of the supplier, description and price of each item sold'. Unfortunately, it would be naïve to assume that these measures have had the effect of severely curbing the trade either in stolen cultural objects or forgeries. This is because criminals have responded to the changes in industry practice by creating false documents relating to provenance.

Money laundering measures cannot be presented as a panacea for all problems. Evidence of an underlying crime will need to be detected. In an area as complex as cultural property, the enforcement agencies may legitimately conclude that there is insufficient evidence to warrant either a criminal prosecution or a civil action to recover the property for the benefit of the state. The result may be that if, for example, employees of a university take possession of a cultural object for the purposes of restoration or research and becomes doubtful of its provenance, they may face a dilemma. They should file a suspicious activity report with the Serious Organised Crime Agency (or, its expected replacement, the National Crime Agency) of course. But SOCA may be disinclined to take the matter further, unless there is compelling evidence. In this example, the employees cannot retain the object indefinitely because their employing university would be sued for conversion; sadly, despite legitimate suspicions, they may have no option but to return the object to the client. The burden would then be on the source state to seek to recover it.

There has been no prosecution of an auction house or art dealer for money laundering in the UK so far. However, it would be a mistake to assume that this state of affairs is likely

[39] See 3.45.

[40] See 3.44.

[41] See 3.34–3.41. For the definition of proceeds of crime, see the Proceeds of Crime Act 2002, s 340(3); see also 3.35.

[42] See 4.14–4.15. Furthermore, if the accused is deemed to have a 'criminal lifestyle,' it is assumed that all of the income gained, or property received, in the previous six years represents the proceeds of crime: see 4.16–4.17.

to continue. A recent prosecution in the United States of three dealers and a collector would suggest otherwise. It was alleged that they were part of a major international smuggling gang. On 13 July 2011, they were indicted before a grand jury in the US District Court, Eastern District of New York: they were accused of conspiring to smuggle antiquities, including sarcophagi, from Egypt, via Dubai, into the United States, and conspiring to engage in money laundering.[43] It was alleged that the antiquities were imported with misleading descriptions on shipping labels and customs documentation (such as 'wooden panels'), but were discovered and seized by the customs authorities. It was also suggested that false provenances had been created by one of the dealers.[44] The United States Government gave notice to the grand jury that all of the antiquities and laundered money would be subject to forfeiture in the event of conviction. Increasingly customs laws, allied to money laundering measures, are the basis for prosecutions in the United States.[45] A combination of charges relating to evasion of customs duties or tax, for example, and money laundering could well form the basis for prosecutions in the United Kingdom in the future.

7.12 Money Laundering Measures and International Co-operation

One significant outcome of international efforts to combat serious crime and money laundering has been the development of greater co-operation between enforcement agencies. It is increasingly recognised that international gangs are attracted to art and antiquities. The conventions which provide underlying principles and a framework for united action in relation to the protection of cultural property, such as the UNESCO Convention, are valuable; yet there is a danger that their focus upon preservation and ownership of cultural property and export controls may be politically divisive. In contrast, international initiatives relating to economic crime, such as the UN Convention against Transnational Organised Crime,[46] have brought nations together. These conventions establish universal principles and make it easier for the police and customs officers in one country to work with their counterparts in another country.

In the past, there was some doubt over the extent to which international criminal networks were involved in the illicit trade in cultural property.[47] The seriousness of the problem has now been recognised by the Convention Against Transnational Crime and by UN resolutions. The lack of information regarding trafficking in cultural property, which made it difficult for police and customs officers to determine its scale, can be linked to a different concern, which is lack of expertise amongst enforcement agencies in relation to art crime. These agencies have not had, and are unlikely to ever receive, the resources necessary to tackle the illicit trade in a comprehensive fashion.[48] Instead, the art market is expected to regulate itself. Money laundering measures assist considerably in dealing with these problems. Police and customs officers are now familiar with the relevant provisions of the

[43] See M Vlasic, 'Stamping out the Illicit Trade in Cultural Artifacts' *The Guardian* (7 August 2011); see also, ICE news release, 'ICE Busts Egyptian Antiquity Smuggling Ring' *Cultural Property and Archaeology Law* (26 July 2011).

[44] *US v Khouli, Alshdaifat, Lewis and Ramadan*, no 11-340.

[45] See also the dispute between the US Government and the St Louis Art Museum in relation to a mask attributed to the Egyptian mummy Ka-Nefer-Nefer. The US Justice Department is attempting to recover the mask using domestic customs laws.

[46] See 2.39.

[47] Select Committee of Culture Media and Sport, First Report of 2003–2004, *Cultural Objects: Developments since 2000*, [22]–[25].

[48] ibid, [16].

Proceeds of Crime Act 2002. They may have no expertise in relation to identifying the age of a cultural object or its source country, but provided that there is evidence of criminal conduct (such as manifestly incorrect statements on import documents), they may be able to take the object into custody. The 2002 Act also gives them wide powers of search and seizure to assist them in bringing charges against suspects, allowing them to interrupt any suspected illicit import or trade through the seizure of artefacts.[49]

V Changing Market Norms

7.13 Ethics

The UNESCO Convention has been criticised quite unfairly for failing to stop the illicit trade in cultural objects. The drafters of the Convention could never hope to do so. After all, the war on drugs has not been won, despite the resources poured in towards fighting it. Repressing the trafficking in cultural property poses far more difficulties than curbing trafficking in drugs. Prohibited drugs are in the main clearly identifiable. In contrast, it may be difficult to distinguish licit from illicit cultural objects, particularly with so many fakes and forgeries in circulation. The expertise required to support a successful legal action is of a far greater order. But the UNESCO Convention was invaluable in reminding the world that there should be an ethical, as well as legal, approach, to dealing with cultural property. The major contribution of the criminal conventions has been to forge greater co-operation between nations and between domestic law enforcement agencies. Voluntary and commercial bodies have also initiated various schemes to prevent trafficking.[50]

The huge profits to be made in dealing in art and antiquities may prove such a distraction to a number of participants in the market that they become indifferent to where an object had originated. It was once commonplace for those dealing in valuable works of art and objects of antiquity to ask no questions. One possible reason for the popularity of this norm was that it might have been assumed by dealers that, if they had no actual knowledge that an item was stolen, they would avoid committing a criminal offence. However, dealers might also fail to keep proper records of sales and purchases, which would mean that the provenance of objects might become increasingly obscure, as they were passed from one dealer to another. The facts of *Kurtha v Marks*[51] are a reminder of a market which has lacked a sufficiently ethical dimension. The claimant sued the defendant to obtain the return of his painting by Souza, which had been stolen. The defendant, a dealer, attempted to persuade the court that the action was time-barred because it had been purchased in good faith by his seller more than six years beforehand. The defendant's seller had bought two paintings by Souza for £25,000 in cash; he then resold them shortly afterwards to the defendant for £124,000 in cash. Both men were dealers. They could not offer a proper explanation relating to why they had paid in cash (rather than using cheques or credit

[49] For details on search and seizure powers, see 4.06.

[50] For example, with the assistance of the Portable Antiquities Scheme, Ebay publishes guidance to discourage sellers offering items for sale on its internet site which should be reported under the provisions of the Treasure Act: http://pages.ebay.co.uk/buy/guides/antiquities.

[51] *Kurtha v Marks* [2008] EWHC 336.

cards, which would leave a documentary trail).[52] The defendant excused his failure to investigate the provenance of the paintings on the basis that this was usual in the trade: he suggested that all dealers were wary of revealing their sources because, as middlemen, they were afraid of being cut out of the picture in other dealings.[53] However, the lack of detail relating to provenance proved to be the defendant's undoing: there was insufficient evidence relating to the date on which, and the person from whom, the painting was acquired to establish the limitation defence. It should also be noted that this type of behaviour, involving cash sales of valuable property, with poor records and no questions asked, would now expose participants to the risk of prosecution for a money laundering offence or a civil recovery order.[54]

The criminal law is now acting as an instrument for change. One of the key characteristics of recent legislation, such as the Bribery Act 2010, is the creation of a line of managerial responsibility so that those involved in the management of companies cannot avoid liability.[55] The details of each legislative measure may vary, but they all create obligations with potential liability for senior management of large organisations, including auction houses. These legislative measures should have a ripple effect on other participants in the market, forcing up standards of behaviour. For example, if one is familiar with money laundering measures, one can see their influence over the whole of the document produced by the DCMS in 2005, which offers guidance to museums on combatting the illicit trade in cultural property.[56] Higher standards of conduct are now expected of dealers, so that the current codes of due diligence are more stringent than those which existed in the last century.[57] Arguably, there should be a code of due diligence for collectors as well, so that they are more alive to the risk of committing an offence.

Sooner or later, a collector will be prosecuted in the UK for collecting illicit cultural objects, and this will have the effect of deterring others, at least to an extent. Even so, one should not lose sight of the global nature of this market: objects can always be diverted to other markets, where the private purchasers are not so fastidious. Consequently, the greater the co-operation between governments, the better. It is a welcome sign that there have been a number of recent repatriations of looted property from museums to source countries such as Greece and Italy. Greece has been able to recover items stolen during the 1990s, including items purchased by the J Paul Getty Museum.[58] UNESCO's Intergovernmental Committee for Promoting the Return of Cultural Property to its Countries of Origin or its Restitution in the Case of Illicit Appropriation has also played a key role in relation to the repatriation of items.

From an economic perspective, for every country, it is important to create the right conditions so that the market in licit cultural property remains a thriving one. However, this concern does not mean that the market may not be regulated. Nor does it logically follow that the intrinsic cultural values of objects, which should prompt an ethical approach,

[52] ibid, [90], [91], [98].

[53] ibid, [101].

[54] See the comments by Tugendhat J to this effect, ibid, [140]. For discussion of civil recovery orders, see 4.20.

[55] As regards the liability of senior officers of a company in relation to tainted cultural objects in contravention of the Dealing in Cultural Objects (Offences) Act 2003, see 3.65. The Money Laundering Regulations require organisations to establish an internal system of monitoring: see 3.45.

[56] For a discussion of DCMS guidance, entitled 'Combating Illicit Trade: Due Diligence Guidelines for Museums, Libraries and Archives on Collecting and Borrowing Cultural Material', see 5.16.

[57] See 5.18–5.21.

[58] UNESCO, Information Kit, *The Fight Against the Illicit Trafficking of Cultural Objects, The 1970 Convention: Past, Present and Future* (2011) CLT/2011/CONF 207/6.

should be neglected. In the past, financial considerations have undermined ethical perspectives in the market. Market norms have encouraged participants to see cultural property as an investment. The lack of regard in relation to an object's provenance has served to commodify it. If its past is unknown, it is likely to be judged on whether it is aesthetically pleasing. The virtue of legislation which puts pressure upon those dealing in cultural objects to check an item's history to the extent that this is feasible, and to maintain written records, is that the unique character of every object will be increasingly recognised. In the context of combatting the illicit trade in art and antiquities, this type of legislation does not appear overly bureaucratic and cumbersome. Rather, it serves a worthwhile end. Every effort is surely worthwhile, in order to protect cultural objects for the benefit of all of humankind. As Paul Bator has observed:

> The very power of art lies in its ability to use symbol and image to give objective expression to the inner life of emotion, to communicate 'felt life' (to use Henry James's phrase) . . . And our encounter with questions such as, who am I, where do I belong, what is my connection to others, is itself a deep and inescapable constituent of every person's felt life. Art speaks directly to the inner consciousness within which we resolve whether we do really feel a sense of belonging to a group or community.[59]

[59] PM Bator, 'An Essay on the International Trade in Art' (1982) 34 *Stanford Law Review* 275, 305.

Appendix A

Convention on the Means of Prohibiting and Preventing the Illicit Import, Export and Transfer of Ownership of Cultural Property 1970

PARIS, 14 NOVEMBER 1970

The General Conference of the United Nations Educational, Scientific and Cultural Organization, meeting in Paris from 12 October to 14 November 1970, at its sixteenth session,

Recalling the importance of the provisions contained in the Declaration of the Principles of International Cultural Co-operation, adopted by the General Conference at its fourteenth session,

Considering that the interchange of cultural property among nations for scientific, cultural and educational purposes increases the knowledge of the civilization of Man, enriches the cultural life of all peoples and inspires mutual respect and appreciation among nations,

Considering that cultural property constitutes one of the basic elements of civilization and national culture, and that its true value can be appreciated only in relation to the fullest possible information regarding is origin, history and traditional setting,

Considering that it is incumbent upon every State to protect the cultural property existing within its territory against the dangers of theft, clandestine excavation, and illicit export,

Considering that, to avert these dangers, it is essential for every State to become increasingly alive to the moral obligations to respect its own cultural heritage and that of all nations,

Considering that, as cultural institutions, museums, libraries and archives should ensure that their collections are built up in accordance with universally recognized moral principles,

Considering that the illicit import, export and transfer of ownership of cultural property is an obstacle to that understanding between nations which it is part of UNESCO's mission to promote by recommending to interested States, international conventions to this end,

Considering that the protection of cultural heritage can be effective only if organized both nationally and internationally among States working in close co-operation,

Considering that the UNESCO General Conference adopted a Recommendation to this effect in 1964,

Having before It further proposals on the means of prohibiting and preventing the illicit import, export and transfer of ownership of cultural property, a question which is on the agenda for the session as item 19,

Having decided, at its fifteenth session, that this question should be made the subject of an international convention,
Adopts this Convention on the fourteenth day of November 1970.

Article 1

For the purposes of this Convention, the term `cultural property' means property which, on religious or secular grounds, is specifically designated by each State as being of importance for archaeology, prehistory, history, literature, art or science and which belongs to the following categories:

(a) Rare collections and specimens of fauna, flora, minerals and anatomy, and objects of palaeontological interest;
(b) property relating to history, including the history of science and technology and military and social history, to the life of national leaders, thinkers, scientists and artist and to events of national importance;
(c) products of archaeological excavations (including regular and clandestine) or of archaeological discoveries;
(d) elements of artistic or historical monuments or archaeological sites which have been dismembered;
(e) antiquities more than one hundred years old, such as inscriptions, coins and engraved seals;
(f) objects of ethnological interest;
(g) property of artistic interest, such as:

    (i) pictures, paintings and drawings produced entirely by hand on any support and in any material (excluding industrial designs and manufactured articles decorated by hand);
    (ii) original works of statuary art and sculpture in any material;
    (iii) original engravings, prints and lithographs ;
    (iv) original artistic assemblages and montages in any material;

(h) rare manuscripts and incunabula, old books, documents and publications of special interest (historical, artistic, scientific, literary, etc.) singly or in collections;
(i) postage, revenue and similar stamps, singly or in collections;
(j) archives, including sound, photographic and cinematographic archives;
(k) articles of furniture more than one hundred years old and old musical instruments.

Article 2

1. The States Parties to this Convention recognize that the illicit import, export and transfer of ownership of cultural property is one of the main causes of the impoverishment of the cultural heritage of the countries of origin of such property and that international

co-operation constitutes one of the most efficient means of protecting each country's cultural property against all the dangers resulting there from.

2. To this end, the States Parties undertake to oppose such practices with the means at their disposal, and particularly by removing their causes, putting a stop to current practices, and by helping to make the necessary reparations.

Article 3

The import, export or transfer of ownership of cultural property effected contrary to the provisions adopted under this Convention by the States Parties thereto, shall be illicit.

Article 4

The States Parties to this Convention recognize that for the purpose of the Convention property which belongs to the following categories forms part of the cultural heritage of each State:

(a) Cultural property created by the individual or collective genius of nationals of the State concerned, and cultural property of importance to the State concerned created within the territory of that State by foreign nationals or stateless persons resident within such territory;
(b) cultural property found within the national territory;
(c) cultural property acquired by archaeological, ethnological or natural science missions, with the consent of the competent authorities of the country of origin of such property;
(d) cultural property which has been the subject of a freely agreed exchange;
(e) cultural property received as a gift or purchased legally with the consent of the competent authorities of the country of origin of such property.

Article 5

To ensure the protection of their cultural property against illicit import, export and transfer of ownership, the States Parties to this Convention undertake, as appropriate for each country, to set up within their territories one or more national services, where such services do not already exist, for the protection of the cultural heritage, with a qualified staff sufficient in number for the effective carrying out of the following functions:

(a) contributing to the formation of draft laws and regulations designed to secure the protection of the cultural heritage and particularly prevention of the illicit import, export and transfer of ownership of important cultural property;
(b) establishing and keeping up to date, on the basis of a national inventory of protected property, a list of important public and private cultural property whose export would constitute an appreciable impoverishment of the national cultural heritage;
(c) promoting the development or the establishment of scientific and technical institutions (museums, libraries, archives, laboratories, workshops . . .) required to ensure the preservation and presentation of cultural property;
(d) organizing the supervision of archaeological excavations, ensuring the preservation `in situation' of certain cultural property, and protecting certain areas reserved for future archaeological research;

(e) establishing, for the benefit of those concerned (curators, collectors, antique dealers, etc.) rules in conformity with the ethical principles set forth in this Convention; and taking steps to ensure the observance of those rules;
(f) taking educational measures to stimulate and develop respect for the cultural heritage of all States, and spreading knowledge of the provisions of this Convention;
(g) seeing that appropriate publicity is given to the disappearance of any items of cultural property.

Article 6

The States Parties to this Convention undertake:

(a) To introduce an appropriate certificate in which the exporting State would specify that the export of the cultural property in question is authorized. The certificate should accompany all items of cultural property exported in accordance with the regulations;
(b) to prohibit the exportation of cultural property from their territory unless accompanied by the above-mentioned export certificate;
(c) to publicize this prohibition by appropriate means, particularly among persons likely to export or import cultural property.

Article 7

The States Parties to this Convention undertake:

(a) To take the necessary measures, consistent with national legislation, to prevent museums and similar institutions within their territories from acquiring cultural property originating in another State Party which has been illegally exported after entry into force of this Convention, in the States concerned. Whenever possible, to inform a State of origin Party to this Convention of an offer of such cultural property illegally removed from that State after the entry into force of this Convention in both States;
(b) (i) to prohibit the import of cultural property stolen from a museum or a religious or secular public monument or similar institution in another State Party to this Convention after the entry into force of this Convention for the States concerned, provided that such property is documented as appertaining to the inventory of that institution;
(ii) at the request of the State Party of origin, to take appropriate steps to recover and return any such cultural property imported after the entry into force of this Convention in both States concerned, provided, however, that the requesting State shall pay just compensation to an innocent purchaser or to a person who has valid title to that property. Requests for recovery and return shall be made through diplomatic offices. The requesting Party shall furnish, at its expense, the documentation and other evidence necessary to establish its claim for recovery and return. The Parties shall impose no customs duties or other charges upon cultural property returned pursuant to this Article. All expenses incident to the return and delivery of the cultural property shall be borne by the requesting Party.

Article 8

The States Parties to this Convention undertake to impose penalties or administrative sanctions on any person responsible for infringing the prohibitions referred to under Articles 6(b) and 7(b) above.

Article 9

Any State Party to this Convention whose cultural patrimony is in jeopardy from pillage of archaeological or ethnological materials may call upon other States Parties who are affected. The States Parties to this Convention undertake, in these circumstances, to participate in a concerted international effort to determine and to carry out the necessary concrete measures, including the control of exports and imports and international commerce in the specific materials concerned. Pending agreement each State concerned shall take provisional measures to the extent feasible to prevent irremediable injury to the cultural heritage of the requesting State.

Article 10

The States Parties to this Convention undertake:

(a) To restrict by education, information and vigilance, movement of cultural property illegally removed from any State Party to this Convention and, as appropriate for each country, oblige antique dealers, subject to penal or administrative sanctions, to maintain a register recording the origin of each item of cultural property, names and addresses of the supplier, description and price of each item sold and to inform the purchaser of the cultural property of the export prohibition to which such property may be subject;
(b) to endeavour by educational means to create and develop in the public mind a realization of the value of cultural property and the threat to the cultural heritage created by theft, clandestine excavations and illicit exports.

Article 11

The export and transfer of ownership of cultural property under compulsion arising directly or indirectly from the occupation of a country by a foreign power shall be regarded as illicit.

Article 12

The States Parties to this Convention shall respect the cultural heritage within the territories for the international relations of which they are responsible, and shall take all appropriate measures to prohibit and prevent the illicit import, export and transfer of ownership of cultural property in such territories.

Article 13

The States Parties to this Convention also undertake, consistent with the laws of each State:

(a) To prevent by all appropriate means transfers of ownership of cultural property likely to promote the illicit import or export of such property;

(b) to ensure that their competent services co-operate in facilitating the earliest possible restitution of illicitly exported cultural property to its rightful owner;
(c) to admit actions for recovery of lost or stolen items of cultural property brought by or on behalf of the rightful owners ;
(d) to recognize the indefeasible right of each State Party to this Convention to classify and declare certain cultural property as inalienable which should therefore ipso facto not be exported, and to facilitate recovery of such property by the State concerned in cases where it has been exported.

Article 14

In order to prevent illicit export and to meet the obligations arising from the implementation of this Convention, each State Party to the Convention should, as far as it is able, provide the national services responsible for the protection of its cultural heritage with an adequate budget and, if necessary, should set up a fund for this purpose.

Article 15

Nothing in this Convention shall prevent States Parties thereto from concluding special agreements among themselves or from continuing to implement agreements already concluded regarding the restitution of cultural property removed, whatever the reason, from its territory of origin, before the entry into force of this Convention for the States concerned.

Article 16

The States Parties to this Convention shall in their periodic reports submitted to the General Conference of the United Nations Educational, Scientific and Cultural Organization on dates and in a manner to be determined by it, give information on the legislative and administrative provisions which they have adopted and other action which they have taken for the application of this Convention, together with details of the experience acquired in this field.

Article 17

1. The States Parties to this Convention may call on the technical assistance of the United Nations Educational, Scientific and Cultural Organization, particularly as regards:

(a) Information and education;
(b) consultation and expert advice;
(c) co-ordination and good offices.

2. The United Nations Educational, Scientific and Cultural Organization may, on its own initiative conduct research and publish studies on matters relevant to the illicit movement of cultural property.

3. To this end, the United Nations Educational, Scientific and Cultural Organization may also call on the co-operation of any competent non-governmental organization.

4. The United Nations Educational, Scientific and Cultural Organization may, on its own initiative, make proposals to States Parties to this Convention for its implementation.

5. At the request of at least two States Parties to this Convention which are engaged in a dispute over its implementation, UNESCO may extend its good offices to reach a settlement between them.

Article 18

This Convention is drawn up in English, French, Russian and Spanish, the four texts being equally authoritative.

Article 19

1. This Convention shall be subject to ratification or acceptance by States members of the United Nations Educational, Scientific and Cultural Organization in accordance with their respective constitutional procedures.

2. The instruments of ratification or acceptance shall be deposited with the Director-General of the United Nations Educational, Scientific and Cultural Organization.

Article 20

1. This Convention shall be open to accession by all States not members of the United Nations Educational, Scientific and Cultural Organization which are invited to accede to it by the Executive Board of the Organization.

2. Accession shall be effected by the deposit of an instrument of accession with the Director-General of the United Nations Educational, Scientific and Cultural Organization.

Article 21

This Convention shall enter into force three months after the date of the deposit of the third instrument of ratification, acceptance or accession, but only with respect to those States which have deposited their respective instruments on or before that date. It shall enter into force with respect to any other State three months after the deposit of its instrument of ratification, acceptance or accession.

Article 22

The States Parties to this Convention recognize that the Convention is applicable not only to their metropolitan territories but also to all territories for the international relations of which they are responsible; they undertake to consult, if necessary, the governments or other competent authorities of these territories on or before ratification, acceptance or accession with a view to securing the application of the Convention to those territories, and to notify the Director-General of the United Nations Educational, Scientific and cultural Organization of the territories to which it is applied, the notification to take effect three months after the date of its receipt.

Article 23

1. Each State Party to this Convention may denounce the Convention on its own behalf or on behalf of any territory for whose international relations it is responsible.

2. The denunciation shall be notified by an instrument in writing, deposited with the Director-General of the United Nations Educational, Scientific and Cultural Organization.

3. The denunciation shall take effect twelve months after the receipt of the instrument of denunciation.

Article 24

The Director-General of the United Nations Educational, Scientific and Cultural Organization shall inform the States members of the Organization, the States not members of the Organization which are referred to in Article 20, as well as the United Nations, of the deposit of all the instruments of ratification, acceptance and accession provided for in Articles 19 and 20, and of the notifications and denunciations provided for in Articles 22 and 23 respectively.

Article 25

1. This Convention may be revised by the General Conference of the United Nations Educational, Scientific and Cultural Organization. Any such revision shall, however, bind only the States which shall become Parties to the revising convention.

2. If the General Conference should adopt a new convention revising this Convention in whole or in part, then, unless the new convention otherwise provides, this Convention shall cease to be open to ratification, acceptance or accession, as from the date on which the new revising convention enters into force.

Article 26

In conformity with Article 102 of the Charter of the United Nations, this 'Convention shall be registered with the Secretariat of the United Nations at the request of the Director-General of the United Nations Educational, Scientific and Cultural Organization.
Done in Paris this seventeenth day of November 1970, in two authentic copies bearing the signature of the President of the sixteenth session of the General Conference and of the Director-General of the United Nations Educational, Scientific and Cultural Organization, which shall be deposited in the archives of the United Nations Educational, Scientific and Cultural Organization, and certified true copies of which shall be delivered to all the States referred to in Articles 19 and 20 as well as to the United Nations.

Depositary:

UNESCO

Entry into force:

24 April 1972, in accordance with Article 21

Authoritative texts:

English, French, Russian and Spanish

Registration at the UN:

9 May 1972, No 11806

Appendix B

Council Regulation (EC) No 116/2009 of 18 December 2008 on the export of cultural goods

10.2.2009 EN Official Journal of the European Union L 39/1

I

(Acts adopted under the EC Treaty/Euratom Treaty whose publication is obligatory)

REGULATIONS

COUNCIL REGULATION (EC) No 116/2009

of 18 December 2008

on the export of cultural goods

(Codified version)

THE COUNCIL OF THE EUROPEAN UNION,

Having regard to the Treaty establishing the European Community, and in particular Article 133 thereof,

Having regard to the proposal from the Commission,

Whereas:

(1) Council Regulation (EEC) No 3911/92 of 9 December 1992 on the export of cultural goods ([1]) has been substantially amended several times ([2]). In the interests of clarity and rationality the said Regulation should be codified.

(2) In order to maintain the internal market, rules on trade with third countries are needed for the protection of cultural goods.

(3) It seems necessary to take measures in particular to ensure that exports of cultural goods are subject to uniform controls at the Community's external borders.

(4) Such a system should require the presentation of a licence issued by the competent Member State prior to the export of cultural goods covered by this Regulation. This necessitates a clear definition of the scope of such measures and the procedures for their implementation. The implementation of the system should be as simple and efficient as possible.

(5) The measures necessary for the implementation of this Regulation should be adopted in accordance with Council Decision 1999/468/EC of 28 June 1999 laying down the procedures for the exercise of implementing powers conferred on the Commission ([3]).

(6) In view of the considerable experience of the Member States' authorities in the application of Council Regulation (EC) No 515/97 of 13 March 1997 on mutual assistance between the administrative authorities of the Member States and cooperation between the latter and the Commission to ensure the correct application of the law on customs and agricultural matters ([4]), the said Regulation should be applied to this matter.

(7) Annex I to this Regulation is aimed at making clear the categories of cultural goods which should be given particular protection in trade with third countries, but is not intended to prejudice the definition, by Member States, of national treasures within the meaning of Article 30 of the Treaty,

HAS ADOPTED THIS REGULATION:

Article 1

Definition

Without prejudice to Member States' powers under Article 30 of the Treaty, the term 'cultural goods' shall refer, for the purposes of this Regulation, to the items listed in Annex I.

Article 2

Export licence

1. The export of cultural goods outside the customs territory of the Community shall be subject to the presentation of an export licence.

([1]) OJ L 395, 31.12.1992, p. 1.

([3]) OJ L 184, 17.7.1999, p. 23.

2. The export licence shall be issued at the request of the person concerned:

(a) by a competent authority of the Member State in whose territory the cultural object in question was lawfully and definitively located on 1 January 1993;

(b) or, thereafter, by a competent authority of the Member State in whose territory it is located following either lawful and definitive dispatch from another Member State, or importation from a third country, or re-importation from a third country after lawful dispatch from a Member State to that country.

However, without prejudice to paragraph 4, the Member State which is competent in accordance with points (a) or (b) of the first subparagraph is authorised not to require export licences for the cultural goods specified in the first and second indents of category A.1 of Annex I where they are of limited archaeological or scientific interest, and provided that they are not the direct product of excavations, finds or archaeological sites within a Member State, and that their presence on the market is lawful.

The export licence may be refused, for the purposes of this Regulation, where the cultural goods in question are covered by legislation protecting national treasures of artistic, historical or archaeological value in the Member State concerned.

Where necessary, the authority referred to in point (b) of the first subparagraph shall enter into contact with the competent authorities of the Member State from which the cultural object in question came, and in particular the competent authorities within the meaning of Council Directive 93/7/EEC of 15 March 1993 on the return of cultural objects unlawfully removed from the territory of a Member State ([1]).

3. The export licence shall be valid throughout the Community.

4. Without prejudice to the provisions of paragraphs 1, 2 and 3, direct export from the customs territory of the Community of national treasures having artistic, historic or archaeological value which are not cultural goods within the meaning of this Regulation is subject to the national law of the Member State of export.

Article 3

Competent authorities

1. Member States shall furnish the Commission with a list of the authorities empowered to issue export licences for cultural goods.

2. The Commission shall publish a list of the authorities and any amendment to that list in the 'C' series of the *Official Journal of the European Union*.

Article 4

Presentation of licence

The export licence shall be presented, in support of the export declaration, when the customs export formalities are carried out, at the customs office which is competent to accept that declaration.

Article 5

Limitation of competent customs offices

1. Member States may restrict the number of customs offices empowered to handle formalities for the export of cultural goods.

2. Member States availing themselves of the option afforded by paragraph 1 shall inform the Commission of the customs offices duly empowered.

The Commission shall publish this information in the 'C' series of the *Official Journal of the European Union*.

Article 6

Administrative cooperation

For the purposes of implementing this Regulation, the provisions of Regulation (EC) No 515/97, and in particular the provisions on the confidentiality of information, shall apply *mutatis mutandis*.

In addition to the cooperation provided for under the first paragraph, Member States shall take all necessary steps to establish, in the context of their mutual relations, cooperation between the customs authorities and the competent authorities referred to in Article 4 of Directive 93/7/EEC.

Article 7

Implementing measures

The measures necessary for the implementation of this Regulation, in particular those concerning the form to be used (for example, the model and technical properties) shall be adopted in accordance with the procedure referred to in Article 8(2).

Article 8

Committee

1. The Commission shall be assisted by a committee.

2. Where reference is made to this paragraph, Articles 3 and 7 of Decision 1999/468/EC shall apply.

([1]) OJ L 74, 27.3.1993, p. 74.

Article 9

Penalties

The Member States shall lay down the rules on penalties applicable to infringements of the provisions of this Regulation and shall take all measures necessary to ensure that they are implemented. The penalties provided for must be effective, proportionate and dissuasive.

Article 10

Reporting

1. Each Member State shall inform the Commission of the measures taken pursuant to this Regulation.

The Commission shall pass on this information to the other Member States.

2. Every three years the Commission shall present a report to the European Parliament, the Council and the European Economic and Social Committee on the implementation of this Regulation.

The Council, acting on a proposal from the Commission, shall examine every three years and, where appropriate, update the amounts indicated in Annex I, on the basis of economic and monetary indicators in the Community.

Article 11

Repeal

Regulation (EEC) No 3911/92, as amended by the Regulations listed in Annex II, is repealed.

References to the repealed Regulation shall be construed as references to this Regulation and shall be read in accordance with the correlation table in Annex III.

Article 12

Entry into force

This Regulation shall enter into force on the 20th day following its publication in the *Official Journal of the European Union.*

This Regulation shall be binding in its entirety and directly applicable in all Member States.

Done at Brussels, 18 December 2008.

For the Council

The President

M. BARNIER

ANNEX I

Categories of cultural objects covered by Article 1

A.	1. Archaeological objects more than 100 years old which are the products of:	
	— excavations and finds on land or under water	9705 00 00
	— archaeological sites	9706 00 00
	— archaeological collections	
	2. Elements forming an integral part of artistic, historical or religious monuments which have been dismembered, of an age exceeding 100 years	9705 00 00 9706 00 00
	3. Pictures and paintings, other than those included in categories 4 or 5, executed entirely by hand in any medium and on any material ([1])	9701
	4. Watercolours, gouaches and pastels executed entirely by hand on any material ([1])	9701
	5. Mosaics in any material executed entirely by hand, other than those falling in categories 1 or 2, and drawings in any medium executed entirely by hand on any material ([1])	6914 9701
	6. Original engravings, prints, serigraphs and lithographs with their respective plates and original posters ([1])	Chapter 49 9702 00 00 8442 50 99
	7. Original sculptures or statuary and copies produced by the same process as the original ([1]), other than those in category 1	9703 00 00
	8. Photographs, films and negatives thereof ([1])	3704 3705 3706 4911 91 80
	9. Incunabula and manuscripts, including maps and musical scores, singly or in collections ([1])	9702 00 00 9706 00 00 4901 10 00 4901 99 00 4904 00 00 4905 91 00 4905 99 00 4906 00 00
	10. Books more than 100 years old, singly or in collections	9705 00 00 9706 00 00
	11. Printed maps more than 200 years old	9706 00 00
	12. Archives, and any elements thereof, of any kind or any medium which are more than 50 years old	3704 3705 3706 4901 4906 9705 00 00 9706 00 00
	13. (a) Collections ([2]) and specimens from zoological, botanical, mineralogical or anatomical collections;	9705 00 00
	(b) Collections ([2]) of historical, palaeontological, ethnographic or numismatic interest	9705 00 00

([1]) Which are more than 50 years old and do not belong to their originators.

([2]) As defined by the Court of Justice in its judgment in Case 252/84, as follows: 'Collectors' pieces within the meaning of heading No 97.05 of the Common Customs Tariff are articles which possess the requisite characteristics for inclusion in a collection, that is to say, articles which are relatively rare, are not normally used for their original purpose, are the subject of special transactions outside the normal trade in similar utility articles and are of high value'.

14. Means of transport more than 75 years old	9705 00 00 Chapters 86-89
15. Any other antique items not included in categories A.1 to A.14	
(a) between 50 and 100 years old	
toys, games	Chapter 95
glassware	7013
articles of goldsmiths' or silversmiths' wares	7114
furniture	Chapter 94
optical, photographic or cinematographic apparatus	Chapter 90
musical instruments	Chapter 92
clocks and watches and parts thereof	Chapter 91
articles of wood	Chapter 44
pottery	Chapter 69
tapestries	5805 00 00
carpets	Chapter 57
wallpaper	4814
arms	Chapter 93
(b) more than 100 years old	9706 00 00

The cultural objects in categories A.1 to A.15 are covered by this Regulation only if their value corresponds to, or exceeds, the financial thresholds under B.

B. Financial thresholds applicable to certain categories under A (in euro)

Value:

Whatever the value

— 1 (Archaeological objects)

— 2 (Dismembered monuments)

— 9 (Incunabula and manuscripts)

— 12 (Archives)

15 000

— 5 (Mosaics and drawings)

— 6 (Engravings)

— 8 (Photographs)

— 11 (Printed maps)

30 000

— 4 (Watercolours, gouaches and pastels)

50 000

— 7 (Statuary)

— 10 (Books)

— 13 (Collections)

— 14 (Means of transport)

— 15 (Any other object)

150 000

— 3 (Pictures)

The assessment of whether or not the conditions relating to financial value are fulfilled must be made when an application for an export licence is submitted. The financial value is that of the cultural object in the Member State referred to in Article 2(2).

For the Member States which do not have the euro as their currency, the values expressed in euro in Annex I shall be converted and expressed in national currencies at the rate of exchange on 31 December 2001 published in the *Official Journal of the European Communities*. This countervalue in national currencies shall be reviewed every two years with effect from 31 December 2001. Calculation of this countervalue shall be based on the average daily value of those currencies, expressed in euro, during the 24 months ending on the last day of August preceding the revision which takes effect on 31 December. This method of calculation shall be reviewed, on a proposal from the Commission, by the Advisory Committee on Cultural Goods, in principle two years after the first application. For each revision, the values expressed in euro and their countervalues in national currency shall be published periodically in the *Official Journal of the European Union* in the first days of the month of November preceding the date on which the revision takes effect.

ANNEX II

Repealed Regulation with its successive amendments

Council Regulation (EEC) No 3911/92 (OJ L 395, 31.12.1992, p. 1)	
Council Regulation (EC) No 2469/96 (OJ L 335, 24.12.1996, p. 9)	
Council Regulation (EC) No 974/2001 (OJ L 137, 19.5.2001, p. 10)	
Council Regulation (EC) No 806/2003 (OJ L 122, 16.5.2003, p. 1)	Annex I, point 2 only

ANNEX III

CORRELATION TABLE

Regulation (EEC) No 3911/92	This Regulation
Article 1	Article 1
Article 2(1)	Article 2(1)
Article 2(2), first subparagraph, introductory wording	Article 2(2), first subparagraph, introductory wording
Article 2(2), first subparagraph, first indent	Article 2(2), first subparagraph, point (a)
Article 2(2), first subparagraph, second indent	Article 2(2), first subparagraph, point (b)
Article 2(2), second subparagraph	Article 2(2), second subparagraph
Article 2(2), third subparagraph	Article 2(2), third subparagraph
Article 2(2), fourth subparagraph	Article 2(2), fourth subparagraph
Article 2(3)	Article 2(3)
Article 2(4)	Article 2(4)
Articles 3 to 9	Articles 3 to 9
Article 10, first paragraph	Article 10(1), first subparagraph
Article 10, second paragraph	Article 10(1), second subparagraph
Article 10, third paragraph	Article 10(2), first subparagraph
Article 10, fourth paragraph	—
Article 10, fifth paragraph	Article 10(2), second subparagraph
—	Article 11
Article 11	Article 12
Annex, points A.1, A.2 and A.3	Annex I, points A.1, A.2 and A.3
Annex, point A.3A	Annex I, point A.4
Annex, point A.4	Annex I, point A.5
Annex, point A.5	Annex I, point A.6
Annex, point A.6	Annex I, point A.7
Annex, point A.7	Annex I, point A.8
Annex, point A.8	Annex I, point A.9
Annex, point A.9	Annex I, point A.10
Annex, point A.10	Annex I, point A.11
Annex, point A.11	Annex I, point A.12
Annex, point A.12	Annex I, point A.13
Annex, point A.13	Annex I, point A.14
Annex, point A.14	Annex I, point A.15
Annex, point B	Annex I, point B
—	Annex II
—	Annex III

Appendix C

Council Directive 93/7/EEC of 15 March 1993 on the return of cultural objects unlawfully removed from the territory of a Member State

Official Journal L 074, 27/03/1993 P. 0074 – 0079
[abbreviated]

THE COUNCIL OF THE EUROPEAN COMMUNITIES,

Having regard to the Treaty establishing the European Economic Community, and in particular Article 100a thereof,

Having regard to the proposal from the Commission (1),

In cooperation with the European Parliament (2),

Having regard to the opinion of the Economic and Social Committee (3),

Whereas Article 8a of the Treaty provides for the establishment, not later than 1 January 1993, of the internal market, which is to comprise an area without internal frontiers in which the free movement of goods, persons, services and capital is ensured in accordance with the provisions of the Treaty;

Whereas, under the terms and within the limits of Article 36 of the Treaty, Member States will, after 1992, retain the right to define their national treasures and to take the necessary measures to protect them in this area without internal frontiers;

Whereas arrangements should therefore be introduced enabling Member States to secure the return to their territory of cultural objects which are classified as national treasures within the meaning of the said Article 36 and have been removed from their territory in breach of the abovementioned national measures or of Council Regulation (EEC) No 3911/92 of 9 December 1992 on the export of cultural goods (4); whereas the implementation of these arrangements should be as simple and efficient as possible; whereas, to facilitate cooperation with regard to return, the scope of the arrangements should be confined to items belonging to common categories of cultural object; whereas the Annex to this Directive is consequently not intended to define objects which rank as 'national treasures' within the meaning of the said Article 36, but merely categories of object which may be classified as such and may accordingly be covered by the return procedure introduced by this Directive;

Whereas cultural objects classified as national treasures and forming an integral part of public collections or inventories of ecclesiastical institutions but which do not fall within these common categories should also be covered by this Directive;

Whereas administrative cooperation should be established between Member States as regards their national treasures, in close liaison with their cooperation in the field of stolen works of art and involving in particular the recording, with Interpol and other qualified bodies issuing similar lists, of lost, stolen or illegally removed cultural objects forming part of their national treasures and their public collections;

Whereas the procedure introduced by this Directive is a first step in establishing cooperation between Member States in this field in the context of the internal market; whereas the aim is mutual recognition of the relevant national laws; whereas provision should therefore be made, in particular, for the Commission to be assisted by an advisory committee;

Whereas Regulation (EEC) No 3911/92 introduces, together with this Directive, a Community system to protect Member States' cultural goods; whereas the date by which Member States have to comply with this Directive has to be as close as possible to the date of entry into force of that Regulation; whereas, having regard to the nature of their legal systems and the scope of the changes to their legislation necessary to implement this Directive, some Member States will need a longer period,

HAS ADOPTED THIS DIRECTIVE:

Article 1
For the purposes of this Directive:

1. 'Cultural object' shall mean an object which:

– is classified, before or after its unlawful removal from the territory of a Member State, among the 'national treasures possessing artistic, historic or archaeological value' under national legislation or administrative procedures within the meaning of Article 36 of the Treaty,

and

– belongs to one of the categories listed in the Annex or does not belong to one of these categories but forms an integral part of:
– public collections listed in the inventories of museums, archives or libraries' conservation collection.

For the purposes of this Directive, 'public collections' shall mean collections which are the property of a Member State, local or regional authority within a Member States or an institution situated in the territory of a Member State and defined as public in accordance with the legislation of that Member State, such institution being the property of, or significantly financed by, that Member State or a local or regional authority;

– the inventories of ecclesiastical institutions.

. . .

ANNEX

Categories referred to in the second indent of Article 1 (1) to which objects classified as 'national treasures' within the meaning of Article 36 of the Treaty must belong in order to qualify for return under this Directive

A.

1. Archaeological objects more than 100 years old which are the products of:

   – land or underwater excavations and finds,
   – archaeological sites,
   – archaeological collections.

2. Elements forming an integral part of artistic, historical or religious monuments which have been dismembered, more than 100 years old.
3. Pictures and paintings executed entirely by hand, on any medium and in any material (1).
4. Mosaics other than those in category 1 or category 2 and drawings executed entirely by hand, on any medium and in any material (1).

5. Original engravings, prints, serigraphs and lithographs with their respective plates and original posters (1).
6. Original sculptures or statuary and copies produced by the same process as the original (1) other than those in category 1.
7. Photographs, films and negatives thereof (1).
8. Incunabula and manuscripts, including maps and musical scores, singly or in collections (1).
9. Books more than 100 years old, singly or in collections.
10. Printed maps more than 200 years old.
11. Archives and any elements thereof, of any kind, on any medium, comprising elements more than 50 years old.
12. (a) Collections (2) and specimens from zoological, botanical, mineralogical or anatomical collections;
    (b) Collections (2) of historical, palaeontological, ethnographic or numismatic interest.
13. Means of transport more than 75 years old.
14. Any other antique item not included in categories A 1 to A 13, more than 50 years old.

The cultural objects in categories A 1 to A 14 are covered by this Directive only if their value corresponds to, or exceeds, the financial thresholds under B.

B. Financial thresholds applicable to certain categories under A (in ecus)

VALUE:

0 (Zero)
– 1 (Archaeological objects)
– 2 (Dismembered monuments)
– 8 (Incunabula and manuscripts)
– 11 (Archives)

15 000
– 4 (Mosaics and drawings)
– 5 (Engravings)
– 7 (Photographs)
– 10 (Printed maps)

50 000
– 6 (Statuary)
– 9 (Books)
– 12 (Collections)
– 13 (Means of transport)
– 14 (Any other item)

150 000
– 3 (Pictures)

The assessment of whether or not the conditions relating to financial value are fulfilled must be made when return is requested. The financial value is that of the object in the requested Member State.

The date for the conversion of the values expressed in ecus in the Annex into national currencies shall be 1 January 1993.

(1) Which are more than fifty years old and do not belong to their originators.
(2) As defined by the Court of Justice in its Judgment in Case 252/84, as follows: 'Collectors' pieces within the meaning of Heading No 99.05 of the Common Customs Tariff are articles which possess the requisite characteristics for inclusion in a collection, that is to say, articles which are relatively rare, are not normally used for their original purpose, are the subject of special transactions outside the normal trade in similar utility articles and are of high value.'

Return of Cultural Objects Regulations 1994, as amended
[abbreviated]
Schedule 1

VALUE: [Whatever the value]
–1 (Archaeological objects)
–2 (Dismembered monuments)
–8 (Incunabula and manuscripts)

–11 (Archives)
[¢15,000.00]
–4 (Mosaics and drawings)
–5 (Engravings)
–7 (Photographs)
–10 (Printed maps)

[¢30,000.00]
– 3A. (Water colours, gouaches and pastels).

[¢50,000.00]
–6 (Statutory)
–9 (Books)
–12 (Collections)
–13 (Means of transport)
–14 (Any other item)

[¢150,000.00]
–3 (Pictures)

Categories of objects are numbered in this Schedule in accordance with the numbering in the Annex to the Directive.

INDEX